HARVARD OBSERVED

An Illustrated History of the University in the Twentieth Century

HARVARD OBSERVED

An Illustrated History of the University in the Twentieth Century

John T. Bethell

Harvard University Press
Cambridge, Massachusetts, and London, England • 1998

Library of Congress Cataloging-in-Publication Data
Bethell, John T.
    Harvard observed: an illustrated history of the university in the
    twentieth century / John T. Bethell
      p. cm.
    Includes bibliographical references and index.
    ISBN 0-674-37733-8 (alk. paper)
      1. Harvard University—History—20th century. I. Title.
LD2153.B48   1998
378.744'4—dc21   98-29816

Previous pages: Harvard Yard and the old College pump, 1898.
Photograph courtesy of the Harvard University Archives.
Following pages: Aerial view of Harvard, Cambridge, and Boston
by Laurence Lowry.

Contents

Prologue

THIS INFORMAL HISTORY chronicles the institutional life of America's oldest university in a century of turbulent change. The narrative begins in 1898, when cities were lamplit, the Wright brothers were flying kites, and the year's snappiest novelty song was "I Guess I'll Have to Telegraph My Baby." A hundred years later, television screens glow in 98 percent of American homes, *Voyager 2* shoots Jupiter's moons, and schoolchildren exchange e-mails with age-mates in what once seemed far-off lands.

Harvard Observed frames the evolution of twentieth-century Harvard in the broader context of national and world events. The intent is to chart some of the interactions between a leading American university and the larger society. As a foray into cultural history, this book also looks at the academic rites, intellectual arguments, sexual mores, fads, and folklore that became touchstones for succeeding generations.

Just over a quarter of Harvard's long history is spanned in these pages. That leaves, in the jargon of present-day script writers, a substantial "back story." Harvard was not always rich and famous, nor was it always Harvard. In October 1636, sixteen years after the Pilgrims arrived at Plymouth, the Great and General Court of Massachusetts Bay Colony voted £400 for "a schoale or colledge." A year later a Board of Overseers was appointed "to take order for a colledge at Newetowne." The first dozen freshmen began recitations in the summer of 1638, and New Town was renamed Cambridge. A single frame house and a one-acre cowyard constituted all of the college property.

The college interested John Harvard, a Puritan minister from neighboring Charlestown. When he died of consumption in the fall of 1638, aged 30, he left it his library of 400 books and half of his estate. The General Court gave the college his name, but for decades people spoke of "the college at Cambridge" or "Cambridge College."

The early college was hard-pressed financially. With New England in the grip of a severe economic depression, fund-raising agents were sent to England. They took with them a pamphlet, *New Englands First Fruits*, that had in it American higher education's first mission statement: "to advance Learning and perpetuate it to Posterity; dreading to leave an illiterate Ministry to the Churches." In 1643 the college found a patron in Ann Radcliffe, Lady Mowlson, who provided £100 to create its first scholarship fund. At home, the General Court issued appeals to New England families for annual aid in the form of "college corn": a quarter-bushel of grain, or its equivalent in currency.

In 1650 President Henry Dunster secured from the General Court a charter incorporating the president, treasurer, and five fellows as "The

President and Fellows of Harvard College." The self-perpetuating Harvard Corporation would become the operating arm of the College, subject to the advice and consent of the Board of Overseers.

"Since Harvard's was the first corporation in the western world," observed the *Harvard Alumni Bulletin* in 1950, "it may be said with truth that it 'brought two new elements into American life'—the corporation as a means of perpetuating an institution beyond the lives and fortunes of mere men; and the independent college, free to conduct teaching and research, supported by individuals and groups outside mere government." In its earliest years of activity, the struggling college thus set a pattern of governance for institutions to come, and began an American tradition of voluntary philanthropic support.

THOUGH THE COLLEGE was not church-sponsored, its students were subject to strict religious discipline. For the better part of two centuries, doctrinal disputes colored faculty politics. The election of a layman, John Leverett (A.B. 1680), as president in 1708 was a milestone. His seven predecessors had been clergymen. A century later Harvard broke with its Calvinist heritage when a Unitarian minister was chosen as president. When the Divinity School was founded in 1816, its constitution stated that "no assent to the peculiarities of any denomination shall be required."

As the institution grew into a university, the College remained at the heart of Harvard. A medical school had opened in 1782, with diminutive Holden Chapel as its base. A law school opened in 1817, a school of applied science in 1847. Advanced study at German universities converted younger Harvard scholars to the cause of academic specialization. They came back eager to enlarge libraries and laboratories, to free more time for research, to build new fields of study. Realms of knowledge were expanding rapidly; the ideas of Charles Darwin were challenging accepted tenets in the sciences and humanities. Harvard's leaders of the Civil War era spoke of creating "an American university in the highest and best sense." But it was Charles William Eliot (A.B. 1853), then teaching chemistry at the new Massachusetts Institute of Technology, who would reform the University and become the commanding figure in nineteenth-century American education.

In choosing Eliot as president in 1869, the conservative Bostonians on the Corporation exhibited—not for the last time—a propensity to take risks. The position had been declined by Charles Francis Adams (A.B. 1825, LL.D. 1864), minister plenipotentiary to Britain during the Civil War. The Corporation now turned to Eliot, who had just been elected an Overseer. Eliot came from a prominent family—his father, Samuel (A.B. 1817), had been mayor of Boston and treasurer of Harvard—but his candidacy was anathema to old-guard faculty members and Overseers. As an assistant professor he had been passed over for a chair in applied science. He had recently published an *Atlantic Monthly* article making the case for extensive curricular change. At 35 he would be younger than any president since Henry Dunster.

After two months of give-and-take the Overseers consented, by a vote of sixteen to eight, to the election of one of their own. In the phrase of Oliver Wendell Holmes, Eliot turned the University over "like a flapjack." Within three years he had reorganized the hidebound schools of law, medicine, and divinity, appointed the first dean of the Faculty of Arts and Sciences, doubled the size of the teaching staff, and launched a graduate school of arts and sciences. By 1886 he had installed the elective system, paving the way for courses in such new subjects as economics, fine arts, archaeology and ethnology, government, social ethics, physiology, and psychology. To bring in more public school students, Greek was dropped as a requirement for admission. Undergraduates gained a further measure of freedom when Harvard became the first college to forgo compulsory chapel.

Scholars from the Universities of Cambridge, Edinburgh, and Heidelberg were among the delegates at a four-day celebration of the College's 250th anniversary in 1886. The ultimate accolade came from Professor Basil Gildersleeve, representing Johns Hopkins University: "We measure everything today by the standard of Harvard."

ELIOT DOMINATED Harvard affairs for four decades. Unlike his predecessors, he chaired the meetings of all of his faculties, and convened them more frequently. His vision of Harvard's role, as expressed in his inaugural address, was clear-cut. A university existed to serve the interests of the nation. Its president "must keep watch on the progress of the age" to ensure that the institution adapts itself to "significant changes in the character of the people for whom it exists." The spirit of democracy was best served by attracting to the College a natural aristocracy of talent, drawn from widely divergent backgrounds; by fostering habits "of independent thinking on books, prevailing customs, current events"; by providing "a training-school in which multitudes learn in many ways to take thought for others, to exercise public functions, and to bear public responsibilities. . . ." Eliot set the direction of twentieth-century Harvard. How his successors carried on and advanced his ideals is a principal theme of *Harvard Observed*.

The book's narrative structure is primarily chronological and necessarily selective. Space constraints made it difficult to trace the evolution of the graduate and professional schools in detail. The complex research life of the University, which deserves a book in itself, gets short shrift. But *Harvard Observed* is not a reference work. It is meant to provide a panoramic view for the general reader.

THE COMPILATION OF THIS BOOK was spurred by the approaching centennial of *Harvard Magazine*, which began life in November 1898 as a four-page weekly called the *Harvard Bulletin*. Frequent deadlines and a birthright of corporate independence invested the *Bulletin*—renamed the *Harvard Alumni Bulletin* in 1910—with vitality and staying power; its issues are a rich source of detail about the quotidian life of a rapidly growing university. In more recent times the grim realities of publishing economics imposed a series of reductions in frequency, but longer intervals between issues let the editors cover their institutional beat with increasing depth and variety. When "bulletin" came to seem an anomalous term, the title was changed to *Har-*

vard *Magazine*. That was in 1973. The journal has published on a bi-monthly basis since 1977, and remains editorially independent.

The ninety-nine bound volumes of the *Bulletin* and *Harvard Magazine* were a basic resource for *Harvard Observed*. Much is owed to the editors and writers whose work this book distills. Other important acknowledgments appear on page 316, but here the compiler must declare his special indebtedness to six stalwarts who preceded him in the editor's chair: Jerome D. Greene (founding editor, 1898-1901); John D. Merrill (1903-1907, 1919-1940); M. A. DeWolfe Howe (1913-1919); David McCord (1940-1946); William Bentinck-Smith (1946-1953); and Norman A. Hall (1953-1966). Bless them all.

THE STORY OF TWENTIETH-CENTURY Harvard begins when the *Bulletin* did, in 1898. After four months of fighting, the Spanish-American War was over. The Treaty of Paris would transfer much of Spain's dwindling empire to the United States. Congress's war resolution had renounced any claim to Cuba, but Puerto Rico, the Philippines, and Guam would become U.S. dependencies. Expansionist zeal had led to the annexation of Hawaii in July; in a year the United States and Germany would divide the archipelago of Samoa. For the first time, the nation would be a major stakeholder in the Caribbean and the Far East.

"The march of events rules and over-rules human action," President William McKinley told U.S. peace commissioners leaving for Paris. "Without any design or desire on our part the war has brought us new duties and responsibilities which we must meet and discharge as becomes a great nation." Most Americans and their leaders could not have imagined what intervention in Cuba's revolution might lead to. One who did was Colonel Leonard Wood (M.D. 1884), commander of the "Rough Riders" regiment and McKinley's personal physician. Taking ship for Cuba, Wood had written his wife, "Hard it is to realize that this is the commencement of a new policy and that this is the first great expedition our country has ever sent oversea and marks the commencement of a new era in our relations with the world."

Whatever the new era might bring, Harvard would expect to play an increasing role in it. Many Harvardians already regarded the spheres of influence of nation and University as indistinguishable. In a mock-heroic poem composed for a 1901 football banquet, F. J. Stimson (A.B. 1876) would declaim that

> In these three years we've come to man's estate
> And on our brow the cares of Empire wait...
> Let each freshwater college own our sway,
> Each Tagalog or Cuban or Malay
> Come in—for like the Peace of Rome of yore
> Fair Harvard's peace is o'er the world once more.

In point of fact the most violent and complex century in history had begun. Global warfare, vast social changes, and the effects of accelerating technological innovation form the backdrop of *Harvard Observed*. How the institution adapted is the book's overarching concern.

The Reformers

I do not know how it is with you, but I know that I am unable to keep up in mind or memory with the expansion of Harvard University.
—*Charles William Eliot, addressing alumni in 1902*

A CAUSTIC MIDWESTERN HISTORIAN would observe that "the sharpest criticism of Harvard, as well as of the rest of the universe, has come from Harvard men." But as the nineteenth century ended, Harvard men had reason to approve of their alma mater. Charles William Eliot, rounding out his third decade as president, had led it to the forefront of American higher education. The University was the nation's largest, with an enrollment of 4,000 and a $12 million endowment. Eliot's teaching appointments had made his faculty the envy of other institutions. His reforms in graduate and undergraduate education had been widely emulated.

With the best-funded financial aid program of any private institution, Harvard College was attracting an increasingly national student body. The "Annex," now renamed Radcliffe College, provided instruction to women. The Graduate School of Arts and Sciences was the nation's leading producer of Ph.D.s. The schools of medicine and law were the leaders in their fields.

The elective system was Eliot's best-known reform. It allowed undergraduates to design their own

Opposite: A turn-of-the-century view of the Johnston Gate (1890), main entrance to Harvard Yard. Automobiles and buses had not yet overrun Harvard Square.

At right: Charles William Eliot, foremost educational reformer of his era. Louis Potter's bust stands in the Faculty Room of University Hall.

LOWELL IN 1898

Academic Warrior

Born and bred on Beacon Hill, A. Lawrence Lowell had the courtly manner and broad "a" of a typical Boston Brahmin. But "Mr. Lowell is no mere conservative," noted the *Harvard Bulletin;* "he has always had that gleam of radicalism so often found in able men whose environment would seem naturally to foster only tradition and stability." As a reformer, Lowell was never daunted by the size of the task at hand. *At War with Academic Traditions in America* was the revealing title of one of his books.

Lowell was 40 when he began his academic career. He seemed intent on making up for lost time. He disliked small talk and could be brusque to the point of rudeness. Early on, associates sensed that he hoped to become Harvard's president. In 1908, when Charles W. Eliot announced his impending retirement, Lowell was ready to step in.

studies, choosing freely from more than 450 course offerings. This break with the rigidly prescribed curricula of the past had begun before Eliot became president, but he had implemented it and proselytized for it.[1] In practical terms, the elective system liberated students and teachers from outworn pedagogical practices, enabling them to acquire the new knowledge and specialized skills demanded by an industrial and scientific age. Eliot thought of it as the product of three and a half centuries of social change. "The elective system is, in the first place, an outcome of the Protestant Reformation," he had written in 1895. "In the next place, it is an outcome of the spirit of political liberty."

By the turn of the century the concept had been taken up by every large college or university in the country, with the exception of Yale. Harvard College's last course requirements, other than freshman English and a foreign language, were dropped in 1899. But old-guard defenders of "classical learning" did not capitulate, and even liberal-minded faculty members were troubled by the number of undergraduates who abused the freedom of the elective system to coast through Harvard. The most persistent critic was A. Lawrence Lowell (A.B. 1877, LL.B. 1880), professor of the science of government.

At Eliot's behest, Lowell had left his Boston law practice in 1897 to teach in the new department of government. His teaching had confirmed his belief that the intellectual and social life of the College was in decline. As Lowell saw it, Eliot had gone overboard on the elective system and ignored the importance of residential facilities. The two men would grapple over these issues for almost a decade.

TO ELIOT AND OTHER leading educators, it was axiomatic that American universities should serve the national interest. For one of the newly built gates to the Yard he would compose the inscription

Enter to grow in wisdom
Depart better to serve thy country and thy kind.

"A true university is a school of public spirit for its governors, benefactors, officers, graduates, and students," Eliot had written in 1895. "We seek to train doers; achievers, men whose successful careers are much subservient to the public good. We are not interested here in producing languid observers of the world, mere spectators in the game of life, or fastidious critics of other men's labors." To Eliot, the University's 20,000 alumni were "the living Harvard force."

The same theme was sounded by another tireless reformer, Theodore Roosevelt (A.B. 1880), the first American president to urge collegians to enter public service. "If you become so overcultivated . . . that you cannot do the hard work of practical politics," TR would tell Harvard students, "then you had better never have been educated at all."

Roosevelt had entered politics at 22. After a year at Columbia Law School he successfully ran for the New York legislature. In 1884 he was the youngest delegate at the Republican national convention in Chicago. Stricken by the sudden deaths of his mother and his young wife, he left politics for a time to ranch and hunt in the Dakota Badlands. He returned to become a reform Civil Service Commissioner in Washington, then New York City's crusading police commissioner, then assistant secretary of the navy in President William McKinley's administration. When the Spanish-American War began, Roosevelt quickly resigned to join the Rough Riders. His famous charge up San Juan Hill led to his election as governor of New York four months later.

In a move to sidetrack his onrushing political career—"silent and awful like the Chicago Express," in the words of his friend Henry Adams (A.B. 1858)—Republican bosses drafted Roosevelt as McKinley's running mate in 1900. Thanks in part to TR's tireless campaigning, McKinley defeated William Jennings Bryan in November. "This election means my political death," groaned Roosevelt. But McKinley was shot by an anarchist ten months later, and TR became president at 42.

Senator Mark Hanna, the Ohio millionaire who had been McKinley's political patron, had fought to keep "that wild man" off the ticket. "Now look," he fumed on the funeral train, "that damned cowboy is president of the United States!" Six months later Roosevelt justified Hanna's fears by invoking the little-used Sherman Antitrust Act to dissolve a giant holding company formed by J. P. Morgan and rail barons James J. Hill and E. H. Harriman. TR's zeal and combativeness inspired reformers within both parties and at every level of government. He was a man perpetually in motion. News photographers followed him on his frequent hikes, horseback rides, and hunting trips. Mass-circulation newspapers and magazines were a new force in American culture; the phrase had not yet been coined, but presidential appearances became media events.

Two months before he became president, Roosevelt completed a six-year term on Harvard's Board of Overseers. He continued to visit Cambridge, lecturing and taking part in academic exercises. At the Commencement of 1902 he was awarded an LL.D. The president showed his institutional loyalty when Harvard's new football coach requested that Ernest Graves, formerly of West Point, be temporarily detached from his army post to serve on his coaching staff. TR wrote to Secretary of War Taft, "I was a Harvard man before I was a politician. Please do what these gentlemen want."

Theodore Roosevelt's hyperactive political life inspired "Vacation," drawn for *Puck* by Joseph Keppler and now in Harvard's Theodore Roosevelt Collection.

ONLY AT HARVARD, some might have said, could two of the nation's most resolute educational reformers meet on familiar terms with its most energetic exponent of economic and political reform. The triangle was an odd one. Wary of Roosevelt and his "lawless mind," Eliot still wrote avuncular letters advising the president on social policy. Lowell was friendly with TR, who lectured to some of his government classes, but disagreed with his view of the federal government as the guardian of the public interest. As for Roosevelt, his genuine concern for higher education was sometimes outweighed by his interest in football. When Eliot sought to abolish the game because of its roughness, it was said that TR had privately called him a mollycoddle. Each man had his own agenda. As the dominant figure in national politics, Roosevelt was determined to use his power and influence to advance social progress and enlarge America's role in world affairs. Lowell was absorbed by educational issues. He saw flaws in the College and wanted to correct them. Eliot took a more serene view of the College and had further reforms in mind; Lowell's complaints puzzled him. In the new century's first decade, academic politics at Harvard would come down to a test of strength between the two men, with Lowell gaining the upper hand. By the fall of 1908, when Eliot announced his resignation, Lowell would be seen as the heir apparent.

Dr. Eliot's Unfinished Business

FORMAL PHOTOGRAPHS—an informal one was a rarity—captured the public persona of Charles William Eliot: aristocratic, high-minded, patient, unbending. Less evident were the personal characteristics that informed his administrative decisions and his day-to-day dealings with members of the Harvard community: his libertarian views, his flashes of dry wit, the agility of his mind and body.

Eliot had turned 65 in the spring of 1899. He had no thought of retiring. His was the most influential voice in American education. He had just published *Educational Reform: Essays and Addresses, 1869-1897,* and he meant to keep up his writing and speaking—not only on educational matters but also on social, moral, and cultural issues, foreign affairs, and religion. Always interested in reform at the elementary and secondary-school levels, he was working to extend the free elective system to high schools. At the college level, he hoped to reduce the standard course of study from four to three years.

To increase Harvard's strength in science and technology, he intended to renew his efforts to join forces with the Massachusetts Institute of Technology. He was considering a new graduate school of diplomacy and public service. He hoped to curb the excesses of intercollegiate athletics—especially football.

He still had remarkable stamina. Like Roosevelt, Eliot was an exponent of strenuous exercise. In 1858, as a young instructor, he had rowed for a Harvard crew that broke the course record in the Boston City Regatta.[2] For much of his life he had ridden horseback almost daily. At sixty he had taken up bicycling. He spent summers cruising the Maine coast in his 43-foot sloop, *Sunshine.* He slept soundly, rose early, and refreshed himself by taking ten-minute catnaps.

His national reputation continued to grow. Other educational leaders asked his advice. The press sought him out for oracular statements on every subject—marital happiness, labor disputes, "race suicide," Prohibition, the religion of the future. He became, as philosophy professor Ralph Barton Perry would later put it, "adviser-at-large to the American people on things-in-general." With his faculty, with members of the Board of Overseers, with administrators and students, Eliot was now on warmer terms than in the past. Yet these groups—particularly the faculty—could and did resist many of the changes he proposed.

As president, Roosevelt enjoyed dressing the part. But he kept a wrestling mat in the White House.

OUR PORTRAIT GALLERY. No. 1.

"*A semely man oer haelt was withal,*
Bold of his speche and wise and wel y taught;
And of manhode lakked him right naught."
PROLOGUE, OF CANTERBURY TALES.

During his last decade in office most of his initiatives would be stymied. In terms of personal power and influence, the apex of Eliot's forty-year presidency had come just before the turn of the century.

IN 1869, AT THE START of his presidency, the ranks of the Faculty of Arts and Sciences had included 45 "teachers of professorial grade." Now there were 135. Eliot had hand-picked most of them.

Some of his best appointments were from outside the academy. In 1870 he had invited Henry Adams, then a reform-minded political journalist in Washington, to create a course in medieval history.* He got Charles F. Dunbar (A.B. 1851) to leave the editorship of the conservative *Boston Advertiser* to become America's first professor of economics. Dunbar became dean of the faculty and one of the president's closest associ-

---

*A famous exchange ensued. *Adams:* "But, Mr. President, I know nothing about medieval history." *Eliot:* "If you will point out anyone who knows more, Mr. Adams, I will appoint him."

The English Department's Barrett Wendell (top) was supercilious and foppish in manner, but got high marks as a teacher of composition. The ferocious "Kitty"–George Lyman Kittredge (above)–taught Shakespeare for nearly fifty years. The correct way to spell it, he insisted, was "Shakspere."

"Copey"–Charles Townsend Copeland (below)–had a large and devoted following. Adoring students and auditors filled his English courses, poetry readings, and soirées. But President Eliot disliked his posturing and refused to promote him.

Charles R. Lanman taught Sanskrit. A devoted rower, he was known as "Charles River" Lanman.

ates. In an obscure New York law firm Eliot found Christopher Columbus Langdell (A.B. 1851, LL.B. 1853), whom he had known in College. Langdell returned to teach at the Law School and become its first dean.

Other early appointees included the peripatetic William James (M.D. 1869), founder of America's first psychological laboratory, and the three other members of Harvard's "Philosophical Four": George Herbert Palmer (A.B. 1864), Josiah Royce, and George Santayana (A.B. 1886, PH.D. 1889). Oliver Wendell Holmes Jr. (A.B. 1861) was hired to teach courses on the American constitution. Young Henry Hill (A.B. 1869), son of former president Thomas Hill, offered the first course in organic chemistry. For the aesthete Charles Eliot Norton, his cousin, Eliot established Harvard's first chair in fine arts. For the composer John Knowles Paine he created America's first professorship in music.

Eliot raided other leading institutions for scholars. He brought Charles Lanman (Sanskrit) from Johns Hopkins; Charles Haskins (medieval history) from Wisconsin; Bliss Perry (English) from Princeton. Kuno Francke (German) and Hugo Münsterberg (psychology) were imported from Munich and Freiburg respectively. Charles Parker (classics) and Roger Merriman (history) had been at Oxford.

In the 1880s came a generation of young Harvard graduates who became institutional icons: Le Baron Russell Briggs (A.B. 1875), Barrett Wendell (A.B. 1877), George Lyman Kittredge (A.B. 1882), and George Pierce Baker (A.B. 1887) in English; Edward Channing (A.B. 1878, PH.D. 1880) and Albert Bushnell Hart (A.B. 1880) in history; Frank Taussig (A.B. 1879, PH.D. 1883) in economics; Charles Grandgent (A.B. 1883) in Romance languages. More home-grown talent arrived in the 1890s: Charles Townsend Copeland (A.B. 1882) in English; Theodore Richards (A.B. 1886, PH.D. 1888) in chemistry; Archibald Cary Coolidge (A.B. 1887) in history; Irving Babbitt (A.B. 1889) in French.

Eliot had gone outside the academy to hire Lawrence Lowell. In 1901 Lowell made his presence felt as the head of a faculty committee that blocked the last of Eliot's major reform proposals.

STRICTER ADMISSION STANDARDS had raised the average age of entering freshmen, pushing the average age at graduation to 22. Many graduates of the professional schools did not begin their careers until they were in their late twenties, an increasing source of concern to professional-school educators. Eliot favored a three-year A.B. program,

Left: Josiah Royce, George Herbert Palmer, and William James. With George Santayana, they made up the celebrated "Philosophical Four." The portrait is by Winifred Rieber.

Santayana, perceptive and caustic, left for Europe in 1912.

Le Baron Russell Briggs, professor of English, got the new post of dean of the College when the faculty was reorganized in 1891. His empathy with undergraduates was legendary. A Harvard student, it was said, would rather be dismissed by Briggs than kept on by another dean.

As dean of the Faculty of Arts and Sciences from 1902 to 1925, Briggs chaired most of its major committees. For much of that time he was also president of Radcliffe College; in 1904 he became Boylston professor of rhetoric and oratory.

like those of Oxford and Cambridge, because it would shorten the course for those seeking advanced degrees, while adding rigor to undergraduate education. He could not have foreseen that his losing battle for a three-year A.B. would lead to a sweeping reexamination of the College's educational program.

By 1900 a quarter of the members of each class entered Harvard with advanced standing and met the A.B. requirements in three years, though many opted to take more courses and graduate with the rest of their classmates. In his annual reports, and in speeches to students and alumni, Eliot pushed hard for the three-year A.B. "The growing habit of spending long years in preparation for a life work is a grave error," he told arriving members of the Class of 1904—among them Franklin Roosevelt, a future president, and Percy Bridgman, a future Nobel Prizeman. "A course of study should only be long enough to win power; the sooner you begin to use it the better. Do not get in four years what you can get in three."

In 1901 the Faculty of Arts and Sciences narrowly defeated a proposal to regularize a three-year residency for the A.B. The debate brought out rising concern about academic standards. Eliot insisted that the elective system had raised the quality of instruction so much that the level of work required for the A.B. was higher than ever. But faculty members knew that too many students were abusing the system by larding their study cards with "snap" or "cinch" courses. Undergraduate wags snickered about "the Faculty of Larks and Cinches."

A committee was appointed to explore ways of "improving instruction in Harvard College." Its chairman was Le Baron Russell Briggs, dean of the College. The driving force was Professor Lowell. In what was then a novel procedure, the committee sent questionnaires to students and teachers. The returns revealed that the average number of hours that most students invested in study was "discreditably small." Lowell wrote the committee's report. "Too much teaching and too little studying" was its terse verdict on the state of undergraduate education.

The three-year A.B. was doomed. Few now cared to argue that the College could accomplish in three years what it was failing to do in four.[3] The Briggs Committee's report also provided a baseline for later committees, led by Lowell, that examined the elective system and proposed measures to reshape and stiffen the College curriculum.

THE THREE-YEAR A.B. got some of the blame for a financial crisis in 1903-1904, when the University ran a deficit of $43,000. Rapid expansion in Eliot's time had often caused deficits, but not on that scale.[4] The causes included declining tuition income and increased costs incurred by additions to the teaching staff, predicated on enrollment increases that did not materialize. Undergraduate enrollment had begun slipping in 1901. In 1904, the year of the big deficit, the College had 205 fewer students than in 1903. An increase in three-year A.B.s accounted for some of the decline, but the number of entering freshmen

Harvard at the Turn of the Century

William James, professor of philosophy, was completing *Varieties of Religious Experience.*

The Charles River was tidal; a dam had been proposed.

John Brice Gordon Rinehart '00 was not in his Grays Hall room on a June evening in 1900, but his classmate Ralph R. ("Railroad") Kent persisted in calling his name from below. Others took up the chant, and the

night filled with "Rineharts." For decades to come, "Oh, Rinehart" would be the rallying cry that summoned restive students into the Yard for nocturnal frivolity.

Harvard Square: Since the West End Railway's conversion of its horsecar routes to electric traction in 1889, the Square had become a major transportation exchange. Lyceum Hall, the building with the pitched roof, now belonged to the Harvard Cooperative Society. To the right is College House, a dormitory for students of modest means.

was falling. Competition from smaller New England colleges, especially Dartmouth, was a factor. Some potential applicants may have been wary of the individualism and heterodoxy that were part of Harvard's milieu. Others, perhaps, were put off by reports of friction between the College's well-heeled prep school crowd and the scholarship students they disparaged as "greasy grinds." Whatever the causes, the problem had to be met. Harvard relied on student fees for 60 percent of its total income. Raising tuition was one option. Retrenchment was another. Seeking funds from alumni was a third.

College tuition had gone from $104 a year to $150 just before Eliot's presidency began. An Overseers' committee now recommended a 50 percent rise. That would make up for cost-of-living increases since 1869 and furnish $150,000 a year in new income. But Harvard was already considered a high-cost college. A survey of fifteen institutions showed that twelve charged lower fees. Yale and Princeton were on a par with Harvard. Eliot opposed any increase, fearing that it would reduce the

Telephones. In 1900 the University had two. One was in the office of C. L. Smith, dean of the Faculty of Arts and Sciences. Harvard's chief engineer had the other.

Memorial Hall and its 190-foot clock tower dominated the Harvard landscape.

Walter Clarkson '03, the premier college pitcher of his era, helped the 1901 baseball team to a record of 18-2. Clarkson captained the team for another two seasons, but lost his eligibility when he signed, for a bonus, with the New York Highlanders.

Hemenway Gymnasium, north of the Yard, was the largest gym in the country and the cradle of physical education in America. Dr. Dudley Sargent was its longstanding director.

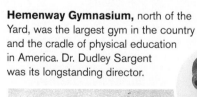

Helen Keller '04 was among 300 students enrolled at Radcliffe College. An illness had left her blind, deaf, and mute before she was two.

The Diary of a Freshman, by Charles Macomb Flandrau (A.B. 1895), sold briskly in Cambridge bookshops.

Future president Franklin Roosevelt enrolled in 1900 and took his A.B. in three years.

Charles Francis Adams was the spokesman for an Overseers' committee that proposed a tuition increase to help ease the financial crisis that arose in 1904. President Eliot objected. "I am inclined to think that you would be more tolerant than I of the presence of stupid sons of the rich," he wrote Adams.

William Lawrence, bishop of Massachusetts and fund-raiser extraordinaire.

proportion of students from public schools, then about 30 percent. To his persistent critic Charles Francis Adams (A.B. 1856), a member of the Overseers' committee, he wrote:

> You said at the start of this discussion . . . that you wanted the College open to young men who had either money or brains. The gist of our difference lies, I think, in this restricted alternative. I want to have the College open equally to men with much money, little money, or no money, provided they all have brains. I care no more than you for young men who have no capacity for an intellectual life. They are not fit subjects for a college, whether their parents have money or not. I am inclined to think that you would be more tolerant than I of the presence of stupid sons of the rich. I care for the young men whose families have so little money that it would make a real difference to them whether the Harvard tuition fee were $150 or $225. You do not seem to care for that large class. To my thinking, they constitute the very best part of Harvard College.

Eliot prevailed. Tuition stayed at $150 until 1916. Against the advice of the Overseers, Eliot held up faculty promotions and cut junior positions and salaries. Noting that the number of arts and sciences courses had risen from 92 to 456 in Eliot's time, the Overseers voted that new ones be added only after the utmost deliberation. The governing boards then turned to the alumni. The first modern capital campaign was announced in 1904. The goal was $2.5 million to increase faculty salaries. Professors' salaries had risen as much as 25 to 40 percent since 1869, but instructors' pay had *declined* by 40 percent.

The campaign was led by a master fund-raiser: William Lawrence (A.B. 1871, S.T.D. 1893), Episcopal bishop of Massachusetts.[5] Then vice president of the Alumni Association, he was also an Overseer; a decade later he would join the Corporation. A core group of twenty alumni, mostly from Boston and New York, contributed $50,000 each; overall, 2,000 alumni gave a total of $2.4 million. It was the first time that an institution of higher learning had raised as much as a million dollars at one time. The campaign eased Harvard's financial crisis, but the University struggled with mounting deficits for the rest of the decade.

Gold Coasters and Greasy Grinds

WAS THE COLLEGE A HAVEN for rich men's sons? Was it "of broad democratic resort," in Eliot's words, or did it, in fact, institutionalize social inequities? The debates over tuition and the three-year A.B., the committee report on academic standards—all raised hard questions about the makeup of the student body and the cultural stratifications within it.

"It is a common error to suppose that the men of this University live in rooms the walls of which are covered with embossed leather; that they have at hand every luxury of modern life," Eliot had told entering freshmen in the fall of 1900. "As a matter of fact, there are but few such. The great majority are of moderate means; and it is this diversity of condition that makes the experience of meeting men here so valuable."

Achieving "diversity of condition" had been one of Eliot's paramount goals. Class subscriptions and individual gifts had provided Harvard with the best-funded financial aid program of any private college. The nationwide expansion of the railroads and the growing number of regional Harvard clubs, energetically raising scholarship money and boosting the College, had increased the geographic and social diversity of the student body. But because its residential facilities were inadequate, Harvard was losing the "collegiate way of living" idealized by its founders.

Enrollment had grown fourfold in three decades. By 1900 it was about 2,000. Less than a third of all undergraduates could be housed in the dozen or so College dormitories, many of them primitively equipped and poorly maintained. Another third of each class lived at home, rented rooms in private residences, or lodged in boarding houses. Wealthier students flocked to the twenty private residence halls that had gone up in recent years. These citified buildings offered luxurious suites, including baths.[6] In one or two, squash courts and swimming pools were among the amenities. The new epicenter of undergraduate life at Harvard was the "Gold Coast," a three-block cluster of residence halls conveniently close to classrooms and clubhouses. The wealthiest stu-

Mount Auburn Street, a block south of Harvard Yard, was lined by luxurious private residential halls that catered to wealthy students.

This photograph of the "Gold Coast," from about 1910, shows Claverly, Randolph, and Russell Halls, all built between 1892 and 1900. At right is the recently completed clubhouse of the Harvard Lampoon. Its fanciful design was the last work of architect Edmund Wheelwright (A.B. 1876), a founding editor of the magazine.

dents dined at one of the more than two dozen "waiting" or "final" clubs, or at private houses or restaurants. Most of the rest took meals at Memorial Hall's dining commons, or the newer and cheaper Randall Hall Commons a block away.

Traditional College activities still helped cultivate class solidarity. Students were urged to compete for class teams, attend smokers and beer nights, and form organized cheering sections at intercollegiate athletic contests. In 1899 Major Henry Lee Higginson (1855, A.M. *hon.* 1882) gave $150,000 to build a social center. Conceived by William Roscoe Thayer (A.B. 1881), editor of the *Harvard Graduates' Magazine,* the Harvard Union represented an earnest effort to heal divisions within the undergraduate body by providing a club that was open to everyone, regardless of social or financial standing. The Union served well as a locus for organizational activities, but did not bridge what Samuel Eliot Morison later called "the social chasm between the clubbed and the unclubbed."

If the fabric of Harvard's collegial life was unraveling, there was no single cause. The defects of the elective system could be blamed for the number of feckless "pass men" who took easy courses and devoted themselves to club life and social events in Cambridge and Boston. Snobbish "society men" could be blamed for ostracizing the studious "grinds." Certain faculty members could be blamed for glorifying the nineteenth-century type of the leisure-class gentleman. And Eliot and the Corporation could be blamed for failing to recognize the importance of residential facilities to a cohesive university community.

Known to generations of students as "The Widow Nolen," W.W. Nolen (A.B. 1884) operated a Mount Auburn Street cram school that provided tutoring, papers, and anything else a lagging student might need to pass courses.

The Widow himself had graduated *summa cum laude.* He used some of his earnings to assemble a notable collection of Lincolniana, which he left to the Harvard College Library at his death in 1923.

THE FIRST YEARS OF Eliot's presidency had seen the completion of four big dormitories: Thayer Hall (the College Yard's first large-scale building, intended to house men who could not afford the rising cost of private lodgings); Matthews and Weld Halls, at the Yard's southern end; and Holyoke House, at Massachusetts Avenue and Holyoke Street. Three more dormitories rose north of the Yard in the 1890s. Conant and Perkins Halls, near the scientific laboratories, foreshadowed the Georgian Revival styling that would dominate Harvard architecture for a half-century. Walter Hastings Hall, near the Law School, became a haven for Jewish students and was known as "Little Jerusalem." Only Holyoke House was built with Harvard money. Eliot was now content to let private enterprise meet the College's residential needs. As he noted in his annual report for 1905-06, dormitories yielded lower financial returns than the University's general investments.

In 1902 a bequest from George Smith (A.B. 1853) of St. Louis provided funding for three new dormitories. Lawrence Lowell was quick to weigh in, writing Eliot to urge that they be located within the Yard. Lowell cited "a growing feeling . . . that the tendency of the wealthy students to live in private dormitories outside the yard, involves great danger of a snobbish separation of students on lines of wealth, and is thereby bringing about a condition of things that would destroy the chief value of the College as a place for the training of character. I fear, that with the loss of that democratic feeling which ought to lie at the basis of university life, we are liable to lose our moral hold upon a large part of

Genial Bully

NO BENEFACTOR had done more for Harvard than Henry Lee Higginson. Head of a Boston investment house, Higginson shared his wealth, vision, and energy with many of the city's cultural institutions—most notably the Boston Symphony Orchestra, which he founded in 1881 and steered for four decades. Elected to the Harvard Corporation in 1893, he was soon recognized as its wisest and most far-sighted financial strategist.

Higginson gave more than financial advice. He acquired and donated the 31-acre tract that became Soldiers Field; funded the Harvard Union as a center for students, faculty members, and alumni; secured the properties that became the sites of the Medical School and the Business School; and endowed a professorship at the Medical School.

The brevity of his undergraduate career made his devotion to Harvard all the more remarkable. Higginson entered with the class of 1855, but an eye problem forced him to leave after six months. He spent four years in Europe, hiking, learning French and German, and gorging himself on operatic and concert music. In the Civil War he served as an officer of the First Massachusetts Cavalry, barely surviving a spinal bullet wound inflicted during a Virginia skirmish in 1863.

For the rest of his life he was *Major* Higginson. Invalided home, he married Ida Agassiz, a daughter of Professor Louis Agassiz. After trying oil drilling and cotton farming, he joined Lee, Higginson, his father's firm, as a partner in 1868. His success as an early venture capitalist provided the wherewithal to launch and maintain the Boston Symphony. Like the BSO, Major Higginson became a Boston institution. He accepted that status with humility, observing that "for most people, the place of second fiddle

Henry Lee Higginson sat for John Singer Sargent's portrait with his Civil War cavalry cloak on his lap. The scar left by a saber wound can be seen on Higginson's cheek.

is preferable to first fiddle."

Old friends of this genial and courteous gentleman remembered that schoolmates had called him "Bully Hig." Tenacious and scrupulously honest, he could be singularly direct. "Cease all hard words about corporations and capitalists," he wrote bluntly to Theodore Roosevelt when the president took on the trust-builders. To a cousin he once wrote, "Nobody knows his duties better than yourself—therefore I presume to admonish you. I want you, as the oldest and richest member of your family and mine, to give to the College $100,000. . . ."

His own largesse brought him to the brink of insolvency more than once. His philanthropic record bore out his belief that "a rich man should give away all of his fortune during his lifetime."

His only Harvard degree was an honorary A.M. conferred after the Boston Symphony Orchestra's initial season. "To the degree of Master of Arts, a title of peculiar fitness," wrote the *Alumni Bulletin* after his death in 1919, "the hearts of a multitude of Harvard men would add, in all affection and gratitude, *summa cum laude*."

The Harvard Union, given by Major Higginson as a "house of fellowship" for students, faculty members, and alumni.

**Robert Woods Bliss (A.B. '00) in
Wytche Hazelle, the Hasty Pudding
Theatricals production of 1900.**

**A class in experimental psychology
led by Professor Hugo Münsterberg
(at head of table). William James
had founded the world's first psychological laboratory in 1875.**

**A student room in the
Yard, with décor typical
of the era, about 1905.**

the students. . . ." Eliot put Lowell on a committee to review the procedure for assigning dormitory rooms. Lowell wrote its report. Going well
beyond its mandate, it stated that Harvard was facing a choice between
two models: the German, in which a university's only responsibility
was instruction, or the English "college system" exemplified by the Ox-
bridge universities.

Lowell's preference was clear. "A college education without a larger
community life cannot permanently succeed," he told New York Harvard Club members in 1904. Many poorer students, said Lowell, "need
a larger social life. The richer men need not only this, but more intellectual stimulus; and all of them need to be shuffled together."

The idea of residential colleges had come up as early as 1871. Lowell
had come out for it in a critique of the elective system written for the
Harvard Monthly in 1887. Now the subject was current again. As Columbia's Phi Beta Kappa orator in 1906, Charles Francis Adams attacked
the elective system as a mischievous fad and endorsed the principle of
residential colleges, each "so limited in size that individuality would be
not only possible but a necessary part of the system."

Eliot was unmoved. "To know by name and pat on the back two
hundred men is not much of an object," he wrote later, "but to know a
few men body and soul, and to have a sympathetic intercourse with
these few, is a large part of what a university can do for youth." Scholarly clubs and debating societies, he believed, promoted that sort of fellowship.

OF GREATER CONCERN to Eliot was the proportion of students
from public schools. To Adams he had stated that young men of limited means "constitute the very best part of Harvard College." He agreed
that the College was obliged to educate the sons of the rich; in his inaugural address he had said that "the country suffers when the rich are
ignorant and unrefined." But Eliot's remarkable patience was wearing
thin. "The striking things about the American boy from well-to-do families," he wrote to one schoolmaster, "are his undeveloped taste and fac-

ulty for individual labor, the triviality of his habitual subjects of thought, the brevity of his vocabulary, and his lack of judgment and sense of proportion in historical, literary and scientific subjects."

To enroll more public school graduates, active measures were called for. Eliot reorganized the College admissions process in 1905. Five committees of "weary professors" were melded into one, largely staffed by administrators. The faculty was persuaded to accept the new College Entrance Examination Board tests as substitutes for Harvard's own. Because the CEEB tests were administered in three times as many locations as Harvard's, the catchment area for prospective students was greatly enlarged. The next year's entering class was almost 10 percent bigger, and the proportion of public school men began to edge upward.

As the public school contingent grew, so did the proportion of Jewish and Roman Catholic students. In 1870, when the College's total enrollment was 563, the student body had included three Jews and seven Catholics. The first black graduate, Richard Greener, took his degree that year. By 1908 about 7 percent of the College's 2,240 students were Jewish and almost 9 percent Roman Catholic. About two dozen were black. The registrar's rolls listed students from all 48 states, Puerto Rico, Hawaii, the Philippines, and thirty foreign countries, including Brazil, China, India, Japan, Siam, and Russia. The Cosmopolitan Club, a new social center for foreign students, had already outgrown its rooms in Holyoke House and was seeking more space.

Boxed in. Forty men, averaging 163.2 pounds each, squeezed into a 36-square-foot box to help Lewis Johnson (A.B. 1887), professor of civil engineering, project the load-bearing capacities of elevators.

Harvard had felt the effects of the massive immigration movements that were changing the nation's sociological mix. The first surge of post-Civil War immigration had come primarily from the so-called Nordic countries of Europe, but by 1905 three-quarters of those in the immigrant pool were from southern and eastern Europe. Some 9 million immigrants arrived between 1900 and 1910. To many native-born Americans the influx of "alien hordes" presaged disaster. Their phobias were fanned by a spate of books and essays purveying pseudoscientific theories of racial hierarchy. The Immigration Restriction League, founded in 1894 and headed by a group of Harvard-educated Bostonians, led a national movement to curtail immigration. A half dozen faculty members, including Lawrence Lowell, were active in it.[7] The tensions and conflicts aroused by large-scale immigration would take decades to play out in the life of the nation, and would vex Harvard and other old-line universities in the early 1920s. In the meantime, social stratification persisted—and years would pass before the College constructed new residential facilities.

The Chinese Club, founded in 1909 with 31 members. The government of China used Boxer Rebellion indemnity funds to send young scholars to Harvard and other American universities.

INTERCOLLEGIATE ATHLETICS was the one force that bridged social divisions and created a sense of solidarity in the College. Spectator sports provided common ground and a source of institutional pride to large numbers of students and alumni. The exploits of college athletes in football, baseball, and crew colored the romanticized vision of American campuses reflected in popular college novels of the day. But to President Eliot, the rise of intercollegiate athletics posed a threat to the intellectual and moral well-being of the University community. The worst example was football.

An Undesirable Game for Gentlemen

A QUARTER-CENTURY AFTER the game's invention, college football held a central position in institutional and national life. Harvard Stadium, heroic in scale and with the classic contours of a Roman circus, was a monument to its importance. America's largest collegiate sports arena, and the world's first massive reinforced concrete structure, it was largely built in four months, in time for the last two games of the 1903 season. A twenty-fifth-reunion gift of $100,000 from the class of 1879 helped meet the $325,000 cost.[8]

Social life on fall weekends was centered on football. Franklin Roosevelt, a sometime usher and cheerleader, took his cousin Eleanor to the new Stadium for the Yale game in 1903 (and proposed the next

A football poster from the early years of the century. "To Hell with Yale," says the dog-Latin motto.

day). The spirit of the times still resonates in the rousing marches composed by young Harvard men when the Stadium was new: "Up the Street," "Soldiers Field," "Gridiron King," "Yo Ho, the Good Ship Harvard," and "Harvardiana," all written between 1904 and 1909. For Harvard and other large colleges, football was a gushing cash cow. Big games almost always sold out. A capacity crowd of 35,000 filled the Stadium for the Yale game in 1903. Gate receipts for the season came to $73,000. With an unbeaten team, Yale took in $103,000, enough to cover the operating expenses of its schools of law, medicine, and divinity.

But college football was also beset by eligibility scandals, slush funds for star players, illegal betting, and injury epidemics caused by overtraining, flimsy equipment, intentional fouling, and the "mass plays" allowed by the rules. Yale's victory over Harvard in 1894 had involved so much bloodletting that the series was suspended for two years. In 1904 the national toll of football deaths reached 21. Only one Harvard player got through the season uninjured.

In *The Varieties of Religious Experience* (1902), William James had written that "what we now need to discover in the social realm is the moral equivalent of war: something heroic that will speak to men as universally as war does." Some saw football as the answer. President Eliot did not. "The ethics of the game, which are the imperfect ethics of war, do not improve," he wrote in his annual report in 1903. His outlook had changed since 1881, when he had stated that sports and games had transformed the ideal student "from a stooping, weak and sickly youth into one well-formed, robust, and healthy." Outdoor sports, Eliot conceded, might "promote vigorous physical development and provide invaluable safeguards against effeminacy and vice." But athletic prowess had little to do with success on the battlefield or in business, and as a spectacle football was "more brutalizing than prize-fighting, cock-fighting or bull-fighting." Harvard had led in regulating athletics. A committee of faculty members and Overseers, formed in 1882, had devised rules to ensure the amateur status of athletes and restrict the number of games played outside Cambridge. Since 1893 a graduate manager had overseen the athletics program. A faculty-student-alumni committee policed eligibility violations. Now Eliot wanted Harvard to take the lead in abolishing football. He almost succeeded in 1905, when mayhem on the gridiron commanded national attention. But a quicker man got around him.

THE SEASON OF 1905 was a turning point for college football. A preseason exposé in *McClure's* magazine emphasized the game's lax ethics and rampant brutality. A *Chicago Tribune* tally of football casualties listed 18 deaths and 159 serious injuries. President Roosevelt intervened in an effort to rescue the game. But it was Harvard's young coach, William T. Reid Jr. '01, A.M. '02, who led the reform movement that saved football from abolition at Harvard and other major colleges.

Reid had excelled in football and baseball at Harvard, and had been volunteer coach of the unbeaten 1901 football team. Officials of the Athletic Association of Harvard Graduates, dismayed by three straight losses to Yale, lured him away from a schoolteaching job in California to become Harvard's first salaried football coach in 1905. With a stipend and expense account of $7,000, the 26-year-old Reid earned more than any faculty member and nearly as much as President Eliot.

Reid was one of six Harvard, Yale, and Princeton officials summoned to the White House in the fall of 1905. The nation had recoiled at a gruesome news photo of a Swarthmore lineman who had been mauled by Pennsylvania's team. President Roosevelt had just mediated an end to the Russo-Japanese War and would earn the Nobel Peace Prize for his work. He now sought to bring concord to American football. If violent play continued, he warned, he might bar the game by executive edict. As an advocate of the strenuous life, TR did not object to rough games, nor did he want his alma mater to abolish football. That would be "doing

Brute force counted more than skill in turn-of-the-century football, and offensive "mass plays" resulted in an epidemic of fouls and injuries.

Dedicated to "the joys of manly contest," Harvard Stadium was built in the fall of 1903. It was topped off with a colonnade in 1910.

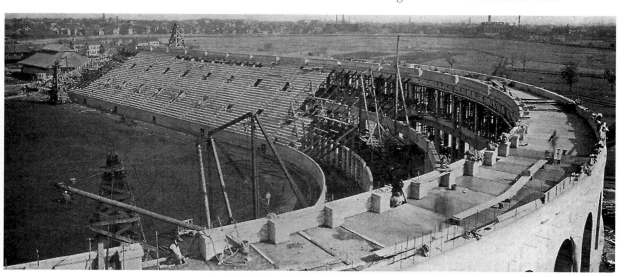

A record crowd, estimated at 43,000, trooped to the two-year-old Stadium for the 1905 Harvard-Yale game. The Eli prevailed, 6-0. The contest was marred by a flagrant foul that provoked widespread concern about the rules of the game.

Bill Reid, then 26, revamped Harvard's football program in 1905. The young coach's maneuverings at a national rule-making convention helped deflect pressures to prohibit football.

the baby act." He did want strict adherence to the rules. From the representatives of the Big Three he exacted a pledge to "play football honestly" and honor the rules against roughness, holding, and foul play.[10]

Reid knew it would take more than that to satisfy Harvard's president. "I have come to believe that the game ought to be radically changed," he wrote in an open letter to John D. Merrill (A.B. 1889), secretary of the Athletic Association and editor of the *Harvard Bulletin*. Reid was appointed to chair a committee to recommend "thoroughgoing" rule changes. A flagrant foul in that year's Yale game underscored the need to stiffen the rules. Freshman Francis ("Hooks") Burr, an all-America lineman and punter, was struck in the face by Yale's J.J. Quill after signaling for a fair catch. Burr was stunned and his nose broken, but because Quill's "hands were open," no penalty was called.[9]

Reid's committee proposed rule changes aimed at making football a test of skill, not brawn. Time was running out. An Overseers' subcommittee reported in January 1906 that "the present method [of football] is thoroughly bad and ought to be stopped absolutely and finally." The full board voted to permit no further games unless and until the governing boards approved changes in the rules.

Reid then executed a series of maneuvers that secured the adoption of most of his proposals at the national level. Doing so meant dislodging Yale's powerful Walter Camp, who wanted only minor rule changes, as secretary of an intercollegiate rules committee. Reid helped form a new committee and took over as secretary. A new rulebook based on the proposals developed at Harvard was approved in May 1906. New eligibility requirements barred graduate students and freshmen from competing on varsity teams. The Overseers agreed to sanction another year of competition. Reid led his 1906 team to a 10-1 season and went back to teaching in California. Columbia, Northwestern, California, and Stanford were among major colleges that gave up football after the 1905 season. Had Harvard done so, more would have followed.

Though eligibility issues and payoffs still plagued the game, the rule changes made a difference. Harvard's team injuries fell from 145 in 1905 to 31 in 1906. The new-style game, which legalized forward passing, was also more interesting to watch. The *Nation* acknowledged that "football was much improved by the new rules that emphasize brain over brawn" —while agreeing with President Eliot that "intercollegiate sport is an unnecessary distraction of students from their studies."

Eliot continued to inveigh against football.[10] Writing in 1907, he credited the new rules—"extorted . . . from [football's] creators and managers by the pressure of public opinion"—with improving the techniques of the game. But he added:

> The spirit of the game, however, remains essentially the same. It is properly described by the adjective "fierce,"—a term which is commonly applied to the game by its advocates. It therefore remains an undesirable game for gentlemen to play, or for multitudes of spectators to watch. No game is fit for college uses in which men are often so knocked or crushed into insensibility or immobility, that it is a question whether by the application of water and stimulants they can be brought to and enabled to go on playing. . . . An extreme recklessness remains a grave objection to the game of football, and it also makes basketball and hockey, as developed in recent years, undesirable games.

Misalliance with MIT

ELIOT HAD ALWAYS HOPED to join forces with the Massachusetts Institute of Technology, where he had taught chemistry before his election as Harvard's president. In his first year he had proposed a partial merger of the six-year-old Institute and Harvard's Lawrence Scientific School. MIT president John D. Runkle (S.B. 1851) rejected the proposal. Eliot renewed it when James Mason Crafts (S.B. 1858) became president in 1897. Again he was turned down. But in 1904 Crafts's successor, Henry Pritchett, was tempted.

The Lawrence Scientific School would soon receive income from an enormous bequest to promote applied science. The donor was Gordon McKay (A.M. *hon.* 1896), an inventor of shoe machinery who had died in 1903. His benefaction, the largest yet received by Harvard, was to be paid out over many years and would later be valued at more than $16 million. Offering undergraduate and graduate courses, Lawrence had an enrollment of 530 and was now Harvard's third largest school. During the twelve-year deanship of Nathaniel Southgate Shaler (S.B. 1862), professor of geology, it had added four-year programs in mechanical engineering, mining and metallurgy, architecture, landscape architecture, and forestry. With millions available for its Scientific School, Harvard might begin to take students away from MIT. The Institute was outgrowing its buildings on Boston's Copley Square, and its finan-

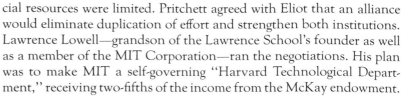

Gordon McKay. His multimillion-dollar bequest to promote applied science at Harvard was the largest yet received by the University.

Henry Lee Higginson organized the purchase of Charles River marshland as a new site for MIT. "It seems to me an essential part of the plan, if the University and the Technology are to get together, that the Technology should live on the marsh, for I know of no other place where they can squat," he wrote to President Eliot in the summer of 1904.

cial resources were limited. Pritchett agreed with Eliot that an alliance would eliminate duplication of effort and strengthen both institutions. Lawrence Lowell—grandson of the Lawrence School's founder as well as a member of the MIT Corporation—ran the negotiations. His plan was to make MIT a self-governing "Harvard Technological Department," receiving two-fifths of the income from the McKay endowment.

When the plan became known, there was hell to pay. MIT alumni, faculty members, and students saw the proposed alliance as subverting the Institute's independence. Many of those on the Harvard side saw it as breaching the spirit and terms of McKay's bequest. Harvard and MIT students made plans to settle the matter with sticks after a torchlight procession from Cambridge to Boston on the eve of the 1904 elections. At the eleventh hour Major Higginson got word and persuaded the Harvard paraders to alter their route and bypass MIT. The Tech students tussled with Boston policemen instead.

Lowell's brother Percival (A.B. 1876), an MIT astronomer, was indignant. "That a corporation avowedly has no soul does not condone an act by which money secured on certain representations is unblushingly pocketed to other purposes," he wrote the *Boston Transcript.* "To speciously name it an alliance deceives no one not a dullard or a dupe to the fact that it is a merger, intended to be all the more complete as time goes on. To call a spade a shovel only adds to the offence."

News of the plan alarmed Dean Shaler. His friendship with Gordon McKay had secured McKay's bequest to Harvard. Breaking off a visit to Italy, he rushed back to marshal faculty opposition.

Overriding a faculty vote, the MIT Corporation agreed to proceed if the Institute could legally sell its Boston property, obtained under a grant from the legislature, to help pay for a new campus. The courts ruled that out in the fall of 1905.

Lawrence Scientific School did not survive the mating dance. It was replaced in 1906 by a new Harvard Graduate School of Applied Science. Lawrence's instructional functions, facilities, and endowment funds were divided between the new graduate school and the College, which began granting a bachelor's degree in science. Shaler became dean of the new school, but within a month he developed appendicitis and died of postoperative pneumonia. A captivating teacher and energetic field geologist, he had been a colorful presence at Harvard for forty years (see page 31). Wallace Sabine (A.M. 1888), a physicist and expert on architectural acoustics, succeeded him.

The prime beneficiary of the institutional courtship was a graduate school that had not yet been born. With a handful of Harvard and MIT alumni and friends who favored the alliance, including Lawrence Lowell and Andrew Carnegie, Major Higginson had raised a subscription of $240,000 to purchase 1.3 million square feet of Charles River marshland as a site for the relocated Institute. A planned dam was expected to stabilize the river and render its marshlands buildable. The parcel remained in trust until 1918, when Lowell, who had become Harvard's president, persuaded his fellow trustees to transfer their shares to Harvard "for future inevitable extensions of the University." Seven years later the Allston marshland became the new campus of the Harvard Business School.

Powerful Connections

THE NEWS OF GORDON McKAY's huge bequest, reported for the first time in 1893, heralded a new age of philanthropic giving for Harvard. But McKay lived on for ten years, and no income from the bequest was paid until 1909. The new era really arrived when President Eliot rose at the Commencement of 1901 to read a cable from J. Pierpont Morgan confirming his $1 million gift of "the centre pavilion and two buildings for the new Medical School." Mindful of the power of example, Morgan had added, "You can announce this."

New industrial wealth was now flowing to colleges and universities in sums of unprecedented size. Much of it came from men without previous ties to the institutions they aided. Members of Harvard's governing boards, ever alive to new sources of support, were adroit at developing links to the rich and powerful.

The business and industrial boom of the post-Civil War era had generated immense family fortunes derived from mining and oil, steel and chemicals, railroads and shipping, meat-packing, communications, real estate, banking, and stock speculation. By 1890, one percent of the nation's families owned 51 percent of its total wealth. The formation of holding companies enlarged existing fortunes, gave rise to new ones, and kept the stock market buzzing.

Not yet burdened by personal income taxes, the newly rich lived extravagantly. They erected mansions, traveled in private railroad cars, sailed enormous yachts, assembled vast art collections. Their campaign contributions helped return Theodore Roosevelt to the White House in 1904, but their attempts to rig markets and control competition led the president to denounce them as "Wall Street conspirators" and "malefactors of great wealth" as he pressed for stronger regulation of business behavior. Yet many high-living capitalists took up civic causes, gave liberally to churches, and extended their patronage to cultural and educational institutions. Some, like Johns Hopkins, Paul Tulane, Ezra Cornell, and Leland Stanford, used their millions to found new colleges and universities. Others helped older ones.

By 1902 the nation's financial and commercial life was dominated by two interrelated groups of Wall Street titans. At the head of one group was J.P. Morgan. He had just formed the world's largest corporation, United States Steel, by buying out Andrew Carnegie's holdings: mines, mills, railroads, steamships. Associated with Morgan were George F. Baker, president of New York's First National Bank, and western railroad builder James J. Hill. In the other group were James Stillman, president of National City Bank; Jacob Schiff, of Kuhn, Loeb, and Company; railroad tycoon E.H. Harriman; and the Rockefeller family.

Morgan, who had spent two years at the University of Göttingen, was the son of a millionaire. The others were self-made men; none had gone to college. Some would have agreed with Chauncey Depew, presi-

J. Pierpont Morgan, "monarch of Wall Street," was the colossus bestriding the financial world of his day. Astute and unflappable, he sought to stabilize American business by "re-Morganizing" chaotic industries and using his credit and influence to halt financial panics.

Morgan's gift to Harvard of more than $1 million, pledged in 1901, funded three of the five buildings on the Medical School's new campus. It was the largest donation for current use that Harvard had yet received.

Within a year of his graduation, James Hazen Hyde (A.B. 1898) inherited control of the Equitable Assurance Society of New York, as well as seats on the boards of 46 large corporations. An ardent Francophile, Hyde used some of his wealth to give Harvard an exchange professorship with France. He also donated a library to the Harvard Union.

Above, Hyde appears dressed for a $200,000 costume party he threw in 1905. The ballroom of Sherry's hotel became a wing of Versailles in the reign of Louis XV; the Metropolitan Opera orchestra and corps de ballet entertained until midnight, and 350 guests danced until dawn.

The use of Equitable funds for Hyde's partying–and for dubious financial maneuverings–caused a scandal that led to a sweeping investigation of the insurance industry. Hyde retreated to Paris, where he spent the last forty years of his life and extended his lavish hospitality to visiting Harvardians.

dent of the New York Central Railroad, that the classical learning dispensed by old-line colleges was "the veneer of the quack, and . . . the decoration of the dude." The old education, said Depew, "gave the intellect a vast mass of information useful in the library and useless in the shop." In their benefactions to higher education, hard-headed businessmen leaned toward technical and professional schools.

By raising the financial stakes for schools of all kinds, they also changed the nature of educational fund-raising. The professionalized "development office" was still far in the future, but institutions now began to venture beyond local and regional canvassing to prospect for donors in the goldfields of New York City. Tactical planning and contact work was done by members of governing boards who knew the business community. Major Higginson, a Harvard Corporation member for 26 years, sat on corporate and institutional boards with Morgan, Carnegie, Schiff, and others. Robert Bacon (A.B. 1880), a three-term Overseer who joined the Corporation in 1912, had been a Morgan partner. As Overseers in later years, J. Pierpont Morgan Jr. (A.B. 1889) and Thomas Lamont (A.B. 1892), another partner in the house of Morgan, kept up Harvard's ties with 23 Wall Street.

Harvard could work both sides of the street. The General Education Board, first of John D. Rockefeller's foundations, supplied half the seed money for the future Harvard Business School. George F. Baker Jr. (A.B. 1899) was one of the school's early donors; his father would later give $5 million for a new campus. A James J. Hill professorship of railroad transportation was founded with $125,000 raised by Lamont and $125,000 from Hill himself. James Stillman gave the College an infirmary and endowed a chair of comparative anatomy at the Medical School. Jacob Schiff funded Harvard's Semitic Museum and the first archaeological excavations at Samaria, ancient capital of the kings of Israel.

It made sense for colleges and universities to try to lock in big donors by making them trustees. Conceding that "the personal presence of a living benefactor is apt to be troublesome in the management of an institution of learning," President Eliot could still describe the ideal trustee as "the highly educated, public-spirited, business or professional man . . . who has been successful in his own calling." The historian Laurence Veysey would note that powerful trustees "might be dignified and responsible (as at Harvard) or they might be petty tyrants (as at Ohio and West Virginia), but in any event their presence served to remind the university what was expected of it by the 'real' world."[11]

AS HIGHER EDUCATION became more enmeshed with business and spectator sports, the spirit of competition had a catalytic effect on institutional fund-raising. If Morgan could give Harvard a million, so could Rockefeller. His gift to the Medical School took the form of a challenge grant, requiring Harvard to raise $500,000 in endowment funds.

The school's rebirth capped the university-building efforts begun by Eliot in the early years of his presidency. In 1869 the 86-year-old Medical School had been a proprietary establishment, run by Boston physicians and financially independent of the University. The Corporation had no funds to put into it; outside support was almost nonexistent.[12]

When a larger building was needed, $200,000 was raised by a subscription campaign that dragged on for seven years. By the 1890s the need for more classroom and laboratory space was pressing. Enrollment exceeded 300; the faculty had grown to fifty. Instructors were needed in new specialties like histology, gynecology, and neurology.

Drs. Henry Pickering Bowditch (A.B. 1861), the school's former dean, and J. Collins Warren (A.B. 1863), professor of surgery, created a plan for a large new campus, including a fully equipped general hospital. Eliot and the Corporation were fazed by the scale of the proposal. But Overseer Robert Bacon introduced Bowditch and Warren to J.P. Morgan, who liked their enthusiasm. He agreed to fund three central buildings in memory of his father, Junius Spencer Morgan. Charles Harrison Tweed (A.B. 1865), a former associate of the western rail and shipping magnate Collis P. Huntington, persuaded Huntington's widow to fund a fourth building. A fifth was given by the Sears family in memory of three members, each named David Sears (A.B. 1807, 1842, and 1874).

A group led by Major Higginson bought the 26-acre Francis estate in Boston's Fenway district as a site for the school's new campus. The $2.7 million plant was America's largest and costliest medical complex. In time it would become the nucleus of a major medical center made up of a dozen teaching hospitals, professional schools, and research institutions. The new campus was dedicated in September 1906 with two days of academic festivities. President Eliot, who had taught Medical School classes as a young faculty member, spoke presciently of the need for preventive medicine and the value of multidisciplinary research. The

The Medical School's new campus was dedicated in September 1906. President Eliot, speech in hand, can be seen on the top step of the administration building.

The $2.7 million, 26-acre medical complex was America's largest and costliest. Below: the school's central quadrangle. The imperial styling of the buildings was a new departure in Harvard architecture.

school, he concluded, needed youthful leaders "whose chief interest lies in medical and surgical progress rather than in the cautious application of what is now supposed to be known." He soon appointed Dr. Henry Christian, a 32-year-old assistant professor, as dean.

A University in the Largest Sense

THE ROBUST EXPANSION of Harvard's professional schools and allied institutions in the latter years of Eliot's presidency recalled his words at the Commencement of 1870: "We mean to build here, securely and slowly, a university in the largest sense." The Medical School had its new campus; the Law School was adding a large new building. Austin Hall, its headquarters, had been enlarged in 1902, but the school's enrollment was almost 700, the faculty numbered fifteen, and more classroom and library space was needed. The solution was Langdell Hall, a $380,000 white limestone edifice built in 1907. Its scaling and classic porticoes, like those of the Medical School buildings, were in marked contrast to Harvard's traditional red brick. Coldly formalistic, these imperial structures proclaimed that the schools they housed were instruments of high national purpose.[13]

The school of divinity remained Harvard's smallest. It had thirty students and a faculty of six. In 1908 an affiliation with Andover Theological Seminary enlarged enrollment and provided a new building, Andover Hall, erected by the seminary's trustees. The Divinity School had been a Unitarian seminary when Eliot took office; it was now a nonsectarian school of theology with electives in science, "practical ethics," history, philosophy, and psychology that were open to students from the College and the Graduate School of Arts and Sciences.

The school of arts and sciences, formed in 1872, had grown from an initial enrollment of 28 students to more than 400. It was turning out about thirty Ph.D.s a year; no other university trained as many. The school was an important source of teachers for the nation's expanding schools, colleges, and universities. But educational theory and practice was not yet an advanced field of study at Harvard. The Summer School, begun in 1874, enrolled many teachers who wished to learn more about the subjects they taught. It could not equip them with classroom skills or instruct them in educational history and policy issues. In 1891 a faculty committee called for "courses of instruction in teaching,"

Langdell Hall was built on Holmes Field, where Oliver Wendell Holmes once gardened. Completed in 1907, it was named for the Law School's first dean.

Below: Andover Hall, constructed at the Divinity School in 1910, was a rare example of neo-Gothic architecture at Harvard.

The Radcliffe Yard took shape in the century's first decade. Andrew Carnegie (inset), a philanthropist who usually preferred to support small "fresh water" colleges, gave the college library, at far left, in 1908.

The other buildings, from left, are Elizabeth Cary Agassiz House (1903), Harriet Lawrence Hemenway Gymnasium (1898), and Fay House (1807).

and Eliot hired Paul H. Hanus, professor of pedagogy at Colorado State Normal School, to develop them. For six years Hanus single-handedly ran a non-degree-granting graduate department. Unlike other Harvard graduate schools, it admitted women. When Hanus proposed a degree-granting program in 1903, Eliot told him to hold off because of Harvard's financial worries. But in 1906 the Faculty of Arts and Sciences created a "division of education" for Hanus; a decade later a new graduate school was born.

The Summer School, the University museums, the Arnold Arboretum, and Radcliffe College—all begun or significantly enlarged in Eliot's time—were flourishing. And a school of business was on the way

THE NEW PROMINENCE of the corporation in American life, frantic activity in the stock market, revelations of unethical practices and grim working conditions, increasing rapport between captains of industry and captains of education—these factors made it inevitable that business would become a focus of academic training and scholarly study.

The acerbic Thorstein Veblen would write in *The Higher Learning in America* (1918) that the elective system had helped create the demand for "schools of commerce" by nurturing careerism at the college level. "Affecting their choice of electives, has [been] the laudable practical interest that these young men take in their own prospective material success. . . . The college student's interest in his studies has shifted from the footing of an avocation to that of a vocation."

At Harvard, student interest in business had spurted. The proportion of College graduates entering business rose from less than one-fifth in 1897 to about one-half in 1904. If money was what these graduates wanted, managing capital funds was a way to make lots of it. Men with social connections could make good use of them in a banking or brokerage house. Of the 55 members of the Porcellian and A.D. Clubs—the most elite of the ten final clubs—in the classes of 1904, 1905, and 1906, nearly half went into finance after graduation.

It was evident that universities could assist American business by training future managers in sound methods, defining higher standards of conduct, and applying analytic techniques to the operations of corporate organizations. But planning for Harvard's school of business began with a proposal for a school of public service. Settlement of the Spanish-American War and the annexation of Hawaii in 1898 had left the United States with island empires in the Caribbean and the Pacific. Anticipating the development of a colonial system, President Eliot suggested the possibility of "a training school for diplomacy and the government service" to Archibald Cary Coolidge (A.B. 1887), an instructor in history and student of international diplomacy. Coolidge, who imagined a counterpart of the Sorbonne's Ecole Libre des Sciences Politiques, helped outline a plan for a "school of public and private business" in 1906. Frank Taussig, Lee professor of economics, chaired a study committee whose recommendations, in Eliot's words, "[took] the direction of a general training for business pursuits without any special regard to government service." The Corporation approved a five-year trial, on condition that most of the funding be raised by subscription.

"CHINESE" WILSON

Field Work

The growth of new subjects of study, advances in long-distance transportation, and access to new sources of philanthropic support enlarged the geographic range of university scholarship. The Arnold Arboretum's E.H. ("Chinese") Wilson (above) gathered plants in China, Tibet, and Japan. Archaeologist Alfred Tozzer (A.B. 1900) made extended trips to Central America. The Medical School opened a branch in China. The Zoölogical Museum sent a team to the Arctic aboard the schooner *Polar Bear*.

Archaeological excavations at Giza, Egypt, were overseen for more than forty years by George Reisner, Harvard's first—and last—professor of Egyptology. For most of his adult life Reisner gave his address as "Pyramids, Cairo, Egypt."

Frank Taussig, senior member of the economics department, raised funds for the future Business School.

Economist Edwin Gay was the school's first dean.

The Harvard Crimson

PRES. ELIOT RESIGNS

Crimson **extra, November 4, 1908.**

With occasional help from Lawrence Lowell, Taussig set out to raise $125,000. The Wall Street panic of October 1907 set him back. Rockefeller's General Education Board came through with a $62,500 matching grant, but in May the Corporation got cold feet and voted to withhold support unless all the funding was completed forthwith.

Again Major Higginson came to the rescue. He authorized Taussig to tell Eliot that "a donor whose name you are not at liberty to state, but whose financial ability you can guarantee, has underwritten the entire sum remaining to be raised."* Eliot and the Corporation accepted Taussig's verbal assurance. Edwin F. Gay, a professor of economics, was named dean of the faculty of business administration. He assembled a teaching staff of fifteen and set up a first-year curriculum. Taussig had hoped for a "completely separate organization," but Gay and Eliot agreed that the school should begin as a department of the Faculty of Arts and Sciences, using College classrooms.

The new school's two-year program led to a master's degree. Business-related curricula existed at other universities, but at the undergraduate level. Harvard's would be the first business school to require a college degree for admission. The school opened on October 1, 1908, with 24 regular and 35 special students. More than half were graduates of Harvard College.

The Personified Ideal

SPEAKING AT THE COMMENCEMENT of 1908, President Eliot solicited the "special sympathy and attention" of his audience for the Business School, "a novel experiment in our country because it is a graduate school." The schools of law and medicine had become graduate schools by requiring the bachelor's degree for admission, in 1899 and 1901 respectively. With the absorption of the Lawrence Scientific School by the Graduate School of Applied Science, all undergraduate instruction was now consolidated in the College. That department had thus "become a single gate to the professional schools of the University, with one exception." This was the Dental School, where a high-school diploma sufficed for admission. "When that school is put on the basis of the graduate schools," said Eliot, "then will Harvard have accomplished, first and alone in our country, the true organization of a university—a single undergraduate department and all the professional schools on top of that department—all of them requiring a degree in arts, letters, or science for admission. What a contrast to the condition of things forty years ago!"

To some of his hearers, those words surely had a valedictory ring. The 74-year-old Eliot had been president far longer than any of his predecessors. That fall he tendered his resignation.

His brief letter to the Corporation, dated October 10, 1908, was signed "your friend and servant, Charles W. Eliot." The president

---

*Taussig managed to raise all the required funds from other sources. In a letter to Taussig, Higginson elaborated on his desire for anonymity. "People get so sick of my meddling with matters that they don't like to hear my name," he wrote, "and the President is one of them. I am a kind of nurse, and nobody likes nurses unless they are young and pretty."

wished to retire no later than May 1909, the fortieth anniversary of his election. On November 4, the morning after Election Day, the Overseers were informed. Judge Robert Grant (A.B. 1873, LL.B. 1879), beginning a second term on the board, whispered to the man beside him, "That means Lawrence Lowell as president of Harvard."

The *Crimson* put out a special noontime edition. Evening papers ran the story on front pages dominated by election results. (William Howard Taft, President Roosevelt's secretary of war and chosen successor, had defeated William Jennings Bryan). "Quite naturally," noted the *Harvard Bulletin*, "the thoughts of the people were diverted for a time from a great change in a political administration to the termination of an intellectual administration which for forty years had vitally and pervasively affected the welfare of the American people.

"It would be a difficult task indeed," the *Bulletin* added, "to describe the shock which President Eliot's resignation, in spite of his advanced years, inflicted upon the members of the University, the alumni, his neighbors and friends, and the community at large; to voice the individual regret, the sense of common loss, and that first helplessness that an army feels without its accustomed and triumphant leader . . ."

Students gathered at Eliot's house on Quincy Street the next night and cheered until he came out and spoke. "I have heard a number of reasons suggested as the explanation of my resigning," said Eliot. "Now I am not sick, I am not tired. . . . My faculties and health are still good, I am glad to say. My resignation is meant to precede the time when they may cease to be so. Dr. Arnold, of Rugby, used to say that a man was no longer fitted to be headmaster of a public school when he could not come up the steps two at a time. Now I can still do that.

"I don't like to have my coming retirement spoken of with regret. . . . Forty years of service has been given me in the pursuit of a profession that has no equal in the world. This university has grown into great proportions. It is now the task of all of us to find a man who can enlarge it still more and make it still greater. Good night."

For forty years, observed a *Bulletin* editorial, "he has not been president of Harvard University only; he has been president of all the colleges and all the schools in the United States. . . . It is the glory of Harvard University that she gives all she has to the service of the world, that she does her best to raise other institutions into rivalry with herself, that her greatest greatness is in teaching others to be great. This is the spirit she has caught from her leader.

"President Eliot speaks of a certain loss in modern times from the disappearance of feudal devotion to 'an idealized person'; but 'better than devotion to an idealized person,' he adds, 'is devotion to a personified ideal.' We may distrust the unchecked freedom of his elective system; we may not love his three year degree; we may condemn as unsound much

John Singer Sargent painted President Eliot's portrait in 1907, when Eliot was visiting London. The gown was sent from Cambridge to London for the sitting, but Eliot had left by the time it arrived; Sargent painted the body from a model. The background was the artist's invention. Students and members of Harvard clubs paid Sargent's commission by subscription, and presented the painting to the Harvard Union.

of his reasoning on athletics: he remains beyond all men we have seen or shall see the personified ideal of an American university."

LAWRENCE LOWELL, who had sparred with Eliot for a decade, had shown his capacity for forceful leadership. His colleagues respected his self-made scholarship; he had just published a major work, *The Government of England*. His bearing was presidential. And he wanted the job.

"On the whole, my candidate is Lawrence Lowell," Frank Taussig wrote Eliot. "I wish he were ten years younger," Taussig went on, "and I should not be sorry if he were not a Brahmin-born. But he has qualities of the highest order. He is an experienced and successful teacher; he has academic training and academic interests; he is a distinguished scholar, an able man of affairs, a devoted son of the University; he is known to the alumni and to the public; he has ideas and ideals; he has great nervous vigor and endurance. I do not agree with him upon all matters of academic policy, and have thrashed some of them out with him. I always respect his judgment and admire his spirit. I do not think we can have a better chief."

Eliot had reservations about Lowell's judgment and impulsiveness. He would have preferred Jerome Greene (A.B. 1896), his right-hand man for the past seven years, as his successor. Greene was an astute and worldly administrator who knew Harvard intimately. As a law student he had been the *Harvard Bulletin's* first editor, leaving in 1901 to become Eliot's secretary. Now secretary to the Corporation, he kept the list when the six voting members began the presidential selection process in January 1909. There were 24 names, including those of Bishop Lawrence, Charles Francis Adams, Deans Briggs, Sabine, and Gay, and Lowell. "It took about one look at the list to make it clear that the only real candidate was A. Lawrence Lowell," Greene wrote later. "There was no subsequent urging of the merits of any other candidate."

As Taussig sensed, the only obstacles might have been Lowell's age and the closeness of his ties with Harvard's Brahmin governors. He was 52; Eliot had been 35 at the start of his presidency. One Corporation member, Judge Francis Cabot Lowell (A.B. 1876), was his brother-in-law, ex-law partner, and third cousin; another, Dr. Arthur Tracy Cabot (A.B. 1872), was related to Lowell's wife. Four earlier Lowells had been on the Corporation. John Amory Lowell (A.B. 1815), Lowell's grandfather, had held his seat for forty years and was Senior Fellow when Eliot was elected. Lawrence Lowell's maternal grandfather had founded the Lawrence Scientific School. But his attainments and force of character obviated any suspicions of boardroom bias. The Overseers accepted Lowell's election as a matter of course and confirmed it unanimously.

THE LOWELLS WERE one of New England's most remarkable families. The first arrivals, who spelled the name *Lowle*, had come to Boston from Bristol, England, in 1639. Later generations had produced parsons, jurists, soldiers, scientists, industrialists, financiers, philanthropists. The Massachusetts textile cities of Lowell and Lawrence had been developed by Lawrence Lowell's grandfathers, mill owners who became business associates and dispensed large portions of their great fortunes

"OLD JONES"

"Hell-Banger"

O nly the retirement of a Harvard president could have overshadowed that of Austin Kingsley Jones. For fifty years he rang the Harvard Hall bell to wake students and call them to morning chapel, "giving an example of fidelity and punctuality to all members of the university," as a faculty resolution noted when he retired in 1908.

Jones was hired as a janitor in 1858, the year Charles William Eliot became assistant professor of mathematics and chemistry. He proved adept at circumventing repeated attempts to still the bell. Students, who called the bell-ringer "the Hell-Banger," stole the clapper so often that Jones kept a spare at home.

"Old Jones," who died in 1913, was the last of the celebrated College characters—John the Orange Man, Johnny Cocoanut, Jimmy the Paperhanger, Billy the Postman, "Poco," and others—who enriched the Harvard scene in the late nineteenth century.

Eliot and the Harvard Classics

IN HIS LAST MONTHS as president of Harvard, Charles William Eliot undertook a mass-market publishing venture. Begun early in 1909, it was a fifty-volume library of world literature titled "The Harvard Classics" and advertised as "Dr. Eliot's Five-Foot Shelf."

Eliot had said in a public speech that a five-foot shelf would hold enough books to provide the essentials of a liberal education to anyone who would give fifteen minutes a day to reading. The head of P. F. Collier & Sons, a large New York publishing house, dispatched Norman Hapgood (A.B. 1890), the editor of *Collier's Weekly*, to invite Eliot to winnow the world's best literature and select a five-foot shelf of books. Collier would publish them as a set.

Hapgood pointed out that the books would extend Harvard's presence into countless American homes. Eliot liked the notion, and secured the Corporation's permission to use Harvard's name. As assistant editor he picked William Allan Neilson (PH.D. 1898), a young professor of English who later became president of Smith College.

The project took a year. Eliot consulted faculty members on certain choices, but Neilson was the workhorse. Their selections ranged from Homer and Aesop to such nineteenth-century authors as Emerson, Darwin, Alessandro Manzoni, and

Richard Henry Dana. In keeping with Eliot's precept that selections should be printed in full, the series included all the poetry of Milton and Burns. The last volume contained Eliot's introduction and a reading guide. The entire set ran to more than 22,000 pages of text.

The undertaking generated immense publicity, not all of it favorable, and was a commercial success.[14] Collier's sold more than 350,000 sets, or almost 18 million volumes, over the next fifteen years. Eliot and Neilson later collaborated on a twenty-volume "Harvard Classics Shelf of Fiction," published by Collier in 1917.

A full-page advertisement in the *Harvard Bulletin* described the Harvard Classics as "the crystallization of a lifetime of leadership in education."

Dr. Eliot's Five-Foot Shelf of Books

"The Harvard Classics"

"It is my belief that the faithful and considerate reading of these books, with such rereadings and memorizings as individual taste may prescribe, will give any man the essentials of a liberal education, even if he can devote to them but fifteen minutes a day."

Charles W. Eliot

"Liberal education accomplishes two objects. It produces a liberal frame of mind and it makes the studious and reflective recipient acquainted with the stream of the world's thought and feeling, and with the infinitely varied products of the human imagination."

This Free Book is Valuable

to schools, colleges, hospitals, and libraries. Lawrence's brother Percival was a famous astronomer; his sister Amy would be a famous poet.

Lawrence's had been the sixth generation of Lowells at Harvard College. Schooled in Boston, he enrolled in 1873. Like other Lowells, he excelled in mathematics and history. Graduating second in his class, he took highest honors in mathematics. His thesis, *Surfaces of the Second Order, as Treated by Quaternions*, was published by the American Academy of Arts and Sciences. He finished Harvard Law School in two years, ranking second in a class of nineteen; married his third cousin Anna Parker Lowell; bought a house on Marlborough Street in Boston; and formed a law partnership with Francis Cabot Lowell.

"When I started life my ambition would have been rather a seat on the Supreme Court," he wrote much later, "but as I never made any success in the law any dream of that kind long ago vanished." Underworked at the office, Lowell took up writing. Increasingly interested in comparative government, he published a two-volume survey, *Governments and Parties of Continental Europe*, in 1896. It was favorably noticed at Harvard. At 40 Lowell happily gave up the law and accepted Presi-

As a collegian, Lowell ran track and set records in the half-mile and mile. Social life did not interest him much; he did not join a final club.

dent Eliot's invitation to teach introductory classes in government.

Enrollment in his large courses rose steadily. Lowell found himself teaching in cramped classrooms, without nearby space for small-group sessions. His solution was to donate a lecture hall big enough to hold almost a thousand students, with recitation rooms in the basement. Its classical design, blending red brick with baroque ornamentation, was the work of his cousin, Guy Lowell (A.B. 1892). The donor's only condition was that his part in providing the hall be kept secret. "New Lecture Hall" was completed early in 1903, at a cost of $85,000.

Eliot was well aware that Lowell was critical of the state of the College. That he named him to every major committee formed between 1902 and 1909 testified to the president's impartiality. In 1906 it was Lowell who proposed the idea of an "honors concentration" in history and literature, and who chaired the standing committee to oversee it. In 1908, impatient with the slow progress of committees seeking ways to encourage honors work, Lowell asked Eliot to name a special committee—with Lowell picking the members. He sent a list the next day. "As I have an idea of what this committee can accomplish," Lowell added, "I desire to be made chairman of it myself." Again Eliot acquiesced.

Polling faculty members, students, and recent alumni, the committee concluded that "contentment with mediocrity is perhaps the greatest danger that faces us, and it is closely connected with the feeling among the students that college is a sort of interlude in serious life, separated from what goes before and dissociated with what follows." Fewer than 20 percent of undergraduates sought to take their degrees with honors. Athletic competition, active or vicarious, was important to most of the College's students. Intellectual competition was not.

As a corrective to the systemless elective system, the Lowell Committee's report endorsed concentration and distribution requirements, and proposed an expanded staff of advisers. It called for less pedagogical emphasis on factual detail and more on broad principles and ideas. With near unanimity, the faculty approved the report in the fall of 1909, effectively ending the era of "free electives."

"On a New Tack"

LOWELL MOVED INTO the president's office on May 19, 1909. His formal investiture was held in October. In the interim Lowell made it clear that the University was under new management. As a member of Harvard's Phi Beta Kappa chapter, he used his influence to secure the poet and orator for the annual Literary Exercises in June. The program was obviously intended to mark a break with the Eliot era and to validate Lowell's agenda for change. Lowell's classmate Barrett Wendell, one of the English department's imperious stars, delivered the Phi Beta Kappa poem. In satirical couplets, De Praeside Magnifico bade a teasing farewell to Eliot, but the ending suggested that it was the "clear-eyed, clear-voiced, pure-hearted" Lowell who was the real magnifico. Princeton's president, Woodrow Wilson, was the orator. "We have fallen of late into a deep discontent with . . . the life and work of the undergraduates in our universities," he declared. American col-

New Lecture Hall, built in 1903, was given anonymously by Professor and Mrs. Lowell. The donors and the architect, Guy Lowell, hoped it would be located in Harvard Yard. Instead the Corporation selected a site at the corner of Oxford and Kirkland Streets, north of Memorial Hall.

As Phi Beta Kappa Orator in 1909, Princeton president Woodrow Wilson deplored the "all but complete disorganization" of American colleges.

leges had lost "definiteness of aim" and were in "all but complete disorganization." Most students did not want to learn; they simply wished "to be made men of, not scholars." These ills could be cured only by "new processes of authoritative direction."[15]

The former *praeses* was better treated at Commencement, where he received two doctorates. Harvard did not customarily grant the degree of M.D. *honoris causa*, but an exception was made "for one who, in the opinion of professors of medicine, has accomplished more for the progress of medical education than any other living man, Charles William Eliot. Not in its buildings alone, but also in the instruction and research within its walls, he found our Medical School brick, and left it marble." The other doctorate was an LL.D. The citation read, "Teacher, administrator, orator, prophet; forty years the leader and guide of Harvard, and in the single-minded elevation of his character a model to her sons; the father of the present American university, the brother of all teachers, and the friend of every lover of his country."

Serviceable as ever, Eliot accepted a one-year term as president of the Alumni Association. Lowell spoke at the alumni dinner, declaring that "the object of a college is to produce well rounded manhood, men each as perfect as may be in body, mind, and soul." William James lost no time in writing to congratulate Lowell on his "every-inch-a-king appearance," adding, "The total result of today's ceremony was that everyone now *feels* that *we've got a new president.*"

ELIOT'S INAUGURAL HAD BEEN held in the First Parish Church, across the street from the College Yard. Lowell's took place in the Old Yard itself, with some 13,000 spectators on hand. The academic festivities, meticulously planned by Jerome Greene, lasted two days. Inauguration day was sunny and warm. The College band and a 160-member alumni chorus provided music. After receiving the College charter, seal,

A platform with a sounding board overhead was erected in front of University Hall for President Lowell's inaugural ceremony in October 1909. A crowd of 13,000 filled the Old Yard to see and hear the proceedings.

Lowell and Eliot on inauguration day.

Jerome D. Greene, secretary to the Corporation, was in charge of Lowell's inaugural. President Eliot had privately favored Greene as his successor.

The inaugural procession crossing the Old Yard. In the lead, carrying the College seal, was Jerome Greene. Behind him were Bursar C. F. Mason, with the keys; librarian W. C. Lane, with the charter of the College; and senior L. B. Struthers, the orator of the day. In the background are Hollis Hall (left) and Holden Chapel.

and keys from former governor John D. Long (A.B. 1857, LL.D. 1880), president of the Board of Overseers, Lowell delivered his inaugural address. He then conferred thirty honorary degrees on scholars from Cambridge and Oxford, other foreign universities, and eighteen American institutions. In the afternoon Eliot chaired a meeting of the Alumni Association in Memorial Hall; the Boston Symphony Orchestra gave an evening concert in Sanders Theatre. Undergraduates then marched from the Yard to the Stadium, each carrying a torch and wearing a red sash. The Stadium's colonnade was festooned with red Japanese lanterns; one set of goalposts was hung with lanterns forming a fiery red H. The undergraduates marched twice around the track and assembled to cheer the new president, who responded with a brief speech. The evening was climaxed by fireworks and a blazing set piece in the open end of the Stadium that spelled out *Lowell, Harvard*.

The second day began with exercises in Sanders Theatre. Delegates representing thirty foreign and 216 American institutions mounted the stage to shake Lowell's hand. After luncheon in University Hall, guests were conveyed to the Medical School ("by special electric cars and automobiles," noted the *Harvard Bulletin*), where thousands were served tea. A dinner for delegates at the Harvard Union brought the inaugural blowout to a close.

IN HIS INAUGURAL SPEECH, Lowell left no doubt that the individualized college of Eliot's era demanded resocialization. "Among his other wise sayings," he began, "Aristotle remarked that man is by nature a social animal; and it is in order to develop his powers as a social being that American colleges exist. The object of the undergraduate department is not to produce hermits, each imprisoned in the cell of his own intellectual pursuits, but men fitted to take their

places in the community and live in contact with their fellow men."

Since the introduction of the elective system, said Lowell, "college life has shown a marked tendency to disintegrate, both intellectually and socially." The process had been hastened by "the great increase in numbers, and . . . by an abandonment of the policy of housing the bulk of students in college dormitories." A consequence of the fragmentation of college life was "the overshadowing interest in athletic games," which gave students "the one common interest, the only striking occasion for a display of . . . solidarity." The task ahead was to create a new solidarity: "to frame a system which, without sacrificing individual variation too much, or neglecting the pursuit of different scholarly interests, shall produce an intellectual and social cohesion, at least among large groups of students, and points of contact among them all."

Lowell outlined his plan for concentration and distribution requirements. "The best type of liberal education in our complex modern world," he declared, "aims at producing men who know a little of everything and something well." He called for an integrated curriculum like the Oxford Honours School's—six out of sixteen elective courses to be taken in a single field, such as history, chemistry, or economics; the balance to be made up of general courses in unrelated fields. He sketched out plans for tutorial instruction and for freshman residence halls.

His phrasing was as forceful and resonant as Eliot's had been in 1869:

- It will no doubt be argued that a university must reflect the state of the world about it; and that the tendency of the times is toward specialization of functions, and social segregation on the basis of wealth. But . . . one object of a university is to counteract rather than copy the defects of the day.
- All the activities of a university are more or less connected with, and most of them are based upon, the college. It is there that character ought to be formed, that citizens ought to be trained and scholarly tastes implanted.
- The essence of a liberal education consists in an attitude of mind, a familiarity with methods of thought, an ability to use information rather than in a memory stocked with facts, no matter how useful such a storehouse may be.
- The change from the life of a school to that of a college is too abrupt. . . . Taken gradually, liberty is a powerful stimulant, but taken suddenly in large doses, it is liable to act as an intoxicant or an opiate.
- Progress means change, and every time of growth is a transitional era; but in a peculiar degree the present state of the American college bears the marks of a period of transition. This is seen in the comparatively small estimation in which high proficiency in college studies is held, both by undergraduates and by the public at large; for if college education were now closely adapted to the needs of the community, excellence of achievement therein ought to be generally recognized as of great value.

Bishop Lawrence closed the exercises with a benediction. He crossed paths with his second cousin minutes later. "Lawrence, your address is a pretty radical break with the past," said the bishop. "No," replied Lowell, "the same old ship on the same course, only on another tack." Rising to preside at the afternoon meeting of the Alumni Association,

The Stratford Connection

On the day of President Lowell's inauguration, Harvard House at Stratford-on-Avon, England, was formally opened and placed in trust for the University.

The half-timbered structure (below) was built in 1596 for Thomas Rogers, John Harvard's maternal grandfather and a Stratford neighbor of William Shakespeare. By the early 1900s the house was in disrepair.

The popular novelist Marie Corelli conceived the idea of reclaiming the house as a rendezvous for Americans visiting Stratford. Edward Morris, a wealthy Chicagoan, provided funds to acquire and restore it. On October 6, 1909, the premises were opened and transferred in an elaborate ceremony that included an exchange of cables with President Lowell.

Eliot was cheered to the rafters. Commending Lowell as "a scholar through and through," he sought to reconcile their views on the state of the College. What Eliot had begun, Lowell would continue. "We have heard him say it is a period of transition," Eliot told the alumni. "How natural it sounded to me when he used the word transition. It has been a period of transition for the last forty years. It is going right on."

The Lowell Era

MOST OF THE CHIEF academic figures of the post-Civil War generation had died or retired by 1910, and younger educators had come to the fore. Their rise had been marked in a 1907 *Atlantic* article that stated, "The old type of [university] leader, learned and temperate, fast yields to the new type,—self-confident, incisive, Rooseveltian."[16] Not as voluble as TR, but no less sure of himself, Lawrence Lowell fit the description. As Harvard's president he inherited a position of almost papal prominence in American education. In a time of ferment and reappraisal, a leader with energy, a firm tone, and a forthright agenda could accomplish much. And Lowell intended to.

The new president made his energetic presence felt throughout the University. As Elliott Perkins '23, historian and second master of Lowell House, would later put it, "Harvard was still small enough, but only just, to be run as a one-man show. He seemed to be everywhere, to know everything, to have his finger in every pie, and as far as the College was concerned, he was and he did."

Childless himself, Lowell enjoyed mixing with undergraduates. With faculty members he could be disconcertingly direct. Some were taken aback when he inquired about the length of their working day.* Unlike Eliot, Lowell started his own work day at a relatively late hour, though he was always at Appleton Chapel for daily prayers at 8:45. In morning coat, striped trousers, and starched shirt, set off by a bright red tie, he cut a striking figure. Subordinates found him difficult. He was notoriously unpunctual, and was apt to lose himself in administrative detail. "He converses rapidly and listens little," wrote Samuel Eliot Morison, "[and] is inclined to draw conclusions from limited observations of his own, rather than from the prolonged research of an expert." Jerome Greene, Eliot's good right arm for nearly a decade, lasted just a year under Lowell. In 1910 he resigned as secretary to the Corporation to become business manager of the Rockefeller Institute.

Yet Lowell's effectiveness was apparent to all. While reshaping the College curriculum, he oversaw the inception of an inter-university program in extension studies and the founding of the Harvard University Press. He negotiated a new alliance with MIT. He found sources of funding for three freshman halls, four new laboratories, a music building, the Huntington Memorial Hospital, and a new library.

His proposal for an honors college, and his plans for new halls to democratize undergraduate life, suited the temper of the times. "College

32,000 Men of Harvard

The first *Harvard Alumni Directory*, published in November 1910, listed 32,193 living alumni who had studied at Harvard long enough to be listed in the registrar's annual catalog. Alumnae of Radcliffe College were not included.

Compiling the 1,292-page directory took six years. Jerome Greene, then secretary to the Corporation, was in charge of the project. Before it began, the number of living alumni had been reckoned at about 20,000.

Demographic data showed that more than a third of all alumni lived in Massachusetts, and that almost one-sixth were in the legal profession. Education and medicine were the next largest callings.

The University printed 7,500 copies of the *Directory*. It was priced at $2 a copy. Subsequent editions were normally published at five-year intervals.

*Lowell's biographer, former dean of the College Henry Yeomans (A.B. 1900), recorded that "one professor, who did not like the question, replied that his day's work was of twenty-four hours, as many of his best ideas came to him in his sleep."

Eight Minutes to Park Street

PRESIDENT Thomas Hill had lamented in 1863 that "the passage of horse-cars to and from Boston, nearly, if not quite, a hundred times a day, has rendered it practically impossible for the Government of the College to prevent our young men from being exposed to the temptations of the city."

In 1889, when the West End Street Railway converted its horsecar routes to electric traction, the forty-minute tram ride to the city was cut almost in half. The march of modern technology continued. In 1909 the Boston Elevated Railway began constructing a subway line connecting Cambridge and Boston.

The photo above, taken in 1910, shows excavations in progress between Brattle and Harvard Squares. A corner of the Harvard Cooperative Society building can be seen at upper left. Yard dormitories and gambrel-roofed Wadsworth House—once the president's residence, but providing student housing in 1910—appear in the background. Trolley tracks have been rerouted along Mount Auburn Street; earth from the forty-foot trenches is being trucked away as fill for the Charles River embankment and Soldiers Field.

G.F. Swain, a professor at MIT, was principal consulting engineer for Boston's subway system. In the fall of 1909 he became Harvard's first McKay professor of civil engineering. Cambridge-Boston trains began running in 1912. President Hill would have been pained to find that the temptations of the city were now a mere eight minutes from Harvard Square.

Edward Waldo Forbes, art collector and painter, formed a consortium to acquire riverside property on Harvard's behalf. Appointed director of the Fogg Art Museum in 1909, he built it into one of the nation's great teaching museums.

Charles Coolidge's 1910 plan for freshman halls facing the river. The final layout was less palatial, in part because the University could not obtain all of the needed parcels of land.

Fourteen residential buildings, a planing mill and a coal wharf owned by Harvard were razed to make way for the new halls.

students were accused of being increasingly lazy and vice-ridden," Laurence Veysey would write: calls for disciplinary emphasis on hard work, "rooted in the conscience of the Progressive Era," were accompanied by "a democratic outcry against snobbishness and luxury."

Concentration and distribution requirements were prescribed for the class of 1914, arriving in the fall of 1910. Undergraduates were also required to pass a language examination in French or German by junior year. The advising system was enlarged. Lowell followed up with two further reforms: comprehensive examinations and tutorial instruction.

"The ordinary student is too apt to treat courses as Cook's tourists do the starred pictures in foreign galleries, as experiences to be checked off and forgotten," Lowell wrote in his first annual report. General examinations, oral and written, would measure "comprehension, judgment, and skill," while training the examinee in organizing and expressing information and ideas. The medical and divinity schools instituted general examinations for degree candidates in 1912. In arts and sciences, the Division of History, Government, and Economics was the first to require comprehensive exams, effective with the class of 1917. With the exception of mathematics and natural sciences, all other divisions and departments adopted "generals" over the next four years.

Lowell saw tutorial instruction as a vital part of the process he termed "self-education." "There must be tutors," he wrote in 1913, "who confer with the students frequently, not about their courses alone, but also about their outside reading and the final test that lies before them." All divisions or departments requiring general exams would be provided with tutorial staffs, proportionate in size to the number of concentrators. The program got off to a wobbly start. As Professor Morison wrote, "Most students and alumni were against it, partly as a new burden, partly because it seemed a retrograde step from the free election of the Eliot era. Not many members of the faculty cared to undertake tutorial instruction, and new men had to pick up tutorial technique as best they could. . . . There was so much tutorial turnover in the first fifteen years (as in the early days of Harvard College) that a student seldom had the same preceptor for three years."

If Eliot's "free electives" owed much to German *Lernfreiheit*, Lowell's quest for curricular cohesion drew heavily on the English universities.

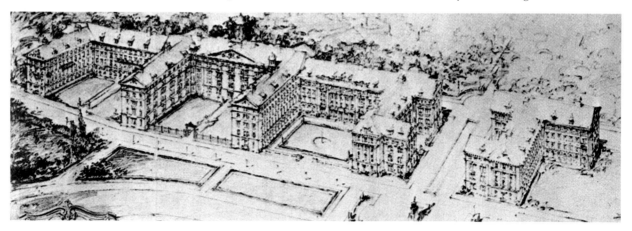

Faculty members were sent to Oxford and Cambridge to observe the tutorial system in action and talk with examiners. In designing a residential system to foster social cohesion, Lowell also looked to the English colleges, where scholarship and gracious living seemed so harmoniously conjoined.

LOWELL'S GOAL WAS TO create a system of Oxbridge-style colleges. It had to be done incrementally, partly because of the cost, partly to avert opposition from wealthy alumni and students who would perceive the colleges as a threat to the club system. At Princeton, Woodrow Wilson had failed in his crusade to abolish the snobbish eating clubs and install a system of colleges. Irate alumni would not forgive him for trying "to spoil the best country club in America."

Lowell's freshman halls would be the edge of the wedge. Four halls, each with residential suites for at least 150 students, a dining hall, and common rooms, could house most of the first-year class. Eventually the halls could become units of a larger system.

They could stand on riverfront land. The so-called Riverside area, between Mount Auburn Street and the Charles River, consisted of frame houses and wharves, warehouses, and coalyards. In 1902 Edward Waldo Forbes (A.B. 1895) had formed a consortium, the Harvard Riverside Associates, to buy land for the University's later use.[17] Sites for the freshman halls, abutting the West End Street Railway Company's power plant, were the first parcels transferred to Harvard.

To design the halls Lowell chose Charles A. Coolidge (A.B. 1881), whose firm had planned the new Medical School campus, the Law School's Langdell Hall, and the campus of Stanford University. Coolidge argued so strongly for a Gothic Revival style that his partners convened a meeting of Boston architects to talk him out of it. Eventually he agreed that the new halls, though larger in scale, should have the red-brick colonial look of the Yard's oldest buildings. Georgian Revival became Harvard's official architectural style for the next three decades, with most of the commissions going to Coolidge's firm.

The largest of the halls would be funded by the George Smith bequest of 1902, now worth more than $600,000. A gift of $450,000 from Mrs. Russell Sage provided a second hall, to be named Standish. Alumni subscriptions, including $100,000 from Lowell and his wife, funded a third, to be named Gore. A decade would pass before funds for a fourth hall materialized.

Site clearance started in the fall of 1912. The Charles estuary dam, built in 1910, now kept the tidal river in check and covered unsavory mud flats. The architecture and landscaping of the new halls would transform a dingy commercial riverfront into an arcadian shoreline of handsome buildings and stately trees. Construction began in the spring. The halls would open their doors in the fall of 1914.

Lowell had already made a move designed to restore the residential character of Harvard Yard. To promote solidarity, members of the class of 1911 were urged to live in the Yard as seniors. In what Dean Briggs called "a belated tribute to modern civilization," Yard dorms were fitted with bathrooms and showers. Hollis, Stoughton, Holworthy, and Thayer

Prodigies

Billy Sidis qualified for admission at nine, but had to wait two years to enroll at Harvard. A mathematical genius with a stratospheric IQ, he already knew six languages.

William James Sidis—his father was Boris Sidis (A.B. 1894, PH.D. 1897, M.D. 1908), an early psychotherapist and protégé of William James—was the youngest of five prodigies then at Harvard. The others were Cedric Houghton, who died while in college; Adolf Berle '13; Roger Sessions '15; and Norbert Wiener, PH.D. '13. Sidis took the most advanced courses the mathematics department could offer, and graduated in 1914.

Berle became an economist and governmental adviser, Sessions an admired composer. Wiener, whose father was Leo Wiener, professor of Slavic languages and literature, was the founder of cybernetics. Sidis vainly sought seclusion.

In 1924 the *New York Herald Tribune* revealed that the "boy brain prodigy of 1909" was a $23-a-week clerk. As a back-office calculator operator, he went from job to job for the rest of his life, trying to avoid the press and sometimes working as a translator. He brought out one book on physics and another on collecting streetcar transfers, his hobby. His writings in science fiction and history went unpublished. Sidis died of a cerebral hemorrhage in Boston in 1944, at the age of 46.

SIDIS AS A SENIOR, AGED 16

Rearranging Harvard's books: Removal of the University Library's holdings from antiquated Gore Hall (below) progressed at a rate of 40,000 to 50,000 volumes a week.

Gore Hall was torn down in January 1913. Excavations for Widener Library began a month later. At right: placing the cornerstone.

Halls were equipped with electric lighting in 1913. A record 334 seniors, more than 90 percent of the class, roomed in the Yard the next year.

GORE HALL, the seventy-year-old University library, had reached the end of its useful life. A picturesque Gothic building inspired by English chapels, it had overflowed in the 1890s and had twice been rebuilt, most recently in 1907. By 1910 the library system's holdings had grown to 543,000 volumes and Gore was full again. A three-man architectural committee, including Charles Coolidge and Guy Lowell, concluded that it was "hopelessly overcrowded," unsafe, unfit for continued use. Recommending that it be razed, they submitted a plan for a library holding 2,370,000 volumes and requiring almost $2 million to build.[18]

"Will some kind millionaire please give Harvard a new library building?" began a wry article in the *Boston American*. "Tainted money not barred. Mr. Rockefeller, take notice. Mr. Carnegie, please write." Early in 1912 Lowell did write to J.P. Morgan Jr., a member of the Overseers' committee on the library, to ask if Andrew Carnegie might be a potential donor. In April Lowell wrote again to put forward the names of Morgan's father and his associate George F. Baker Sr. Then came the

sinking of the White Star flagship *Titanic* on its maiden voyage from Southampton to New York. On board were wealthy Americans with ties to Harvard: the John Jacob Astors, whose son Vincent was a freshman; Mr. and Mrs. Isidor Straus, whose sons Jesse, Percy, and Herbert were graduates; and Mr. and Mrs. George D. Widener, whose son Harry '07 was with them. Eleanor Elkins Widener and her maid survived in a lifeboat; her husband and son were lost.

Harry Widener had been an ardent book collector. At 27 he owned a superb library of rare volumes. His will left it to Harvard, on condition that proper accommodation could be provided. Mrs. Widener thought of giving a new wing for Gore Hall, or perhaps a small building, to house the collection. Politely encouraged by Lowell and Archibald Cary Coolidge, now the director of the library system, she agreed in June 1912 to provide a full-scale building to be known as the Harry Elkins Widener Memorial Library. As its architect she insisted on Horace Trumbauer, whose work included grandiose public buildings and hotels in Philadelphia, the campus of Duke University, and Pennsylvania mansions for Harry Widener's grandfathers. Contracts were signed; the evacuation of Gore Hall began. Randall Hall, the undergraduate dining commons on Kirkland Street, became a storage center for some 400,000 books. The rest were dispersed among nine other buildings. Interim library service began in the fall term. Gore was torn down in January 1913. Excavations for the enormous new library began in February. In June Mrs. Widener helped lay the cornerstone. The structural work was completed within a year. The interior took another year.

WIDENER LIBRARY was the most monumental of a dozen construction projects begun between 1911 and 1913. Lowell had helped launch the building boom, providing $155,000 for a large, red-brick President's House at 17 Quincy Street. Its colonial styling was the work of Guy Lowell. New quarters for the Varsity Club, adjoining the Harvard Union across Quincy Street, were named for Francis H. Burr, captain of the 1908 football team, who had died of typhoid in 1910. Lowell again was a major donor. South of the Yard the freshman halls took shape. Lowell busied himself with every phase of planning and construction. He could be seen almost any day, wrote Professor Morison, "inspecting operations, deciding details with quick and accurate judgment, and leading perspiring and trembling celebrities across swaying planks and up builders' ladders."

Lowell, who liked to work by a fireplace, had insisted that every study should have one. Each resident was to have his own bedroom and Harvard armchair—a replica of the black chairs in the Faculty Room of University Hall, slightly reconfigured by Lowell himself, and adorned with gold insignia for each residential hall.

North of the Yard, ground was broken for the country's first Germanic Museum, designed by Professor German Bestelmeyer of Munich, and a music building whose principal donor was James Loeb (A.B. 1888), amateur scholar and founder of the Loeb Classical Library. On Radcliffe College's central quadrangle, laid out by Guy Lowell in 1902, construction of Barnard and Whitman Halls raised the number of women's dormitories to four.

The Gray Herbarium was expanded. A new wing connected the Peabody Museum of Archaeology and Ethnology with the Museum of Comparative Zoology. Close by, three specialized science buildings—the Wolcott Gibbs and T. Jefferson Coolidge Jr. laboratories, both for physical and inorganic chemistry, and the Cruft High-Tension Laboratory for electrical engineering—were constructed for the departments of chemistry and physics. Modest in size, the Gibbs and Coolidge Labs were elements of a grand plan to rescue Harvard chemists from inadequate quarters in Boylston Hall and set them up in a quadrangle complex of eight linked buildings with a bell tower. Morris Loeb (A.B. 1883), a pioneer physical chemist and patron of science, helped organize the rescue attempt. The bell-tower quad was never realized, but Loeb and his brother James provided most of the funding for Gibbs Laboratory.

Professor Theodore Richards, the world's leading authority on the determination of atomic weights, was put in charge of the lab. In 1915 he became the first American to win the Nobel Prize in chemistry, and the first Harvard faculty member to win a Nobel.[19] The early years of Lowell's presidency had emphasized the centrality of Harvard College,

Adolphus Busch Hall was built to house the Germanic Museum's collections of sculpture and art objects sent to Harvard by Kaiser Wilhelm as a gesture of friendship in the early years of the century.

The museum's curator was Kuno Francke (left), professor of German.

Gifts of $250,000 from Adolphus Busch, head of the St. Louis brewing family, funded the new hall, designed in a style known as "modern Munich." The building's stucco finish, red tile roof, and enclosed garden set it apart from other structures at Harvard.

but the award to Richards was a reminder to all that Harvard was also a major research university.

ADVANCED RESEARCH in the physical sciences was converging on atomic structure, radiation, and the essence of matter. At the University of Manchester, Ernest Rutherford had used radium emissions to demonstrate the existence of a nucleus within the atom. His findings, published in 1911, launched the nuclear age. In the years ahead, inspired theoretical work and refined instrumentation would lead to epochal revelations about the nature of matter and energy, time and space. At Harvard, Professor Richards and Gregory Baxter (A.B. 1896), his former pupil, revised the classification of certain elements in the periodic table; weighing lead samples found in uranium ores, Richards confirmed the existence of isotopes (atoms of the same element differing in atomic weight). Theodore Lyman (A.B. 1897), director of Jefferson Laboratory, measured ultraviolet radiation; his colleague William Duane (A.B. 1893) studied X-ray emissions. The implications of atomic theory and advances in spectroscopic analysis would soon transform the related fields of astronomy and geology.

In 1915 Professor Theodore Richards became the first American to win the Nobel Prize in chemistry, established at the turn of the century.

But to most Americans, theoretical science was eclipsed by miracles of applied technology. The years between 1901, when Guglielmo Marconi sent the first wireless message across the Atlantic, and 1913, when Model Ts rolled off Henry Ford's first assembly line, were filled with portentous events: the dawn of the age of flight and the first coast-to-coast automobile trip (1903); the first Victrola "talking machine" and the earliest vacuum tubes (1904); the first steam turbine ocean liners (1906); the introduction of electric appliances like washers and vacuum cleaners (1907); newsreels (1909); and transcontinental flight (1911).

The pace of life in the late nineteenth century had been changed by the telephone and the telegraph, typewriters, elevators, and trolleys. Rapid advances in communications and transportation technology would continue to shrink time and distance in the twentieth century.

HARVARD'S CAPACITIES IN applied science and engineering did not satisfy President Lowell. Enrollment in the Graduate School of Applied Science had leveled off at about 110—small compared with the schools of law (780), arts and sciences (430), and medicine (280). Costs of plant and equipment were high. Lowell had done his utmost to effect an

Replacing a wooden drawbridge, a new bridge connecting Boylston Street in Cambridge and North Harvard Street in Boston was completed in 1913. It was donated by Larz Anderson (A.B. 1888) in memory of his father, Nicholas Longworth Anderson (A.B. 1858). Because the Charles River was classified as navigable as far as Watertown, government regulations specified a clear height of twelve feet above water in the central channel.

"DYING HARVARD ELMS," ran a *Boston Transcript* headline in 1910. "Every tree in the yard seems doomed." Cankerworms had eaten the Yard's elms in the 1840s. A leopard-moth blight got them in 1909. By 1914 all but eight or ten Yard elms had died.

A photograph (above) in the *Alumni Bulletin* of October 4, 1911, showed the "Class Day Elm," near Holden Chapel, as a torso. The tree was known to have been in place as early as 1767. The *Bulletin* speculated that Yard squirrels had driven away birds that might have eaten hostile parasites.

Below: the northern part of the Old Yard in 1914. Elms and red oaks were replanted, but by the end of the century Dutch elm disease was killing off the last of the elms.

alliance between Harvard and MIT in 1905. He still regarded it as an ideal arrangement. "The Technology" was about to move closer. An imposing new building would occupy filled land in East Cambridge, fronting the Charles River Basin. In the fall of 1913 Lowell and MIT president Richard Maclaurin agreed on a plan for cooperative instruction in "mechanical, electrical, civil and sanitary engineering, mining and metallurgy." MIT would provide facilities; Harvard would provide funding, including three-fifths of the income from the Gordon McKay endowment, and some of the faculty. The plan was ratified by the governing boards of both institutions and announced early in 1914.[20] The faculty of what had become the Graduate Schools of Applied Sciences was dissolved, Harvard teachers began part-time service at MIT, and laboratory equipment was moved to the Institute. A collaborative arrangement also launched the Harvard-MIT School for Health Officers, America's first professional training program in public health and the forerunner of Harvard's School of Public Health.

But the two institutions had jumped the gun. The President's Report for 1913-14 confirmed that "some friends of the University [i.e., trustees of the McKay endowment] have grave doubts whether the agreement is in accord with the provisions of Gordon McKay's will." The Corporation would seek the opinion of the Supreme Judicial Court of the Commonwealth "in order to set all doubts at rest." In 1917 the court nullified the agreement, rejecting the Corporation's argument that "the school of applied science on the Charles River Embankment is . . . a department of Harvard University." McKay, said the court, had in mind "the advantages of combining training in the exact sciences with liberal culture in the atmosphere of the University" when he made his bequest. The ruling irked and embarrassed officials of both institutions. Harvard had to start over in engineering, but by then America was at war, and laboratories built for the applied sciences had been taken over by the U.S. Navy.

The Golden Years

THE LAST PREWAR YEARS were lively ones. Americans raced automobiles and watched rickety biplanes maneuver at air shows. They tapped their feet to the marches of John Philip Sousa, danced the turkey trot and the tango, bought piano rolls of ragtime music by Scott Joplin and Irving Berlin. The Metropolitan Opera mounted its first opera by an American composer: *The Pipe of Desire*, by Frederick Shepherd Converse (A.B. 1893). The New York Armory Show introduced Americans to modern art; most didn't like it. Books that created a stir included *Three Lives*, by Gertrude Stein (A.B. 1898); *Mr. Faust*, by Arthur Davison Ficke '04; *A Boy's Will* and *North of Boston*, by Robert Frost '01; and *Sword Blades and Other Poems*, by Amy Lowell, sister of Harvard's president. Clark University president G. Stanley Hall (PH.D. 1878) brought Sigmund Freud over to lecture. "The future of psychology belongs to your work," William James told Freud. The temperance movement gained momentum; women's suffrage was a heated issue. Theodore Roosevelt, who had most recently held the presidency of the Harvard Alumni Association, bolted the Republican Party to run against President Taft as a "Progressive" candidate in 1912. In America's first Harvard-Yale-Princeton election, he and Taft split the Republican vote and Woodrow Wilson led the Democrats to victory.

Harvard vibrated with the times. "Never was College so exciting," wrote Professor Morison, who had graduated in 1908, "or drunks so drunken, or the generous feeling of ardent youth so exalted, as in those golden years before the World War." The dance mania "hit the College hard, and more students acquired cars, since Henry Ford had invented the Model T for the impecunious; whilst Nationals, Renaults, and Mercedes began to be seen parked along the Gold Coast."

President Lowell had ushered in his reforms with the declaration that "college life has shown a tendency to disintegrate, both intellectually and socially." But contemporary accounts now began to reflect a degree of intellectual seriousness and an interest in social interchange that was new. "Surely nothing in the last five years has approached the criminal stupidity of the horseplay which was constant in the preceding decade," wrote Eugene Hecker '05 in a 1914 *Alumni Bulletin* article titled "Saner College Life."[21] New courses in fields like history and economics, wrote Hecker, had given students "something in which they could become genuinely interested, and that promotes seriousness of purpose."

Earnest undergraduates were reading Santayana's *The Life of Reason*, Nietzsche and Schopenhauer, and the poems and plays of Yeats, Synge, and Dunsany. "There was talk of the world, and daring thought, and intellectual insurgency; heresy has always been a Harvard and New England tradition," wrote the radical journalist John Reed '10. Reed conceded that the elective system had carried individualism "to the point where a man who came for a good time could get through and graduate without having learned anything," but he prized Harvard's libertarian climate and its eclectic mix of students:

All sorts of strange characters, of every race and mind, poets, philosophers, cranks of every twist, were in our Class. . . . What is known as "col-

The Harvard Aeronautical Society sponsored its first air meet at Squantum, Massachusetts, in September 1910. English aviator Claude Grahame-White took prizes in seven of nine events (including one of $5,000 for accuracy in dropping bombs on a dummy battleship). Above: Grahame-White at the controls of his Farman biplane, with passenger A.A. Merrill, D.M.D. '07.

The start for the Country Club

The first gasoline-powered cars were still being road-tested when the class of 1896 graduated. By the time of the class's fifteenth reunion, automobiles were transforming American life.

lege spirit" was not very powerful; no odium attached to those who didn't go to football games and cheer. . . . Students themselves criticized the faculty for not educating them, attacked the sacred institution of intercollegiate athletics, sneered at undergraduate clubs so holy that no one dared mention their names. No matter what you were or what you did—at Harvard you could find your kind. It wasn't a breeder for masses of mediocrely educated young men equipped with "business" psychology; out of each class came a few creative minds, a few scholars, a few "gentlemen" with insolent manners, and a ruck of nobodies. . . . [22]

Out of Reed's own class came more than a few creative minds. The men of 1910 included Walter Lippmann, who became the nation's most influential journalist; T.S. Eliot, perhaps the century's most influential poet; Alan Seeger, a poet who lost his life as a Foreign Legionnaire in the Great War; Robert Edmond Jones, who revolutionized theatrical stage design; Hans von Kaltenborn, pioneer radio commentator; Heywood Broun, reporter and columnist; Bronson Cutting, senator from New Mexico; Willard Gibbs, designer of wartime Liberty Ships; Carl Binger, influential psychiatrist; and Alfred Kuttner, translator of Freud's *Interpretation of Dreams*.

Light drama: Alanson Sturgis, class of '14, as Amorita Carramba in the Hasty Pudding Theatre's *The Legend of Loravia*.

Reed himself came to Harvard from Portland, Oregon, determined to make the most of his college days. He was an editor of the *Harvard Monthly*, the *Advocate*, and the *Lampoon*; a football cheerleader; a lyricist for the 1910 Hasty Pudding show; and a member of the Socialist Club. Reed became a war correspondent and wrote a noted book on the Russian Revolution, *Ten Days That Shook the World*. He died of typhus in 1920 and was buried outside the Kremlin wall.

The reputation of Harvard's English department attracted an exceptional number of young men and women who became major figures in literature and the theater. Among those whose Harvard careers overlapped Reed's were poets John Hall Wheelock '08 and Conrad Aiken '11, cultural historians Van Wyck Brooks '08 and Frederick Lewis Allen '12, editor Maxwell Perkins '07, and humorist Robert Benchley '13. The serious study of theater arts began when Professor George Pierce Baker founded his "47 Workshop" in playwriting in 1905. Among his star pupils were Edward Sheldon '08 and Lee Simonson '09. The Harvard Dramatic Club was founded in 1908 to produce "original plays by undergraduates or graduates of the University." The first undergraduate group to admit Radcliffe students, the HDC mounted plays by Shakespeare and Shaw (though the Corporation refused to permit the club to present Shaw's provocative *Mrs. Warren's Profession* with Radcliffe actresses in the female roles).

Serious drama: George P. Baker, professor of English, and students enrolled in his "47 Workshop" course.

The Delta Upsilon Club put on Elizabethan drama; the Cercle Français, Circolo Italiano, Deutscher Verein, and Sociedad Española offered plays in French, Italian, German, and Spanish.

The Pierian Sodality of 1808 was reorganized as a serious orchestra interested in introducing music by undergraduate composers. A new Debating Club, formed to "serve as a forum where questions of University interest may be freely discussed," drew an audience of 800 to an ini-

tial discussion of social divisions within the student community. In the spring of 1908, Walter Lippmann and eight fellow undergraduates organized the Socialist Club, to consider "all schemes of social reform which aimed at a radical reconstruction of society." Membership grew to more than fifty. "He who listens carefully enough," wrote Lippmann in a come-on to fellow students, "will hear at Harvard heresies about private property which ten years ago would have been denounced by the public press as leading straight to atheism, to free love, and all the other horrors that terrified ignorance can conjure up."

Other new groups reflected a rising level of social consciousness. Reed credited Lippmann and his associates with inspiring them. "Under their stimulus the college political clubs, which had formerly been quadrennial mushroom growths for the purpose of drinking beer, parading, and burning red fire, took on a new significance," he wrote. "Out of the agitation sprang the Harvard Men's League for Women's Suffrage, the Single Tax Club, [and] an Anarchist group. . . . Prominent radicals came to Cambridge to lecture, [and] all over the place radicals sprang up, in music, painting, poetry, the theater." The Dramatic Club's spring production in 1911 was *Manacles*, a socialist play by Hiram Moderwell '12. Even the senior class poems of those years were socialistic, thought Reed. Lippmann helped found the Social Politics Club—which included faculty members—"to bring together men who believe the world is not finished." Then came a Progressive Club, a Diplomatic Club, and an International Polity Club. In the *Harvard Monthly*, the *Advocate*, and the *Harvard Illustrated Magazine*, undergrad-

Harvard's Overseers, meeting in the Faculty Room of University Hall on November 1913. Nearest the camera are President emeritus Eliot, President Lowell, and former Massachusetts governor John D. Long, president of the board.

J.P. Morgan Jr. and Theodore Roosevelt were among the eight members who missed the meeting. The photograph was believed to be the first ever taken of the board.

Closed Shop

In 1911, making a brief visit to the United States between jail terms in her own country, the courageous English suffragette leader Emmeline Pankhurst altered her plans

EMMELINE
PANKHURST

and accepted an invitation from the Harvard Men's League for Women's Suffrage to speak at Sanders Theatre. The Corporation refused her the use of the hall. Because Harvard was not coeducational, women could not lecture to College groups unless they were "officially invited." The League had to hire a hall.

Protests from students and alumni were unavailing. Revising its policy to avoid the women's issue, the Corporation stated in March 1912 that "the halls of the University shall not be open for persistent and systematic propaganda on contentious questions of contemporaneous social, economic, political, or religious interests." But as government professor William Bennet Munro put it, "Nowadays every request raises the question as to what is propaganda and what is not. Every speaker on every topic is a propagandist to some degree."

Opposite: Harvard's junior varsity eight rocked the rowing world by winning the Grand Challenge Cup at Henley-on-Thames, July 1914. Boston's Union Boat Club trailed by a length and a quarter.

uate writers exhorted the University to pay its workers a living wage, offer a course on socialism, extend the use of its halls to women speakers. In the *Illustrated*, Gerard Henderson '12 lamented the "false and humiliating position in which Radcliffe stands with regard to the University," and urged full acceptance of women in the life of the College.

"Of course all this made no ostensible difference in the look of Harvard society," wrote Reed, "and probably the clubmen and the athletes, who represented us to the world, never even heard of it." Though the Progressive Era was at its height, the majority of American college students remained politically conservative or indifferent.

HARVARD ATHLETES were riding high. Percy Haughton (A.B. 1899), a football and baseball star of the late 1890s, had become head coach of football in 1908. His squads were competing successfully against teams like Michigan and Penn State. Haughton, whose vocation was banking, was an inventive tactician and stern disciplinarian. Between 1911 and 1915 his teams rolled up an unbeaten streak of 33 games. The stars of that era included linemen Hamilton Fish '10, Bob Fisher '12, Huntington ("Tack") Hardwick '15, and Stanley Pennock '15, and running backs Hamilton Corbett '11, Percy Wendell '13, Charlie Brickley '15, and Eddie Mahan '16. Each earned all-America recognition at least twice. Hockey, tennis, and golf came into their own as intercollegiate sports, and Crimson teams consistently achieved winning records. Harvard baseball improved under Dr. Frank Sexton, a former major-league pitcher who was the team's first paid coach. Later, when a dispute with the team's advisory committee cut short Sexton's tenure, Percy Haughton stepped in to help salvage the season.

The rowing record was unspectacular, but from 1908 to 1913 Harvard's varsity boat won every race against Yale. The streak ended when Yale won the 1914 race by one-fifth of a second, the shortest interval possible on stopwatches of the day. Harvard's junior varsity beat Yale and went on to compete in England's Henley Royal Regatta. (Under Henley rules, the varsity crew was ineligible because it was professionally coached). With Robert F. Herrick Jr. (A.B. 1890) as their amateur coach, the J. V. rowers crossed the Atlantic on the *Olympic*, sister ship of the *Titanic*. They defeated Winnipeg Rowing Club and Leander in trial heats and found themselves facing the Union Boat Club of Boston in the Grand Challenge Cup finals. Union's crew was made up of former Harvard rowers. In Henley's first all-American final, held on the Fourth of July, Harvard came from behind to win by a length and a quarter. No American crew had ever won the Grand Challenge Cup.

Henley had become a truly international regatta; the total of 77 entries made 1914 a record year. The Grand Challenge heats had included British, Canadian, American, and German crews. But within a month the guns of August had shattered international comity. Kaiser Wilhelm II's army was invading Belgium, and the British grand fleet was steaming across the North Sea toward the coast of Germany.

The Great War

Between the closing of the University at the end of June and its opening at the end of September the face of the world has suffered the most sudden and complete change that has visited it in modern times.
—*From the* Harvard Alumni Bulletin *of September 30, 1914*

T HE OUTBREAK OF WAR IN EUROPE took America by surprise. There was war talk in the spring of 1914, but it was about Mexico, where U.S. troops had landed to cut off munitions shipments to dictator Victoriano Huerta. Tensions in Europe were high, but the continent had seen no full-scale war for a century. It was widely assumed that diplomats would control events, and that Britain's naval supremacy would keep German imperialism at bay.

In 1906 the British navy had launched the 17,900-ton, steam-turbine-driven H.M.S. *Dreadnought,* the largest, fastest, most heavily armed warship ever built. It revolutionized naval architecture and set off a worldwide naval arms race.

"The great nations of Europe," warned Foreign Secretary Sir Edward Grey, "are raising enormous revenues to kill each other." By the summer of 1914, Britain had twenty *Dreadnought*-class battleships, with four superdreadnoughts abuilding. Germany had thirteen dreadnoughts, and the world's largest army.

But when the killing began, it was not at sea. The shooting started in the Bosnian city of Sarajevo, where Serbian nationalists gunned down the heir to the throne of Austria-Hungary in June

Detail from *The Coming of the Americans to Europe,* one of two murals painted by John Singer Sargent for the main staircase of Widener Library. The soldiers' identical faces were intended to suggest Everyman; the figures at right symbolize France, Belgium, and Britannia. President Lowell commissioned the murals to memorialize the 373 Harvard men who died in World War I.

1914. The war went on for four and a half years, and left more than ten million dead.

Many Harvard alumni and students volunteered for military or relief work when the war began. Once the nation entered the war, Harvard and other American universities became virtual arms of the government. Research and teaching were redirected toward military ends. Three-fifths of the student body left for active service; most of those who stayed did so as military trainees. Educators did little to mitigate the anti-German hysteria that swept the American public, creating a climate of intolerance, suspicion, and racial animosity that continued to trouble American society—and Harvard itself—long after the war.

The Clash of Rival Powers

AS ROWERS FROM TWELVE NATIONS gathered at Henley-on-Thames in late June, Kaiser Wilhelm II held his own regatta at Kiel, with the men of a British navy squadron as guests. The Kiel Canal, linking the North Sea and the Baltic, had been enlarged to accommodate German dreadnoughts, and the Kaiser seized the occasion to show off some of his new fighting ships.

The two navies competed in sailboat races and held shipboard banquets and dances. The regatta ended abruptly on the afternoon of June 28, when a launch brought word to the Kaiser, who was entertaining the British ambassador aboard the imperial racing yacht *Meteor*, that Austrian Archduke Franz Ferdinand and his wife had been assassinated. Wilhelm II left for Berlin, and the dreadnoughts and cruisers of the British Grand Fleet took up battle stations in the North Sea.

In the United States the assassination made headlines for a day and was soon forgotten. Three weeks passed. Austria-Hungary issued an ultimatum to Serbia; rejecting a compliant reply, the Dual Monarchy declared war on its small neighbor. Within days a complex web of treaties and alliances, intended to deter war, drew the major powers of Europe into conflict.

In aid of Serbia, Czar Nicholas II—the Kaiser's cousin—ordered the mobilization of Russia. As Austria-Hungary's ally, Wilhelm II declared war on Russia and her major ally, France. Britain entered the war when Germany threatened to march through Belgium and strike at France. On August 4, as German brigades marched on the Belgian city of Liège, President Wilson issued a formal proclamation of U.S. neutrality.

Most Americans saw the war as a European affair, but its economic repercussions shook the nation. The disruption of foreign trade slowed business activity. To ward off a financial panic caused by foreign investors liquidating securities, the New York Stock Exchange closed down for months. Wheat, cotton, and other commodity prices fell. Unemployment rose. The recession lasted almost a year.

The first British units reached Belgium in mid-August. In the east, a 650,000-man Russian force met German divisions at the Prussian frontier. The largest armies ever assembled in Europe were about to collide. Each side had staked its hopes on a lightning victory. That possibility vanished in early September, when French and British forces halted the

Kaiser Wilhelm II (left) entertaining his cousin, Czar Nicholas II of Russia, aboard the imperial yacht.

advancing Germans in the First Battle of the Marne. The Allies failed to exploit their advantage, but the Germans backed off. By the end of the month both sides were entrenched along the Aisne River, shelling each other from heavy gun emplacements behind the front lines. The war had gone underground, and a long stalemate had begun.

The Volunteers

A FEW HARVARD MEN WERE IN COMBAT within weeks of the first fighting, in units of the French infantry, the Foreign Legion, the Royal Scots Fusiliers, the Royal Canadian Highlanders, and the German army. Most were foreign citizens with military obligations to their countries, but some were Americans who ignored President Wilson's warning that the federal penal code barred U.S. citizens from serving the belligerents "directly or indirectly." Wilson's interpretation would have applied as well to the hundreds of Harvard men and women who volunteered to drive ambulances in the war zone, work in hospitals, or perform other kinds of relief work.

Many alumni and students were in Europe in the summer of 1914. Among the first volunteers were vacationers who acted as attachés at overtaxed U.S. embassies and consular offices. Physicians left their practices to assist at French and British hospitals. Dr. Richard Derby '03 was one of the first to answer a call for surgeons put out by the four-year-old American Hospital in Paris. His wife, Ethel, Theodore Roosevelt's younger daughter, volunteered as a nurse. The American Distributing Service, directed by Russell Greeley '01 and manned by a staff of six, provided hospital relief. Founded and largely funded by Mildred Barnes Bliss, wife of Robert Woods Bliss (A.B. 1900), counselor at the

Outside the American Military Hospital in Paris, ambulance drivers mobilized for service at Dunkirk in January 1915. Fourth from left is former Harvard economist A. Piatt Andrew, a newly arrived driver who would soon become inspector general of the American Ambulance Field Service. Under his direction, the A.F.S. grew into the most fully developed American volunteer organization in France.

"Doc" Andrew (right), an expert on monetary policy, had been director of the U.S. Mint and an adviser to the Senate committee that planned the Federal Reserve System. After the war he served for fourteen years as a Massachusetts congressman.

American embassy in Paris, the A.D.S. procured supplies for more than 700 French hospitals.

Of the 3,500 American volunteers who went to the front as ambulance drivers from 1914 to 1917, about 450 were alumni or undergraduates of Harvard. Most saw duty with one of three major services formed in the fall of 1914: an American Hospital squad, later reorganized by A. Piatt Andrew (PH.D. 1900) as an autonomous corps called the American Ambulance Field Service; the Harjes Formation, run by the senior partner of the Morgan-Harjes Bank in Paris; and the American Volunteer Motor-Ambulance Corps, founded by Richard Norton (A.B. 1892). These services met a vital need. France's ambulance corps had forty motorized vehicles when the war began. The rest were horse-drawn wagons built for the Franco-Prussian War of 1870.

Norton and Andrew were adventurous academics. Norton, a son of Professor Charles Eliot Norton, had done archaeological research in Central Asia. Seeking work as a war correspondent, he was moved by the sight of Marne wounded arriving in Paris. He proceeded to raise $17,000 to assemble a fleet of ten ambulances. By October 1917, when American relief units were absorbed by the military, the combined Norton-Harjes units had 200 ambulances and 700 volunteers. Andrew, who had taught economics at Harvard and been director of the U.S. Mint, volunteered as an American Hospital driver. He went on to build a recruiting and fund-raising system that supported a corps of 1,000 ambulances and 1,200 drivers—almost 350 of them from Harvard—and a truck fleet with 800 drivers.[1] With its own training school, repair depot, hospital, and recreation center, the Ambulance Field Service was the most extensive American volunteer organization in France.

Ambulance work was demanding and dangerous. Volunteers drove Ford, Packard, Daimler, and Sunbeam vans rigged to transport three or four wounded men. Narrow roads were often pitted by shell holes or awash in mud. Tires blew out, engines overheated. Though American ambulances carried wounded German prisoners in addition to British and French troops, they were shelled by German artillery units. Much of the driving had to be done at night, without headlights.

Norton recorded that his drivers carried almost 28,000 cases in the first year of the war. Driver Dallas McGrew '03 described in a letter the "feverish work, mainly at night, driving up unlighted roads to the field dressing stations, getting our gruesome cargoes and wallowing back— dodging ammunition trains of charging great motors, as well as hurrying columns of infantry and artillery—hub-deep in mud, blindly, to the evacuation hospitals at the nearest railway point. Over and over again until daylight, when we shall sleep, patch our racked ambulances, refill with oil and essence, and prepare for the next night's work! It's inglorious, unseen drudgery. . . ."

Yet the work appealed to restless young men and women who wanted to help France and Britain.[2] Among the first Harvard volunteers were John Paulding Brown '14, who looked in at the American Hospital "and fifteen minutes later was an ambulance driver"; McGrew, Richard Lawrence '02, and Lovering Hill '10, former students of Piatt Andrew; and Waldo Peirce '08, an ebullient painter and irrepressible

Richard Norton, trained as an archaeologist, ran an ambulance service that ultimately became the Norton-Harjes Corps.

mimic. Many drivers would make their names as literary men: novelists Charles Nordhoff '09 and John Dos Passos '16; playwright Sidney Howard, GSAS '16; critic Malcolm Cowley '19; editor Edward Weeks '22; and poets E.E. Cummings '15, Robert Hillyer '17, Archibald MacLeish, LL.B. '19, and Harry Crosby '22, whose bohemianism hid the fact that he was a nephew of J.P. Morgan. Not all volunteers were young. As "an avowed unneutral," Robert Bacon—former ambassador to France, president of the American Hospital, and member of the Harvard Corporation—left for France as soon as the war broke out, arriving in time to drive an ambulance at the Marne. He was then 54.

AVIATORS OF THE LAFAYETTE ESCADRILLE were the first to show the American flag in France. Founded by Norman Prince '08, LL.B. '11, an amateur pilot who had trained under the Wright brothers, the Escadrille drew many of its early members from American ambulance units and the French Foreign Legion.

Eager to get into the war, Prince sailed for France in December 1914. In Paris he talked the French war office into letting him form a French Flying Corps squadron manned by American aviators. For his six-man squadron Prince recruited three Americans who had transferred from the Foreign Legion to a French aviation school, and his friends Frazier Curtis (A.B. 1898) and Elliot Cowdin '09, an American Hospital ambulance driver. Curtis washed out after several crashes, and on a training flight one of the ex-Legionnaires was downed and captured behind German lines. But at length the Lafayette Escadrille took wing.

Five of the original members—including Prince and Victor Chapman '13, formerly of the Foreign Legion—would die in action. But the Escadrille was a magnet for adventurous young Americans. By 1918, when the squadron was absorbed by the U.S. Army, 325 men had been members. Some 25 had been killed, others wounded or taken prisoner. The squadron was officially credited with destroying 199 German planes.

Aerial warfare was still in its infancy. Aviators flew scouting patrols, dropped small bombs on ground targets, and attacked enemy observation balloons and aircraft. Instrumentation was minimal, communication was by hand signals, and armor was almost nonexistent. Open

Norman Prince founded the Lafayette Escadrille. In 122 aerial engagements he was credited with downing five German planes. Handicapped by poor depth perception, he died after a night crash in 1916.

Victor Emmanuel Chapman. To admiring French aviators he was known as *le roi de l'air.*

Left: The Lafayette Escadrille. From left: Chapman, Elliot Cowdin, Bert Hall, William Thaw, Captain Thenault and Lieutenant de Laage de Mieux (French officers), Norman Prince, Kiffin Rockwell, James McConnell.

cockpits exposed pilots to subzero temperatures and enemy bullets. Engines stalled and guns jammed. The slow-moving wood-and-canvas planes were easy targets, and incendiary bullets could set them afire. Even so, the letters and journals of early military pilots are full of ecstatic descriptions of the joys of flying. Victor Chapman, who had been studying architecture in Paris when war broke out, wrote his brother:

> Over the field we soared, and due east for B—. . . . The earth seemed hidden under a fine web such as the Lady of Shallot wove; soft purple in the west changing to shimmering white in the east. Under me on the left, the Vosges, like rounded sand dunes cushioned up with velvety light and dark mosses (really forests). . . . Ah, there are quantities of worm-eaten fields— my friends, the trenches,—and that town with the canal going through it must be M—. Right beside the capote of my engine, shining through the white silk cloth, a silver snake: the Rhine! "What, not over quarter to six, and I left the field at five! Thirty-two hundred metres. Let's go north and have a look at the map. Boo, my feet are getting cold!"

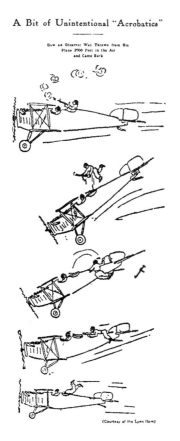

A Bit of Unintentional "Acrobatics"

How an Observer Was Thrown from His Plane 2000 Feet in the Air and Came Back

(Courtesy of the Lynn Item)

Flying as an observer in aerial combat was risky. These sketches from the Lynn (Massachusetts) *Item* depict an incident that occurred in France in 1918. The airman who barely escaped a 2,000-foot fall was Lieutenant Gardiner Fiske '14. His aircraft was piloted by Lieutenant Samuel Mandell II '19.

Attached to the U.S. 20th Aero Squadron, Mandell (right) flew in the war's last American air mission on November 5, 1918. Badly injured when his plane crashed near enemy lines, he was shot to death by a German officer.

First-hand accounts of aerial combat were vivid and searing. A.L. Cunningham '18, who joined the Escadrille after serving in the Foreign Legion, described the death of his friend Philip Davis '08 in a battle with six German planes over enemy territory:

> We were nothing but a whirl of machines diving, firing, and zooming up again. . . . Suddenly a tiny flame spurted out of Davis's machine just behind the pilot's seat, and began to lick its way around the fuselage. Instantly he dove toward the earth. Powerless and horrified I followed. A few hundred feet further down his machine burst into a mass of flames and then . . . out of all control, dropped into a *vrille* or nose spin; righted itself, slid off on what was left of its wings, and dropped again into a *vrille*. It continued to fall tumbling from *vrille* to wing slide, then back again to *vrille* until it crashed in a little meadow a few miles back of the German lines and at the edge of a wood. I saw some human figures running towards it, but could distinguish nothing else. I circled overhead . . . while the machine smoked and smouldered on the ground.[3]

Minutes before taking off, wrote Cunningham, Davis had "characteristically remarked how lucky we were to be in the air service instead of among those poor devils in the trenches."

VOLUNTEERS WENT INTO THE TRENCHES bravely and insouciantly. Alan Seeger '10, who had gone to Paris to write, joined the Foreign Legion in August 1914. He found himself in a company that included Joseph Ganson (A.B. 1892), James Carstairs '11, and David King '16. By October they were in front-line trenches at Champagne. "Imagine how thrilling it will be tomorrow marching toward the front with the noise of battle growing continually louder," Seeger wrote his mother. "I go into action with the lightest of light hearts."

"Just back from my first experience of the real thing," wrote Harry Byng '13, an Englishman who had captained Harvard's soccer team and was at the front as a private in the London Artists' Rifles. "Quite good fun, but heavy rain does not improve a narrow clay trench." As the weather got worse, so did trench duty. "It is the damnedest life imaginable," wrote André Chéronet-Champollion '02, a great-grandson of the Egyptologist who deciphered the Rosetta Stone. He had enlisted in the French army in August and gone to the front six months later. "We live like swine," Champollion wrote his friend Anton Schefer '03.

> There is no water, so we never wash or even brush our teeth. . . . We simply live in filth. At night we are huddled together in a small bomb-proof or covered trench. Though we are pretty well protected from the weather and bullets, we have hardly room enough to turn around in. . . . We eat from the pail, and can get or send for all the red or white wine we want. In the morning, besides tepid coffee, we are given a swig of rum which warms our stomach and starts the blood going. . . . Write often, old top. Your faithful friend, CHAMPY.

Three days later, shifting sandbags before an expected German assault, Champollion was shot in the forehead and killed.

The principal task of infantrymen in the trenches was to withstand constant shelling. Barrages from artillery units behind the lines caused the most casualties of the war, but it was an inefficient means of killing. "It is surprising how many shells it takes to kill or even wound one man," noted Charles Morgan '06, who got into the war as an ambulance driver but later gained a commission in a British artillery unit.

"When there is an attack on, the scene is quite indescribably unreal," wrote C.S. Forbes '00, an American Hospital ambulance driver.

> The din is most awe-inspiring. Seemingly from almost every square yard for miles around the French guns belch forth a continuous stream of death into the inferno in front, and the Germans answer in like manner with their shrieking and shattering shells. From all sides rockets shoot up into the sky as if celebrating some gala performance of the Devil himself. White rockets that remain in the air for about a minute, red balls of fire, green lights, great flares of bengal lights, and some fiendish looking things, that zigzag across the sky like some gigantic snake. . . . When all this bedlam dies down we get the miserable results that are carried in, covered with mud and blood.

"The shrapnel wounds simply defy description," wrote George Benet, M.D. '13, a volunteer in an American Hospital surgical unit.

> You see a boy of eighteen with his lower jaw, floor of mouth, and half his tongue blown away. He lives, but for what? Another young man of 24 with both legs gone at the thighs, and his right arm crippled for life. . . . One chap told a nurse that he saw his captain killed (by shell) and his head blown off. When he ran to him his "trachea said squeak—squeak." I have no doubt it did; but imagine scenes like that to think about the rest of your life.

George Williamson '05, a British army lieutenant who died of wounds in November 1914, was believed to be the first graduate of an

Alan Seeger, who joined the Foreign Legion as a private in August 1914, fought in five major battles. He was killed July 4, 1916, as the six-month Battle of the Somme began.

> I have a rendezvous with Death
> At some disputed barricade
> When Spring comes back with rustling shade
> And apple-blossoms fill the air—
> I have a rendezvous with Death
> When Spring brings back blue days and fair.
> —Alan Seeger, *Poems* (1916)

American college to die in the war. A Montreal lawyer, Williamson had become a reserve officer in the Duke of Wellington's West Riding Regiment while studying at Oxford. He was buried in Flanders. Fritz Daur, s.t.m. '14, died of wounds in Flanders the following week. Returning to his native Germany after graduating from the Divinity School, he had been called up and sent to the Belgian front. Edward Stone '08, fatally wounded by shrapnel in February 1915, was the first American-born Harvard soldier to die in the war. Then living in France, he had joined the Foreign Legion in August 1914 and gone to the front in October.

The deaths of Champollion and Harry Byng were reported that spring. Byng, now an officer in the King's Own Scottish Borderers, had been married in London in March; back at the front, he recorded the grisliness of war in letters and journal entries ("There are dead bodies hanging on the barbed wire—one Gurkha strangling a German. Then there is a little grave bearing the epitaph, 'Some one's leg.'"). Byng was killed leading an attack at Festubert in May. "I must confess I don't like the life a great deal," he had written not long before, "and after the war, I shall get out of the regular Army, as soon as I can."

For most volunteers, idealistic hopes gave way to disillusionment and despair. "For a decadent race, the French are doing well," wrote the French-born Robert Pellissier '04, formerly an assistant professor of Romance languages at Stanford, now a French army sergeant:

> But good heavens, what a futile and criminal thing war is. No one who has not seen it can realize how wicked it is. Only an ass or a bandit can talk about the necessity or beauty of war. . . . The one decent thing that may come out of this horrible mess may be the discrediting of war in Europe, and perhaps elsewhere. It's an idea which keeps up French soldiers at present. One often hears them say, "Well, whatever happens to us, our children at least will be freed from the curse of militarism . . ."

Alan Seeger now wrote in his diary, "We are not living the life of men at all, but of animals, living in holes in the ground, and only showing outside to fight and to feed." To his mother he wrote, "You are quite wrong about my not realizing what I was getting into when I enlisted. I knew that it would be a fight to the finish, just as our Civil War was. The conflagration, far from diminishing, seems to be spreading. The lull during the winter has allowed each side on this front to fortify itself so strongly that, in my opinion, the deadlock here is permanent."

"An Oasis of Peace and Concord"

ADDRESSING THE FRESHMAN CLASS as the fall term of 1914 began, President Lowell spoke briefly but strongly about the war. "It is destroying the flower of the youth of Europe," said Lowell. "It is blotting out lives that would otherwise be destined to be of incalculable value to mankind. . . . If the torch of civilization is to be carried forward, a certain responsibility rests upon us, who are not being killed, to fill the gaps in the ranks of civilization which those men would have filled. . . . Men who would otherwise be eminent in science, in lit-

Early casualties of the war (clockwise from top left): George Williamson '05, Edward Stone '08, André Chéronet-Champollion '02, and Harry Byng '13.

erature and in art, are now having their young lives torn out of them by
shells, and it is for the youth of America to take their place. You are
recruited and are now in training."

The *Alumni Bulletin* assured readers that "returning members of the
University will find, beyond their immediate work, many things to turn
their thoughts from the tragedy of Europe." The new freshman residence halls had opened. The exterior of Widener Library was done, but
labor troubles had slowed work on the interior. New trees had replaced
some of the Yard's blighted elms. The cooperative agreement with MIT
was not fully implemented, "but the two institutions are now closely
related, and the students are fraternizing in some of their activities."
Tech students would be allowed to apply for tickets to "the important
football games." The team's prospects were bright. "Football critics
generally agree that Brickley, Mahan, and Bradlee constitute the most effective and versatile backfield ever known since American college football
began," crowed the *Bulletin.* "Francke, who is a son of Professor Kuno
Francke, has all the qualifications for the rush line. He is heavy, well
formed, and unusually intelligent."

An editorial note addressed the issue of institutional neutrality.
"The University enrollment includes members of every one of the
nations involved [in the war]," it began, "and its obvious part is to observe the strict neutrality which President Wilson has urged upon all
Americans."

> Open meetings in behalf of one side or the other would invite many diffi-
> culties. While actual war, in which millions of men are engaged, is in
> progress, there can be no dispassionate discussion here. . . . Harvard is a
> great centre of neutrality, an oasis of peace and concord, to which the sons
> of twenty different races and countries repair. Here they should both find
> and practise that mutual toleration and good-will for lack of which Europe
> has been turned into the slaughterhouse at which the world stands aghast.

Wilson had urged Americans to "be impartial in thought as well as
in action." But at Harvard and most eastern colleges, the ideals of
impartiality and "mutual toleration" faded fast. Truculent public statements by German leaders aroused Americans; accounts of the brutal
invasion of neutral Belgium elicited shock and anger. At Harvard,

**Grander in scale than anything
Harvard had built in the past, the
new freshman residence halls
opened in the fall of 1914.
Above: Gore Hall and the entrance to
its courtyard. Below: Standish Hall's
common room. These two Halls
would later form the main buildings
of John Winthrop House.**

where a vast new library loomed in the Yard, students and faculty members recoiled at news that German troops had gutted the medieval library of the University of Louvain. President Lowell responded by creating visiting lectureships for two scholars from Louvain.

"Not for a moment was the Harvard community neutral in thought or deed," Samuel Eliot Morison would later write. Returning to teach at Harvard after a stint at the University of California, Morison was struck by the intensity of pro-Allied feeling. At Berkeley, the European war had "seemed to the average student as unreal as the Wars of the Roses." Here "one was on the outskirts of battle."

Hugo Münsterberg, a pioneer in applied psychology, alienated faculty colleagues when he pleaded the German cause. As an exchange professor in Berlin in 1910, Münsterberg had founded the Amerika Institut to promote interchange between his native and adopted countries.

Members of the community bridled when Professor Hugo Münsterberg, a pioneer in applied psychology, rushed into print a pro-German book called *The War and America*. Colleagues stopped speaking to him; rumors circulated that the German-born scholar was in the pay of the Kaiser's secret service. A member of the class of 1900 threatened to cancel a $10 million bequest to Harvard if Münsterberg were allowed to remain on the faculty. Calling the bluff, Münsterberg offered to resign if his antagonist would remit $5 million forthwith.[4] President Lowell, much annoyed, had the Corporation announce "that, at the instance of the authorities, Professor Münsterberg's resignation has been withdrawn, and that the University cannot tolerate any suggestion that it would be willing to accept money to abridge free speech, to remove a professor or to accept his resignation."

Students threw eggs at a bronze lion that the Duchy of Brunswick had given the Germanic Museum. Kuno Francke, the museum's curator and Harvard's ranking professor of German, had advocated the German cause. Professor Kuno Meyer of the University of Berlin, who was to give a lecture on Celtic literature, was disinvited because of his "active propaganda among the Irish on behalf of Germany." But when the Medical School formed a surgical unit to serve for three months at the American Hospital in Paris, Lowell felt bound to state that if Germany asked for similar help he would undertake to arrange it.

The unarmed Cunard liner *Lusitania*, largest steamer in the Atlantic service, left New York for Liverpool on May 1, 1915. Six days later the ship was torpedoed by a German U-boat eight miles off the Irish coast. Among the 1,198 passengers and crew who lost their lives in the sinking were five alumni of Harvard, including Elbert Hubbard, class of 1897, a popular inspirational writer, and Carlton Brodrick '08, who had been working for Herbert Hoover's Belgian relief commission.

The Medical School team, led by Moseley professor of surgery Harvey Cushing (M.D. 1895), sailed for France in March. Events in Europe that spring heightened anti-German feeling. The Kaiser decreed that the waters surrounding the British Isles were a war zone where enemy ships would be sunk without warning. An American citizen drowned when a U-boat sank the British liner *Falaba* in St. George's Channel. American papers denounced the sinking as a crime against humanity.

In April the Germans used poison gas against Allied forces defending Ypres, a Belgian gateway to the Channel ports. Dr. Cushing treated some of the victims in Paris. "A huge, rolling, low-lying greenish cloud of smoke with yellowish top, began to roll down on them from the German trenches, fanned by a steady easterly wind," he wrote in a memoir published in the *Alumni Bulletin* that spring:

The smoke was suffocating and smelled to one like ether or sulphur, to another like a sulphur match times one thousand—to still another like burning rosin. One man said that there were about one thousand Zouaves of the Bataillon d'Afrique in the lines, and only sixty got back—either suffocated or shot as they clambered out of the trenches to escape. . . . In any event, there's the devil's work going on around Ypres. . . .

The "smoke" was chlorine gas. It brought shock, agonizing invalidism, and slow death to 15,000 French colonial and Canadian troops. Worse asphyxiants were to come, and gas would be used by both sides for the rest of the war. Lawrence Brokenshire '16, of the Canadian Royal Highlanders, was a gas victim at Ypres. He recovered and later served in the Royal Flying Corps. One of those who died was Calvin Wellington Day, a lieutenant in the Princess of Wales's Own Rifles who had been a Harvard graduate student and research assistant in physics.

On May 1 the American tanker *Gulflight* was sunk without warning. A week later the British Cunard liner *Lusitania*, en route from New York to Liverpool, was torpedoed in the Irish Sea. Among the 1,198 passengers and crew members lost were 128 Americans. The sinking demonstrated the lethal effectiveness of submarines, and was an ominous sign that in modern war civilian lives were expendable. Led by Theodore Roosevelt, interventionists called for a declaration of war. Wilson clung to his principle of neutrality. "There is such a thing as a nation being so right that it does not need to convince others by force," he declared; "there is such a thing as a man being too proud to fight." He did seek assurances that such acts would not recur. Months later, after the sinking of the White Star liner *Arabic* with two American lives lost, German ambassador Count von Bernstorff announced that liners would not be sunk without warning or respect for the lives of noncombatants.

SOMBER VERSES BY FORMER Oxford don Alfred Noyes, the Phi Beta Kappa poet, set the tone for a restrained Commencement in 1915:

> Music is dead, while half the world is dying.
> Shreds of Uranian song, wild symphonies
> Tortured with moans of butchered innocents,
> Blow past us on the wind.

"The future is dark," President Lowell told his audience on the afternoon of Commencement day. "We know not whether we shall be entangled or escape being entangled in this war. But our duty is just as great in the one case as it is in the other. Whether we fight or whether we do not fight, we fight or we do not fight for civilization."

The day's major event was a noontime ceremony to dedicate Widener Library. Eleanor Elkins Widener presented President Lowell with the key; Archibald Cary Coolidge, director of the University Library, carried into the building John Downame's *Christian Warfare*, the only surviving volume from the library that John Harvard had left to the College in 1638.[5] In an eloquent speech, Senator Henry Cabot Lodge quoted Milton: "There are certain books which being sown up and

The Gas Fiend, one of many grim war cartoons by the Dutch artist Louis Raemakers, was inspired by the Germans' use of poison gas against French and Canadian troops at Ypres, Belgium, in April 1915.

Dr. Harvey Cushing (below), in charge of Harvard Medical School's first surgical unit to serve in France, was among the physicians treating a trainload of soldiers said to have been felled by German *"gaz asphyxiant."* "I hardly believed the tale," Cushing wrote in his journal, "or thought I had misunderstood, until this evening's *communiqué* bears it out."

"A University in Itself"

Faculty members, dignitaries, and alumni assembled at noon on Commencement Day, 1915, for the dedication of the Harry Elkins Widener Memorial Library. Senator Henry Cabot Lodge (A.B. 1871, LL.B. 1874, PH.D. 1876, LL.D. '04) was the principal speaker. "A great library draws men and women in search of education as a garden of flowers draws the bees," said Lodge. "Carlyle indeed went even further when he said 'the true university of these days is a collection of books.' Such a library as this is not only a pillar of support to learning but it is a university in itself. . . ."

Stocking the new library with the 645,000 volumes temporarily housed in outlying buildings took fourteen weeks. A single truck, making ten to twelve trips per day, moved an average of 46,000 books a week. The transfer of the three-million-card catalog was completed in a day.

Harry Widener's collection was housed in a central suite of rooms beneath a rotunda (below).

Dedication of the Harry Elkins Widener Memorial Library, June 24, 1915.

down may chance to spring up armed men." Hours later, trucks began to arrive with boxes of books that had been stored in more than a dozen outlying buildings.

Horace Trumbauer, the library's architect, received an honorary M.A. at the morning ceremonies. The University did not award such degrees to women, so Mrs. Widener was not among the day's twelve honorands. Harvard did confer an M.A. on Alexander Hamilton Rice (A.B. 1898, M.D. 1904), physician and South American explorer, who went on to marry Mrs. Widener. Among the graduating seniors were E.E. Cummings, who gave a Commencement oration titled "The New Art," and Lionel de Jersey Harvard, collateral descendant of John Harvard. Lionel composed the class hymn and the class poem, and briefly addressed the assembled alumni at the afternoon ceremonies.

ABOUT 85 HARVARD STUDENTS went to Plattsburg, New York, that summer for a month of intensive military training. Major General Leonard Wood (M.D. 1884) had run the first summer program for 160 collegians at Gettysburg, Pennsylvania, in 1913. Enrollment had since soared to 620. After the sinking of the *Lusitania*, a group of New Yorkers led by Robert Bacon and Grenville Clark '03, LL.B. '06, had met to discuss preparedness measures. With Theodore Roosevelt, they persuaded General Wood to conduct a reserve officers' training camp for business and professional men at Plattsburg in August. More than 1,200 enrolled; about 500 trainees came from Harvard, including one faculty member, two Overseers, and a member of the Corporation (Bacon). An overflow camp was held the next month for 600 men who hadn't applied in time for the first session. The following summer no fewer than 16,000 men trained at twelve camps modeled on Plattsburg, and assistant secretary of the navy Franklin D. Roosevelt '04 assembled a squadron of private vessels for a "naval Plattsburg" cruise. President

Lowell had been an early advocate of the Plattsburg idea, and had served on an advisory committee formed by General Wood in 1913. In the fall of 1915 he persuaded Wood to be a guest instructor in the College's first elective course in military science. Some 560 students enrolled in the course, which was given for credit.

AMERICA'S BUSINESS RECESSION was over. A war boom had begun. The British fleet was securing sea lanes for American shipping; New York displaced London as the center of world finance. Allied orders for munitions, agricultural products, and other goods kept American industries humming. The house of Morgan had played a pivotal role in the upturn. The firm acted as purchasing agent for the governments of Britain and France; at the same time, it extended bank credits, sold foreign-owned U.S. securities, and formed large syndicates to float long-term loans to the Allies. The Federal Reserve System, then in its second year, facilitated the expansion of currency and credit. Encouraged by economic conditions, the Harvard Corporation began planning a massive, $10 million endowment campaign. The younger J. P. Morgan's right-hand man, Thomas Lamont, agreed to serve as chairman.

The summer of 1915 brought a surge of domestic terrorism and subversion. New York City was rocked by bombings. On July 3 the morning papers reported that an explosion had shattered a reception room in the Senate wing of the Capitol. In Glen Cove, Long Island, Morgan and his houseguest, British ambassador Sir Cecil Spring Rice, were discussing the news over coffee when an intruder burst in. "So you are Mr. Morgan," the man said, waving a brace of pistols. The husky Morgan wrestled him to the floor, but the pistols went off and Morgan received flesh wounds in his thigh and abdomen. In custody the assailant gave a

Harvard at the Front

Official picture: Clubmen Mellen '17, Walker '11, Galatti '10, Suckley '10, Rice '12, Carey '14, Hale '14, Hill '10, and (in wooden shoes) Peirce '08.

The Harvard Club of Alsace Reconquise was born November 19, 1915–the eve of that year's Harvard-Yale football game. The club's 25 members were American Field Service ambulance drivers who were billeted in a small town in the Vosges sector.

Stephen Galatti '10, one of the organizers, informed the *Alumni Bulletin* that club members had performed "three official acts, namely: to send a telegram to [head coach] Percy Haughton advising him how to beat Yale by Joffre tactics; secondly, to drink the health of the team after said game; thirdly, to have their photograph taken. The first act was censored by unsympathetic officials, the second was suc-

cessful, and the third I enclose for your judgment.... With the moving of [our] section to another army, the Harvard Club of Alsace Reconquise ends its active career (but expects to have even

more active meetings in New York or Boston). It was perhaps only a name, but its members enjoyed the name as signifying that Harvard was there too in reconquered territory...." [6]

false name and said he had planned to halt munitions shipments to Britain by taking the Morgan family hostage. He turned out to be Erich Muenter, a University of Chicago graduate who had once been an instructor in German at Harvard. Muenter had vanished from Cambridge in 1906 as police investigated the arsenic poisoning of his wife. Having claimed responsibility for the Capitol bombing, he soon died, mysteriously, in jail.

At about the same time, Treasury agents recovered a briefcase left on a New York elevated train by a German embassy attaché. In it they found plans to foment strikes in arms plants, rig the cotton market, corner chlorine supplies, and purchase munitions to keep them out of Allied hands. With the concurrence of government officials, the papers were leaked to the *New York World*. Disclosures of German intrigue were a boon to the cause of military preparedness. Theodore Roosevelt and Leonard Wood were its leading proponents. TR, nearing the end of his second term on the Board of Overseers, insisted that military training should be a required part of the curriculum. "Harvard should take the lead in every real movement for making our country stand as it should stand," he wrote in the *Harvard Advocate* of December 1915.

Unfortunately prominent Harvard men sometimes take the lead the wrong way. This applies pre-eminently to all Harvard men who have had anything to do with the absurd and mischievous professional-pacifist movements which have so thoroughly discredited this country during the past five years. . . . The pacifist of this type stands on an exact level with the poltroon. His appropriate place is with the college sissy who disapproves of football or boxing because it is rough. . . . No man is worth his salt who is not ready at all times to risk his body, to risk his well-being, to risk his life, in a great cause. No nation has a right to a place in the world

Theodore Roosevelt leaving University Hall in the spring of 1916 after his final meeting as a member of the Board of Overseers. The Overseers' meetings, he told his friend Owen Wister (A.B. 1882), made him feel "like a bulldog who had strayed into a symposium of perfectly clean, white Persian cats."

TR wanted Harvard to take the lead in preparing the nation for war. "Let Harvard men, graduates and undergraduates alike, start at once to practice and to preach that efficient morality which stands at the opposite pole from the milk-and-water doctrines of the professional pacifists," he wrote in a *Harvard Advocate* article.

Volunteers for the newly formed Harvard Regiment reporting at Briggs Cage in January 1916.

unless it has so trained its sons and daughters that they follow righteous-ness as the great goal. . . .

WITH AN ELECTION YEAR APPROACHING, President Wilson was under fire from two sides. Roosevelt attacked him as the cynosure of "mollycoddles" and "flapdoodle pacifists" who were afraid to fight. Senator Robert La Follette and William Jennings Bryan, who had re-signed as Wilson's secretary of state, pictured the president as the dupe of profiteers and warmongers. Early in 1916 Wilson made a speaking tour to promote preparedness, arguing that the way to stay out of war was to become invincible. That summer Congress acted to strengthen the nation's armed forces. But Roosevelt wouldn't let up. When Wilson sought respite at Shadow Lawn, his summer home in New Jersey, TR made his famous "Shadows" speech:

> There should be shadows enough at Shadow Lawn—the shadows of men, women, and children who have risen from the ooze of the ocean; the shadows of the helpless whom Mr. Wilson did not dare protect lest he might have to face danger; the shadows of babies gasping pitifully as they sank beneath the waves. . . . Those are the shadows proper for Shadow Lawn; the shadows of deeds that were never done; the shadows of lofty words that were followed by no action; the shadows of the tortured dead.

Roosevelt was eager to take on Wilson in the election of 1916, but the Republican Old Guard would not excuse him for leaving the party in 1912. In November Wilson narrowly beat former New York governor Charles Evans Hughes. After the election he pleaded for international compromise—"peace without victory"—and put forward a series of war and peace aims that became known as the Fourteen Points.

The German government now resumed unrestricted submarine war-fare. Wilson responded by breaking diplomatic relations. In the first four months of 1917, German U-boats sank an average of ten ships a day. Four American ships were torpedoed in February and March. "There is no question about going to war," Theodore Roosevelt told re-porters: "Germany is already at war with us." Though he was 58, TR was now proposing to raise a volunteer regiment of "horse-riflemen" in the spirit of San Juan Hill. On April 2 Wilson sent Congress a war message. "We have no quarrel with the German people," he declared, but "the world must be made safe for democracy." At 3 A.M. on the morning of April 6, Congress voted to declare war on Germany. In the Christian calendar the day was Good Friday.

Cogs in the War Machine

CALLING WILSON'S WAR MESSAGE "a great state paper," Roosevelt rushed to Washington to seek presidential approval of his plan for a volunteer regiment.[7] Harvard was also quick to mobilize. A "Harvard Regiment," formed in January 1916 with more than 1,000 student members, had become the first unit of the army's new Reserve Officers' Training Corps. On the day of the diplomatic break with Germany, President Lowell had written French ambassador Jules Jusserand to say that Harvard would welcome invalided French officers as military instructors. Six officers arrived in mid-April, and other American schools soon made similar arrangements.[8] Under their French mentors, trainees drilled and practiced bayonet work in the Stadium, dug model trenches near Fresh Pond, and slept in pup tents during field maneuvers in western Massachusetts.

The University held a convocation in May 1917 to award an LL.D. degree to Joseph Joffre, Marshal of France (third from left). The aging hero of the Marne also made a brief appearance at Harvard Stadium, where he was cheered by a crowd of 22,000.

French Lieutenant André Morize, instructor in military science, showing plans of trainees' model trenches at Fresh Pond to Secretary of War Newton D. Baker on an inspection tour in the fall of 1917.

Minutes after the declaration of war, Dean Briggs had told an inquiring *Crimson* reporter that intercollegiate athletics would be suspended. The Business School quickly set up a course for supply officers. To assist students enlisting in military or relief units, the Faculty of Arts and Sciences voted to give final exams in April and May. Many upperclassmen left to attend officers' training camps or to begin active duty; others were commissioned after taking an intensive three-month summer program. Enlistments and draft calls halved the University's total enrollment of 4,700 in the spring and summer of 1917.

Only the Medical School, with about 400 students, remained at roughly its normal size: the draft laws encouraged medical students to continue their studies as army officers "detached for special service." Leaves for duty in army, navy, and Red Cross medical branches depleted the school's teaching faculty. More than two dozen Harvard doctors staffed four volunteer surgical and dental units attached to British, French, and American base hospitals in France.[9] Dr. Varaztad Kazanjian, D.M.D. '05, a Dental School faculty member who had sailed with the first Harvard hospital unit in 1915, was hailed as "the miracle man of the Western Front" for his reconstructive techniques.

Regular enrollment at the Business School fell precipitously, from a pre-war level of 232 to 32 in the fall of 1918. All but three of the school's faculty members eventually left to join the war effort, and Dean Edwin Gay took a leave of absence to direct the U.S. Shipping Board's division of planning and statistics. By the fall of 1917, the Law School's enrollment had dropped from 850 to about 250. Many faculty members left to serve in the Judge Advocate General's department.

Chemists and physicists conducted secret research. Professor Elmer Kohler oversaw poison-gas research for the Chemical Warfare Service.

The Harvard Regiment's thousand members marching down Columbus Avenue, Boston, in a "preparedness parade" in May 1916.

Another professor, Arthur Lamb, headed a government laboratory that designed and produced gas masks. James Conant '14, Ph.D. '16, a young instructor in chemistry, synthesized a scarce drug at the Bureau of Chemistry in Washington. He later did gas research at a secret laboratory in Ohio. Percy Bridgman '04, Ph.D. '08, assistant professor of physics, worked on sound-detection systems for anti-submarine warfare, and developed a technique for pre-straining gun barrels.

Harvard's Psychological Laboratory devised aptitude tests for aviation trainees. Teachers of German translated papers found on interned ships. Two of the French department's native speakers were sent to West Point to help cadets with conversational French. In France, a Harvard geographer made topographical studies from observation balloons; professors of physiology studied traumatic shock.

Harvard also ran a course for naval reservists, and furnished classrooms and quarters for two government schools: one for navy radio operators, the other a program for future ensigns. Headquartered in Pierce Hall and Cruft Laboratory, the radio operators' school had a complement of 250 enlisted men when it started in May 1917. Over the next eighteen months the number rose to almost 5,000. The program used all or part of twenty University buildings; a temporary barracks for trainees was erected on Cambridge Common.

The Summer School held a series of 24 lectures on "historical aspects of the present conflict," and sponsored a course on nutrition. Harvard heeded Herbert Hoover, the nation's food czar, and observed "meatless Tuesdays" and "wheatless Wednesdays." Harvard University Press employees farmed a plot of land between Memorial Hall and Kirkland Street. Dining halls salvaged peach pits to fabricate gas mask linings. The University, and many local and regional Harvard clubs, suspended the serving of spirits at social functions.

BY SEPTEMBER 1917, Harvard's enrollment had dropped by 40 percent. A census taken by the *Alumni Bulletin* and the Alumni Office showed that almost 5,500 alumni and former students were in some form of national service. All undergraduates who completed twelve courses, as opposed to the usual sixteen, received "war degrees." Faculty members entering national service received Harvard checks to cover the difference between their regular salary levels and government pay. About 235 out of a teaching force of 1,000 were listed as engaged in

Naval Radio School trainees mess at Memorial Hall in the fall of 1917.

war research or in the military; almost 130 were on leave from the University.

The war's known toll of Harvard lives had reached 44. Among the dead were poet Alan Seeger, killed on July 4, 1916, as the Somme offensive began, and Robert Pellissier, the former Stanford French teacher, killed at the Somme two months later. Norman Prince, the founder of the Lafayette Escadrille, had died of injuries after striking an aerial cable in a night landing attempt. Prince's place in the squadron was taken by his older brother, Frederick '08. Victor Chapman, at 26 the Escadrille's youngest member, had been killed in an aerial dogfight in the summer of 1916. Chapman's father, the often acerbic essayist John Jay Chapman, wrote that "Victor's entry into [aviation] was, to him, like being made a Knight. It transformed— one might almost say—transfigured him." As a memorial to his son the elder Chapman endowed a Harvard fellowship for French students.

ALMOST 600 ALUMNI AND STUDENTS had volunteered during the period of neutrality. With the arrival of American troops in France in the summer of 1917, hundreds more went to the front. In the vanguard was army ambulance driver Paul Cody Bentley '17, the first member of the American Expeditionary Forces to die of battle wounds. His unit, supporting French army detachments, was under fire near the Aisne River throughout the summer. During a German gas attack in early September, Bentley's vehicle was approaching a stretch of road called "Dead Man's Curve" when it was raked by heavy artillery. Bentley died of a chest wound inflicted by a gas-bearing shell.

Technology was transforming the nature of war. The Germans had introduced poison gas in 1915 and flamethrowers ten months later. The British introduced armored tanks in the six-month Battle of the Somme in 1916. Both sides had wireless communications to supplement field telephones, dogs, and carrier pigeons. The range and firepower of aircraft had increased; so had the number of planes in action.

Trench warfare remained grisly and primitive. "It's strange the way we have gone back to ancient methods of fighting," wrote Braxton Bigelow '09, of the 170th Tunneling Company, British Royal Engineers. "We carry loaded sticks, spiked and knobbed clubs, daggers, and knives of all sorts and shapes, and I have even seen brass knuckles." Bigelow, who spent twenty months at the front before he was lost in a raid on a German trench system, had previously described "the most intense bombardment and machine gun fire I had ever seen. . . . Our front lines, support lines, and communications trenches were simply a mass of flying sandbags, earth, and flame. You would think nothing could live through it. No wonder they take men out raving mad."

American troops tried to show that no matter how bad it got, they could take it. Early in 1918, from a front-line artillery post near Toul,

Lieutenant Douglas Campbell '17, Harvard's ranking air ace, was credited with downing six German planes. Shot in the back during a dogfight in June 1918, he recovered and was awarded the Croix de Guerre, Légion d'Honneur, and Distinguished Service Cross. Campbell was attached to the 94th ("Hat-in-Ring") Pursuit Squadron, the first American military air unit to become operational at the front.

War Stories

MORE THAN 11,000 Harvard men, from 55 College classes and the six graduate and professional schools, served in the war. Their doings filled 1,083 pages in *Harvard's Military Record in the World War*, edited by Frederick Mead (A.B. 1887) and published by Harvard University Press in 1921. These were some of them:

JOHN GALLISHAW '18. A Newfoundlander, he joined a Canadian motorcycle unit as a dispatch rider in November 1914. Discharged after being wounded at Gallipoli, he joined the U.S. Army, was gassed in France, and returned to Harvard as an instructor with the Student Army Training Corps.

Morgan

CHARLES MORGAN '06. He volunteered as an American Hospital ambulance driver in 1914 and became a British artillery officer the next year. Wounded three times, Morgan was awarded the Military Cross. He remained in service until April 1919.

HENRY FARNSWORTH '12. A *Providence Journal* correspondent in Mexico when the European war began, he sailed for France and joined the Foreign Legion early in 1915. "As long as you are soldiering," he wrote, "I think it as well to do it with people who are soldiers to the very marrow of their bones." An avid reader, he lamented that books were too heavy to march with. But "the State of the German Mind, Plato or Kant, are not necessary for the moment," he wrote, "and I have read Milton, Shakespeare, and Dante." In September 1915 Farnsworth's battalion was wiped out in the Battle of Champagne. His parents gave Widener Library a reading room in his memory.

Farnsworth

Lieutenant GEORGE PLUMMER HOWE (A.B. '00, M.D. '04). A Boston physician and amateur archaeologist, he joined the Medical Officers' Reserve Corps, was sent overseas in May 1917, and was attached to a battalion of British Royal Fusiliers. In British units, medical officers went over the top with their men to render first aid and direct stretcher-bearers. Howe suffered a head wound at the third battle of Ypres in September 1917, but remained at his aid post until he was killed by shellfire. He was believed to be the first American officer to lose his life in the war.

Ensign ALBERT STURTEVANT. A Harvard law student in 1916, he was a former Yale crew captain who had rowed in the famous Yale-Harvard race of 1914. On escort duty early in 1918, his navy seaplane was attacked by German aircraft and shot down over the English Channel. Sturtevant was the first aviator serving with American forces to die in action.

LIONEL DE JERSEY HARVARD '15. Known as "Johnny" to his College contemporaries, Harvard had planned to become a medical missionary. After graduation he had returned to his native England, married, and received a commission in the Grenadier Guards. Harvard was shot in the chest in the 1916 Somme offensive, but later fought at Ypres and Cambrai. His company was in the front line when the German armies launched the major offensive of March 1918. After ten days of heavy bombardment, he was killed by shellfire near Arras.

Harvard

Colonel RAYNAL C. BOLLING (A.B. '00, LL.B. '02). He was planning Air

Ambulance driver Paul Bentley '17, the first A.E.F. member to die of wounds sustained in battle.

Lieutenant Jeff Feigl '18 wrote his family, "If any of you could see me now, you wouldn't recognize me, let alone speak to me. I haven't had a bath since January first. I haven't had my clothes off for 27 days, and I live in, on, and look like mud. Not that all artillery men are like that—quite the contrary. I am now doing liaison work for my battery. That is, I live with the Infantry and brace up their morale by my inspiring presence. In other words it is a sort of diplomatic job....I never felt better in my life, nor enjoyed myself more."

Feigl was killed by shrapnel on March 21, when the German army launched a major offensive. He had been at the front for eleven weeks. Posthumously awarded the Croix de Guerre, he was the first American artillery officer to die in battle. "He was known to the men

Colonel Raynal Bolling's monument in Greenwich, Connecticut.

Service operations in France when his automobile was caught in an ambuscade near the front in March 1918; he died exchanging revolver fire with German officers. Colonel Bolling was the first high-ranking U.S. officer to be killed in the war. Bolling Field, in Washington, D.C., was later named in his honor.

GUY LOWELL (A.B. 1892). The architect of many Harvard buildings, he was chief of military affairs for the American Red Cross in Italy. Lowell's ambulances carried an estimated 150,000 sick and wound-

ed soldiers, and his rolling canteens served some 750,000 men per month.

Major HANFORD MACNIDER '11. He led infantry troops in seven major engagements in France and won the Distinguished Service Cross for his single-handed capture of a German machine-gun emplacement. After the war he was one of the first national commanders of the American Legion.

WALTER LIPPMANN '10. As confidential clerk to Secretary of War Newton D. Baker, he was recruited for "The Inquiry," a secret intelligence-gathering group. Later, as an army captain, he was an attaché at the Paris Peace Commission.

Lieutenant QUENTIN ROOSEVELT '19. He shot down one German plane before dying in a dogfight in July 1918. His aircraft crashed in enemy territory; the Germans buried him **Roosevelt** with full military honors. Quentin, who left Harvard to enlist in April 1917, was the youngest of Theodore Roosevelt's four sons. THEODORE JR. '09, KERMIT '12, and ARCHIBALD '17 all fought in France; Theodore and Archibald were both wounded.

Major CHARLES WHITTLESEY, LL.B. '08, and Captain GEORGE MCMURTRY (A.B. 1899). They commanded the 77th Division's "Lost Battalion." Cut off from supplies and surrounded for five days in the Meuse-Argonne fighting, Whittlesey refused to surrender. McMurtry was wounded

Whittlesey

twice. Both were awarded the Congressional Medal of Honor.

Captain EDWARD GRANT '06, LL.B. '09, was killed by shellfire as he led a battalion attempting to rescue Whittlesey's unit. A former National League infielder, Grant was memorialized by a monument at New York's Polo Grounds, where he finished his baseball career.

Grant

Lieutenant F. R. AUSTIN '20. Among the thousands of Americans who died in the Meuse-Argonne fighting—the final battle of the war— were 36 Harvard men. One was Larry Austin, who was killed on November 11, 1918 (see page 86).

Austin

in the Battery," wrote Feigl's orderly, "as the officer who wore the smile that never came off."

HUGO MÜNSTERBERG HAD DIED lecturing to a Radcliffe psychology class in 1916. Two years earlier, attacks on Münsterberg had elicited a terse affirmation of free expression from President Lowell. In his annual report for 1916-17, Lowell elaborated on the necessity of ensuring freedom of speech for faculty members.

"The objections to restraint upon what professors may say as citizens seem to me far greater than the harm done by leaving them free," he wrote. "If a university or college censors what its professors may say, if it restrains them from uttering something that it

Only twenty-two, but a finished life;
Here in school, scholarship, off to Harvard,
Graduated, off to France, dead.
... Gone out like a shadow, and emptiness
in the home. . . .
—*Edgar Lee Masters*, "Paul Cody Bentley"

does not approve, it thereby assumes responsibility for that which it permits them to say."

It is sometimes suggested that the principles are different in time of war; that the governing boards are then justified in restraining unpatriotic expressions injurious to the country. But the same problem is presented in war time as in time of peace. . . . There is no middle ground. Either the university assumes full responsibility for permitting its professors to express certain opinions in public, or it assumes no responsibility whatever, and leaves them to be dealt with like other citizens by the public authorities according to the laws of the land.

Recruiting appeals. Harvard librarians assembled a collection of hundreds of wartime posters.

MANY COLLEGES AND UNIVERSITIES had become cogs in the American war machine. The *Princeton Alumni Weekly* noted proudly that "every day Princeton becomes less an academic college and more a school of war." At state-supported institutions in California, Illinois, Michigan, and Missouri, faculty members were subjected to doctrinal inquisitions. Columbia president Nicholas Murray Butler acceded to trustees' demands that three professors be dismissed for "treason and sedition." At Harvard, superpatriots like Professors Albert Bushnell Hart (A.B. 1880) and Richard Clarke Cabot (A.B. 1889, M.D. 1892) denounced those who were against the war or undecided about it.

The larger society was gripped by anti-German hysteria. In 1917 Congress passed an espionage act imposing a $10,000 fine and twenty years in jail for interfering with the draft or encouraging disloyalty. A sedition act extended such penalties to the use of "disloyal or abusive language" about the government, flag, or uniform of the United States. Conscientious objectors were sent to prison. State laws forbade schools to teach German. Public libraries jettisoned books by German authors. Reports of German atrocities were reflexively accepted as true. Hoodlums stoned stores whose owners had German surnames.

The Committee on Public Information, under Colorado journalist George Creel, fed war news to reporters, coined slogans, subsidized patriotic films, and trained "four-minute men" to hawk Liberty Bonds at cinemas. Americans tried to efface all Teutonic influences on their culture. Sauerkraut became "liberty cabbage"; children caught "liberty measles." Churches did without hymns set to German music. The Metropolitan Opera and major orchestras stopped performing works by German composers.

The Boston Symphony Orchestra, with a German-born conductor, Karl Muck, and 22 German members, did not. Henry Lee Higginson, the orchestra's founder, patron, and chief administrator, was attacked for refusing to fire Muck and resisting demands that the national anthem be played before every concert. Charles William Eliot and Lawrence Lowell supported their old friend. "The continuance of the Symphony Concerts, and the retention of Dr. Muck as Director is a very important matter for our community," Lowell wrote Higginson. "Music is one of the things in which America is singularly backward," he added. "I do not see how German music, or German musicians, can corrupt America, or Germanize us. Because we quarrel with a nation because their conduct is outrageous and requires to be suppressed by force, is no reason why we should deprive ourselves of their art."

Continuing outcries forced the cancellation of the orchestra's planned midwestern tour in the spring of 1918. Barraged by abusive mail, the 83-year-old Higginson reluctantly decided that his conductor should step down. Muck agreed to do so after the concert season. But in March, as he rehearsed Bach's *St. John Passion*, Muck was arrested for internment as an enemy alien. In May, after the final concert, Higginson went onstage at Symphony Hall and announced that after almost four decades he was giving up his work with the orchestra.

THE COURSE OF THE WAR IN EUROPE was changing. The Bolshevik revolution in November 1917 had taken Russia out of the fighting. Shifting troops from the eastern to the western front, the Germans began a series of large-scale spring offensives. Static trench warfare now gave way to a war of maneuver and open fighting.

For the first time since 1914, German forces menaced Paris. The city was shelled for a week by "Big Bertha," a gigantic gun with a range of 75 miles. In their first extended fighting of the war, American troops helped halt the advance in May. General John J. Pershing, commanding the A.E.F., estimated that he would need another eighty divisions to win the war by the end of 1919. He then had fewer than twenty. In July the Germans mounted a massive offensive that was repulsed at the Second Battle of the Marne. An Allied counterthrust in September culminated in the six-week-long Meuse-Argonne battle, pitting a force of unprecedented size—1.2 million American and 135,000 French troops—against two stubborn German armies.

To the west, American, British, and Australian units breached the Germans' last line of defense, the Siegfried Line. Swiftly, unexpectedly, the empire collapsed. German sailors mutinied. Revolts broke out in Berlin, Munich, and Rhineland cities. Austria, Bulgaria, and Turkey,

Brisk Bond Market

Congress authorized the first Liberty Loan bond issue in April 1917. Aggressively promoted, with the help of popular entertainment figures like Charlie Chaplin, Mary Pickford, and Douglas Fairbanks, a series of bond "drives" raised $21 billion—almost two-thirds of the cost of the war—over the next eighteen months. The fourth and last campaign, in October 1918, was so effective that more than half the nation's adult population bought bonds.

Through the Liberty Loan campaigns, men and women who had never before invested their take-home pay or their savings were introduced to money markets. A key administrator of the huge and intricately organized program was John Price Jones '02, a pioneer in the new field of professional fund-raising. After the war he would adapt techniques developed in Liberty Loan campaigns to raise countless millions for Harvard and many other colleges, universities, and nonprofit organizations.

Jones

"Publicity," explained Jones, "provides a certain amount of mental ammunition that is shot at the mind and heart by constant repetition." A new era in fund-raising was at hand.

A Liberty Loan parade on Garden Street, Cambridge, in 1918. The vehicle belonged to a local manufacturer of machinery, engines, and pumps.

More than a thousand strong, the Students' Army Training Corps unit and its brass band formed up on the steps of Widener Library in November 1918.

Germany's allies, sued for peace. In early October an interim German government asked Woodrow Wilson for armistice terms.

The Khaki College

IRONICALLY, HARVARD and more than 500 other American colleges and universities were now fully militarized. "It is only for the first week of the [fall term] that the College will stand in anything like the place it has always held as an autonomous institution," the *Alumni Bulletin* informed readers. On October 1 the government would take over Harvard's academic programs and most of its institutional life. "All the inconveniences and disruptions entailed are accepted, not grudgingly or of necessity, but in the true spirit of the cheerful giver," reported the *Bulletin*.

In summer session, Congress had created the Students' Army Training Corps to mobilize all physically fit college men over eighteen. Participating colleges would receive funds to instruct, house, and feed members of SATC. The army, in turn, would induct thousands of college-educated officers, trained under standards set by the War Department.

In retrospect, SATC would be seen as an arrangement that undermined the academic integrity of American educational institutions. At the time it was welcomed as a patriotic initiative that provided much-needed financial relief to hard-pressed schools. Enlistments and draft calls were depopulating every college and university; with the draft age reduced to eighteen, colleges would lose all their students except those who were physically unfit or still too young for service. Food and fuel costs were rising sharply. After much debate, the College tuition fee had been raised in 1916, for the first time in 47 years. The increase from $150 to $200 a year had been expected to yield more than $100,000 in additional income. But as enrollment

continued to drop, Harvard found itself with a $400,000 shortfall.

SATC branches were organized at 540 colleges and universities, enrolling about 140,000 men. Participation was compulsory for all physically fit students of draft age. Harvard's army unit numbered 1,265 men; another 600 joined naval, Marine Corps, and Junior SATC units.* Military discipline prevailed at all times. Exercise drills began at 7 A.M.; morning chapel was shifted to 7 P.M. Bugle calls summoned faculty members and students to classrooms. Infractions of military rules meant confinement to barracks and fatigue duty on weekends.

Course requirements for future infantry officers were representative of the SATC curriculum: "Military Instruction (eleven hours a week); Problems and Issues of the War (nine hours); Military Law and Practice (nine hours); Sanitation and Hygiene (nine hours); Surveying and Map-Making (twelve hours); Unassigned (three hours)." The course on issues of the war, taught by a faculty committee that included President Lowell, covered "historical and economic causes of the war," "the study of the points of view of the various nations as expressed in their governmental institutions," and "the study of their points of view as expressed in their philosophies and literatures."

Regular courses in mathematics, physics, and chemistry were oversubscribed; faculty members from other departments were called in to help teach them. The department of Romance languages taught "military French"; German 1b covered "subjects in military science and history." An educational psychology class taught new techniques of standardized intelligence testing developed for army use. Fine Arts 2, a drawing class, was devoted to military sketching. Composition students in English A, now merged with the war-issues course, were required to write "war arguments, Liberty Loan appeals, war stories,

*Harvard's first ROTC unit had already commissioned more than 1,200 officers, and a second unit had begun training men under draft age.

and technical expositions of modern warfare."

Many course offerings in the liberal arts were suspended for the duration. The only medieval history course was one on the constitutional history of England. Gone were social-ethics courses on poor relief, criminology, housing, rural development, and immigration reform.

With the advent of the SATC the academic year had been redivided into trimesters. Before the first term was over, so was the war. The Corps was demobilized in December, and standard courses were reinstated in January 1919. The SATC's most useful function, concluded President Lowell, had been to increase the public's respect for university professors. "It is now generally recognized," he wrote, "that university professors have shown themselves highly efficient in the most exacting practical affairs, even in matters far removed from their special fields." But Lowell conceded that "even a small amount of drill in term time interferes with the regular college duties more than it contributes to military training." The wry epitaph for the short-lived SATC was that it had required just enough academic work to unmake the curriculum, but not enough drill to make soldiers.[10]

Death and Victory

PEACE NEGOTIATIONS WERE STALLED for a month while Allied statesmen and generals argued about armistice terms. The weather worsened. Fighting in the Meuse-Argonne and other sectors went on. On November 7 a rumor that the Germans had signed an armistice sparked premature celebrations around the world. In Cambridge the Harvard Hall bell pealed; a company of future ensigns broke ranks outside Matthews Hall and cheered lustily.

The next day a German armistice delegation sought an immediate cease-fire. The request was refused. For their own histrionic reasons, Allied leaders had decided to end the war on the eleventh day of the eleventh month, at 11 A.M. The Germans were given 72 hours to accept peace terms that would prostrate their nation. Kaiser Wilhelm abdicated and fled to the Netherlands.

The Armistice was signed before dawn on November 11. Fog overhung the frontier. Most troops on both sides lay low all morning, but a few ruthless commanders relentlessly pushed ahead. East of the Meuse River, units of the U.S. 28th Division were sent to attack well-fortified German lines. The 109th Infantry Regiment's headquarters company silenced a German machine-gun nest, but Lieutenant Larry Austin '20, commanding the company, was killed shielding his men from a crossfire. His death came fifteen minutes before the war's end.

THE TOLL OF THE DEAD was staggering. Germany's losses were estimated at 1.8 million or more, Austria-Hungary's at 1.2 million. Russia lost an estimated 1.7 million, France 1.4 million, Great Britain almost a million. The United States, with 4.8 million men under arms, sent almost 1.4 million to the front and lost 115,000. In four and a half years of fighting, an estimated 6 million men were disabled. Another 5 million civilians in war zones died of exposure, disease, or starvation. A

The Morning After

When we first heard of the Armistice we felt a sense of relief too deep to express, and we all got drunk. We had come through, we were still alive, and nobody at all would be killed tomorrow. The composite fatherland for which we had fought and in which some of us still believed—France, Italy, the Allies, our English homeland, democracy, the self-determination of small nations—had triumphed. We danced in the streets, embraced old women and pretty girls, swore blood brotherhood with soldiers in little bars, drank with our elbows locked in theirs, reeled through the streets with bottles of champagne, fell asleep somewhere. On the next day,

after we got over our hangovers, we didn't know what to do, so we got drunk. But slowly, as the days went by, the intoxication passed, and the tears of joy: it appeared that our composite fatherland was dissolving into quarreling statesmen and oil and steel magnates. Our own nation had passed the Prohibition Amendment as if to publish a bill of separation between itself and ourselves; it wasn't our country any longer. Nevertheless we returned to it: there was nowhere else to go.

—Malcolm Cowley '19, *Exile's Return* (1934). Above, Cowley as an American Field Service ambulance driver.

global pandemic of virulent "Spanish flu," reaching its peak in the last months of 1918, killed as many as 25 million more.[12]

Almost 11,400 Harvardians served in the war. About two-thirds of those in the military received commissions. Of those in military or relief services, 418 were decorated. Some 400 were wounded; 373 died in service. Forty-three of the dead had not yet graduated.

President Lowell wrote to every mother of an undergraduate lost in the war. Above the main staircase of Widener Library he memorialized the Harvard dead with two murals commissioned from John Singer Sargent, D.ART. '16. One showed marching men on their way to rescue France and Belgium; a dying soldier appeared in the other. For the second mural Lowell and Sargent jointly composed the inscription, "Happy those who with a glowing faith / In one embrace clasped Death and Victory." Lowell had written to Sargent, "Faith that what one is doing is worth doing is the most important practical motive in life. It was strong at the time of the war . . . That is the reason I feel that the men who died in a glowing faith were happy."

The letters and journals of many of the dead did attest to a faith in the rightness of their mission. Calvin Wellington Day, called "Happy" Day by the soldiers in his Canadian battalion, wrote before his death at Ypres that "the men of the contingent, have gone into this thing coolly and calmly. . . . In being given the responsibility and opportunity of being a very junior officer of such men I get great satisfaction." "It is much more than *patria* we are fighting for now," wrote Howard Clapp '16, a 22d Aero Squadron pilot who was lost on a bombing mission in the last week of the war; "it is the ending of such horrible pain and sorrow for all the generations that are to come after us."

Larry Austin, killed on the morning of Armistice Day, had written proudly of the infantrymen he commanded. "I shall never be more happy than as the leader of these boys if I am worthy," his letter ended. "In this game as a platoon leader the chances are pretty good of being killed, but it is the dandiest of them all...."

The poignancy of lives unfulfilled haunted Lawrence Lowell. In *What a University President Has Learned,* published twenty years later, he would write:

> During the World War one thought of the moon shining upon the pale faces of the dead on the battlefield—faces of young men who would have been the thinkers and statesmen of the future, killed by conditions which neither they, nor perhaps anyone else, could have controlled. They are gone, and how much may have been lost to the world with them we shall never know, for they were among the choicest of their kind.

"Death and Victory," the second of two Widener Library murals painted by John Singer Sargent.

Between the Wars

War is hell and no war is ever over. Its baneful ripples forever leave their imprint on mankind.
    —*Dr. Wilfred Grenfell*, A.M. hon. '09, Among the Deep-Sea Fishers (*1920*)

T HE NIGHTMARE WAS ENDING. No war had ever wrought such devastation. Hopes for a lasting peace faded as the victors bickered about settlement terms; the provisions they finally agreed on made it impossible to restore political and economic stability in Europe. Historians would view the next two decades as a truce between stages of a single conflict.

Fighting continued even during the peace talks. In northern Russia a joint British-French-American force pursued Bolshevik soldiers. Ethnic hatreds set off border skirmishes in the Balkans.

The United States, now the world's strongest nation, declined to participate in postwar peacekeeping. Henry Cabot Lodge would be remembered as the politician who kept America out of the League of Nations, but President Wilson doomed his own cause by refusing to compromise. The political battle over the proposed League covenant wrecked Wilson's precarious health and brought on a national leadership crisis.

Wilson's most outspoken opponent, Theodore Roosevelt, had been silenced. Overcoming the shock of his son Quentin's death in combat, he had re-entered national politics, blasting Wilson's

Courtyard of Adolphus Busch Hall: in the center, a replica of the twelfth-century "Lion of Brunswick." Completed in 1917, the new Germanic Museum remained closed for four years because of anti-German hostility.

high-handedness in a Carnegie Hall speech before the congressional election of 1918. At 60 TR was scarcely too old for a presidential run, but his health was failing. On the day of the armistice he was hospitalized with fever and muscular pain. Bedridden for weeks, he jotted down plans for a party platform. "I cannot go," he told visitors, "without having done something to that old gray skunk in the White House." On Christmas Day he went home; ten days later he died in his sleep. General Leonard Wood, TR's commandant in the Spanish War, wrote in the *Alumni Bulletin* that "his death coming at this time, perhaps the greatest crisis in our national life, is a calamity." A memorial notice to members of the class of 1880 quoted the words of Mr. Valiant-for-Truth in *Pilgrim's Progress*: "My sword I give to him that shall succeed me in my pilgrimages and my courage and skill to him that can get it. My marks and scars I carry with me, to be a witness that I have fought His battles that will now be my rewarder."

In a curious twist of political fate, another Roosevelt ran for national office in 1920. Franklin D., who had held his fifth cousin's old post of assistant secretary of the navy, was the Democrats' vice presidential nominee. Between that campaign and his ascent to the White House twelve years later, American life underwent wrenching change.

Anti-German enmity whipped up during the war was transferred to Bolshevik sympathizers, immigrant groups, and black citizens. Prohibition became the law of the land, but Americans partied with a vengeance. Women got the vote, and with it a growing sense of emancipation. Radio, films and newsreels, and fast cars accelerated the pace of everyday life. For the well-to-do, a seven-year business boom fostered a sense of cozy security. Then came the stock-market crash of 1929, a worldwide economic breakdown, and a protracted period of depression that ended only with the renewal of war in Europe.

The turmoil of the times resonated at Harvard. President Lowell had a prominent part in the League of Nations debate, setting the stage for his successor's active involvement in public affairs. Lowell defended academic free speech resolutely, but did not resist the pervasive racial and religious prejudices of his day. In the boom years of the 1920s, Lowell the builder transformed the physical campus, and the residential House system was born. On that base, the modern University began to take shape during the presidency of James Bryant Conant, even before the crucial influence of the second world war.

LIKE OTHER UNIVERSITIES, Harvard emerged from the Great War with its population diminished, its curriculum out of joint, its capital depleted. The war had checked academic initiatives and suspended the $10 million endowment campaign begun in 1916. Restoring standard courses, preparing for steeply increasing enrollment, and resurrecting the campaign were major concerns. But there was much more to do. The state supreme court had ruled out the coordinate relationship of Harvard and MIT. Harvard now had to restore its engineering programs. The war had suspended a Law School fund appeal. The Medical School needed funds, and the Dental School was close to penniless: it had almost no endowment, and most of its 89 faculty members were

Ohio governor James Cox was the Democratic presidential nominee in 1920, with a rising young politician named Franklin Roosevelt (left) as his running mate. They campaigned for the League of Nations treaty, but Republicans Warren Harding and Calvin Coolidge got the isolationist vote, and a resounding victory.

Lowell and the League of Nations

FOR EIGHTEEN MONTHS the nation was deeply divided over the Treaty of Versailles and its provision for international peacekeeping. As executive chairman of the League to Enforce Peace, an influential group founded in 1915, President Lowell was a staunch advocate of the proposed League of Nations. No Harvard president had involved himself so actively in a controversial national issue.

Headed by former President Taft, the League to Enforce Peace stood for an international court of justice and for military or economic sanctions against any nation that resorted to war without first submitting to international arbitration. In 1919 Taft and Lowell endorsed the League of Nations at a series of regional congresses and "ratifying conventions" in fifteen states. Before an overflow audience at Boston's Symphony Hall, Lowell debated with Senator Henry Cabot Lodge, whose hostility to President Wilson had led him to oppose the League covenant.

Wilson took his case to the people in a fall tour of midwestern and western states where isolationist resistance to the League of Nations was strong. If the treaty went down, he told audiences, "I can predict with absolute certainty that within another generation there will be another world war."

The president had made forty speeches in three weeks when he collapsed on his special train near Wichita, Kansas. Three days later he suffered a stroke. Wilson was still partially paralyzed when a Senate vote made it clear that the treaty could not pass without amendments. The president refused to compromise. Lowell returned to Symphony Hall to make a fighting speech on behalf of the League. Once a warm admirer of Wilson, he privately lamented his fellow political scientist's poor statecraft. By making himself chief delegate at the Paris conference and trying to play a lone hand as international peacemaker, Wilson had antagonized senators whose votes he needed.

In March 1920 the treaty was beaten again in Congress. Wilson expressed hope that the coming election might serve as a "great and solemn referendum" on the League, but as Lowell observed, that was politically naive. The administration was enfeebled, and the electorate was sure to get rid of the Democrats. If the election were cast as a vote on the League, pro-Leaguers were finished.

Ohio governor James Cox and Franklin Roosevelt, the Democrats' sacrificial offerings, campaigned for the treaty without amendments. Senator Warren Harding, the Republican candidate, polled 16 million votes to 9 million for Cox, the largest plurality yet given an American president.

"There will be no betrayal of the deliberate expression of the American people in the recent election," Harding told Congress in April 1921. "The League covenant can have no sanction by us." That fall the Senate approved a separate peace with Germany, leaving the League to limp along as best it could.

teaching without pay. The Business School had been all but wiped out by the war. Edwin Gay, its dean, was about to become president and de facto editor of the *New York Evening Post*, now owned by banker and Business School backer Thomas Lamont. To succeed him, Lowell chose Wallace Brett Donham (A.B. 1898, LL.B. '01), Boston banker, Harvard College fund-raiser, and Business School lecturer.

Plans to establish a graduate school of education had been hanging fire since 1916. Rockefeller's General Education Board had promised a $500,000 matching grant to honor Charles William Eliot and Paul Hanus, who had devised Harvard's first teaching courses. But a million more had to be raised for endowment.

Gold Coast real estate opportunities beckoned. Required residence in the new freshman halls and the wartime enrollment drop had hurt the privately owned apartment buildings. The University had obtained Randolph Hall, built in 1897 by Archibald Cary Coolidge and two of his brothers, in a swap for College House, an aging dormitory on Harvard Square. Apley Court, Craigie Hall, Westmorly Court, and other Gold Coast buildings were now available on favorable terms.

The Corporation looked to the Harvard Endowment Fund to ease financial pressures. About four-fifths of the amount originally sought was to provide a 50 percent raise in faculty salaries, which had been unchanged since 1905.[1] The rest would benefit the cramped and undermanned chemistry department and the schools of dental medicine and education; support a new physical fitness program for undergraduates; and create an unrestricted "mobile fund" yielding $50,000 a year. The campaign was restarted in the spring of 1919. Its $10 million goal, the highest ever set by a university, was raised to $15 million.

John Price Jones '02, who had helped plan the Liberty Loan drives, was engaged to manage the campaign, making Harvard the first academic institution to employ a professional fund-raiser.[2] In another nod to professionalism, Frederick Lewis Allen '12, the newly appointed secretary to the Corporation, was put in charge of the University's first news office. Though President Lowell took a dim view of institutional publicity, the wartime Committee on Public Information had shown what a systematic communications program could achieve.

THE COMMENCEMENT OF 1919 blended homage to the past with high resolve for the future. To the *Alumni Bulletin*, it reflected a spirit of "prodigious exaltation." All but one of fourteen honorary degree recipients had been selected because of their heroism in war.[3] Cabot Lodge, chairman of the Senate foreign relations committee, spoke at the afternoon exercises. He did not refer to the League of Nations covenant, which his committee would soon take up. Lodge did tell his hearers that "if you would be . . . of the largest service to mankind, be Americans first, Americans last, Americans always. From that firm foundation you can march on. Abandon it and chaos will come as when the civilization of Rome crashed down in irremediable ruin."

Reign of Terror

THE SUCCESS OF THE Russian Revolution, uprisings in Europe, and a wave of industrial strikes brought on the nation's first "red scare" in 1919. Terrorist bombings and the presence of radical elements in the labor force led millions to equate strikers with Bolsheviks. The Red Menace replaced the Hun as the national phobia. Harvard was not immune. Reporting on the 1919 Class Day exercises, the *Alumni Bulletin* noted that the senior who sang the class ode then "burst forth into a severe arraignment of Bolshevism and Anarchy."

On May Day, mobs led by soldiers and sailors had attacked socialist groups in New York, Cleveland, and Boston. One Harvard radical who suffered for his beliefs was William Sidis '14, the prodigy who had enrolled at eleven (see page 49). Sidis was at the head of a May Day parade in Roxbury, carrying a red flag, when police with drawn guns ordered

More than three hundred members of the Associated Harvard Clubs marched into Buffalo in June 1919 for their first postwar meeting.

the marchers to disperse. A daylong melee broke out. Sidis was beaten, arrested, and jailed, along with more than a hundred others. Blaming him for provoking the riot, a presiding judge set bail at $5,000. Classmate Leverett Saltonstall arranged Sidis's bond the next day.

A thousand Boston policemen struck in September, seeking a pay increase and the right to unionize. Almost 400 Harvard faculty members, students, and alumni answered Police Commissioner Edwin Curtis's call for volunteers to uphold law and order. Edwin Hall, Rumford professor of physics, was the first to sign up. He was 63. President Lowell set aside a room in University Hall as a volunteer center. His cousin, industrialist and pioneer aviator Godfrey Lowell Cabot (A.B. 1882), reported for duty with two pistols strapped to his belt.

A two-day looting and rioting spree ensued. Members of one Harvard volunteer unit, including the football all-American Tack Hardwick '15, were taunted, trampled, and beaten by a mob of thousands in Scollay Square. Declaring that "There is no right to strike against the public safety by anybody, anywhere, any time," Governor Calvin Coolidge called out the State Guard. Eight rioters were killed, and scores of volunteers injured, in the worst days of the disorder.

Harold Laski spoke out on the strikers' behalf. A 26-year-old Englishman, he had taught political theory at Harvard since 1916. Professor Hall likened Laski to a rattlesnake; Thomas Nixon Carver, professor of political economy, called him a "boudoir Bolshevist." The *Crimson* and the *Alumni Bulletin* defended his right to speak. Laski was hauled up before an Overseers' committee at the Harvard Club of Boston. "If the Overseers ask for Laski's resignation, they will get mine," Lowell told former *Bulletin* editor Mark DeWolfe Howe (A.B. 1887). The committee backed off. "Lowell was magnificent," Laski wrote Justice Oliver Wendell Holmes. But at the end of the year Laski left for the London School of Economics, where he became the Anglo-American world's leading theorist of democratic socialism.

Helmeted guardsmen patrolled Boston's streets until December. All the strikers were fired. Coolidge's handling of the strike brought him

Harvard's medical faculty opened its ranks to a black instructor in 1918, and to a woman the next year. William A. Hinton '05, M.D. '12, a bacteriologist and immunologist whose parents were born in slavery, taught until 1950. Hinton devised a widely used syphilis test; his will left a scholarship fund for graduate students in any Harvard department.

Alice Hamilton, who had pioneered the study of industrial epidemiology, was appointed assistant professor in the Medical School's new department of industrial hygiene in 1919. Her field investigations and teaching revolutionized practices in the field of occupational health.

Hamilton's appointment did not entitle her to use the Faculty Club, sit on the Commencement platform, or apply for football tickets. In 1935, when she retired at 65, Harvard lost its only female faculty member. She was still an assistant professor. An ardent feminist and birth-control advocate, Hamilton lived to be 101.

national prominence and helped gain him the Republican vice presidential nomination in 1920. Newspaper editorials declared that Boston had halted the "Russianizing" of America; Senator Lodge hailed the city's victory over "Soviet government by labor unions."

MORE THAN 4 MILLION American workers struck or abstained from work in 1919. When 400,000 coal miners prepared to walk out, Attorney General A. Mitchell Palmer used wartime emergency powers to stop them. Suspected Communists were rounded up in the notorious "Palmer raids." Some 10,000 were arrested and illegally jailed; 250 "undesirables" were deported to Russia. The Ku Klux Klan, revived in 1916, hounded individuals and organizations it saw as un-American. To Frederick Lewis Allen, who wrote popular histories of the time, "it was an era of lawless and disorderly defense of law and order, of unconstitutional defense of the Constitution, of suspicion and civil conflict—in a very literal sense, a reign of terror."

Books and magazines, plays and films were scrutinized as sources of Soviet propaganda. The *New Republic*, edited by Herbert Croly (A.B. 1890), and the *Nation*, under Oswald Garrison Villard (A.B. 1893), were branded as "revolutionary" by the American Defense Society. The repressive political climate spurred the formation of the American Civil Liberties Union in 1920. Its founders included Jane Addams, Clarence Darrow, John Dewey, Law School professor Felix Frankfurter, LL.B. '06, Helen Keller '04, and Roger Baldwin '05, who would be its executive director for more than forty years.

Colleges and universities were attacked as seedbeds of socialism. "Enemies of the Republic," a series of articles published under Vice President Coolidge's byline, warned of radicalism in women's colleges, noting that Radcliffe debaters had argued the affirmative on the topic, "Resolved, that the recognition of labor unions by employers is essential to successful collective bargaining." Urged to rebut the vice president, Charles William Eliot declined in Olympian fashion ("Mr. Coolidge's views on the women's colleges, if they are his, are completely insignificant, and not worth the trouble of refutation"). But when New York lawyer Austen Fox (A.B. 1869, LL.B. 1871) was irked by a *Harvard Law Review* essay criticizing the trial judge in a deportation case, the Overseers confronted the author, law professor Zechariah Chafee, LL.B. '13, in a second "Trial at the Harvard Club." Again Lawrence Lowell intervened. "Hardly had the proceedings begun," wrote his biographer, Henry Yeomans, "before he was acting as chief counsel for the defense." The Overseers' committee voted 6-5 to close the case.[4]

Chafee dedicated his next book, *Free Speech in the United States*, to Lowell, "whose wisdom and courage in the face of uneasy fears and stormy criticism made it unmistakably plain that so long as he was president no one could breathe the air of Harvard and not be free."

LESS HEROIC WAS LOWELL'S ROLE in two disputes that became public in 1922. One arose from the discovery that black students had been barred from the freshman residence halls. The other stemmed from Lowell's attempt to impose a quota for Jewish applicants to the College.

Harvard in the Rose Bowl

AFTER TWO wartime seasons of informal competition against teams like Dean Academy and Bump Island Naval Reserve, Harvard resumed intercollegiate football in 1919. The first postwar squad, under new coach Robert Fisher '12, was a powerhouse. Compiling a record of 9-0-1, it shut out seven opponents, tied Princeton, 10-10, and defeated Yale, 10-3. The season was climaxed by Harvard's first and last Rose Bowl invitation.

In a private railroad car coupled to the Wolverine, the 22-man squad headed west on December 20. Facing Oregon on New Year's Day, Harvard hadn't scrimmaged for almost six weeks.

The East's first Rose Bowl representatives, Brown and Penn, had left Pasadena without scoring a point. Harvard held the Webfoots to two second-period field goals and had a 7-6 lead at halftime, on the strength of Fred Church's twenty-yard sweep and Arnold Horween's conversion kick. Wilting in 70-degree weather, the Crimson players kept Oregon at bay in the second half, blocking two field goal tries, hurrying another, and driving to the opponents' one-foot line as the clock ran out. The *Alumni Bulletin's* writer described Harvard's 7-6 victory as "a desperate contest."

Stanley Burnham '19, a reserve back who did not see action, celebrated the event in Kiplingesque verse: "East is East, and West is West / And never the twain shall meet; / But East went West at the West's behest / And gave the West defeat."

In a climate of intolerance, Harvard had shown its liberality with the election of Judge Julian Mack (LL.B. 1887) as the first Jewish Overseer, in 1919, and of James Byrne (A.B. 1877, LL.B. 1882) as the Corporation's first Roman Catholic member, in 1920. That Lowell would countenance exclusionary policies angered many alumni and friends.

Reports of discrimination against blacks began circulating in 1921, when applicant William Knox Jr. was asked to return a room confirmation issued on the assumption that he was white. Former Overseer Moorfield Story (A.B. 1866), president of the National Association for the Advancement of Colored People, was one of the sponsors of a petition demanding an end to the College's "Jim Crow policy" and a return to the Harvard tradition of "liberalism, tolerance, and justice." It was signed by 143 alumni, representing classes from 1850 to 1920.

Roscoe Conkling Bruce '02 then submitted a room application for his son, a freshman at Phillips Exeter. A black high school principal in West Virginia, Bruce had been a debater, Phi Beta Kappa member, and Class Day orator at Harvard. His application was rejected by Lowell himself. "In the Freshman Halls, where residence is compulsory, we have felt from the beginning the necessity of not including colored men," wrote Lowell. "I am sure you will understand why . . . we have not thought it possible to compel men of different races to live together."

Bruce did not understand. "To proscribe a youth because of his race is a procedure as novel at Harvard until your administration as it is unscientific," he wrote back. "However unpopular the Jew, the Irishman, and the Negro may be in certain minds and in certain sections and at

Law School alumnus Julian Mack, judge of the U.S. Circuit Court, Chicago, was elected an Overseer in 1919. The first Jewish member of the board, he was past president of the American Jewish Congress and former head of the Zionist Organization of America.

James Byrne, New York lawyer and classmate of President Lowell, was the Corporation's first Roman Catholic member. Elected in 1920, he succeeded the late Henry Lee Higginson. To Charles C. Burlingham (A.B. 1879), Overseer and fellow New York lawyer, Byrne was "a stout, unfailing, and never-quitting defender of the wronged."

Harvard Square, about 1920. The oval subway kiosk, built in 1912, would be replaced in 1928. Old Lyceum Hall (pitched roof), home of the Harvard Cooperative Society, would also give way to a new and larger structure.

The four-story Abbot Building, constructed in 1908, still stood at the end of the century.

Youthful fitness. Herbert Hoffleit, 14, and Frederick Santee, 15, were among 115 freshmen in the class of 1924 who signed up for lawn tennis to meet stiffened physical training requirements.

certain times (wartime not being one), the fact remains that the distribution of human excellence in each of these races, as in the case of every other race, begins at zero and ends in infinity. . . ."

The exchange was covered in Boston and New York papers and in the *Alumni Bulletin*, which ran more than sixty letters from aroused readers. Several recalled that Lowell's inaugural address had stressed the value of "throwing together youths of promise of every kind," and had stated that "one object of a university is to counteract rather than copy the defects in the civilization of the day." A *Bulletin* editorial deplored what "appears inevitably as a reversal of policy if not as positive disloyalty to a principle for which the University has hitherto taken an open and unshaken stand." Charles William Eliot told the *Nation*, "I am opposed to every form of racial discrimination in the universities of our heterogeneous democracy. Any such discrimination would violate very precious Harvard traditions."[5]

The Corporation, which had backed Lowell, now voted somewhat confusingly that freshmen "of the white and colored races shall not be compelled to live and eat together, nor shall any man be excluded by reason of his color." Thereafter, wrote Henry Yeomans, blacks "were so skillfully located in the Halls that no susceptibilities were hurt."

LOWELL WAS ATTEMPTING another social engineering project: reducing the College's Jewish component. Alumni in certain areas had complained that potential applicants were put off by the number of Jews at Harvard. The proportion had risen from just over 7 percent at the start of Lowell's presidency to 20 percent or more.[6]

"Foreign elements" had worried officials of private colleges since the war years. Columbia and New York University had Jewish quotas. Yale kept its proportion of Jewish students below 12 percent. Princeton keyed its acceptances to the representation of Jews in the nation: about 3 percent. At the national level, beginning in 1921, Congress passed stringent immigration laws to pinch off the flow of eastern and southern European immigrants, many of them Jews. Lowell, who had become national vice president of the Immigration Restriction League in 1912, thought the new laws "very sensible."*

Noting the rise of anti-Semitism in the larger society, he wrote in 1922 that "anti-Semitic feeling among students is increasing, and it grows in proportion to the increase in the number of Jews." His solution, "in the interest of the Jews as well as of everyone else," was to hold the Jewish presence to 15 percent. As a first step he instructed Chester Greenough, dean of the College, to limit scholarship awards to Jewish students. When Judge Mack and others objected, Lowell suggested to admissions chairman Henry Pennypacker (A.B. 1888) that if acceptances of provisionary freshmen and transfers "excluded all but the clear-ly desirable Jews," the proportion would drop to 15 percent. Aware that Lowell was trying to bypass the Overseers and facul-ty, Pennypacker replied that his committee was unwilling to "practice discrimination without the knowledge and assent of the Faculty."

Lowell put the matter before the Faculty of Arts and Sciences. The upshot was a thirteen-man committee formed "to consider principles and methods for more effectively sifting candidates for admission in respect to character." Three members were Jewish. Lowell's announcement of the committee brought a torrent of criticism from the press, politicians, and labor leaders. Angry Jewish alumni appealed to Charles William Eliot for help. Eliot wrote a series of letters to the committee arguing against any enrollment limitations.

The committee's report, approved by the Corporation and faculty in April 1923, recommended that Harvard "maintain its traditional policy of freedom from discrimination on grounds of race or religion." But it also proposed a trial policy allowing ap-plicants in the top one-seventh of their class to be admitted with-out examination. This was a device to draw students from southern and western schools where Jews were sparsely represented. As it turned out, more than 40 percent of those admitted under the plan were Jewish. The proportion of Jews in the College rose to 27 percent in 1925.

But Lowell got his way. A faculty committee now proposed that lim-iting class size to 1,000 would let the admissions committee select "the best" candidates. An Overseers' committee chaired by lawyer Henry James (A.B. 1899, LL.B. '04) considered the measure for almost two years before endorsing a three-year trial.[7] In the meantime the admissions committee adopted an application form requiring candidates to submit information on ethnic identity, religious affiliation, and any change "in your own name or that of your father (explain fully)." A photograph was required. After a visit with Pennypacker, Yale's new dean of the col-lege noted that "they are . . . going to reduce their 25 percent Hebrew total to 15 percent or less by simply rejecting without detailed explana-tion." When the three-year trial period ended, the class-limitation poli-cy was continued without consulting the governing boards. The pro-

Edward Orval Gourdin '21, LL.B. '24, was among the great track stars of his day. When the Harvard-Yale-Oxford-Cambridge meet was revived in 1921, he won the 100-yard dash and set a world record of 25 feet, 3 inches in the broad jump (above). Gourdin was national pentathlon champion in 1921 and 1922; at the 1924 Olympics in Paris he was a sil-ver medalist in the broad jump.[8] The Harvard record he set in 1921 was still unbroken at century's end.

In later life Gourdin made his mark as the first African American appointed to the Massachusetts Superior Court. He died in 1966.

*President Eliot, who favored unlimited immigration, called the policies of the Immi-gration Restriction League "vicious—economically, politically, and sentimentally."

portion of Jews dropped to 15 percent or less until World War II, when numbers rose again.[9] Even after the war, internal memoranda would refer explicitly to a "quota for a certain type," and Jewishness would be taken into account in balancing residential assignments.

Boom Times

A SPIRIT OF EXUBERANCE was displacing the tension and turbulence of the nation's early postwar years. New possessions—radios, cars, airplanes—and more leisure time helped Americans forget Europe's problems. They took up tennis and golf, defied Prohibition in speakeasies, danced the Charleston, and watched Harry Houdini wriggle out of handcuffs, straitjackets, and locked containers. Silent movies like *Brown of Harvard* and songs like *Doin' the Raccoon* and *Collegiate!* reflected a popular infatuation with college life.

"The Twenties, reversing age-old custom, Biblical precept, and familiar adage, was a period in which, in many respects, youth was the model, age the imitator," wrote Mark Sullivan (A.B. '00, LL.B. '03), *New York Herald Tribune* columnist and cultural historian. "On the dance-floor, in the beauty parlor, on the golf course; in clothes, manners, and many

Harvard in the Movies

HOLLYWOOD didn't take long to discover Harvard. A Selig film version of the 1909 play *Brown of Harvard* premiered in 1917. In 1926 a remake cast William Haines as the obnoxious hero, contesting with a studious rival for athletic success and the affection of a professor's daughter. Location shots showed Harvard-Yale football at the Stadium, a New London boat race, Harvard Square, Widener Library, Memorial Hall, and the Hasty Pudding Club.

In 1922 "Rockett Film Corp." made *Keeping Up with Lizzie*, in which young Harvard graduate Dan Pettigrew (Edward Hearn)

Valentino as rowing rajah.

won ambitious Lizzie Henshaw by unmasking a phony count who was out to steal her dowry.

Paramount's *The Young Rajah* (1922) featured Rudolph Valentino as a princely Hindu who went to Harvard, became a star athlete, and fell for a Brahmin, Molly Cabot.

In *Birthright* (Micheaux Film Corp., 1924), Peter Siner played an idealistic black graduate facing the bigotry and brutality of both races in a southern town. In flashbacks, *Forever After* (First National, 1926) replayed scenes from the life of an infantry captain (Lloyd Hughes) wounded in France. His father's financial reverses had forced him to leave Harvard.

A Harvard-Yale boat race ended *For the Love of Mike* (First National, date uncertain), starring Claudette

William Haines as bullyboy *Brown of Harvard*.

Colbert. Columbia's *Flight* (1929) was an early talkie, directed by Frank Capra, with Ralph Graves as "Lefty" Phelps. After a misplay in the Harvard-Yale game, Lefty joined a Marine flying squad, was sent to quell an uprising in Nicaragua, and was lost in the jungle. Lucky Lefty: his pal Williams (Jack Holt) found him, then let him have the girl they both coveted.

Columbia made the last prewar Harvard picture: *Harvard, Here I Come* (1941), in which Maxie Rosenbloom won a Harvard athletic scholarship but failed as a student.[10]

Harvard celebrated President Eliot's ninetieth birthday with special ceremonies in Sanders Theatre and the Yard on March 20, 1924. Eliot received greetings from around the world. The dignitaries above are (from left) Massachusetts governor Cox; Supreme Court Chief Justice Taft; Charles T. Greve (A.B. 1884), president of the Associated Harvard Clubs; Eliot; Supreme Court Justice Edward T. Sanford (A.B. 1885), president of the Alumni Association; President Lowell; President Angell of Yale; and Dean Le Baron Russell Briggs.

points of view, elders strove earnestly to look and act like their children, in many cases their grandchildren."

With their ukuleles and hip flasks, collegians of the time appeared insouciant. College and university administrators, in contrast, were struggling. Enrollments were higher than ever, but facilities were overtaxed. Harvard's endowment campaign had languished when a postwar business boom fizzled in 1920. Extended for more than a year, the drive fell short of its $15 million goal by well over $1 million. The University reported record deficits in 1919 and 1920. The fund-raising case had rested partly on the premise that increasing tuition would make Harvard look like a school for the rich. Now the Corporation's members swallowed hard and raised tuition from $200 to $250 a year.

With the economy picking up again, the Corporation announced a $3 million campaign for Harvard chemistry and approved the fine arts department's plans to seek $2 million for a building to replace its outgrown art museum. Dean Donham was also anxious to raise funds for the Business School. Enrollment had jumped from 160 to 400 in a single year; the school was dispersed in six far-flung University buildings, and needed dormitories. With sketches for a new plant in hand, Donham persuaded the Corporation to add a $5 million Business School appeal to the chemistry and fine arts drives. To reach prospective donors who were not affiliated with Harvard, Donham suggested that the three-sided campaign be billed as a plan "to Extend the National Service of Harvard University." Bishop Lawrence, a member of the Corporation since 1913, agreed once more to act as chief fund-raiser. Announcement of the campaign coincided with a gala celebration of President Eliot's ninetieth birthday in March 1924.[11]

A prime prospect was George F. Baker, 81-year-old chairman of New York's First National Bank. Baker had given millions to the Red Cross during the war years and had generously supported educational, chari-

Moving Day

After almost forty years on the Delta in front of Memorial Hall, Daniel Chester French's John Harvard statue was rolled into Harvard Yard on April 15, 1924. There it was reinstalled between the west steps of University Hall, an area previously occupied by a relief map of the Yard.

"He has stepped from the wilderness into the market place, from without the city to within," the *Alumni Bulletin* wrote approvingly.

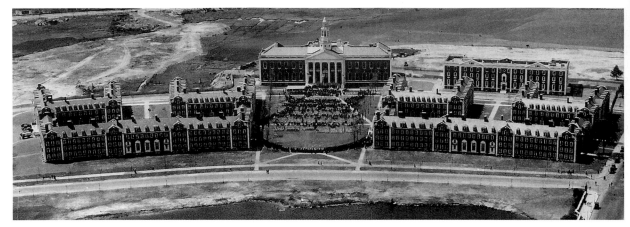

An audience of 4,000 attended
the dedication of the new Business
School campus. Acres of marshland
east of the campus still had to be
filled. Below: George F. Baker, the
campus's principal donor. Known as
"the Sphinx of Wall Street," he was
one of America's richest men.

The John W. Weeks Bridge
connected the Business School
with Harvard's central campus.
It was dedicated in May 1927.

table, and medical institutions. Through Thomas Lamont, Bishop Lawrence let Baker know that he was angling for a gift of $1 million. When they met in April 1924, Baker told the bishop that he did not wish to contribute a million, or even a half million. "I have no interest in the Chemistry or the Art," Baker told Lawrence—but in the Business, yes: "If by giving $5 million I could have the privilege of building the whole school, I should like to do it."

Donham threw himself into the process of planning a campus for 1,000 students on the reclaimed marshland that Henry Lee Higginson had secured for Harvard (see page 32). An architectural competition was held in the fall; the New York firm of McKim, Mead & White, planners of the neighboring Harvard Stadium, submitted the winning entry. The firm of Frederick Law Olmsted, planners of Boston's "Emerald Necklace" park system, was chosen to do the landscaping.

Ground was broken in June 1925. Work was slowed by the sogginess of the site. As construction went forward, some features of the original plan had to be dropped, to Donham's dismay. These included a model factory, which the Corporation deemed unsuitable for the grounds of a school, a recreational facility, and a chapel. A Georgian-style footbridge with conduits for steam and electrical lines linked the new plant to the central campus. It was given by friends of John W. Weeks, former secretary of war and Massachusetts senator, in Weeks's memory.

The new campus opened in the fall of 1926. A formal dedication was held in June 1927, in the presence of the 84-year-old George Baker, his son George F. Baker Jr., and 4,000 guests. At the senior Baker's request, the administration building was named for his friend J.P. Morgan. The library was named for Baker. The school's six dormitories took their names from secretaries of the Treasury: Morris, Hamilton, Gallatin, Chase, McCulloch, Mellon.[12]

Since the senior Baker had insisted on building "the whole school," Donham had to persuade some would-be donors to reassign their pledges. President Lowell wanted to screen out rising traffic noise in Harvard Yard by adding buildings to "cloister" it; funds originally designated for the Business School now helped realize his aim. Lehman Hall, a new bursar's office, rose on a site near the center of the Square. The donors were Arthur Lehman (A.B. 1894), a New York financier, and his wife, Adele. Straus Hall, a four-story residence for underclassmen, was built to the north. The $300,000 construction cost had been pledged for a Business School dormitory by three Straus brothers, Jesse (A.B. 1893), Percy (A.B. 1897), and Herbert '03, as a memorial to their parents. Isidor Straus, the New York retailer who built Macy's into the world's largest department store, and his wife, Ida, had been lost on the *Titanic* in 1912. The Yard's west side was screened by two smaller residence halls, Lionel and Mower. Lionel Hall was given by Lowell himself in memory of Lionel de Jersey Harvard '15, killed in France in 1918. The four new buildings helped unify the Yard and formed three compact quadrangles on its west side.

The new halls eased Harvard's chronic housing shortage. From 1916 to 1926 the undergraduate body had increased from 2,580 to almost 3,300. Straus, Lionel, and Mower provided beds for 135 students; 300 sophomores were to be housed on an interim basis in new Business School residence halls. McKinlock Hall, fourth and last of the freshman residence halls, was another important addition to Harvard's housing stock. The parents of George Alexander McKinlock Jr. '16, an infantry officer killed in action in France in 1918, were the principal donors. Built on the riverbank at a cost of $810,000 and opened in 1926, McKinlock housed about 150 freshmen. Like the halls to the west of it, it was designed by Coolidge, Shepley, Bulfinch & Abbott, a firm that would soon have all the Harvard work it could handle.

THE PACE OF CONSTRUCTION in the middle and late 1920s matched that of the early Lowell years. The new Fogg Art Museum, a Coolidge project, rose on Quincy Street lots where frame buildings had stood. Behind its Georgian exterior was a serene courtyard inspired by a sixteenth-century Tuscan loggia. Warburg Hall, the museum's largest exhibition space, had a sixteenth-century carved oak ceiling from Dijon, France. The campaign for Harvard chemistry funded Mallinckrodt and Converse Laboratories, built for $2.1 million. A $1.6 million extension of Langdell Hall, begun soon after a Law School endowment drive that raised $2.4 million, more than doubled the building's size. The Medical School, long in need of a dormitory, finally got one when a sluggish subscription campaign was topped off by a $700,000 gift from Harold Vanderbilt '07, New York Central Railroad director, inventor of contract bridge, and America's Cup yachtsman.

Harvard's building boom was helped by a buoyant stock market, vigorous business expansion, and frenetic merger and acquisition activity. Thanks in part to professional publicists like John Price Jones and the New York consultant Ivy Lee, who helped guide Harvard's campaigning, public confidence in American business was at a new high. Indifferent political leadership did not deter economic growth. President Harding had died in office, before the full extent of his appointees' corrupt dealings was disclosed. Business indicators continued to climb when Vice President Calvin Coolidge, described by Frederick Lewis Allen as a man of "uncompromising unoriginality," succeeded him.

Though the University's yield on capital investments rose to 5.4 percent in this period, Harvard was still hard put to cover faculty salaries.

VANZETTI (LEFT) AND SACCO
AS DRAWN BY BEN SHAHN

Guilty as Charged?

The pending execution of Nicola Sacco and Bartolomeo Vanzetti, convicted of murder in a 1920 payroll holdup in South Braintree, Massachusetts, stirred worldwide protests. Felix Frankfurter, Byrne professor of law, was one of many liberal lawyers who believed the immigrant anarchists had been framed and sought to avert the execution.

In May 1927, their counsel petitioned for clemency to Governor Alvan Fuller. To advise him on the appeal he appointed a committee made up of President Lowell, retired probate judge Robert Grant (A.B. 1873, LL.B. 1879), and Samuel W. Stratton, LL.D. '23, president of MIT. The "Lowell Committee" concluded that the men had been fairly tried, and Sacco and Vanzetti were executed in August.

Much harsh criticism was directed at Lowell. Demands for Frankfurter's dismissal came from the other side. Lowell stood firm for Frankfurter, as he had done in the cases of Harold Laski and Zechariah Chafee.

Every anniversary of the execution, wrote Henry Yeomans, President Lowell's biographer, "brought to Lowell as long as he lived, letters and telegrams, usually anonymous, of bitter, personal abuse."

Citing "want of sufficient income," Lowell announced another tuition increase in 1926. The Harvard Fund Council was formed that year to solicit individual giving on a class-by-class basis. It raised $123,544 in its first year. It would also be the first alumni fund to record 10,000 givers in a single year. Alumni giving was increasing, but one of Harvard's most princely benefactors, soon to make his surprising appearance, was not an alumnus. He was Edward Harkness, a Yale man.

HARKNESS PROVIDED the residential Houses that Lawrence Lowell had long dreamt of. "What we want," Lowell had said in a speech at Yale in 1907, "is a group of colleges, each of which will be national and democratic, a microcosm of the whole university." When the last freshman hall was completed, Lowell acknowledged that he had conceived the halls "with a view to building upon them a set of colleges for the remaining three years." In 1926 he sought support for an experimental "honors college" from Rockefeller's General Education Board, but the board turned him down.

At Yale, president James Rowland Angell (A.M. 1892, LL.D. '21) was proposing a residential college plan to his trustees, and Edward Harkness had come forward as a possible donor. Heir to a Standard Oil fortune, Harkness had graduated from Yale in 1897; his family had given the college a residential quadrangle housing 600 students. But to Harkness's annoyance, academic politics stalled Angell's plan.

In October 1928 he called on Lowell in Cambridge. When Lowell described his proposal for an honors college, Harkness offered $3 mil-

Edward Harkness, a Yale graduate, paid for the Harvard Houses. To the *Yale Record*, it was "a Princeton plan done at Harvard with Yale money."

"I Breathe"

THE DRINKER RESPIRATOR, better known as the iron lung, was invented in 1928 by Philip Drinker, then assistant professor of ventilation and illumination at Harvard's School of Public Health. Before an effective vaccine was cultured in the 1950s, his respirator saved thousands of polio victims.

Collaborating with Louis Shaw '09, instructor in physiology, Drinker used cast-off vacuum-cleaner motors to pump air in and out of an airtight box and force anesthetized cats to respirate. He imagined that the technique might be employed to treat cases of asphyxiation resulting from gas leaks, electric shocks, or attempted suicides.

The respirator was first tried on an eight-year-old polio patient at Children's Hospital, Boston, in October 1928. She rallied, but did not survive. The next polio victim to use the new device was a Harvard junior, Barrett Hoyt '30, who was on the verge of suffocation. Within a few minutes he

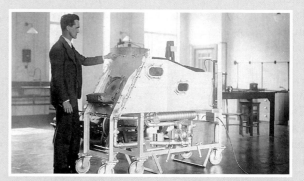

Philip Drinker and the iron lung he pioneered.

told his attending doctors, "I breathe." Hoyt lived until 1972.

When a polio epidemic swept northeastern states in 1932, the Boston firm of Warren E. Collins, Inc., was licensed to manufacture the Drinker respirators. More than 3,000 were eventually made. Iron lungs filled entire hospital wards. Drinker went on to do pathfinding research on the measurement and reduction of fumes, smoke, and dusts.

Eliot House, one of three Houses built from the ground up, nearing completion in 1931. It occupied a large triangular tract, purchased in 1930, where the West End Street Railway's power plant had stood.

lion to fund it. But he had hoped to do more for the average student. Lowell showed him working plans—drawn up by the Coolidge firm six years earlier—for two large residential complexes. Harvard already owned or had access to the required land. Three months later Harkness offered a gift of $11 million to fund seven residential Houses.[13] Three would be built from the ground up. The freshman halls and Gold Coast residences would form the principal elements of the other four.

The Faculty of Arts and Sciences approved the plan unanimously. Undergraduate and alumni clubmen looked askance at it. The *Crimson* declared that the College needed no "broad undergraduate intercourse" or "artificial cross-sectioning." A Student Council report compiled in 1926 strengthened Lowell's hand. It recommended that the College "be divided for social and residential purposes, into several smaller units." A subsequent report suggested that a residential House plan might remedy some of the adverse effects of the club system.

Charles Coolidge's firm designed the new Houses and the changes to existing structures. Construction started early in 1929. The president and his cocker spaniel, Phantom, were daily visitors at the work sites. Two new Houses, Dunster and Lowell, were ready in the fall of 1930. Other Houses opened a year later. Each had suites for students and tutors, with shared sitting rooms and fireplaces, and comfortable lodgings for the Master, common rooms, library, and dining hall. Unlike Standish, Gore, and McKinlock Halls, which were laid out with open courtyards facing the river, Houses built from the ground up were quadrangular, with enclosed courtyards like those of Oxonian colleges. The new Houses also had towers, another Oxonian feature.

Critical to the idea of the Houses was the concept that each should be a self-contained community, oriented not to the surrounding streets but to courtyards within.

No two plans were alike. Some had to be fitted to irregular sites. Exteriors and interiors bespoke elegance. "One ought to eat only venison, drink only champagne in the Eliot dining room," wrote undergraduate columnist George Homans '32, later a prominent Harvard sociologist, in the *Harvard Graduates' Magazine.* In staffing the Houses Lowell favored men with Oxford connections; most of the original Masters were scholars of English literature or of history.[14]

The seven Houses' titles evoked Harvard history. Dunster, Eliot, Kirkland, and Leverett bore the names of former presidents. Adams,

Lowell, and John Winthrop honored families long involved with the College. The Houses held 1,700 students, or about two-thirds of College upperclassmen. Despite early grumblings, fewer than eighty upperclassmen chose not to apply when the Houses opened.[15] With the four freshman halls now forming the cores of Kirkland, Leverett, and John Winthrop Houses, entering classes were assigned to the Yard. The "cloistering" effort had been completed in 1930, when Wigglesworth Hall was built along Massachusetts Avenue. The Harvard Union's great hall now became a dining commons. These arrangements created a collegiate structure that helped prepare freshmen for House life.

The House system was widely hailed as a forward step in American education. Harkness would later write to Lowell, "How fortunate for me that you were there when I appeared . . . and found that you had set the stage so completely for my project." His $13 million project goaded Yale into action. President Angell convened a committee to plan a system of eight residential colleges; Harkness, reconciled with his alma mater, found $15.7 million to fund the plan.

Living Dangerously

THE NATION WAS NOW HAVING the time of its life. In the summer of 1929 the securities market went wild. Speculators and everyone else watched, tantalized, as market indices soared, fell, and soared again. Like the bull market, sports were a national mania. Babe Ruth's legs had begun to go, but he still drew capacity crowds to every ball park he played in. In August he hit the five hundredth home run of his career. Big Bill Tilden won his seventh amateur tennis title. Robert Tyre (Bobby) Jones '24 enjoyed his seventh consecutive year as winner of either the U.S. open or amateur golf title.

A $1.3 million Indoor Athletic Building, largely funded by three anonymous alumni and by football revenue, was under construction at Harvard. It occupied an entire block. New steel stands, accommodating 3,000 more spectators, replaced wooden bleachers at the open end of Harvard Stadium. "This increase will be only a drop in the bucket of demand for tickets to the important games of the season," opined the

With Byrd at the Pole

In June 1929 the pioneer radio station KDKA, Pittsburgh, beamed a special program dedicated to five Harvard men accompanying Commander Richard E. Byrd, G'17, on his first expedition to the South Pole. The program included Harvard songs by "Madame Louise Homer and the Harvard Quartet," and salutations from President Lowell and A. Chester Hanford, dean of the College.

BYRD

In the Harvard contingent were Dr. Francis Coman, A.M. '20, medical director, and F. E. Crockett '30, Joe de Ganahl '25, E. E. Goodale '28, and Norman D. Vaughan '29, dog-drivers.

In 1994, aged 88, Vaughan returned to Antarctica to cross the interior and make the first ascent of 10,300-foot Mount Vaughan, so named by Byrd in the 1930s.

The Indoor Athletic Building (1930) provided Harvard's first intercollegiate swimming facility, three basketball courts, and rooms for fencing, wrestling, boxing, and physical training. Located between Kirkland and Lowell Houses, the I.A.B. was planned by Coolidge, Shepley, Bulfinch & Abbott, architects of the Houses.

Opposite: The great court of Lowell House, 1930.

Harvard athletes were part of the sports-crazy 1920s. Above: George Owen '23, a nine-letter man, captained the Boston Bruins.

Bobby Jones '24, who had come to Harvard from Georgia Tech, dominated the world of golf.

Palmer Dixon '25 twice won the national squash championship.

Pitcher Charles Devens '32 had three seasons with the New York Yankees.

Alumni Bulletin. The team would travel to Michigan in November, and the Boston and New York Harvard clubs had booked private railroad cars to Ann Arbor.

Serious readers were talking about Walter Lippmann's best-selling *A Preface to Morals,* which explored the postwar malaise that had pervaded American culture. "What most distinguished the generation who have approached maturity since the debacle of idealism at the end of the war is not their rebellion," wrote Lippmann, "but their disillusionment with their own rebellion." Other books that everyone seemed to be reading were Remarque's *All Quiet on the Western Front,* Renn's *War,* and Hemingway's *Farewell to Arms.*

The Great War now seemed remote to many. In the fall of 1929, ten years after the League of Nations debate, the *Bulletin* could observe that

the men who are this week entering the College and Professional Schools at Harvard were boys between the ages of eight and twelve when the Treaty of Versailles was signed. They may faintly recall it, but they did not understand it. Of the world as it was before 1914 they know nothing except what they read in books or hear from the tedious reminiscences of their elders. The hopeful liberalism of pre-war days and the passionate idealisms or bitter partisanships of the War itself mean little or nothing to them. The world of bolshevism, of the new nationalism of the East, of post-war disillusionment, of radio, aeroplane, and investment trusts, of short skirts, bobbed hair, and the one-piece bathing suit, of petting and bootlegging . . . is the only world they have ever known.

American life had changed greatly in a decade. The Republican Party was pleased to take credit. "Republican efficiency has filled the workingman's dinner pail—and his gasoline tank *besides*—made telephone, radio and sanitary plumbing *standard* household equipment," boasted a 1928 campaign advertisement for presidential candidate Herbert Hoover. "Republican prosperity is . . . written in the peak value of stocks and bonds. Republican prosperity has *reduced* hours and *increased* earning capacity, silenced *discontent,* put the proverbial 'chicken in every pot.' And a car in every backyard, to boot."

Hoover, who had made a prewar fortune in mining, was the "Great Engineer" who would install prosperity on a permanent basis. His victory over New York governor Al Smith in 1928 delighted investors.

On September 3, 1929, stock market averages hit an all-time high. Red flags were flying: brokers' loans now exceeded $8 billion, more money than the Treasury had in circulation. Yet Irving Fisher, a Yale economist, could insist in mid-October that stock prices had reached "what looks like a permanently high plateau." The bulletin of the Harvard Economic Society, an enterprise launched after the war by the economics department, advised subscribers that "if recession should threaten serious consequences for business (as is not indicated at present) there is little doubt that the Reserve System would take steps to ease the money market and so check the movement."

Just before noon on October 24, Richard Whitney '11, acting president of the New York Stock Exchange, crossed the street to tell J.P.

Morgan's head men that a rash of distress selling had begun. The ticker was virtually paralyzed; no one knew what his holdings were worth. The Morgan men, among them Whitney's brother George '07, had already called leading bankers to an emergency meeting. Because Morgan himself was in Europe, Thomas Lamont presided. The Morgan firm had arrested the panic of 1907 by arranging new funds for banks that were out of cash. Now the assembled bankers agreed to provide $240 million to prop up the market. Whitney, who normally acted as Morgan's main broker, returned to the floor of the exchange and placed orders for large blocks of stock. Prices steadied. "RICHARD WHITNEY HALTS STOCK PANIC," read a headline the next day. But when the ticker caught up it listed a record 13 million shares sold, and a net loss of $11 billion. The day would go down as "Black Thursday."

"Despite its severity," the Harvard Economic Society told subscribers, "we believe that the slump in stock prices will prove an intermediate movement and not the precursor of a business depression such as would entail prolonged further liquidation." The market crashed again the next week, with a 16-million-share day on October 29. Liquidation continued; price averages hit bottom on November 13. More than $30 billion in capital values—exceeding the national debt, and roughly the cost of the war against Germany—had been wiped out in less than three weeks. The collapse set off a downward spiral in prices, production, employment, and foreign trade. Corporate profits fell from $10 billion in 1929 to $3 billion in 1932.

Europe's economies tumbled too. Many people believed the capitalist system was done for. The worldwide depression that followed the crash would last until the renewal of war in Europe.

Richard Whitney, acting president of the New York Stock Exchange, tried to restore confidence when the market collapsed in October 1929. A decade later he was convicted of misappropriating funds from his own firm and its customers. Whitney was expelled from the stock exchange and sent to Sing Sing prison.

The Lean Years

THE DEPRESSION's immediate impact on Harvard was limited. Even in the leanest years administrators balanced budgets without extreme measures. Enrollment rose modestly, though the registrar recorded a slight drop in the number of states and countries represented. Construction projects went on.

The University had changed treasurers early in 1929. Charles Francis Adams (A.B. 1888, LL.B. 1892), treasurer since 1898, had joined Hoover's cabinet as secretary of the navy. His successor was Henry Lee Shattuck '01, LL.B. '04, a partner in the Boston law firm of Ropes & Gray and a member of the state legislature. When the crash came, about 60 percent of the University's endowment was safely invested in bonds; only 27 percent was in stocks. Shattuck did not join the selling wave. He bought up more common stocks at bargain prices, and did so throughout the 1930s. The equity portion of the portfolio grew to 44 percent; the value of stockholdings increased from $21.3 million to $45.1 million. Class gifts to the College held up well: even in grim 1932, the twenty-fifth reunion Class of 1907 was able to raise $100,000. The Harvard Fund recorded steady increases in participation.[16]

Unlike many universities, Harvard did not cut faculty salaries, which had been raised in 1928 and 1930.[17] As a form of financial assis-

Harvard's Barry Wood and Yale's "Little Boy Blue," Albie Booth: elusive backs in football, power-hitting shortstops in baseball.

Founded at Harvard in 1925, the Harvard Flying Club was not only the first college flying organization; it was also the first to purchase its own aircraft—a Whirlwind Travel-Air biplane (above). With forty licensed pilots, the club survived the disastrous spring of 1931, when three of its planes (including the Travel-Air) crashed. The Flying Club was still aloft in the late 1950s.

tance the College lowered room and board rates in the Houses. A scholarship student could live in a single room on the fifth floor of Lowell House for $120 a year; a third-floor suite cost $360. Tuition had gone to $400 in 1928, but would not be raised again for two decades. The Student Employment Office, under Russell Sharpe '28, scrambled to find jobs for students of limited means.[18]

Unemployment statistics made students more serious about their studies, as President Lowell and other administrators assured alumni and the public. But not all the fun and frolic evaporated from college life. In the spring of 1932, persons unknown stole the Memorial Hall bell's 45-pound clapper. A rumor that it had turned up in Matthews Hall drew hundreds of students into the Yard, and a nocturnal rumpus spilled into the Square. Eggs were thrown and trolleys rocked off their wires. Rioters invaded Radcliffe dormitories and set fire to the gates of the University Theatre. Police used tear gas to restore order, arresting nine students and one officer of the College.

The heroics of W. Barry Wood '32, perhaps the best all-around athlete in Harvard history, provided excitement for sports followers. From the fall of 1928 to the spring of 1932, Harvard-Yale contests in football and baseball were spiced by the rivalry between Wood and Yale's Albie Booth. In 1931, when the two young paladins met in football for the last time, a Stadium crowd of 58,000 saw Booth kick a late field goal that gave Yale a 3-0 victory, robbing Harvard of an unbeaten season. Wood and Harvard won the 1932 baseball series with Yale, that year's Eastern champions. Having earned his tenth varsity letter—three each in football, hockey, and baseball, plus a minor 'H' for playing in a 1929 Harvard-Yale tennis match against Oxford-Cambridge—Wood graduated *summa* the next day. He went on to take his M.D. at Johns Hopkins and do advanced research on infectious diseases.

House life helped offset anxiety about the future by providing a cohesive social structure, an organized base for extracurricular activities, and a variety of cultural offerings. As Samuel Eliot Morison noted, the timing of the Harkness gift had been a near thing. After 1929 the economic climate might have discouraged so ambitious an undertaking.

LIKE THE HOUSES, other building projects of the early 1930s were products of 1920s prosperity. The $2 million Biological Laboratories, a vast U-shaped building guarded by life-sized bronze rhinoceroses, was largely funded by Rockefeller's General Education Board. The board also helped fund the ninety-room Research Laboratory of Physics, which was linked to two other physics labs.

Allston Burr (A.B. 1889), Boston investment banker and former Overseer, was principal donor of the Faculty Club, on Quincy Street opposite the President's House. In addition to dining and meeting rooms, a reading room, and a library, it provided two dozen guest rooms. Another of Coolidge's neo-Georgian structures, it occupied a lot where Henry James Sr., and his famous family had once dwelt.

To the north, on Divinity Avenue, the Institute of Geographical Exploration was the gift of Dr. Alexander Hamilton Rice, the gentleman explorer who had married Eleanor Elkins Widener in 1915. Horace

Trumbauer, Mrs. Widener's choice to design her library, imparted his imperial styling to the two-story Institute. It housed an 80,000-book library, a map collection, and rooms for short-wave radio and photographic, cartographic, and surveying equipment.*

THE MEMORIAL CHURCH, the last building of Lowell's era, was the most controversial. Few opposed a memorial to Harvard men who had died in the Great War, but a long-running dispute over the form it should take hindered planning. Many alumni favored a chapel; others wanted a monument, a carillon tower, or some kind of utilitarian building. The *Crimson* rejected a chapel as "the most ignominious of tributes." Harvard, after all, had been the first American college to abandon compulsory religious services. And it already had a chapel.

But a chapel was what President Lowell wanted. "A war memorial which did not have a moral influence would be worthless," he wrote in 1927. "The policy [at Harvard] has been very vocational and materialistic. We are now striving to make it more cultural and spiritual. All but the younger alumni were hatched in a materialistic temperature and it is not always easy to persuade them that there is something in life more important than athletic victories." The Corporation finally approved a proposal for a chapel in 1928. Allston Burr, who was paying most of the cost of the Faculty Club, agreed to lead a $2 million appeal. Preliminary designs from Charles Coolidge's firm were shown in a descriptive book-

Katharine Lane Weems's architectural reliefs and sculptures decorated the Biological Laboratories, one of Harvard's largest facilities. Its portals were guarded by two life-sized rhinos.

The departments of biology, botany, physiology, and zoology, formerly scattered among seven buildings, were consolidated in the five-story, 214,000-square-foot structure. It provided lecture rooms, a library, dark rooms, cold rooms, animal rooms, greenhouses, and aquaria. Designed by Coolidge, Shepley, it opened in 1931.

*With his wife's money, Rice gave Harvard the Institute and more: as a condition of the gift he also funded a professorship of geographical exploration to be held by Rice himself.

The Memorial Church, built in 1931. The church would be described by Paul Hollister '13 as "the Dormitory of the Immortals, with its stout Doric ankles and its tiara of stars."

Below: Appleton Chapel, constructed in 1858, was razed to make way for the new church.

Names of Harvard's war dead were inscribed in the church's memorial room. Joseph Coletti, the young Boston sculptor who was commissioned to detail the room, rejected architect Charles Coolidge's Georgian styling and imposed a classic design that contrasted with the interior of the church. The centerpiece of the chamber was Malvina Hoffman's *The Sacrifice*.

let. The alumni community now became furiously divided over architectural issues. The booklet's second edition omitted the sketches.

Seventy-five-year-old Appleton Chapel was torn down after the 1931 Commencement. The new church rose on its site. Its spacious nave, illuminated by splendid arched windows and seating about 1,200, was designed in the manner of an American Protestant meeting house. An English-style chancel, to be used for morning prayers, perpetuated the name of Samuel Appleton, the old chapel's donor. The names of 373 war dead were set into the marble walls of a coldly formal transept conceived as the student entrance to the church.[19] Its centerpiece was sculptor Malvina Hoffman's *The Sacrifice*, commissioned by the widow of Robert Bacon and depicting a fallen crusader and grieving woman. Completed in 1922, the six-ton monument had been placed temporarily in New York's Cathedral of St. John the Divine. The Memorial Church was dedicated on Armistice Day, November 11, 1932.

The church defined the northern side of a large quadrangle bounded on the south by Widener Library. The relatively massive scaling of its Doric portico helped tame the overwhelming proportions of Widener. The elegantly detailed 197-foot tower, recalling the spire of Boston's Old North Church, became the focal point of Harvard's central campus. The tower's two-and-a-half-ton bell, five feet in diameter, was cast at Loughborough, England. Given by President Lowell, it bore the inscription *In Memory of Voices That Are Hushed*.

THE SOCIETY OF FELLOWS, Lowell's last academic innovation, began as his presidency ended. Modeled on the Prize Fellows program of Trinity College, Cambridge, it was an attempt to release unusually promising graduate students from the necessity of teaching or meeting Ph.D. requirements, while giving them regular contact with eminent scholars. Two dozen Junior Fellows, not over 25 when appointed, would be free to pursue three years of study in any department of the University. The Senior Fellows would include Harvard's president, the dean of arts and sciences, and five faculty members. Lowell, who did not have a Ph.D. and regarded most standard doctoral programs as fussy and restrictive, saw the Society as promoting self-education for the "rare and independent genius."

Like the House plan and the new church, the Society had a long incubation period. Lowell had alluded to "prize fellowships" in his annual report of 1915. Lawrence J. Henderson (A.B. 1898), professor of biological chemistry, helped revive the idea after an exchange with Alfred North Whitehead, who had come from Cambridge University to the philosophy department in 1924. Apprised of their interest, Lowell asked Henderson to head a study committee. When construction of the Houses began, a suite in Eliot House was reserved for the future society's use. Lowell then applied unsuccessfully for supporting grants. In the fall of 1932 he told Henderson's committee that an anonymous donor would fund the Society.

Lowell was the donor. He gave $1.5 million to launch the new venture, and later bequeathed $800,000 as an added endowment in memory of his wife. "There being no visible source of the necessary funds,"

A first design for the Memorial Church. The styling of the tower and colonnade was inspired by the eighteenth-century church of St. Paul, Deptford, London. Like the London church, Harvard's was to have been built of stone.

he wrote afterward, "I gave it myself in a kind of desperation, although it took nearly all I had." There were six original Junior Fellows, and three became distinguished Harvard professors: Garrett Birkhoff '32 (mathematics), Willard Van Orman Quine, PH.D. '32 (philosophy), and B.F. Skinner, PH.D. '31 (psychology). In the next group were sociologist George Homans '32 and Harry Levin '33, later a dominant figure in Harvard's department of comparative literature. Later Fellows included historian Arthur Schlesinger Jr. '38; Walter Jackson Bate '39, PH.D. '42, biographer of Keats and Johnson; economist and Nobel Prize winner James Tobin '39, PH.D. '47; Thomas Kuhn '44, PH.D. '49, author of *The Structure of Scientific Revolutions*; Richard Wilbur, A.M. '47, future poet laureate; linguist Noam Chomsky; E.O. Wilson, PH.D. '55, founder of sociobiology; and economist Henry Rosovsky, PH.D. '59, future dean and Harvard Corporation member. Within the Faculty of Arts and Sciences, one out of ten full professorships would eventually be held by a former Junior Fellow; over the next sixty years the Society's members would win nineteen Nobel Prizes.

The new Society's only firm requirement was attendance at weekly dinners in Eliot House. By the time the first one was held, Lowell had become Harvard's president emeritus.

EPOCHAL CHANGE WAS AT HAND in the fall of 1932. Germany's Weimar Republic was foundering. Adolf Hitler was on his way to the chancellorship. China and Japan were in conflict over the province of Manchuria. In the United States, President Hoover was running for re-election. Franklin D. Roosevelt, governor of New York, was challenging him, promising a new deal for the "forgotten man."

In October Lowell broached the idea of retiring to his doctor, Roger I. Lee '02, M.D. '05, who had recently joined the Corporation. Lowell was 76. His wife of 51 years had died in the spring of 1930. He was increasingly deaf. But he was not pleased when Lee encouraged him to step down. He tendered his resignation reluctantly.

Lowell's decision was made public on November 21. Admirers deluged him with messages. "Of course one regrets not having achieved

President Lowell, then 72, taking ship for Europe in June 1930.

The Society of Fellows, 1933. Though the number of Junior Fellows was to be 24, the first year's group numbered only six.

Front row: Thomas Chambers; President Conant; President Lowell; John L. Lowes, professor of English; Alfred North Whitehead, professor of philosophy; John Chester Miller; Lawrence J. Henderson, professor of biological chemistry. Henderson was the Society's chairman.

Second row: B.F. Skinner; W.V. Quine; Kenneth Murdock, dean of the Faculty of Arts and Sciences; Garrett Birkhoff; Fred Watkins; and Charles P. Curtis, Fellow of Harvard College.

more," he wrote back to Thomas Nelson Perkins (A.B. 1891, LL.B. 1894), a Corporation member since Eliot's time. All Lowell had done was preside over the most spectacular growth period in Harvard's annals. In his 24 years in office, total enrollment had risen from 4,000 to more than 8,000. The ranks of the faculty had more than doubled, from 743 to 1,635. The value of the endowment had grown fivefold, from $22 million to $126 million. More than sixty new buildings had been added: the Houses, laboratories, museums, Widener Library, the Business School plant—more buildings than Harvard had put up in the previous 273 years. Lowell's administration had raised $35 million for construction in the last decade alone.

Curricular standards had been raised, general examinations begun, the tutorial system installed. Since 1927 the College's academic calendar had included another Lowell innovation, a three-week "reading period" before exam time. Professional training had been expanded by the creation of the Graduate School of Education in 1920, the Medical School's school of public health the next year, and a School of City Planning in 1929. Lowell's Society of Fellows, in the words of Corporation member Charles P. Curtis '14, LL.B. '17, had "put a steeple on the edifice of his achievements at Harvard."

The search for a successor took five months. This time there was no Lowell-like figure, primed and ready to step in. The Corporation nar-

Prominent in this 1934 view of the area south of Harvard Yard are the seven residential Houses and the large, square Indoor Athletic Building; across the river, the Business School campus and (at right of Harvard Stadium) Briggs Cage and Dillon Field House. All these buildings were added to Harvard's plant during the 24 years of the Lowell administration.

Scoop

With convincing gravity, a phony issue of the *Crimson* put out by the *Harvard Lampoon* on February 22, 1933, announced the election of "Henry Eliot Clarke '04," of Evanston, Illinois, as Harvard's new president. The hoax fooled the Associated Press, which put the news on the national wire. The *Crimson* office had closed for the Washington's Birthday holiday, but telephone queries were courteously answered by a *Lampoon* editor who had gained entrance to the alien sanctum.

"A financier replaces a long line of scholars," declared the extra. The fictitious Clarke was identified as a midwestern "business messiah" who sat on the boards of nine banks and corporations. His friend and classmate, President-elect Franklin D. Roosevelt, was reported to have wired congratulations to the Board of Overseers.

Hours after the extra's appearance, a *Lampoon* editor eavesdropping on a House dining-hall conversation was amused to hear a senior faculty member say, "Oh yes, I've known Henry Clarke for years. He's a fine fellow."

rowed the field early on; in the spring its members elected a 40-year-old faculty member, James Bryant Conant. Like Eliot, he was a chemist.

President Conant

UNLIKE LOWELL, CONANT had not coveted the presidency. He had assumed the Corporation would seek someone more prominent. Conant was aware that he had recently been passed over for a trusteeship at Roxbury Latin, his old school, because he was not well known.

Organic chemists did know his research on the structure of chlorophyll, hemoglobin, and the blue blood of horseshoe crabs. Colleagues and students knew him as an effective teacher. Born in Boston in 1893, Conant had grown up in Dorchester, attended Roxbury Latin, and entered Harvard with advanced standing in the class of 1914. He was elected to the *Crimson* and the Signet Society, a literary luncheon club where, he later wrote, "I found my general education." Conant graduated *magna cum laude* in 1913, took his Ph.D. in 1916, and became an instructor in chemistry. When America went to war he did chemical research in Washington, ending up as an army major in charge of a secret plant making lewisite gas in Willoughby, Ohio. In 1921 he married Grace Richards, daughter of Nobel laureate Theodore Richards. Professor Kenneth Murdock, a boyhood friend from Dorchester, had been his best man. Conant was appointed to the Emery chair of organic chemistry in 1929, and became chairman of his department in 1931.

He was not Lowell's chosen successor. Conant had been influential in a chemistry department decision not to use tutors. He thought Lowell's eagerness to ensure the success of the tutorial system had filled the faculty's younger ranks with mediocre men "whose merit consisted largely in their willingness to be tutors." When Corporation members Charles Curtis and Robert Homans (A.B. 1894) sought his views on the presidential search, Conant stated his preference for Kenneth Murdock and candidly gave his opinions on the quality of faculty appointments. Homans and his colleagues took note.

They were also mindful of charges that Harvard was losing primacy in science. This gave Conant a slight edge in what came down to a four-horse race. The other contenders were Murdock, who had introduced the study of American literature at Harvard, dean of the Faculty of Arts and Sciences since 1931; Kirkland House master Edward Whitney, professor of history and literature; and Corporation member Grenville Clark, a New York lawyer.

On April 24 Lowell appeared at Conant's lab and brusquely announced that the Corporation had elected Conant president. His selection, announced early in May, evoked general satisfaction. Conant, for his part, could take satisfaction in the financial buoyancy of his institution. Thanks in part to an effective system of accounting installed in the 1920s by comptroller Frederick Mead (A.B. 1887), Harvard had showed operating surpluses for a half-dozen years. At a small retirement dinner tendered to Lowell by the governing boards, the president emeritus even stated that Harvard now had as much money as it would ever need. (Lowell was persuaded to omit his references to Harvard's financial security in a published version of his remarks.)

IN FACE AND FIGURE, Conant resembled the popular image of a man of science: gaunt, bespectacled, high-strung, exuding nervous energy and intellectual power. He took up his duties on September 5, 1933, after a summer of travel and "cogitation" in Europe. Hitler had seized power in Germany, and the political and economic outlook seemed worse than ever. Roosevelt had won the White House, and the Democrats had gained majorities in both houses of Congress. But before the new chief executive was sworn in, the bank closings of February 1933, cascading business failures, and widespread unemployment accelerated America's economic tailspin. Walter Lippmann, the leading vote-getter in Harvard's Overseers' election that year, had imparted some chilling advice to Roosevelt: "The situation is critical, Franklin. You may have no alternative but to assume dictatorial powers."[20]

Yet the mood in Cambridge was surprisingly cheerful in the fall of 1933. Entering freshmen applauded wildly when the youthful-looking president welcomed them to Harvard, saying that he would always feel a special bond with the class of 1937. In October he ingratiated himself further by abolishing the College's rising bell, a fixture of almost three hundred years' standing. This elicited almost as much enthusiasm as Congress's repeal of Prohibition on December 5.*

Conant's installation, in early October, replicated the simple ceremony used for John Leverett's inauguration in 1708. With a Tercentenary celebration coming up in 1936, Conant wrote later, "it seemed foolish to stage the kind of elaborate academic gathering which in those days usually marked the entry into office of a new man."

The ceremony was held in the faculty room of University Hall, with about 150 attending. George Agassiz (A.B. 1884), president of the Overseers, presented the insignia of office with a brief charge that ended, "Sir! Do not forget that the duty of this great institution is, not to follow, but to lead the way in freeing mankind from the shackles of superstition and stupidity. In these days of stress, when the world is struggling in a storm that threatens to destroy it, the sons of Fair Harvard charge you to remember that if our civilization is to survive, one of the bulwarks of its salvation will be our Alma Mater, if by wise guidance she stands a firm oasis for straight thinking, courage, and high ideals."

In his response, Conant pledged his "entire strength and devotion to the leadership of this community of scholars and students." He would write in *My Several Lives: Memoirs of a Social Inventor* (1970), "I had not the slightest interest in trying to emulate President Lowell's oratorical success in addressing a large gathering out of doors. Since I had no plan for reforming the college or the university, I was grateful that I had a good excuse for not making an inaugural address."

In fact Conant did have plans. His first report to the Overseers, in January 1934, was a call for new directions in admissions, faculty re-

James Bryant Conant, Harvard's 23d president, on the steps of University Hall in the late summer of 1933.

---

*A Kirkland House drama group was presenting Fielding's *Tom Thumb* that night, and a spontaneous eruption of applause greeted King Arthur's lines in act I, scene 2: "Today it is our pleasure to be drunk, / And this our queen shall be as drunk as we."

MINOT AND MURPHY

A Pair of Nobelists

The first Harvard Medical School researchers to win the Nobel Prize were doctors George R. Minot '08 and William P. Murphy, M.D. '22, who shared the 1934 prize in medicine with Dr. George Whipple, dean of the medical school at the University of Rochester.

Clinical trials conducted by Murphy and Minot confirmed Whipple's experimental finding that pernicious anemia could be cured by a liver diet. Harvard's only previous Nobel laureate, chemist Theodore Richards (see page 53), had died in 1928.

cruitment, tenure appointments, undergraduate instruction, and standards for graduate education. To stimulate advanced research, Conant proposed to create a few select professorships that would free leading scholars from departmental responsibility. To broaden the makeup of the College, he proposed "national scholarships" to bring in promising high school graduates from the hinterlands.

Conant anticipated limited growth and a long-lasting era of retrenchment. His expectation was predicated on two related assumptions that proved erroneous. One was that the nation was entering "a static period in our history." The other was that the United States would keep clear of European and Asian conflicts.

LIKE MOST AMERICANS, people at Harvard—especially those of military age—were alarmed by the rise of totalitarianism abroad. Accounts of the treatment of Jewish populations in Germany and Austria were a shock, but too many Americans reacted passively. When astronomer Harlow Shapley lobbied Conant to bring Harvard into a consortium of universities offering honorary chairs to refugee scholars, the new president and the Corporation temporized. (Conant did lend active support to a plan developed by Shapley in 1939 to raise $150,000 for "asylum fellowships" at Harvard.)[21]

Academic exiles still found their way to Cambridge. The influential economist Josef Schumpeter, a visiting tutor in the late 1920s, had left the University of Bonn in 1932 to take a Harvard professorship. Other exiled scholars who accepted permanent appointments included Heinrich Brüning, ex-chancellor of the Weimar Republic; psychologist Erik Erikson, from Vienna; classical philologist Werner Jaeger, from Berlin via Chicago; theoretical physicist Philipp Frank, Einstein's friend and biographer, from Prague; Walter Gropius and Marcel Breuer, from the Bauhaus-Dessau; and art historian Jakob Rosenberg, from Berlin.[22]

The Fogg Art Museum's associate director, Paul Sachs (A.B. '00), used his extensive connections to find places for refugee scholars at other institutions. When the Nazis began confiscating modernist art, Germanic Museum director Charles Kuhn, PH.D. '29, mounted German modernist exhibitions and purchased works by such artists as Beckmann, Grosz, Heckel, Kandinsky, and Klee. In 1934 the Corporation peremptorily refused the gift of a traveling fellowship to Germany from the eccentric Ernst F. Sedgwick Hanfstaengl '09. "Putzi" Hanfstaengl was a crony of Hitler who pounded out Harvard marches on the piano for the Führer. "We are unwilling," the Corporation stated, "to accept a gift from one who has been so closely associated with the leadership of a political party which has inflicted damage on the universities of Germany through measures which have struck at principles we believe to be fundamental to universities throughout the world."

The next year Harvard gave honorary degrees to former chancellor Brüning, Albert Einstein, and novelist Thomas Mann, all outspoken opponents of National Socialism. The planners of the Tercentenary celebration made a point of inviting prominent German scholars.

Undergraduate reaction to the European situation ran the gamut from lethargy to histrionics. Six hundred signed an "Oxford Oath" that they would never fight. They were mocked by parading members of the "Michael Mullins Chowder and Marching Society." When the local chapter of the Communist-led National Student League held a mass meeting in front of Widener, it was hastened to a hooting, vegetable-throwing conclusion by a bugler in Boy Scout uniform and a student dressed as Hitler, who punctuated antiwar speeches with militaristic rhetoric. The Debate Council drew a capacity audience to a mock trial of Hitler for his purges of June 1934.

For the most part, staffers and students cared more about making the new Houses work than about the peacekeeping weaknesses of the League of Nations, the Nazi Anschluss of Austria, Italy's invasion of Ethiopia, or Spain's civil war. Japan's actions in China were overshadowed by new developments in the physical and social sciences: atom-smashing, synthesizing organic compounds, applying the analysis of interpersonal dynamics to real-life situations, the New Deal's expanded opportunities for careers in public service and administrative law.

"To accomplish its mission Harvard must be a truly national university," Conant had written in his first annual report. "We should be able to say that any man with remarkable talents may obtain his education at Harvard whether he be rich or penniless, whether he come from Boston or San Francisco. . . . Today our fellowship and scholarship funds are woefully inadequate."[23] At his first Corporation meeting, Conant had suggested using Harvard's three-hundredth anniversary as a fulcrum for fund-raising. The weak economy made Corporation members dubious. In the fall of 1935, heartened by an improving stock market, they authorized what Conant described as "a campaign but no intensive drive."

"The Three Hundredth Anniversary Plan of University Professorships and National Scholarships at Harvard" was announced in November. Pamphlets were sent to 65,000 alumni, but the fund-raisers aimed primarily at a thousand top prospects, carefully analyzed, rated, and personally solicited, in ten regional areas. No previous campaign

Albert Einstein and astronomer Harlow Shapley at Harvard, 1935. The world's leading physicist was diffident about accepting Harvard's offer of an honorary degree, but Shapley lured him to Cambridge by inviting him to bring his violin and enjoy an evening of chamber music with Boston Symphony Orchestra string players. "We had taken advantage of his weakness," Shapley wrote in his memoirs.

Returning for his twenty-fifth reunion, Ernst Hanfstaengl '09, a friend of Adolf Hitler, offered $1,000 to create a traveling fellowship to Germany in his name. The Harvard Corporation wanted no part of it.

had been run with such efficiency. Though no dollar amount was specified, the goal was $6 million, to endow six professorships and fund thirty scholarships.

The appeal emphasized Harvard's role as a national institution. But the campaign bogged down. Adverse economic conditions were an obvious reason. Low-key publicity was another. A third was the conviction of many wealthy alumni that Harvard was too much identified with Franklin Roosevelt's New Deal. "As the presidential election of 1936 approached, the tension between New Dealers and anti-New Dealers mounted," Conant wrote in his memoirs. "Harvard was blamed for the active part its professors and recent graduates had been playing in President Roosevelt's alphabetical agencies." At a New York Harvard Club dinner, Conant was confronted by an elderly alumnus with drooping white mustache and ruddy face. "Speaking loudly above the hubbub," wrote Conant, "he leaned across the table and declared, 'I want you to know that I and my friends *hate* the Harvard Law School.' That declaration of alumni hostility was hardly a good omen for the success of the Three Hundredth Anniversary Fund."

That Man in the White House

FRANKLIN D. ROOSEVELT, the fifth president to hold a Harvard degree, was the first to make systematic use of university expertise. "The country is being run by a group of college professors," complained West Virginia senator Henry Hatfield, adding, "This Brain Trust is endeavoring to force socialism upon the American people." The best-known brain-trusters in Roosevelt's inner circle were from Columbia, but Harvard was well represented.

Law School professor Felix Frankfurter, who had helped found the American Civil Liberties Union, was "a one-man recruiting agency for the New Deal" and served as an all-purpose adviser. Among his recruits were Law School graduates Benjamin Cohen, s.j.d. '16, and Thomas ("Tommy the Cork") Corcoran, s.j.d. '26, two of the president's most valued aides. Alvin Hansen, professor of economics, was a principal architect of New Deal policies. Adolf A. Berle Jr. '13, a former Business School lecturer, was resident expert on corporate behavior.

Roosevelt's ebullient optimism had lifted the nation's morale even as the Depression deepened. His emergency measures shored up a chaotic banking industry and a sinking stock market; his massive spending programs helped restart a stalled economy. The New Deal saved the free enterprise system at a time when other industrialized nations were succumbing to totalitarianism. But in boardrooms, clubrooms, and parlor cars all over the country, "that man in the White House" was reviled for taking the nation off the gold standard, truckling to organized labor, bullying the financial community, and "soaking the rich" by raising income and inheritance taxes. Descended from old New York families, educated at Groton and Harvard, Roosevelt was "a traitor to his class." Some of his harshest critics were Harvard men.

Roosevelt's affection for Harvard was lifelong. As an undergraduate he had been one of the busiest members of the class of 1904. A slender

The China Trade

Just east of University Hall, an excavation crew digging trenches for Harvard's steam-tunnel system in 1926 struck a kitchen midden filled with broken crockery. Some of the fragments were pieces of Staffordshire plates with early nineteenth-century views of Harvard that President Quincy had bought for the College commons almost a century earlier.

Having picked through the shards, President Lowell commissioned a new series of plates combining original borders with new views by Kenneth Conant '15, a young professor of architecture. Harvard sold 6,800 sets of Wedgwood plates at $12 each, retaining some for dining-hall use. Like the earlier plates, they were dark blue in color.

Subsequent sets of plates, platters, and coffee cups were issued from 1932 to 1951, and sold for the benefit of the Alumni Association. By popular demand, the color was changed to red.

Harvard's success with china prompted many other schools and colleges to commission their own Wedgwood ware.

Harvard Crimson president Franklin Roosevelt, front row center, and his senior board in the fall of 1903.

six-footer with patrician features and an engaging smile, he wore pince-nez like those of his admired distant cousin Theodore. The *Crimson* was his chief interest, but he was determined to be "always active" and belonged to a dozen other extracurricular groups. He was elected managing editor of the paper in January 1903. Having entered with sophomore standing, he would complete his A.B. requirements four months later, but the *Crimson's* presidency was his if he wished to stay on. In order to do so he took economics and history courses as a graduate student. In his final year he also became engaged to his distant cousin Eleanor Roosevelt, TR's "favorite niece."

As class committee chairman, Roosevelt kept in touch with classmates during his years as a practicing lawyer and New York assemblyman. He regularly attended Harvard Club events in New York, Boston, and Washington, and returned to Cambridge for reunions and Fly Club and *Crimson* dinners. He went to Harvard-Yale crew races and football games. In 1917, at 35, he was elected an Overseer.

He was then assistant secretary of the navy, a post that TR had held. At the Democratic convention of 1920, political horse-trading made him the running mate of Ohio governor James Cox. A year later he was stricken with polio while vacationing at his family's summer home on Campobello Island, New Brunswick. His ailment was misdiagnosed by two physicians before Dr. Robert Lovett (A.B. 1881), professor of orthopedic surgery at Harvard Medical School and chairman of the Harvard Infantile Paralysis Commission, reached Campobello and recognized it as poliomyelitis.

Roosevelt began a second term as a New York state senator in 1913. He resigned his seat to join the Wilson administration as assistant secretary of the navy.

Roosevelt's illness was the defining event in his life. Until then he had struck many as cocky, superficial, a bit of a playboy, a political lightweight exploiting his family name. His infirmity and his arduous rehabilitation changed him physically and mentally. Suffering toughened his character and stiffened his political will. He gained a new empathy with those whose lives had been ill-favored. His unquenchable

optimism, and his refusal to regard himself as an invalid, would become legendary.

In 1928 he ran for governor of New York, making light of his handicap in a winning campaign. That spring his classmates chose him as chief marshal of Commencement at their twenty-fifth reunion. Harvard's Phi Beta Kappa chapter selected him as the orator at its annual Literary Exercises, and made him an honorary member. Helped onstage at Sanders Theatre by his son James, then a rising senior, Roosevelt got a lengthy standing ovation when he was introduced. His oration, titled "The Age of Social Consciousness," blended a hopeful meliorism with the complacencies of a generation that would soon be wondering how things got so bad so fast.

He received an LL.D. on Commencement day. President Lowell's citation read, "Governor of New York; a statesman in whom is no guile." It was a curious way to describe a man who would be known for his genial deviousness and political legerdemain. At the afternoon meeting of the Alumni Association, Roosevelt presented the class gift of $150,000 and was one of five speakers. The theme of his address was the need to shift the focus of higher education from "teaching . . . directed to cooperative and mass effort" to "the stimulation and strengthening of the will and the power of the individual to act as an individual." To some of his hearers that must have sounded strangely like Republican ideology.

Re-elected governor by a record plurality, Roosevelt emerged as the Democrats' likeliest presidential nominee in 1932. Walter Lippmann, who had urged him to run for governor in 1928, now called him "an amiable boy scout," "a pleasant man who, without any important qualifications, would very much like to be President." Among Roosevelt's backers was Joseph P. Kennedy '12, a millionaire real estate speculator and movie mogul. Joe Kennedy got the California delegation into camp. Other states fell in line, and Roosevelt was nominated on the fourth ballot. In a dramatic gesture, he flew from Albany to Chicago to accept the nomination.

Lippmann did a *volte-face* in October, telling readers that he would "vote cheerfully for Governor Roosevelt." Ted Roosevelt Jr. '09, who had lived in the White House and yearned to reclaim it, endorsed Herbert Hoover, writing his mother that he was "distinctly hopeful . . . about November. Franklin is such poor stuff it seems improbable that he should be elected President." In November Ted's distant cousin carried all but six states and his alma mater. The electorate gave Roosevelt 23 million votes to Hoover's 16 million. Harvard students went strongly for Hoover, a Stanford man, in a *Crimson* straw poll. Even Norman Thomas, making the second of six presidential bids as the Socialist Party candidate, outran Roosevelt in five of the seven Houses.

As SQUIRE OF THE WHITE HOUSE, FDR welcomed Harvard visitors. Among those signing the executive mansion's guest book were two dozen Crimson rowers (including Franklin Roosevelt Jr. '37), who came to dine after racing at Annapolis in May 1935. To the surprise of Bill Bingham '16, Harvard's director of athletics, the president greeted

Opposite: Governor Roosevelt accepting the Democratic Party's nomination at its 1932 convention at Chicago Stadium. The nominee promised "a new deal for the American people."

fifteen of the oarsmen by their first names as they filed in. When senior Tommy Hunter came through the line, Roosevelt leaned from his chair to embrace him. The 96-pound coxswain had been a polio patient.

In April 1934, a month before the class of 1904's thirtieth reunion, the president put on a White House reception for 936 classmates, wives, and children from 26 states and five countries. The receiving line wound through the Blue Room for an hour. On the south lawn a Marine band played Harvard marches. "The president had a genial word for everybody," wrote class secretary Edward Taft, "appearing for all the world as if he had never had so good a time."

A *Boston Transcript* writer had observed before the event that the guests would be better off than the host, since "they are going to get more food out of him than he got votes out of them." The *Transcript* man had a point. Most of Roosevelt's classmates opposed him politically, and some loathed him. Walter Russell Bowie '04, dean of Union Theological Seminary, recalled "the rancorous and almost hysterical political animus which rose against him and what he stood for among the privileged groups to which many of the Harvard graduates happened to belong. I was amazed and disgusted to hear the way men talked of him when he was at the Harvard Tercentenary."

Harvard's Tercentenary bash offered endless variety. In April 1936 the Classical Club presented the *Mostellaria* of Plautus as the Tercentenary Latin Play. A special orchestral score was composed by Elliott Carter '30. Above, from left: masked actors David H.H. Ingalls '36 as Theoproprides, an elderly Athenian gentleman, and Ralph Lazzaro '36 as Phaniscus, a slave.

ROOSEVELT'S OFFICE made him the principal figure at the Tercentenary celebration. Lawrence Lowell, its honorary chairman, treated him rudely in an exchange of letters before the event. Lowell's letter of invitation, addressed to "Mr. Franklin D. Roosevelt," described the Tercentenary as an "opportunity to divorce yourself from the arduous demands of politics and political speech-making," and suggested that the president speak for no more than ten minutes.

To Felix Frankfurter FDR wrote, "I felt like replying—'if I am invited in my capacity as a Harvard graduate I shall, of course, speak as briefly as you suggest—two minutes if you say so—but if I am invited as President to speak for the Nation, I am unable to tell you at this time what my subject will be or whether it will take five minutes or an hour.' I suppose some people with insular minds really believe that I might make a purely political speech lasting one hour and a half."

Roosevelt sent a polite reply seeking assurance that he was being invited as president of the United States. Lowell confirmed that he was, adding, "In that capacity I suppose you will want to say something about what Harvard has meant to the nation," and again suggesting a time limit. "Damn," wrote FDR to Frankfurter. To Lowell he responded curtly, "Thank you for your letter of April 14. You are right in thinking that I will want to say something of the significance of Harvard in relation to our national history. Yours very sincerely, Franklin D. Roosevelt."

The *Crimson's* editorial board was as contumacious as Lowell. "Perhaps those who have repeatedly told us that educated men should go into politics were on the wrong track," sneered an editorial in January 1936. "In the midst of our great Three Hundredth Anniversary Celebration, let the presence of this man serve as a useful antidote to the natural overemphasis on Harvard's successes."

Part tortoise, symbol of long life and endurance, and part dragon, symbol of power and happiness, this 20-ton marble monument was presented during the Tercentenary exercises by Fred Sze '18, president of the Harvard Club of Shanghai, on behalf of alumni in China.

Dating from the Ch'ing Dynasty (1796-1821), the monument had been sent by the emperor to one of his provincial governors.

The Tercentenary

HARVARD CELEBRATED its anniversary in the grand style. The Tercentenary was a brilliant show, spread out over ten months and international in scope. Though an approaching hurricane drenched spectators and dignitaries at the closing session, the observance was a rousing success.

Planning had begun in 1924, when Samuel Eliot Morison was appointed Tercentenary Historian.[24] Jerome Greene, who had organized Lowell's inaugural and Eliot's ninetieth birthday celebration, was the Tercentenary's chief designer. He had returned to his old job as secretary to the Corporation in 1934, and was largely responsible for the decision that the events should emphasize Harvard's current resources and future prospects rather than past achievements, while linking Harvard and American higher education with international scholarship.

The celebrating commenced on November 7, 1935, when Morison spoke at exercises in honor of John Harvard's birthday, and ended with three days of festivity in mid-September. During the summer Harvard placed itself "on view." Escorted by red-jacketed student guides, nearly 70,000 visitors toured University buildings and special exhibits. Professional societies scheduled meetings to dovetail with Tercentenary events. The Law School and Medical School sponsored conferences

Festival Rites

Harvard's Tercentenary drew many distinguished outsiders, and brought thousands of alumni back to celebrate their alma mater. Some festival touches recalled the past: a lion borrowed from the Emmanuel College arms capped the tallest flagpoles; the official flag of Harvard's bicentennial celebration was unsealed and raised at the meeting of the Associated Harvard Clubs on September 17.[25] Greetings arrived from around the world; so did presents. Alumni in Japan sent a 300-year-old stone lantern (below).

and symposia. Boston museums displayed Harvard treasures; organ and chamber music concerts featured works by Harvard composers. The Boston Symphony presented three Tercentenary Concerts.

More than seventy scholars from fifteen countries took part in a two-week Tercentenary Conference of Arts and Sciences in September. Scientists in academic regalia expounded on cosmogony, cosmic radiation, communications engineering, nuclear physics, experimental morphology, parasitism, and more; humanists and social scientists took up such topics as "Authority and the Individual," "Independence, Convergency, and Borrowing in Institutions, Thought, and Art," and "Stability and Social Change." Their scholarly outpourings were preserved in three thick volumes issued by the Harvard University Press.

An audience of 15,000, including some 10,000 alumni, attended the three concluding "Tercentenary Days." The central part of the Yard, now christened the "Tercentenary Theatre," was festooned with gonfalons and banners bearing heraldic devices of the various Houses and professional schools. A dais seating 840 persons was erected on the por-

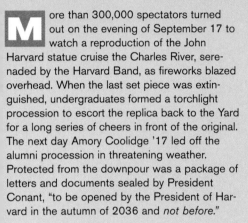

More than 300,000 spectators turned out on the evening of September 17 to watch a reproduction of the John Harvard statue cruise the Charles River, serenaded by the Harvard Band, as fireworks blazed overhead. When the last set piece was extinguished, undergraduates formed a torchlight procession to escort the replica back to the Yard for a long series of cheers in front of the original. The next day Amory Coolidge '17 led off the alumni procession in threatening weather. Protected from the downpour was a package of letters and documents sealed by President Conant, "to be opened by the President of Harvard in the autumn of 2036 and *not before.*"

tico of the Memorial Church. In front of it was a prominent speaker's stand with a high, gabled canopy. The wiring of the outdoor area for amplification and recording was described by a New York paper as "the most elaborate ever attempted in the United States." Cameramen and radio technicians perched on platforms rigged to trees.

At an opening exercise in Sanders Theatre, 547 delegates—representing 530 universities, colleges, and learned societies from 46 states and 40 foreign countries—filed onstage in order of institutional seniority. First came the delegate from Cairo's Al-Azhar University, founded in the year 970. An hour later President Conant shook the hand of Hu Shih, professor of Chinese philosophy at the University of Peking.

The Associated Harvard Clubs held an outdoor meeting the next day. The sky was leaden, but rain held off. That evening a fireworks display drew more than 300,000 spectators to the banks of the Charles.

The final day of celebration began ominously. A hurricane off the Virginia coast was moving rapidly northward. "Light and intermittent rain" was forecast, with heavier rainfall after noon. Defying the ele-

As the rain came down on the last day of the Tercentenary exercises, the president of the United States joked with his former law partner Grenville Clark, a member of the Harvard Corporation.

"We saw the rain beating gustily in so many venerable faces; we saw it pattering down on rank on rank of gray heads which we knew contained as precious an agglomeration of brains as the world has ever seen gathered in one spot . . . and we noted the truly aristocratic disdain with which the demigods on the platform met the dull fury of the heavens."

–From the Alumni Bulletin of September 30, 1936

ments, Conant chose to keep the proceedings in the Tercentenary Theatre. By noon his chilled guests had been thoroughly wetted. Conant, Lowell, and Roosevelt sat stoically at the front of the platform, declining the protection of umbrellas.

A peal of bells, transmitted by radio from London's Southwark Cathedral, John Harvard's baptismal place, began the exercises. Following a series of brief addresses, England's poet laureate, John Masefield, LITT. D. '18, read lines composed in celebration of John Harvard's legacy (". . . this scene of living corn made bread, / This lamp of human hope become a star"). Conant then delivered the first major public speech of his presidency. Titled "The University Tradition in America—Yesterday and Tomorrow," it was a plea for "learning," not mere "training," and for universities as "sanctuaries of the inner life of the nation . . . concerned with things of the spirit."

"The future of the university tradition in America," Conant declared, "depends on keeping a proper balance between the four essential ingredients—the advancement of learning, the liberal arts college, professional training, and a healthy student life. If such a balance can be maintained, the private and public universities of the nation will function both as instruments of higher education and as centers for developing a national culture worthy of this rich and powerful land."

He concluded by emphasizing the need for freedom in the search for truth: "The origin of the Constitution [and] the functioning of the three branches of the Federal Government, the forces of modern capitalism, must be dissected as fearlessly as the geologist examines the origin of the rocks. On this point there can be no compromise; we are either afraid of heresy or we are not. If we are afraid, there will be no adequate discussion of the genesis of our national life; the door will be shut to the development of a culture which will satisfy our needs. . . . Harvard was founded by dissenters. Before two generations had passed there was a general dissent from the first dissent. Heresy has long been in the air. We are proud of the freedom which has made this possible even when we may most dislike some particular form of heresy we may encounter."

The president then awarded honorary degrees to 62 eminent scholars. He had written all the citations himself. Among the recipients were the Cambridge scientist Sir Arthur Eddington, philosophers Rudolf

Carnap and Étienne Gilson, psychoanalyst Carl Jung, immunologist Karl Landsteiner, anthropologist Bronislaw Malinowski, psychologist Jean Piaget, and Harvard's Howard Mumford Jones, scholar of American literature. With the singing of "O God, Our Help in Ages Past," the morning exercises ended, and the rainfall became torrential. Forced indoors, a thousand privileged guests witnessed the afternoon proceedings in Sanders Theatre. Others listened to public address systems set up in University buildings, or to the radio broadcast.

LAWRENCE LOWELL, as President of the Day, spoke first. The measured phrases with which he began would be widely quoted. "As wave after wave rolls landward from the ocean, breaks and fades away sighing down the shingle of the beach, so the generations of men follow one another, sometimes quietly, sometimes, after a storm, with noisy turbulence. But, whether we think upon the monotony or the violence in human history, two things are always new—youth and the quest for knowledge, and with these a university is concerned. So long as its interest in them is keen it can never grow old, though it count its age by centuries. The means it uses may vary with the times, but forever the end remains the same. . . ."

Conant made a report, announcing that almost 9,000 donors had given $2.8 million to the Three Hundredth Anniversary Fund.[26] Again Lowell spoke, glancing once or twice at his watch because his words had to dovetail with a live radio message from Stanley Baldwin, prime minister of Britain and chancellor of the University of Cambridge.

After a speech by Judge Learned Hand (A.B. 1893, LL.B. 1896), president of the Alumni Association, Lowell rose once more. "The next speaker it would be impertinent for me to introduce to you, or to any American audience," he announced. "He is the fourth graduate of Harvard College to hold the office of Chief Magistrate in our nation—two of them named Adams, and two Roosevelt. Gentlemen, the President of the United States!" Roosevelt received a standing ovation.

Omitting Lowell's name from his salutation, FDR noted that he was speaking "in a joint and several capacity": as president of the United States, as chairman of the U.S. Harvard Tercentenary Commission, and as "a son of Harvard who gladly returns to this spot where men have sought truth for three hundred years."

"This meeting is being held," he went on, "in pursuance of an adjournment expressly taken one hundred years ago on the motion of Josiah Quincy. At that time many of the alumni of Harvard were sorely troubled concerning the state of the nation. Andrew Jackson was President. On the 250th anniversary of the founding of Harvard College, many alumni again were sorely troubled. Grover Cleveland was President. Now, on the three hundredth anniversary, I am President."

This disarming opening prefaced a well-turned speech, partly written by Felix Frankfurter, stressing the need to "train men to be citizens in that Athenian sense which compels a man to live his life unceasingly aware that its civic significance is its most abiding." The speech lasted barely ten minutes. "It was really a great triumph," Frankfurter wired Roosevelt the next day. "You furnished a striking example of the

Sow It with Salt

George Bernard Shaw, then the foremost playwright of the English-speaking world, made it amply clear that he did not wish to be among those honored at Harvard's Tercentenary.

John B. Sears '23, M.D. '27, wrote Shaw in the fall of 1935 to ask if he might suggest him to the Corporation as a candidate for Tercentenary honors.

GBS

"Dear Sir," GBS wrote back in an imperfectly typed letter: "I have to thank you for your proposal to present me as a candidate for an honorary degree of D.L. of Harvard University at its tri-centenary celebration. But I cannot pretend that it would be fair for me to accept university degrees when every public reference of mine to our educational system, and especially to the influence of the universities on it, is fiercely hostile. If Harvard would celebrate its 300th anniversary by burning itself to the ground and sowing its site with salt, the ceremony would give me the greatest satisfaction as an example to all the other famous old corrupters of youth, including Yale, Oxford, Cambridge, the Sorbonne, etc. etc. etc. Under these circumstances I should let you down very heavily if you undertook to sponsor me . . . ."

Appended in tidy handwriting was a postscript: "I appreciate the friendliness of your attitude."

civilized gentleman and also of the importance of wise sauciness."

Next came a greeting from Harvard's "dearest enemy," Yale. The emissary was President Angell, who ad-libbed that "as I was drawing about me my bedraggled robes at the close of the [morning] ceremonies, I overheard one of your distinguished graduates, who was exhibiting a condition of complete saturation, remark, 'This is evidently Conant's method of soaking the rich.'"[27] The last speaker was Alexander Dunlop Lindsay, vice-chancellor of Oxford and master of Balliol College, who paid tribute to Harvard and its place in "this strange Utopian flower, this free commonwealth of universities all over the world."

The meeting was now prophetically adjourned, with Conant moving to reconvene on September 18, 2036. "Before putting the motion," said Lowell, "I want to say a word in its favor. If I read history aright, human institutions have rarely been killed while they were alive. They commit suicide or die from lack of vigor, and then the adversary comes and buries them. So long as an institution conduces to human welfare, so long as a university gives to youth strong, active methods of life, so long as its scholarship does not degenerate into pedantry, nothing can prevent it from going on to greater prosperity. In spite of the condition of many things in this world, I have confidence in the future. Those of you, therefore, who believe that the world will exist one hundred years hence, and that universities will then be faithful to their great purpose, will say 'Aye'; contrary-minded, 'No.'"

It was a unanimous vote. The meeting stood adjourned.

Up or Out

A FTER THE TRIUMPHS of the Tercentenary, Conant found himself in a three-year tiff with the Faculty of Arts and Sciences over appointment policies. Eventually it led to a showdown that might have ended his presidency. At stake were issues of academic freedom, administrative control, and constitutional principle.

As Conant had pointed out during the presidential search, the faculty had become overloaded with men hired to staff the tutorial program and assist in large introductory courses in economics, government, history, and English. It also suffered from cronyism. Harvard had always had room for men willing to teach or administer for low salaries, or even gratis. Some, like Theodore Lyman in physics, Paul Sachs and Edward Waldo Forbes in fine arts, Thomas Barbour of the Museum of Comparative Zoology, and the Harvard College Library's Archibald Cary Coolidge, had rendered great service. But many others were undistinguished.

Planning for the Tercentenary, Conant later wrote, "distracted my attention from what should have been my first order of business." When George Birkhoff '05, Perkins professor of mathematics, succeeded Kenneth Murdock as dean of the faculty in 1935, the president and his new dean began "groping our way toward a solution."

To avoid freezing a large group at the instructor level, younger men would have to move on after a few years' teaching experience. That meant starting the appointment process sooner. This led to the policy

As the skies darkened, England's poet laureate, John Masefield, read his "Lines on the Tercentenary of Harvard College in America." The poem paid homage to John Harvard, "whose dead hand brings / These thousands in his honour and his praise."

that became known as "up or out." The well-staffed department of economics was the first to feel it.

In March 1937 Birkhoff overrode a departmental recommendation and informed two young instructors that they would be proposed for two-year "terminating" appointments. Alan Sweezy '29, PH.D. '34, and Raymond Walsh, PH.D. '34, were among the few economics instructors who had dared to introduce students to Marxist analysis. They were popular teachers. They were also officers of a new teachers' union that had campaigned for better salaries in the lower ranks.

The new appointments policy had not been announced officially, and the administration's action was inevitably seen as politically motivated. Conant dug himself in deeper by issuing a statement contending that the economists' cases presented "no unusual features" and that the decisions rested "solely on grounds of teaching capacity and scholarly ability." The teachers' union charged that the statement was libelous. Students formed protest committees. A petition demanding a formal investigation by a panel of senior professors was signed by 131 faculty members. Conant agreed to the inquiry, with Ralph Barton Perry, Pierce professor of philosophy, chairing the panel.[28]

Known as the Committee of Eight, the panel took almost a year to report. It found no abridgment of academic freedom, but was sharply critical of "defective administrative procedure." Because of "the injustice as well as unwisdom" of the administration's handling of the case, the panel recommended giving Sweezy and Walsh unconditional appointments. Backed by the Corporation, Conant rejected this "unwise and impractical" course. Again protests erupted.

The Committee of Eight spent another year reviewing "the tenure, promotion, and general status of the younger teaching members." Its 200-page report called for "more orderly and methodical procedure" rather than "oral rulings," but tacitly accepted the up-or-out principle, recommending that the maximum stay for nontenured faculty members be limited to eight years.

Determined to defend the Harvard tradition that faculty appointments and promotions were the prerogative of administrative officers, Conant refused to allow the full faculty to consider the report. In the meantime, ten more terminating notices had been sent to junior faculty members, including the president of the teachers' union.

When the faculty met for the first time in the fall of 1939, it was on the verge of open rebellion. Carl Friedrich, professor of government, was known to be working on a motion calling for a broad inquiry into University governance. Friends of Kenneth Murdock were touting him as Conant's replacement. Conant prepared for "a knockdown fight" at the next meeting.

Business School dean Wallace Donham warned the president that he had lost the confidence of a majority of the faculty, and that the relationship of the faculty and the governing boards was in jeopardy. He urged Conant to admit his mistakes to the faculty and to ask its members not to challenge the Harvard constitution because of his errors.

Harvard's Byrne professor of administrative law, Felix Frankfurter, was President Roosevelt's choice to fill the Supreme Court seat vacated by the death of Justice Benjamin Cardozo in 1938. Frankfurter assumed the "scholar's seat" that had been held by Justices Joseph Story (A.B. 1798), Oliver Wendell Holmes (A.B. 1861, LL.B. 1866), and Cardozo (LL.D. 1927).

Fallen trees in front of Eliot House showed the force of the hurricane that swept the East Coast on September 21, 1938, taking almost 600 lives. Some 1,500 trees at Harvard's Arnold Arboretum were uprooted or severely damaged.

"In my experience," Donham told Conant, "if one admits a mistake to a faculty group, they will usually rally in support."

Conant wrote in his memoirs that he "had no stomach for apologizing to the faculty, particularly when I was under violent attack." But he did not want a divisive inquiry into Harvard's governance. Before a meeting of record size he acknowledged mistakes and requested the faculty not to take "a hasty step which might affect Harvard for years to come." A professor of government moved to table the motion for an inquiry. By a voice vote that was close to unanimous, it was tabled.

Conant still had to act on almost two dozen appointments expiring in 1939. About two-thirds were continued, but there were more harsh criticisms of the "inflexible slide-rule principle" of up or out.

The path was now clear, however. Reform of the appointments system was completed within two years, largely owing to the tactful work of assistant deans Paul H. Buck, PH.D. '35, professor of history, and William Caspar Graustein '10, professor of mathematics. The so-called Graustein Formula gave flexibility to the new rules. Based on the assumption that a departmental vacancy would occur every four years for every eight permanent staff members, it utilized interdepartmental "loans and credits" to permit appointments before or after an actual vacancy. This allowed a degree of long-range planning that Harvard departments had never enjoyed.

Interfaculty Initiatives

WHILE SKIRMISHING with the Faculty of Arts and Sciences, Conant managed to reorganize the faculties of education, dental medicine, and city planning, and explore the feasibility of new ventures in public policy and journalism. To maximize resources, he favored joint programs that bridged the common interests of separate faculties. In this he was ahead of his time.

President Lowell had told certain Overseers that he was leaving two kittens for his successor to drown. One was the Graduate School of Education. The school was underendowed and chronically short of funds; its tiny faculty was at odds about its mission. Like Lowell, Conant doubted the suitability of educational theory as an academic field, but his national scholarships program had increased his interest in the quality of teaching in high schools.

To the extent that Harvard trained teachers, it did so in two places: the School of Education and the Graduate School of Arts and Sciences. Conant convened an interfaculty group to study ways to combine forces. The result was a new joint degree of master of arts in teaching. Departments in arts and sciences would set standards for the degree and examine candidates; the education school would provide research materials and coordinate practice teaching assignments in local schools. The first degrees were awarded in 1937.

The school's financial woes continued. Unsatisfied with the waning leadership of Henry Holmes '03, the school's dean since its founding in 1920, Conant persuaded him to step down in favor of Francis Spaulding, a young faculty member who was about to accept an offer from the

Lothrop Withington Jr. '42 gulped down a goldfish in March 1939. Withington's publicity stunt did not secure his election as freshman class president, but he did collect a $10 bet from a classmate and start a nationwide college craze.

The national goldfish-swallowing record was reportedly set by a student at MIT who devoured 42 fish in rapid succession.

University of Chicago. Spaulding assumed the deanship in 1940.

The New Deal had greatly increased the scope of government in American life. Programs providing training for public service had sprung up in the departments of government, history, and economics, the division of engineering, and the schools of business, law, city planning, and public health. Dean Donham of the Business School argued forcefully for a new school of public administration, envisioning it as a research facility for various departments and faculties. Lucius Littauer (A.B. 1878), a wealthy glove manufacturer and former congressman from upstate New York, responded with a pledge of $2 million for a building and endowment.[29] Littauer wanted a school with a faculty of its own, but Conant eventually sold him on an interfaculty program. A dozen professors from the departments of government, economics, and sociology, and the faculties of law and business, would make up the teaching staff. The small student body would include places for fourteen "in-service" fellows, as well as graduate students and, later, a limited number of "high-ranking" college graduates.

Littauer gave another $500,000 to ensure a building big enough to house most of the faculty members concerned with the new program. The Littauer Center for Public Administration opened in the fall of 1938. Its building, erected on parkland south of the Law School, was done in the spring. It was designed by the Coolidge firm in a classic style suggesting the Washington headquarters of a federal agency.

The Littauer Center's "in-service" fellowships prefigured mid-career programs later developed by other faculties. With a $1 million bequest from Agnes Wahl Nieman, widow of the *Milwaukee Journal*'s founder, Conant created a parallel program for newspaper reporters. The Nieman Fellowships enabled nine journalists to spend a year at Harvard, attending courses and faculty seminars on a noncredit basis. Conant engaged Archibald MacLeish, LL.B. '19, poet and former *Fortune* magazine writer, as the Nieman Foundation's "curator." He would later hold the venerable Boylston professorship of rhetoric and oratory.

In another move to unite common interests in separate faculties, Conant merged the departments of architecture and landscape architecture with the School of City Planning to form the Harvard Graduate

School of Design in 1937. As chairman of its architecture department he brought in the German designer Walter Gropius, who had founded and led the famous Bauhaus school until the Nazis closed it in 1933. The Bauhaus had revolutionized contemporary art, architecture, and graphics by integrating design with craftsmanship and technology. Gropius, his colleague Marcel Breuer, and a coterie of former students attracted a vibrant community of creative designers that made Cambridge a world center of architectural ideas and discourse.

Girding for War

THE LATE 1930S WERE A TIME of heightened political activity. The number of students drawn to radical politics was still small, but the isolationist American Independence League could claim 700 members in 1939.[30] The pacifist Student Union, with 500, sent two ambulances to aid the Loyalists in the Spanish Civil War. The Nazi attacks on German universities in November 1938 led to the formation of the Harvard Committee to Aid German Student Refugees. Supported by a dozen student organizations, it raised almost $20,000 from students, faculty members, and alumni to fund scholarships and living expenses for European victims of persecution. The Corporation added $10,000, providing a total of twenty scholarships. The movement became a model for refugee scholarship programs in more than 300 colleges.

In July 1939, on the twenty-fifth anniversary of the 1914 Henley victory, a Harvard crew won another Grand Challenge Cup. In a minor historical irony, the world was again at war within weeks. Hitler's Panzer divisions and Luftwaffe bombers and fighters attacked Poland on September 1. Britain and France declared war on Germany two days later.

"In the minds of the 3,500-odd undergraduates now beginning a new year at Harvard, as in the minds of most American citizens, one thought is uppermost," wrote William Frye '40, the *Alumni Bulletin's* undergraduate correspondent: "'Will the United States enter the European war?' The undergraduates know only too well that if such a tragedy ever does occur, they will be in the first draft." Isolationist sentiment remained strong. "We are frankly determined to have peace at any price," declared a *Crimson* editorial. "We intend to resist to the utmost any suggestions that American intervention is necessary to 'save civilization' or even to 'save democracy and freedom.'"

Generations clashed at the 1940 Commencement. Insisting that it was too late for such "fantastic nonsense" as aid to the Allies, class orator Tudor Gardiner '40 said the nation's best course was to get set for the next war by "making this hemisphere impregnable." David Sigourney '15, a World War I veteran who had been class orator 25 years earlier, delivered a counterblast at a meeting of reunion classes. "Take it from me, you boys of 1940," said Sigourney, "the boys of 1915 are far from senescent or from being armchair patriots. We were not too proud to fight then and we are not too proud to fight now." Every sentence, reported the *New York Times*, "was met with a round of boos and hisses, making it almost impossible to hear the speaker"; most of the heckling came from "the classes recently graduating." On the afternoon of

Speaking as a private citizen in a national radio broadcast in May 1940, President Conant urged all possible forms of aid to the Allies. Relentlessly attacking him for his efforts to prepare the nation for war, the *Crimson* declared that Conant was part of a "road gang which is trying to build for the United States a super-highway straight to Armageddon."

Commencement day, Secretary of State Cordell Hull condemned isolationism as "dangerous folly." The next day's headlines reported the fall of France.

Led by Ralph Barton Perry, Harvard faculty members formed the American Defense-Harvard Group to promote support for the Allies. As the Battle of Britain began, the group beamed daily short wave broadcasts of news and opinion to British listeners. President Conant waged a personal campaign to alert the United States to the need for preparedness. As an officer of the University he had been reluctant to speak out on a controversial public issue, but his stance changed when the Nazis invaded France and the Low Countries in May. Conant joined the newly formed Committee to Defend America by Aiding the Allies, chaired by William Allen White, LL.D. '25, editor of the *Emporia* (Kansas) *Gazette*; at White's behest he addressed a national radio audience on May 29. "We must rearm at once," Conant declared. Hitler, he warned, was bent on world domination. Throughout the summer and fall Conant spoke and wrote constantly on the totalitarian threat.

PRESIDENT ROOSEVELT WON an unprecedented third term in the election of 1940.[31] Conant now became an increasingly influential advocate of administration initiatives. He pressed for changes in the Neutrality Act, argued for a military draft, and testified in favor of FDR's lend-lease bill. Early in 1941 he led a mission to England to arrange procedures for exchanging scientific information.

To mobilize the nation's scientific resources, Conant and Vannevar Bush of MIT had organized the National Defense Research Committee in 1940. Conant took charge of its chemistry section in June 1941; a year later he succeeded Bush as NDRC's chairman.

By then Harvard too had begun to mobilize. Under contract to NDRC, Harvard chemists were now conducting explosives research. Physics professor E. Leon Chaffee was running an "electronics radio detection" course for military personnel. Enrollment in ROTC units was rising, and students could take flight instruction at a Harvard summer camp on Cape Cod. Medical School physicians were staffing a Red Cross-Harvard hospital near Salisbury, England, organized to apply

Life's **issue of May 5, 1941, featured an admiring photoessay on Harvard. "Today it stands alone," declared** *Life.* **"Its gravest concern as a world university is that freedom to teach and discover the truth shall not die throughout the world as it has on the European continent. To this end it is meeting the challenge . . . with the full resources of its brains and laboratories, an endowment of $141,000,000 and a collection of 4,000,000 books."**

Conant and Lowell (third from left and far right) at a review of Harvard's 467-member Army ROTC unit in May 1941. The third civilian was Robert Hallowell (A.B. 1896), chairman of the Overseers committee to visit the departments of military and naval science and tactics.

Opposite: President Conant addressing a mass meeting at Sanders Theatre on the evening of December 8, 1941.

When the battleship *Arizona* exploded and sank after being hit with an armor-piercing bomb during the surprise attack on Pearl Harbor, Ensign Philip Gazecki '41 (inset) was among the thousand men who were lost.

The 21-year-old Gazecki, first Harvard man to die in the war as a member of an American military unit, had planned a naval career. As an undergraduate chemistry concentrator, he had developed an anti-fouling paint that was later used on all the navy's big ships.

preventive measures against the predicted outbreak of epidemics in bombed cities.

Hitler startled the world by breaking his pact with Joseph Stalin and invading Russia on June 22, 1941. Addressing entering freshmen that fall, Conant said Harvard would back the national defense effort "in every way possible." He added, "To my mind, until Congress does declare war, we are a people dwelling in an ambiguous halfway house. By failing to act with our full force, we are delaying the hour of final victory, the hour of peace."

Crimson president John C. Robbins Jr. '42 now perceived a "seemingly drastic shift" in undergraduate attitudes. The necessity of resisting Hitler was increasingly recognized. Isolationism was in retreat.

Conant had appointed a seven-man Committee on Civilian Defense. Its members' duties included safeguarding Harvard's museum and library holdings in the event of an attack on the North Atlantic coast. On October 11 civil defense officials staged an air raid drill. While the football team battled Cornell at the Stadium, high-explosive bombs and incendiaries theoretically wrecked Massachusetts Hall, set the President's House ablaze, severed water and gas mains, and left seven casualties. Chief warden Aldrich Durant '02, the University's business manager, declared himself satisfied with the performance of firefighters and first-aid teams. "Had there actually been a raid," he announced, "the situation would have been well under control."

REAL BOMBS FELL on Hawaii on Sunday, December 7. Japanese dive bombers and torpedo planes sank or disabled eighteen U.S. ships, destroyed 350 aircraft, and took 2,403 American lives in a two-hour attack on the Pearl Harbor naval base. An attack on the U.S. airfield at Luzon demolished half of General Douglas MacArthur's Philippine air force. The news spread rapidly through the Harvard community. Extra watchmen were assigned to laboratories where defense research was going on. Undergraduates abandoned their books and stayed close to their radios.

"By Monday," reported the *Alumni Bulletin*, "the shock of surprise had crystallized into a feeling of unity." At noon more than 1,200 students crowded Sanders Theatre to hear a broadcast of President Roosevelt's war message to Congress. A mass meeting in Sanders that evening was relayed by wire to New Lecture Hall and Memorial Church.

President Conant, the principal speaker, pledged Harvard's full resources to help gain a speedy and total victory. "There is little indication that this will be a short war," he concluded. "The period of waiting may try our souls. But patience, fortitude, and courage are required of us all. In every preceding ordeal of battle Harvard has stood in the forefront of those who toiled and sacrificed that liberty might survive. There can be no question that in the days ahead this University and its sons will bring new honors to justify the expectations of ten generations of Harvard men."

"Conant's Arsenal"

To speed the day when we can once more walk in the full sunlight of human liberty, we stand ready to make whatever sacrifice is required.
—*President Conant, speaking at Harvard's Commencement of 1942*

THE MOBILIZATION OF HARVARD went rapidly in the weeks that followed Pearl Harbor. "A speedy victory is the prerequisite to any postwar world worth organizing," wrote President Conant in his annual report to the Board of Overseers, presented in January 1942. "It is for war, therefore, and not for peace that we must now lay our immediate educational plans."

Courses in navigation, camouflage, meteorology, and other subjects of wartime importance were added to the curriculum. As the war went on, almost eighty University laboratories participated in military research projects. Radar jamming, sonar devices, explosives, napalm, a proto-computer, antimalarial drugs, blood derivatives, and new treatments for burns and shock were among the products of Harvard labs. By 1945, University income from government research contracts would reach $33.5 million, a sum exceeded only by MIT and Cal Tech. In *Time* magazine's phrase, Harvard became "Conant's Arsenal."

Medical School physicians manned the first American field hospitals. An astrophysicist taught code-breaking to Radcliffe students. Harvard scientists helped create the first atomic bombs. Almost 27,000 University alumni, students, employees,

Navy cadets drill in the Old Yard, December 1943. No tally was kept, but the number of military trainees who passed through Harvard in the war years was estimated at 45,000 or more.

and faculty members served in the armed forces; 697 lost their lives.

The war had a lasting impact on Harvard and American higher education. It brought universities, government, and industry into a powerful and continuing partnership. It fostered collaborative research and interdisciplinary cooperation between physical scientists, engineers, and social scientists, spawning new fields of advanced study—biophysics, nucleonics, systems research, cybernetics, computation, game theory—that took off in the postwar years.

The war stimulated the development of improved instructional methods, and cleared the way for curricular renewal. It opened Harvard classrooms to women, and later to thousands of veterans whose presence transformed the demography and culture of the University community. Such changes tied Harvard more closely to the larger society, itself much altered by the war.

Bugles in the Yard

NEVER HAD THE INSTITUTION undergone so drastic a change in program in so short a time. Students returned from Christmas vacation to find that the academic schedule was now on a year-round basis, with a twelve-week summer school providing the equivalent of a third semester. (The calendar was later redivided into three segments of sixteen weeks each.) Faculty members accepted a 33 percent increase in teaching loads without extra compensation.

Under contract with the military, Harvard furnished classrooms, laboratories, housing and dining facilities, and instructors for specialized training programs and its own Reserve Officers Training Corps units. "Harvard College has thus become in large measure a military and navy training school," reported dean of the College Chester Hanford. To make room for servicemen, freshmen moved from the Yard to the residential Houses. Eliot House and Kirkland House were occupied by men in the navy V-12 program; Leverett House and most of Winthrop House belonged to the Army Specialized Training Program. The civilian element lived in Adams, Dunster, and Lowell Houses, with an overflow group of freshmen in the Standish Hall wing of Winthrop. The installation of double-decker bunks expanded room capacity in the Yard and the Houses by 30 percent.

Veteran Yard cop John Connolly fends off sports-minded civilians as trainees change classes in the spring of 1942.

The navy's V-12 plan prescribed some required courses, while permitting its 950 enrollees to elect freely from regular course offerings. The navy also sponsored nearly 300 undergraduate reservists in V-1 and V-7 programs. The army emphasized practical skills, but men enrolled in its Specialized Training Program took part of their work in normal academic areas. Most concentrated on personnel psychology, foreign area or language studies, or basic engineering.

ROTC members drilled in Memorial Hall, shouldering Enfield and Springfield rifles manufactured for World War I. Military personnel drilled in the Yard, obliterating most of its grass. Mechanized bugle calls and martial music issued from a Thayer Hall loudspeaker. The chow line replaced the familiar dining hall service, and a charge was imposed

for a second helping. A playpen and sandpile, oddities on a university campus, appeared near Phillips Brooks House.

As a concession to war conditions, the College's entrance requirements were eased. Instead of the former three-hour examinations, the admissions committee required only a school diploma and a satisfactory record in the scholastic aptitude and general achievement tests of the College Entrance Examination Board. Freshmen were permitted to enter in June, beginning in 1942 with the class of 1946, and at the start of any term thereafter. That made it at least theoretically possible to complete work for a bachelor's degree in two calendar years and three months, or a total of seven terms.

Much of the curriculum followed the normal pattern, but the course catalog was enlarged by courses on aerial mapping, aeronautical meteorology, "Camouflage—Protective Concealment" (Fine Arts 1x), "Economic Aspects of War," accelerated instruction in Japanese and Russian, military geology, "Philosophical Aspects of War Issues and Peace Aims," "Navigation and Nautical Astronomy," "The Struggle for World Empire," and "The Development of Modern Armies."

All undergraduates took supervised physical training. Initially graded for fitness by the notorious "step test" devised by a Dr. Brouha, they did calisthenics, worked out with Indian clubs and medicine balls, rowed and played volleyball, and ran obstacle courses and cross-country routes. Introverts who had never gone in for contact sports threw punches under the tutelage of boxing coach Henry Lamar, an affable,

Compulsory exercise: coach Henry Lamar (center) leading a boxing class. Captioned "The Toughening Process Begins," this photo ran in the *Alumni Bulletin* of April 25, 1942. The Harvard student had changed, said the *Bulletin:* "A year ago he was unwilling to believe in the necessity of fighting again for freedom. Six months later his mind was made up."

Chaplains-in-training in a field exercise on the banks of the Charles.

What Victory Requires

Two weeks after Pearl Harbor, President Conant spoke at the annual dinner of the New England Society of New York. His speech was titled "What Victory Requires." A year before the Casablanca conference of January 1943, when President Roosevelt first called for the "unconditional surrender" of Germany, Italy, and Japan, Conant stated that "grim necessity requires that unconditional surrender of the Axis Powers be the first war aim of the United States."

Conant saw the need for a NATO-like alliance to secure the postwar world. "The will to peace of free democratic countries has been proved during the last three years beyond doubt or question," he declared. "A free people will not readily engage in a modern war. This much seems certain. Hence, if freedom is to be protected, once the Axis Powers are beaten, aggressors must be too weak to strike. An armed alliance of free societies must stand ready, once this war is over, to serve together if need be, not for the purpose of imposing their form of government on other people, but protectively against the growth of other challenges to their freedom. If we can do this without malice on the one hand and without sentimentality on the other, we may hope that international order will be restored."

cigar-chomping graduate of the University of Virginia who had lost only one of 39 bouts as a professional light-heavyweight. Lamar, who also coached junior varsity football, took over the varsity when coach Dick Harlow received a navy commission after the 1942 season.

TRAINING COURSES FOR MILITARY PERSONNEL had begun in the spring of 1941, with a Business School program in production and procurement for army quartermasters and navy supply officers. Two temporary structures, Cowie and Carpenter Halls, were erected on former tennis courts for this group of 600 men. The number eventually grew to 1,200. In high secrecy, an "electronics radio detection" course initiated in July 1941 trained as many as 2,000 army, navy, and marine officers per year in the newly developed techniques of radar. Directed by E. Leon Chaffee, Rumford professor of physics, the course was based at the Cruft High-Tension Laboratory, north of the Yard.

A Navy Communications School taught radio transmission and coding techniques to 1,250 officers in five-month courses.[1] Headquarters for this and other navy programs was the President's House at 17 Quincy Street. The Conants had been happy to move to the more modest premises of the Dana-Palmer House, on the site later occupied by Lamont Library. The army and its programs took over the former Sigma Alpha Epsilon fraternity building on South Street, which would later house the department of athletics.

An army chaplains' school, with a non-Harvard faculty and a student body of 330, taught in four-week sessions, was based in the Germanic Museum. Some 10,000 chaplains, representing "all sects, races, and creeds," trained there during the war.

The School for Overseas Administration, directed by Carl J. Friedrich, professor of government, trained officers and enlisted specialists in military government, civil law, languages, and cultural subjects. Three programs for "Cats" (Civil Affairs Training Specialists) focused on Italy, Germany, and Western Europe; two concentrated on Central

Navigation in Cambridge. Navy chief specialist John C. Geston (far right) instructing student ROTC officers. From left: Thomas Gardiner, William Albers, Thomas Godfrey, and Roger Tatton, all of the class of 1942. They are on the roof of the Institute for Geographical Exploration, on Divinity Avenue.

An ROTC artillery unit drilling on Soldiers Field with guns of World War I vintage.

Europe and the Far East. Army amphibian engineers and airstrip soils engineers were taught at the Observatory and at the Engineering School. The School of Public Health instructed navy physicians in tropical medicine. Air force officers learned how to adjust war contracts at the Business School, which also ran a statistical school for about 200 air force officers. A choral group made up of "Stat School" men was known as the Singing Statisticians.

THE ENTIRE UNIVERSITY was on a wartime basis by June 1942. That year's Commencement, reported the *Alumni Bulletin*, was "an intensely solemn and impressive ritual symbolic of a nation at war." To the strains of "Onward, Christian Soldiers," President Conant and President Lowell, now in his eighty-sixth year, led the academic procession into Sever Quadrangle. The thirteen honorary degree recipients included War Production Board chairman Donald Nelson, Secretary of War Henry Stimson, and Secretary of the Navy Frank Knox. Stimson and Knox spoke at the afternoon exercises.

"To speed the day when the Axis powers surrender without conditions," Conant declared in his report to the Alumni Association, "we now dedicate the resources of this ancient society of scholars. To speed the day when we can once more walk in the full sunlight of human liberty, we stand ready to make whatever sacrifice is required." Some 200 faculty members had already joined the armed forces, said Conant; another hundred were serving the government in civilian capacities. Many of those who remained were doing war research. Demands on the scientific laboratories, added Conant, were now so great that "we have been forced to expand into Austin Hall [one of the Law School's main buildings] and the Hemenway Gymnasium, as well as to resort to temporary construction. Of what goes on behind those closed doors, no word may now be told."

Workouts at Soldiers Field.

Opposite: Members of naval and army ROTC and other military units, 1,600 strong, hold a full-dress review at the Soldiers Field baseball diamond, May 11, 1942.

Science under Wraps

OF WHAT WENT ON BEHIND closed doors at Harvard and other research universities, no one knew more than Conant. As chairman of the National Defense Research Committee—a division of the wartime Office of Scientific Research and Development (OSRD)—he supervised a national network of scientists under contract to the military. OSRD would issue nearly 900 contracts during the war. More than a hundred, with a cumulative value of $33.5 million, went to Harvard researchers.

The University's largest projects, the $16 million Radio Research Laboratory and the $8 million Underwater Sound Laboratory, were organized within days of Pearl Harbor. They accounted for 70 percent of Harvard's funding from OSRD. (MIT, producing the most advanced radar research of the war, received 75 contracts with an aggregate value of $117 million. The Harvard-MIT total put Cambridge far ahead of university contractors in other sectors of the country.)

Harvard received its first contracts in late 1940. George B. Kistiakowsky, professor of chemistry, held three of the first five. One of his

tasks was to test new explosives, at $50 a pop. Kistiakowsky would later head the National Defense Research Committee's explosives section, and direct the Manhattan Project's search for a way to trigger a nuclear device.

Louis Fieser, Emery professor of organic chemistry, was another early contractor. Fieser became a Promethean figure in incendiary research. Napalm, lightweight incendiary bombs and grenades, and the M-1 fire starter, used for sabotage and known as the "Harvard Candle," were his inventions. Fieser, who had formerly done cancer research, confessed that he had "always been thrilled by the beauty and power of fire." He had experimented with jellied gasoline to fight crabgrass at his home in Belmont, and his interest was piqued by reports from DuPont of an apparently hazardous gel called divinylacetylene. Fieser found that it burned with "a sputtering, vicious-looking flame. We were impressed by this behavior and greatly intrigued with the idea of a bomb that would scatter burning gobs of such a gel." The result was napalm, used with devastating effect against Japanese islands and cities in the final year of the war. Fire bombs of Fieser's design, engineered by Standard Oil of New Jersey, caused more extensive destruction and loss of life in Japan than the two atomic bombs that ended the war.

Research at high noise levels: Chemist George Kistiakowsky, above, tested new explosives. In the former boiler room of Memorial Hall, psychologist S. Smith Stevens, below, ran a "psycho-acoustic" laboratory.

Fieser's students loved him, but his experiments were often hazardous. One set fire to the roof of Gibbs Laboratory. Another caused a fair-sized conflagration in the baseball stands at Soldiers Field. In addition to his calefactory research, Fieser developed antimalarial drugs and synthesized cortical hormones with the hope of keeping dive-bomber pilots from blacking out.

E. Bright Wilson, another chemist, worked on underwater explosives and designed gauges to measure the pressures of blasts at various depths. Percy Bridgman, who had done military research during World War I, tested armor-plating, experimented with polymers of new plastics, and later assisted the Manhattan Project by making top-secret studies on the compressibility of uranium and plutonium.

Other prewar contracts funded studies of sound control and communications techniques. An "electro-acoustic" lab in Cruft Laboratory was run by physics instructor Leo Beranek '37, a former Harvard Band drummer and a future star of acoustic research. A "psycho-acoustic" laboratory, directed by psychologist S. Smith Stevens, occupied the former boiler room of Memorial Hall. In the words of Harvard war archivist Sterling Dow '25, then an associate professor of history, Stevens's lab was "an inferno of sound."

MUCH OF HARVARD'S PHYSICAL PLANT was under military lease during the war. On Divinity Avenue—in a wing of the Biological Laboratories and a temporary wooden structure behind it, later called the Vanserg Building*—was the Radio Research Laboratory. Headed by Professor Frederick Terman, on leave as dean of Stanford's school of engineering, the RRL was a spin-off of radar development work begun

---

*The names of its postwar users—Veterans Administration, Naval Science, Electronic Research, and Graduate School—gave the acronym Vanserg to this unprepossessing but durable "temporary" building, which still housed University offices in the 1990s.

Louis Fieser had always thrilled to fire. In addition to the invention of napalm, his fire-related research included a manual on arson and feasibility studies on an army scheme to release flame-carrying bats over Japan's home islands. In later years Fieser had a Siamese cat named J.G. Pooh; the initials stood for "jellied gasoline."

at MIT's Radiation Laboratory in the fall of 1940. Aggressively developed by Britain and Germany, radar (an acronym for radio detection and ranging) was the most innovative scientific and engineering development of the pre-atomic phase of the war. Harvard's lab, which eventually had a technical staff of almost 900, concentrated on countermeasures. In a crosstown rivalry between electronic scientists, the Harvard lab sought to frustrate the work being done at the MIT laboratory, where Harvard physicists Edward Purcell, Wendell Furry, Julian Schwinger, and J. Curry Street were among those developing the new science of microwave physics.

Harvard's lab yielded more than 150 anti-radar devices for American and British use. By the end of the war almost every U.S. heavy bomber, naval vessel, and carrier aircraft group had anti-radar equipment designed at Harvard. Radar jamming, an invisible weapon in an increasingly high-tech war, effectively cut Allied losses in the air. One successful technique, code-named "Window," used strips of aluminum foil to dupe enemy radar. The strips were called "chaff," and Fred Whipple, the Harvard astronomer who had helped conceive the idea, was known as the "Air Corps Chief of Chaff." Such countermeasures not only neutralized detection and ranging devices, but also kept much of the enemy's technical manpower busy trying to find ways to overcome jamming.

The Electro-Acoustic Laboratory was in a specially designed building off Oxford Street. The first of Harvard's defense research groups, it was commissioned by the air force in 1940 to find ways of quieting noise in long-range bombers. A second assignment was to improve in-flight and air-to-ground communications systems for high-altitude aircraft. Loudspeakers, microphones, headphones, and sirens were tested in a concrete walled chamber, known as "Beranek's Box" and lined with 20,000 wedge-shaped elements made from eight carloads of spun-glass fiber. Another room could faithfully reproduce the roar of planes in flight.

Astronomer Fred Whipple conceived the idea of using aluminum foil to dupe enemy radar.

The lab studied communications failures and assisted industry in designing, building, and testing new equipment. Devices were sent on to the Psycho-Acoustic Lab for articulation tests.[2] Out of the discovery that the volume of aircraft acoustical fiber should be large in proportion to its weight came a new material that made possible the relative quiet of the Boeing B-29 Superfortress, unveiled in 1943. Called fiberglass, it became a household word in the postwar era.

The Underwater Sound Laboratory, housed in Hemenway Gymnasium, was one of two dozen American university research groups that worked on the submarine-detection system called sonar (sound, navigation, and ranging), originated in World War I. The lab was headed by Frederick Hunt, associate professor of physics and communication engineering (and chief sound-effects man for the Harvard Tercentenary celebration). Eventually it had some 450 employees, many of them women. Tests were run at a field station at Spy Pond, in nearby Arlington, and aboard a small fleet of vessels that included *Galaxy*, a 113-foot steel-hulled yacht built in 1930 for a DuPont executive.

The lab's invention of the bearing-direction indicator for sonar equipment and electronic steering devices for torpedoes helped end the domination of Nazi submarines in the Atlantic. The tide had turned when Allied teams of mathematicians, engineers, and philosophers—including Harvard's W. V. Quine—began breaking coded messages that revealed the whereabouts of German subs. More than a hundred U-boats were tracked down and sunk in a three-month period in mid-1943. All told, the Axis lost 996 subs in a protracted battle for control of the seas that saw the sinking of 4,773 Allied merchant ships. "[Allied] superiority in . . . science," wrote Admiral Karl Dönitz in a dispatch to Berlin, "has torn from our hands our sole offensive weapon in the war against the Anglo-Saxon."

John Pierce, a Harvard research fellow in communication engineering, directed the development of loran (long-range navigation) at MIT's Radiation Lab. Before the war Harvard physicists had designed the first supersonic wind tunnel, used to test bombs and missiles. At the Obser-

The Electro-Acoustic Lab's anechoic chamber was used to test aircraft communications devices. It was nicknamed "Beranek's Box" after physics instructor Leo Beranek (below), the laboratory's director.

vatory, astronomer Harlow Shapley worked on lenses and filters for airfields and aerial photography; James Baker developed wide-aperture, high-resolution lenses for aerial photography. His work laid the foundation for optical systems later used on reconnaissance satellite cameras. Biologist George Wald, a future Nobel winner, studied ways to improve night vision. The Business School's Fatigue Laboratory measured human adaptation to physical stress at high altitudes and to extreme heat and cold.

HARVARD'S MOST PORTENTOUS contribution to postwar science and technology was the "automatic sequence controlled calculator," designed at the Computation Laboratory by associate professor of applied mathematics Howard Aiken, PH.D. '39. The brilliant, abrasive Aiken had left a career in electrical engineering to pursue a Harvard doctorate in mathematics. As a graduate student in 1937 he began planning his giant calculator with the thought that it might aid Harlow Shapley's efforts to calculate the size of the cosmos. He found corporate support for his project when IBM agreed to take a proprietary role in engineering and building the calculator.

Aiken's "mechanical brain" combined electrical and mechanical innovations with standard IBM punch-card technology. The Mark I was unveiled in the summer of 1944. It looked like an overgrown telephone exchange. Its 51-foot-long bank of switches and relays, installed in a soundproofed room, clattered loudly when running a program. Mark I's first task was to compute complex ballistic tables for the navy's Bureau of Ships, which paid Harvard a rental fee of $800 a month, and for the army's Bureau of Ordnance. It also made top-secret calculations for the Manhattan Project.

The official announcement of the "robot calculator" said its applications would extend beyond pure and applied mathematics. The fields of astronomy, atomic physics, optics, and electronics would also benefit. It was not yet clear that computers descended from Mark I and the University of Pennsylvania's ENIAC would eventually run almost

Howard Aiken (above) designed the Mark I calculator. Built with help from IBM and the navy, Aiken's "mechanical brain" was 51 feet long and 8 feet high. Inside it were 72 adding machines mounted in tiers, 500 miles of wire, 2 million wire connections, 1,464 ten-pole switches, and 3,500 multipole relays with 35,000 contacts.

everything in the postwar world, from household finance to the aiming of nuclear missiles and the exploration of outer space. Mark I was soon outdated by all-relay calculators like Aiken's Mark II, and by third- and fourth-generation machines built with electronic components. The momentum of war-driven computation research would put Harvard's applied mathematicians at the forefront of the nascent computer field when hostilities ended.

WAR-DRIVEN RESEARCH also led to major advances in public health. Two 27-year-old junior faculty members, Robert Woodward and William Doering, synthesized quinine, an achievement that had eluded chemists for almost a century. Researchers at the Medical School and its School of Public Health studied malarial parasites and produced new insecticides. The first successful mosquito repellents were byproducts of Professor Paul Bartlett's chemical warfare research. Other researchers devised new burn and shock therapies, designed an oxygen mask that became standard issue, and brewed vaccines for measles and mumps. One of the Medical School's largest contracts supported the derivation of therapeutic blood components—serum albumin, gamma globulins, blood grouping globulins, thrombin, and fibrins—from plasma collected by the American Red Cross. The work enlisted histologists, chemists, immunologists, internists, and surgeons, and yielded new findings about the properties of proteins. Dr. Edwin J. Cohn, professor of biological chemistry, was in charge.

Even the Arnold Arboretum had a part in the war effort. Elmer D. Merrill, its director, prepared "a simple illustrated manual on edible and poisonous plants of Polynesia and Malaysia for emergency rations for troops in the jungles." Three dozen other Harvard botanists also did war-related research.

With a $65,000 contract from the Chemical Warfare Service, a doctor of veterinary medicine named C.A. Brandly worked on vaccines against poultry diseases. His research was top secret. According to war archivist Sterling Dow, anyone able to break into Brandly's lab "could have seized enough concentrated virus to infect and destroy the entire poultry population of the world."

OF ALL THE RESEARCH done at Harvard, work on poison gases—a top-priority field when the war began—was the least rewarding. "Not only was this work utterly fruitless with respect to actual combat," noted Dow, "and not only was it of little or no value for the researchers personally—these things were true of many kinds of war research—but the gas researchers underwent considerable risk. They dealt with gases so strong that the mere vapor of them, present in minute quantities too small to be noticed by the senses, would raise blisters all over the hands and arms. Another type of gas would cause permanent blindness, yet its presence could not easily be detected. One drop of a certain liquid, if it came in contact with the body, would cause terrific results.

"Some men continued in this work as long as three years and a half. They preserved complete secrecy from their colleagues. Thus they got no glory whatever."

Junior faculty members Robert Woodward (left) and William Doering synthesized quinine, an achievement that had eluded organic chemists for almost a century.

At the Medical School, Dr. Edwin Cohn was the director of a research group that developed therapeutic derivatives of blood plasma.

From 1940 until the war's end, President Conant spent more than half his time in Washington as a government science adviser. In his absence, Harvard's academic affairs were handled by Provost Paul H. Buck (above), professor of history and dean of Arts and Sciences. A. Calvert Smith '14 (top right), secretary to the governing boards and Conant's executive assistant, shared administrative responsibilities with University treasurer William H. Claflin '15 (right).

The Home Front

ALMOST EVERYONE GOT INTO the war effort. Faculty and staff members joined civilian defense teams, monitored foreign-language newspapers, helped out blood drives, rolled bandages, salvaged scrap metal, bought War Bonds, raised Victory Gardens, and served on committees organized by the American Defense-Harvard Group (see page 133). These ranged from "Care of European Children" and "Protection of Monuments" to "Press and Writing," "Women's Committee," and "National Morale."

There was a sense of clear and present danger. Off the Massachusetts coast, U-boats had sunk American ships. Leaving the Divinity School tennis courts one summer afternoon, Sterling Dow and associate professor of English Theodore Spencer, PH.D. '28, found themselves talking about defending the area with machine guns. "The possibility seemed real and near," Dow wrote later. "Machine guns lined the Maine coast and even the back roads. Every strategic corner had its sandbags. Young and old took part in airplane spotting, and there was always a chance, you felt, that during your watch the first German raider would be seen coming down the coast."

ON OCTOBER 5, 1942, 340 members of the class of '43 received their degrees ahead of schedule. It was Harvard's first fall Commencement since 1918. With 1,362 members, that fall's freshman class was the College's largest yet. But the ranks of the class of '46 would be thinned at midyear, when Congress lowered the draft age to 18.

The winter was darkened by saddening events. In November a fire at Boston's Cocoanut Grove night club took 500 lives. Among the victims

Philosophy professor Ralph Barton Perry was the unofficial chief marshal of Harvard's home front. A founder and chairman of the American Defense-Harvard Group, he oversaw the work of its many committees. "I have always felt it to be the duty of a philosopher," he later wrote, "to shed what light he could on public issues and to take his stand."

were eight students from Harvard and Radcliffe, seven alumni, and eight military officers assigned to Harvard training programs. Just after Christmas, Lawrence Lowell was found sitting unconscious by the fireside in his house in Boston. A few days later he died, aged 86. The strong-willed old man, who had left the presidency only ten years earlier, had been a dominant figure at Harvard for almost half a century.

A service for Lowell filled the Memorial Church on January 9. Twenty-four hours later came a valedictory ceremony for 1,400 undergraduates who had been called up for military induction. Most were members of the classes of 1943 and 1944. Massachusetts governor Leverett Saltonstall '14 read the lesson from Deuteronomy; President Conant, his classmate, gave a "wartime sermon" contrasting the demands of war and those of a free society. "Gentlemen," Conant concluded, "with anxious pride Harvard awaits the day of your returning."

Farewell party followed farewell party, Commencement followed Commencement. "Exams in all this excitement were an anticlimax," the 1945 class album recorded, "and grades were the worst in years." Before its time, 1945 was now Harvard's senior class. Having had the novel experience of going to college in the summer of 1942 with 1,000 women of Radcliffe and 1,500 military trainees, most of its members were now trying to cram three upperclass years into the fall and winter terms of 1942-43. Of the 997 men who had matriculated in September 1941, less than a quarter were still in college. Now the end was in sight for them. As a *Lampoon* rhymester put it,

> Our youth is spent, our fling is flung,
> We've drained the brimming cup.
> Our whirl is spun, our song is sung,
> Our college days are up.
> So shoot the sheepskin to us, Jim,
> And show us to the door.
> We've clambered out upon the limb
> And now we're off to war.

Hitler's visage helped motivate the 1942 football squad. Harvard gave up intercollegiate football for the duration in 1943, but competed "informally" against nearby colleges and service teams.

By the summer of 1943, draft calls had shrunk civilian enrollment in the College from 3,300 in peacetime to 1,200. As undergraduates disappeared, so did the old collegiate ways. "Harvard was gone," a yearbook writer recalled, and with it "the old easygoing life, the studying for studying's sake, the interest in intellectual subjects without smirking self-consciousness." Men entering the armed forces envied the ones who remained; most of those left "fighting the battle of Harvard Square" hoped to move on as soon as possible.

Most undergraduate organizations either faded away for a time or surrendered their premises for other uses. The Hasty Pudding became an officers' club, the Signet Society a Red Cross center. The *Harvard Crimson* ceased publishing daily. Under a new nameplate, *Harvard Service News*, it came out semi-weekly. The *Advocate* folded under the pressure of personnel and financial problems; the *Lampoon* put out only a few slim issues. The Crimson Network and the Student Council—now a "postwar council" working on future issues of College life—were among the few student groups that maintained continuity. With the undergraduate body shrinking by fifty students a month, the council

Death of a Titan

A GAINST his doctor's advice, A. Lawrence Lowell had marched at the head of the alumni procession at the 1942 Commencement. The former president, who had once seemed tireless, was 85 and in failing health. Returning home in a state of exhaustion, he had handed his silk hat to his housemaid. "Put it away," said Lowell. "I shall not use it again." In spite of his age and the known state of his health, Lowell's death on January 6, 1943, shook the Harvard community. He and his institution had become virtually synonymous, and his death truly marked the end of an era.

A. Lawrence Lowell cutting the cake at Lowell House on his eighty-fourth birthday, December 13, 1940.

"Born to wealth, his tastes were surprisingly simple, in accord with the principle of plain living and high thinking," wrote the *New York Herald Tribune*. President Conant cited his predecessor's faith "that universities would endure so long as they were essential to a developing civilization. To make Harvard a college and a university which would continue to contribute to human welfare and to give youth a strong, active intellectual life, he devoted 24 years of a selfless career."

President Roosevelt sent a telegram praising his former teacher. "As administrator, as author, and as citizen and publicist, Dr. Lowell served many and varied causes with fidelity and distinction," said FDR. "His long life was singularly well-rounded and complete."

"He inherited much, but he gave away even more," wrote *Alumni Bulletin* editor David McCord. "He chose to be rich by making his wants few, as Emerson said of Thoreau. His approach to everything was direct, and his decisions were unconditional. If he believed in a man, he would back him to the limit. He could, on occasion, be brusque almost to the point of rudeness, but he could also be generous to the point of anonymity. We may not know for a long time the extent of his benefactions to the University to which he dedicated his life....From the modified elective system to the Society of Fellows, his influence on scholarship was enormous, though it was not until the midpoint of his career that undergraduate honors and respectability were remarried after a long period of divorce. Character and ability were the twin criteria by which he chose the new men for his powerful faculty. Most importantly of all, he fought consistently and openly for academic freedom."

had six presidents in the course of a single year. In the spring of 1943 the department of athletics suspended intercollegiate football until the end of the war. For three seasons a varsity-level squad under former assistant coach Henry Lamar played an "informal" schedule against nearby colleges and service teams from Camp Edwards, Melville PT Boat Base, New London Submarine Base, and the Coast Guard and Merchant Marine academies. Intercollegiate competition in other sports was limited to local colleges, schools, and service teams. The soccer and rugby squads played Saturday matches against sides made up of sailors from British warships in Boston harbor.

ADMISSION OF WOMEN to Harvard classrooms constituted another marked change in the life of the College. The position of Radcliffe College had long been anomalous. It had not grown closer to Harvard over the decades; the tradition of separate existence had proved remarkably durable. Coeducation remained a Harvard taboo. Some Radcliffe students, mostly doctoral candidates, were admitted to advanced courses and graduate seminars at Harvard. But most of the thousand "Cliffe-dwellers" did not go to Harvard in any real sense. They attended classes given in duplicate at the Radcliffe Yard by Harvard professors. Few upper-level courses were offered. Radcliffe laboratories and facilities for the arts were inferior to Harvard's. Privileged Radcliffe borrowers were confined to a special reading room in Widener Library—for which Radcliffe was assessed an annual fee.

Though he liked the all-male character of the College, President Conant recognized the need for a more rational and efficient relationship with Radcliffe. When he appointed Professor Paul H. Buck as dean of the Faculty of Arts and Sciences in December 1941, Conant told him to find a solution, subject to the approval of treasurer William Claflin. Working "harmoniously and expeditiously," Buck, Claflin, Radcliffe president Ada Comstock, and Radcliffe treasurer Francis C. Gray '12 agreed on a plan to open certain upper-level courses, "in which the enrollment is small and conditions are otherwise deemed suitable by the faculty," to Radcliffe juniors and seniors. Freshmen and sophomores would still take introductory and lower-level courses in duple sessions.[3] Radcliffe would remit most of its tuition income to Harvard to cover administrative and operating expenses.

Approved by the faculty and the governing boards in the spring of 1943, the new plan took effect with the summer term. "Contrary to certain scareheads in the papers," President Conant gruffly assured Harvard alumni, "this date will not mark the beginning of coeducation here in Cambridge." Despite his obvious apprehension, few alumni protested. "Joint instruction" worked so well that by the fall of 1947, all but Radcliffe freshmen were admitted to Harvard courses, and even this limitation soon disappeared. Conant later conceded that "whatever loyal Harvard men might say, the scheme was by all outsiders properly labeled as 'coeducation.'"[4] In Buck's words, it reflected a "recognition, which I do not think we can properly escape in the future, that Harvard assumes an interest in the education of women."

IN ALL PARTS OF THE UNIVERSITY other than Radcliffe, civilian enrollment was plummeting. The graduate and professional school population fell from 7,627 in 1940 to 1,719 in the summer of 1943. The

A Radcliffe "announcerette" helping out at the Crimson Network's studio. The radio station was on the air five nights a week during the war years. As a service to students learning Morse code, it transmitted dots and dashes after signing off at 11 P.M.

The Radcliffe "Ripples" working out in the fall of 1942. The stroke was Maxine Winokur [Kumin] '46, later a well-known poet. The other rowers, from left, were Regula Simons [Boorstein] '46, Eleanor Merrick [Warner] '46, Ann Lynn '46, Virginia Stodder [Hinton] '46, Helen Welch '46, Barbara Ewing [Ylvisaker] '46, and Eileen McGrath '45.

Law School was hardest hit; civilian enrollment dropped from 1,250 to 72. The Medical School had accelerated its M.D. program and was turning out 140 new doctors every nine months. The Business School no longer admitted regular students; its programs were limited to military administrators and "retreads"—above-draft-age men being retrained for war industry. The School of Design had begun to accept women, and now had 35 in its programs.

Faculty members were putting scholarly expertise to new uses. Donald Menzel, a pioneer of modern astrophysics, taught a course in cryptanalysis, a longstanding hobby. It was given at Radcliffe to classes composed entirely of women. Gordon Allport, chairman of the psychology department, specialized in the study of psychological warfare. He served as a consultant to war information officials in Washington, and lectured to army units on propaganda analysis, pamphleteering, and "the organization of rumor clinics." Experts on human vision, architecture, and aerial photography collaborated in planning one of the first military camouflage courses to be taught at a university.

Certain faculty members took on special administrative duties. Elliott Perkins, professor of history and master of Lowell House, was Harvard's draft counselor. In an office at Little Hall, where Holyoke Center would later stand, he gathered and dispensed information. The post of University counselor for veterans, created in 1944, was filled by Payson Wild, professor of government. Wild also directed a new office set up to assist international students. Returning from intelligence work with the Office of Strategic Services in Egypt and Washington, historian-archaeologist Sterling Dow became Harvard's war archivist.[5]

In addition to his Washington duties at the Office of Scientific Research and Development, President Conant had led a comprehensive investigation of the nation's critical rubber shortage. His committee's report, issued in the fall of 1942, endorsed a full-scale program of synthetic rubber production. By then, as chairman of OSRD's secret S-1 executive committee, Conant was deeply involved in the effort to plan and build an atomic bomb. These responsibilities did not keep him from pushing ahead with academic reforms undertaken before the outbreak of war. The first involved the ticklish question of faculty appointments.

To add objectivity and breadth to the tenure review process, Conant created his first ad hoc committees in the 1942-43 academic year. The aim was to allow the Corporation to weigh the recommendations of a specially convened committee along with those of departmental standing committees. The ad hoc group was to consist of leading scholars from related departments or other universities, along with a member of the department concerned with the promotion. By the end of the war, twelve ad hoc committees had met. In Conant's view, the system had convincingly proved its value. It became standard practice at Harvard and was adopted by many other institutions.

The College curriculum was the focus of another major reform initiative. In the spring of 1943 Conant appointed a dozen senior faculty members to review "the objectives of a general education in a free society." Led by Dean Buck, they met regularly over the next two years. The panel's recommendations were published in a report released in the

Psychologist Gordon Allport became an expert on psychological warfare.

spring of 1945. Known as "the Red Book," it stimulated a nationwide review of educational methods and aims, and provided the blueprint for a program of general education that anchored the College curriculum for almost two decades.

ACADEMIC RITES ATROPHIED as the war went on. The 1943 Commencement exercises and Alumni Association meeting were advanced to May 27 and combined in a single afternoon program. The Latin Oration and other student parts were omitted, as was the alumni procession. The costume parade and confetti battle at the Stadium, traditional romps for reunion classes, had been dropped the previous year. They would not be revived in the postwar era.

Some 4,500 military trainees, including 150 WAVES quartered at Radcliffe, received Commencement commissions. Joseph Grew '02, former ambassador to Japan and president of the Alumni Association, received the single honorary degree of the day. It had been voted the previous year, when Grew was still in Japan awaiting diplomatic exchange.

Great Britain's prime minister had also been tendered an honorary degree, but a military strategy meeting in Canada supervened. Three months later he came to collect it.

Churchillian Oratory

THE RIGHT HONORABLE Winston Leonard Spencer Churchill, prime minister of Britain, arrived on a warm September morning in 1943 to accept the LL.D. he had been offered in May. A special convocation had been hastily organized. Last-minute invitations, marked confidential, stated only that an honorary degree would be conferred on Labor Day, September 6. When copy for the programs went to the University Printing Office, the recipient's name was left blank. But at the end stood the text of "God Save the King."

The P.M. came on a private train from Washington, where he was meeting with President Roosevelt. With him were his wife, Clementine, and their daughter Mary. Stepping off at a siding in Allston, Churchill and his entourage were met by President and Mrs. Conant and Governor Saltonstall. At the president's house, the prime minister donned the scarlet gown of an Oxford doctor of laws, hastily sent up from Princeton for the occasion. He was then escorted to Sanders Theatre. After receiving his degree, he was to address a national radio audience.

A capacity crowd of 1,200 had come for the noon ceremony. As the academic procession filed onstage, Churchill got a prolonged ovation. "When the University Marshal had handed Dr. Churchill his diploma," reported the *Alumni Bulletin*, "applause broke out in new strength. It is doubtful if anything in Sanders ever surpassed it." The citation read: *An historian who has written a glorious page of British history; a statesman and warrior whose tenacity and courage turned back the tide of tyranny in freedom's darkest hour.*

Smiling, bowing, and facing a battery of five microphones, Churchill began his speech. He had written it en route to Boston, finishing at 2:45 A.M. A sly private joke at the start was for Conant's benefit. "I am once

Filet de Cheval à la Harvard

World War II ended the use of the horse in the military, in transportation, and in agriculture. But food shortages in the winter of 1943-44 prompted Aldrich Durant '02, Harvard's business manager, to add horse steak to the Faculty Club's menu. The entrée was priced at 75 cents. "Appearance was decidedly appetizing," noted Sterling Dow, the University's war archivist, "and it made by far the most copious meal obtainable at the club." Harvard's openness to culinary experimentation made headlines, and horse steak remained a club fixture until 1981, when a new chef—a Frenchman—refused to serve it because the meat was frozen, not fresh.

Escorted by President Conant, Winston Churchill leaves Memorial Hall after receiving the degree of doctor of laws and making a national radio address at a special ceremony in September 1943.

The Prime Minister's belated response to Harvard's offer of an honorary degree.

again in academic groves—groves is, I believe, the right word," said Churchill. It was a play on the name of General Leslie Groves, head of the army's secret atomic research program and thus an associate of Conant's.*

As chancellor of Bristol University, Churchill recalled, "in 1941, when the blitz was running hard," he had conferred honorary degrees on John Winant, U.S. ambassador to the Court of St. James's, and President Conant *in absentia*.[6] This led into his principal theme: Anglo-American unity, not just in wartime alliance but in peace. Churchill pictured a postwar world in which territorial power struggles were passé. "I like to think of British and Americans moving about freely over each other's wide estates with hardly a sense of being foreigners to one another," he declared. "Such plans offer better prizes than taking away other people's provinces or land, or grinding them down in exploitation. The empires of the future are the empires of the mind." No future system of world security, said Churchill, "will work soundly or for long without the united effort of the British and American people. If we are together, nothing is impossible. If we are divided, all will fail.[7]

"The price of greatness is responsibility," Churchill went on. "One

*The *New York Herald Tribune* reporter was among the many who did not get the joke. No copy of Churchill's text was distributed, and the Trib's account had the prime minister saying, "I am once again in academic robe—robe is, I believe, the right word."

cannot rise to be in many ways the leading community in the civilized world without being involved in its problems, without being convulsed by its agonies and inspired by its causes. If this has been proved in the past, as it has been, it will become indisputable in the future."

"He was cheered to the echo of the old Theatre," reported the *Alumni Bulletin*. "The power of his words had found a mark. He looked pleased." After the ceremony Churchill appeared on the steps of the Memorial Church and greeted a throng of almost 10,000—cadets and officers in parade formation, students and faculty, staff members, alumni, and guests. "The sun was fainting hot," the *Bulletin* noted. "The veteran of older wars and this war spoke briefly to young men who had yet to go out. Cameras clicked and whirred. He rapped with his cane to drive home a point. He looked fiercely into the sun. He looked down and smiled. In his talk he was optimistic, but he emphasized that the end of the war is not yet around any visible corner. Closing, he made the sign of the V twice with the first two fingers of his right hand. The crowd voiced mighty concurrence, and V's appeared everywhere in answer."

On the Stage of History

How proud we ought to be, young and old, to live in this tremendous, thrilling, formative epoch in the human story, and how fortunate it was for the world that when these great trials came upon it, there was a generation that terror could not conquer and brutal violence could not enslave.

"Let all of us who are here remember that we are on the stage of history, and that…whatever part we have to play, great or small, our conduct is liable to be scrutinized not only by history but by our descendants. Let us rise to the full level of our duty."

–Churchill at Sanders Theatre, September 6, 1943

Building the Bomb

THE ALLIES WERE GAINING. British and American air crews were now bombing German industrial cities around the clock. Allied troops had invaded the Italian mainland, and were pushing northward against stiff resistance from Nazi divisions. In the Pacific, American and Australian divisions were island-hopping toward New Guinea and the Philippines, but their progress was costly and slow. As Churchill had told his hearers at Harvard, the end of the war was not around any visible corner. Only a superweapon seemed likely to hasten it.

President Conant was among those who viewed the war as a life-or-death contest between opposing scientists. The differences in the rival

forces' organizational structure were telling. Beginning in June 1940, the National Defense Research Committee had built an unprecedented alliance of universities, research institutes, industry, and government. It was now an enormously powerful scientific and technological enterprise. The Nazis, in contrast, had dispersed research and development among separate groups that were often at odds. Contemptuous of their universities, they banked on state and industrial laboratories for military research. They had also reduced their manpower base by purging Jewish scientists and professionals in the 1930s, and by drafting university scientists for wartime infantry duty. In 1943 the Allied bombings created an armaments crisis, and drafted scientists who were still alive were discharged and sent back to their labs. By then Allied science had gained a decisive edge.

Hitler had spoken menacingly of secret weapons that would strike his enemies dumb. The weapons he meant were products of rocket science, but Allied leaders supposed that atomic research was proceeding apace in Germany, where nuclear fission had been discovered four years earlier.[8] In the fall of 1939, Albert Einstein and other emigré physicists had advised President Roosevelt that Nazi Germany might be developing a uranium bomb. Roosevelt formed a secret advisory committee on uranium fission, restricting its findings to a small "Top Policy Group" that included the president, Vice President Henry Wallace, Secretary of War Stimson, Army Chief of Staff George Marshall, OSRD chairman Vannevar Bush, and President Conant.

In late 1941 a review committee headed by Arthur Compton, a University of Chicago physicist, informed Roosevelt that "a fission bomb of superlatively destructive power will result from bringing quickly together a sufficient mass of element U-235." On December 6, 1941, Vannevar Bush reorganized the government's uranium research program and asked Conant to handle liaison with the physicists involved. The Japanese bombed Pearl Harbor the next day.

America's entry into World War II cleared the way for a full-scale research and production effort. In May 1942 Conant met with OSRD program chiefs to make cost projections. They estimated construction expenses at $80 million, and annual operating costs at $34 million. The first bombs were to be ready by July 1, 1944. The White House approved the estimates, but Conant thought the delivery date was too distant. "Why nearly two years' delay?" he asked Eger V. Murphree, a Standard Oil of New Jersey executive who headed an advisory panel of top-level engineers. "Why is it not possible to speed up the construction?"

"Doctor," replied Murphree, "you can't spend that much money any faster."

The planning group accepted the costly necessity of pursuing four separate programs to develop a fission bomb, using isotopes of uranium-235 or the newly discovered plutonium-239. The activities of American and British scientists were to be organized by the army. The engineer corps would construct production facilities. The corps' Manhattan District was formed in the summer of 1942 to coordinate the overall project, with Brigadier General Groves in command. Groves reported to a four-man Military Policy Committee that included Bush,

Happy Landing

A major event in nuclear science occurred on December 2, 1942, when an atomic pile at the University of Chicago became critical and produced a self-sustaining chain reaction, releasing nuclear power.

Enrico Fermi, the Italian emigré physicist, and the University of Chicago's Arthur Compton, both Nobel laureates, had built the pile in a chamber under the stands of Stagg Field, the university's football stadium.

Compton called President Conant, who chaired a secret committee monitoring atomic-bomb research, to break the news. Conant received the call at Dumbarton Oaks, Harvard's Center for Hellenic Studies, where he stayed during trips to Washington.

"Our Italian navigator has just landed in the new world," said Compton, mindful of security considerations.

"Were the natives friendly?" asked Conant.

"Everyone landed safe and happy," Compton assured him.

Conant, and high-ranking army and navy officers. He was an efficient, tough, headstrong, often tactless officer of the old school. A West Point graduate who had studied civil engineering at MIT, he had just overseen the construction of the Pentagon, one of the biggest building projects in history. In the fall of 1942 Groves arranged the construction of nuclear reactors at pilot plants in Oak Ridge, Tennessee, and Hanford, Washington. With J. Robert Oppenheimer '26, the physicist who would recruit and run the team charged with designing a nuclear bomb, he also selected a laboratory site at Los Alamos, New Mexico.

J. Robert Oppenheimer as a Harvard student. "Although I liked to work," he recalled, "I spread myself very thin and got away with murder."

OPPENHEIMER WAS 38. The son of a wealthy New York textile importer who had emigrated from Germany at fourteen, he had been a precocious introvert as a child. He had concentrated in mathematics at Harvard, but as one of his roommates put it, "he intellectually looted the place." Oppenheimer took six courses per term, audited four more, and worked in the laboratory of physicist Percy Bridgman. Besides math, physics, and chemistry, he studied Latin, Greek, French literature, and Oriental philosophy, and wrote short stories and poetry.

After junior year he had enough credits to graduate. Because he had skipped two required courses, taking graduate seminars instead, the mathematics department would not recommend him for honors. Offered a *summa* in chemistry or in physics, he opted for chemistry and graduated in June 1925. Charmed by relativity theory, he did atomic research at Cambridge University's Cavendish Laboratory and at Göttingen University, where he received a doctorate in 1927. Oppenheimer then returned to the United States and got a dual appointment at Cal Tech and Berkeley. At Berkeley he worked on the separation of uranium-235 with Ernest O. Lawrence, whose invention of the cyclotron had won him the 1939 Nobel Prize. Aware of Oppenheimer's high standing as a theoretical physicist, Arthur Compton recruited him in the summer of 1942 to direct "Project Y," the government's scientific crash program to design and build an atomic bomb.

As director of Project Y, Oppenheimer assembled "the greatest ad hoc physics department in the world" at Los Alamos. (General Groves, however, groused that "at great expense we gathered on this mesa the largest collection of crackpots ever seen.") The laboratory's full staff eventually numbered 120,000. Their work would alter the course of history and change mankind's relationship to the natural world.

Oppenheimer began work at Los Alamos in March 1943. Two months earlier the army had commandeered a four-year-old Harvard cyclotron (see facing page). It had been shipped in parts to Los Alamos. Robert Wilson, who would later join Harvard's physics department, was overseeing its installation. Also present, on loan from Harvard to Los Alamos, was Professor Kenneth Bainbridge, who had helped design the cyclotron.

Before the war Bainbridge had worked independently on the separation of U-235 isotopes, assisted by chemists George Kistiakowsky and Bright Wilson. In 1940 he was the first scientist hired by the new MIT Radiation Laboratory, the nation's major radar research program. In 1943 he was called to Los Alamos. "Hitler's threats and deeds [gave] me

"We certainly fooled them up there at Harvard"

HARVARD's first cyclotron, built in 1939, joined the army in 1943. In *All in Our Time*, a booklet put out by the *Bulletin of Atomic Scientists*, physicist Robert Wilson later recalled a farcical costumed charade staged to procure the cyclotron for secret atomic research at Los Alamos. Assigned to handle the transaction were an army lawyer and doctor, ostensibly civilians, and Wilson. They pretended to represent a St. Louis medical unit that needed the cyclotron for advanced research. Negotiating for Harvard were Dean Paul Buck and physicist Percy Bridgman, whom Wilson revered.

"Transparently, neither Buck nor Bridgman believed a word," wrote Wilson. Having woven a tangled web of patriotic lies, his colleagues finally fell back on a threat to take the cyclotron by eminent domain.

"'Not a chance,' said Buck. 'Why do you think Harvard has the best law school in the land? Do you doubt for a moment that our lawyers can demolish anything you can do?'

"Evidently, my lawyer friend did not doubt it: he raised his offer by a factor of two. Throughout the afternoon the money offered for the cyclotron was doubled and then redoubled. . . . each doubling of the price was met by an equal escalation of the principles of the Harvardians, principles which involved a Free People living in a Free Society, the American Ethic, Home and Country, the Forces of Darkness against the Forces of Light.

"Finally Bridgman, really a Yankee trader at heart, blurted out, 'Well, if you want it for what you say you want it, you can't have it. But if you want it for why I think you want it, then you can have it.' Clearly, President Conant, who could not have been deeper in the Manhattan Project, had dropped a word.

"From then on my friends, who were also pragmatists, left out all reference to their previous story and concentrated instead on the financial terms of the purchase. Throughout this sticky part, the Harvardians prefaced almost every statement with the phrase, 'Harvard has pledged itself to do everything possible for the war effort, but...'

Then they proceeded, or so it seemed to me, to make the most outrageous financial demands.

"Eventually a price was agreed on....It was ten, maybe twenty times what I considered to be the inherent cost of the miserable cyclotron. But as we walked out of the office, my lawyer friend

Associate professors J. C. Street and Kenneth Bainbridge (standing), and Roger Hickman, assistant director of physical laboratories, engineered Harvard's cyclotron, completed in 1939 at a cost of $55,000. Early in 1943 it was shipped to Los Alamos, never to return.

chuckled to me, 'What a bunch of innocents. I was authorized to go much higher!'"

Wilson met General Leslie Groves, the curmudgeonly head of the Manhattan Project, at a conference at New York's Waldorf Hotel the next day. "'Wilson,' he said in his preemptive fashion. 'We certainly fooled them up there at Harvard yesterday, didn't we?' 'Well,' I responded, 'I'm not too sure that we really fooled them.'

"'Wilson,' barked the general. 'We certainly fooled them up there at Harvard.'

"'Yessir,' I replied smartly to his departing back. After all, I would soon be in the army, too."

Wilson did not recall the amount of the purchase price. Professor Kenneth Bainbridge, one of the cyclotron's builders, remembered it as $250,000. Over the protests of Harvard physicists, the 85-ton cyclotron was packed off to New Mexico. The army paid Harvard a dollar a year for it.[9]

a somewhat bloodthirsty outlook on the war," Bainbridge later recalled. He felt "glad to do what I could to help get there first with atomic weapons." In August he and his nine-year-old son drove west with an eight-foot rowboat tied to the top of their car. Then in his late thirties, Bainbridge would be one of the oldest scientists at Los Alamos.

George Kistiakowsky, Bainbridge's Harvard colleague, was then chief of the National Defense Research Committee's explosives section. Early in 1944 he transferred to Los Alamos to help find a way of using conventional explosives to "implode" fissionable material.

Others who played key parts in the Manhattan Project included Paul Nitze '28, who directed the procurement of graphite, beryllium, zirconium, and other esoteric metals. Chemist Donald Hornig '40 designed detonating devices. Norman Ramsey, a Columbia physicist whose postwar research at Harvard would earn him a Nobel Prize, was associate director of the group that planned the delivery of the bomb. And four Harvard undergraduates were among the college-age scientists who were recruited for junior positions at Los Alamos.

WARTIME ATTRITION HAD shrunk Harvard's physics faculty. Only eight of 44 prewar lecturers and instructors were still on hand in the fall of 1943. Enrollment in freshman physics, a required course for army and navy training programs, had tripled. The teaching staff had been reinforced with retirees, refugees from European universities, and volunteers from the departments of English, economics, history, philosophy, and fine arts. "Even three undergraduates and a woman teacher are instructing," reported the *Alumni Bulletin*.

One prominent refugee teacher was Philipp Frank, who had succeeded Albert Einstein as professor of physics at the University of Prague.[10] Harvard's first woman physics instructor was Charlotte Houermans, a Radcliffe appointee. The three undergraduate teaching

Los Alamos National Laboratory in 1944: a town on the frontier of science.

fellows, all juniors, were Kenneth Case, Frederic de Hoffmann, and Roy Glauber. Their stints as instructors were short-lived. Enlisted by the National Roster of Scientific Personnel for an undisclosed research project, they left for New Mexico after Christmas vacation. Riding the Super Chief through the Midwest, de Hoffmann was puzzled when a friendly conductor said, "So you're joining the project!" Said Case, nonchalantly, "You really don't know that we're going to join the atomic bomb project?"

In Los Alamos, Case and de Hoffmann met Glauber and Theodore Hall, an eighteen-year-old Harvard senior. When they reported in, Case later recalled, "a young kid came out of the inner office and said hi." They asked the receptionist who the kid was. "J. Robert Oppenheimer," they were told.

The senior scientists were trying to induce a supercritical mass of fissionable material in a bomb. The junior scientists did lots of number-crunching. Glauber and Case were assigned to Hans Bethe's theory group. Glauber did neutron diffusion calculations on a bulky desktop machine; Case projected destructive yields. In an experimental group led by Bruno Rossi, later a professor at MIT, Hall helped measure reaction cross-sections. De Hoffmann worked with the irrepressible Richard Feynman, a future Nobel laureate, on theoretical fluctuations of chain reactions. After the war de Hoffmann would make calculations that were of major importance to Edward Teller's development of the hydrogen bomb.

The young physicists loved working at Los Alamos. "It was a kind of scientific utopia," recalled Glauber, later Harvard's Mallinckrodt professor of physics. "An open society of the best minds available, freely exchanging ideas without consideration of age, academic rank, or previous achievement." To de Hoffmann, it was "not only a project to end a world war, it was also the beginning of a new technological era." A dozen years later, when he founded a high-technology enterprise that became the General Atomic Division of General Dynamics, de Hoffmann modeled it on Los Alamos.

Hall received his Harvard S.B. *in absentia* in 1944. Case and de Hoffmann received theirs in June 1945, also *in absentia*. Glauber, who was short a few credits, returned to Harvard in 1946. Having headed a staff at Los Alamos, he was startled to find that he still had to pass a swimming test in order to graduate.

"I Know Now Why I Have Been Fighting"

SOME 23,000 HARVARD MEN AND WOMEN were under arms by the beginning of 1944. A section called "Military Intelligence" appeared in each biweekly issue of the *Alumni Bulletin*. It included the names, ranks, and postings of alumni in service, lists of those missing in action or captured, and obituaries. War-related news also dominated the alumni notes pages. An item in the class of 1940 notes began, "The newspapers carried last month an exciting story from the South Pacific: Lieutenant (jg) John F. Kennedy—one of the sons of Joseph P. Kennedy '12, former Ambassador to Great Britain—and twelve of his

On June 29, 1944, more than 5,000 navy and army officer trainees, including a contingent of Radcliffe WAVES, were sworn into the service at Harvard's 293d Commencement. Only nineteen graduating seniors, the smallest number since 1753, received degrees in regular course.

men were thrown into a blazing sea on the morning of August 2, after a Japanese destroyer sliced their PT boat in half. Two of the men were lost and Kennedy personally rescued two others."

First-hand accounts of such landmark events as the taking of Guadalcanal, the defeat of the Nazis' Afrika Korps, and the invasion of Normandy appeared in a section titled "Service Letters." "I have just been present at the reading of the script of the big show on D-Day," began a letter from air force lieutenant Maurice Jack Strauss '38, recounting his unit's briefing on the eve of the Normandy invasion. "At this writing it is the most thrilling experience of my life," wrote Strauss. His squadron towed the first troop-carrying gliders into France in the small hours of June 6, 1944.

Lieutenant Kennedy '40, hero of a tale from the South Pacific.

Harvard resonated to the excitement of the Allies' successful landing. "The strains of the National Anthem and the staccato of early bulletins, flashed from the Cambridge alert center, were electric in more ways than one," noted the *Bulletin*. A week later the Nazis' first V-1 "buzz bombs" fell on London, but by the end of June a million Allied troops were in Normandy and the Red Army was driving hard from the east. In late August German *Wehrmacht* units began to fall back toward the Rhine. When American troops rolled through Paris, they were escorted by a military police battalion commanded by Major David Sigourney '15, the old grad who had chided the "boys of 1940" at the Harvard Class Day exercises four years earlier.

Harvard's civilian enrollment, University-wide, had hit a low of 1,300 in 1943-44. With the opening of a new term on November 1, 1944, it rose to 1,800. Those enrolling included 173 returning veterans, registered in thirteen departments of the University. The office of the University counselor for veterans was now receiving a hundred letters a day from servicemen trying to plan their educational futures.

November brought the nation's first wartime presidential election since 1864. Franklin Roosevelt looked frail, gaunt, and much older than his 62 years, but he was still an exuberant and effective campaigner. Seeking an unprecedented fourth term, with a new running mate, Senator Harry Truman of Missouri, he soundly defeated his Republican challenger, New York Governor Thomas Dewey.

THE PRESIDENT'S HAND had been strengthened in late October, when General Douglas MacArthur's troops invaded the Philippines and U.S. ships and planes won the battle of Leyte Gulf. But stiff German resistance and bad weather slowed the Allied advance in Europe. The Nazis' surprise counterattack in the Ardennes Forest in mid-December brought on some of the fiercest fighting of the war, climaxed by the Battle of the Bulge. The day after Christmas, General George Patton's Third Army rescued encircled troops in the town of Bastogne. Allied forces regrouped, and the Germans drew back.

As American armies pushed eastward, accounts in "Service Letters" took on tones of shock and outrage. "I know now why I have been fighting and I would do it all over again if the same conditions arose,"

Wayne Johnson Jr. '44 negotiating the Parris Island obstacle course as a marine trainee at Quantico, Virginia. A varsity fullback for two years, Johnson also played football at Yale while assigned to a V-12 unit there in 1943. He thus became the only man to win his letter at both Harvard and Yale.

wrote Herbert Stanton '46, a private in the 82nd Airborne Signal Company. "Yesterday I went through a concentration camp that we had just captured. [The prisoners] were living in their own filth, most of them too weak to move out of it. They are starved beyond all recognition, some nothing but bones with waists so thin you could encircle them with your hands. They are living next to dead inmates all over the place. In some buildings the bodies are piled ten high in great areas. . . . All over the camp is the horrible smell of filth and the sickening stench of death."

"When I think of Weimar, I shall not remember Goethe or apple blossoms," Third Army lieutenant Chris Petrow '40 wrote his mother, whose parents were German. "I shall remember only the concentration camp at Buchenwald, just outside the city. Here some 50,000 political prisoners and slave laborers were interned: here they were starved, beaten, tortured, and murdered. . . . I saw the crematory where the victims were burned; the ovens were crammed with charred skulls and an occasional only partly burned corpse. I saw the slaughter house, where men were hung on hooks like sides of beef and then clubbed to death by S.S. men; you could actually see where their nails had clawed the wall in an ecstasy of fear and agony. Most pitiful of all, I saw the quarters where 21,000 men were still living (the Germans had time to evacuate only 29,000 before we arrived). They were living in conditions which no German farmer would tolerate in his pigsty. They lived, 1,600 to a room, in rooms about the size of the common room at Kirkland House. ...When they died, their clothes and the gold from their teeth were salvaged and they were burned in the crematory. The German government offered the ashes of the victim to his family for the price of 1,000 marks. In addition to the normal deaths by starvation and disease, certain of the inmates were selected from time to time for service as human guinea pigs. . . . My personal conviction is that the German nation should be wiped off the face of the earth. They are all as guilty as sin. And, after the war, if I ever hear anyone try to tell me that the Germans are a clean, industrious, good-hearted people who have been persecuted by the rest of the world, I shall slap his face. . . ."

"The average G.I. wants to kill all Germans," wrote Dr. Lawrence Kubie '16, a psychiatrist assigned by the government to report on trauma induced by the stresses of combat. "The beauty of the land increases his rage at the people."

AMERICAN FORCES WERE REACHING the Elbe River on April 12, 1945, when the world was stunned by the news that President Roosevelt had suffered a fatal stroke.

He had gone to his winter home in Warm Springs, Georgia, for a fortnight's rest before traveling to a San Francisco conference inaugurating the United Nations. Before luncheon on the 12th the president was reading the day's mail while having his portrait painted. He was wearing a double-breasted suit and a Harvard tie; the portraitist thought his color was better. Suddenly he collapsed, clasping his head and saying he had "a terrific pain." Physicians' attempts to revive him were unavailing. Within two hours he was dead of a cerebral hemorrhage. The news

Dumbarton Oaks, Harvard's research center in Washington, D.C., was the site of international talks aimed at planning a global peacekeeping organization to succeed the League of Nations. Convened by Secretary of State Cordell Hull in the late summer of 1944, the six-week conference involved four "major powers"–the United States, Great Britain, the Soviet Union, and China–and laid the groundwork for the United Nations.

Dumbarton Oaks, a Georgetown mansion built in 1800, included a research library, museum, and elaborate gardens. It was given to Harvard in 1940 by Robert Woods Bliss '00 and his wife, Mildred, as a center for Byzantine and medieval studies. President Conant, who had made Dumbarton Oaks a base for his wartime work in Washington, offered the mansion as a site for the four-power conference. Above: the opening meeting in the large music room, August 21, 1944.

Monumental Service

FACULTY MEMBERS played key parts in the quest to salvage, preserve, and return looted works of art hidden in occupied Europe and Japan.

Paul Sachs, professor of fine arts, helped organize the hunt for looted works of art.

Paul Sachs, professor of fine arts and associate director of the Fogg Art Museum, was one of the art historians and archaeologists named by President Roosevelt to an advisory commission on the protection of artistic and historic monuments in war areas. At Sachs's suggestion, the American Defense-Harvard Group prepared lists of important buildings, libraries, and collections in various theaters of war. These lists were later elaborated into cultural atlases and included in civil affairs handbooks distributed by the War Department.

Sachs also helped recruit monuments officers from civilian sources and from the ranks of those already in service. Among them were classicist Mason Hammond '25, later Pope professor of the Latin language, and Norman Newton, a professor at the School of Design. Both tracked down art works in Italy. Charles Kuhn, curator of the Germanic Museum, was deputy adviser on monuments, fine arts, and archives in France and Germany. George Stout, A.M. '29, head conservator at the Fogg Museum, had a major role in preserving art works in northwest Europe and later moved on to Japan, where he was joined by Langdon Warner '03, professor of history.

James Plaut '33, peacetime director of Boston's Institute of Contemporary Art, became a monuments officer when he was detached from his naval unit and assigned to the Office of Strategic Services. Plaut was a field operative for "Project Orion" (so named because "we were hunters"). In the spring of 1945, a large cache of art works was found in a salt mine near the Austrian village of Alt Ausee, east of Salzburg. German S.S. security troops had been ordered to blow up the mine if Allied forces approached, but they fled to the hills instead.

"When I entered, it was truly a Hollywood scenario," Plaut recalled. "You walked through a dark passage and suddenly you were in a blinding light. In huge caves, on different levels, the Germans with their great sense of order had put in racks for all the paintings and sculpture. It looked like the storage in a major museum. There were things like the Michelangelo from Bruges on its side, the Van Eyck altarpiece, and thousands of works of art that had been looted from France, Italy, Belgium, and Holland.

"I've often been asked what happened to the art that had been looted from Eastern countries," added Plaut. "We could do nothing about it at the time, because it was in the Russian zone. Most of what disappeared into the Eastern bloc was never found. I've also been asked what proportion of works we were able to save. It came out to about 80 percent of the great art that had been taken from Western Europe."

---

went out by radio just before six. It flashed around the world almost instantaneously, producing shock and consternation everywhere. In London the hour was midnight; the British Broadcasting Company's announcement called it "the darkest night of the war."

"Because this war is a greater war than any war that has gone before it," said the *New York Times,* "because the central issue of the war has been the very life or death of the civilization we have built, Franklin D. Roosevelt will take the honored role in history that belongs to the chief author of the democratic coalition. Certainly in the eyes of the people of the free world beyond our shores no more towering figure has come upon the American scene in the times of men now living." Members of

Questionnaires sent out by the University's War Records Office requested information about the military activities of Harvard alumni. The form at right, filled out in President Roosevelt's own hand, gave his peacetime occupation as "lawyer," his military rank as "Commander-in-Chief of the Army and Navy," and his rank at the time of enlistment as "Same."

Please fill out this form, using typewriter or ink if possible, and return it promptly to Harvard War Records Office, 3d Floor, Lehman Hall, Cambridge, Mass.

FEB 8 1943

HARVARD MEN IN WAR SERVICE

Franklin Delano Roosevelt
Washington
D. C.

Here are your name, mailing address, and class or graduate school affiliation as recorded in our files. Please note any corrections on the lines immediately below.

04
A.B. 04 (03)

Permanent Address (No. and Street)...Hyde Park, Dutchess County
(City or Town)...............................(State)...New York
Peace-time occupation...Lawyer
Branch of military service (state corps, regiment, company or other unit):
Commander in Chief of the Army and Navy

Regularly organized civilian war activity or war industry (give pertinent details):
....

Date and place of enlistment or entry into military service...Since 1933

Rank on enrollment...Same...............................Official No...............
Where stationed in this country (give dates of transfer)...
Washington D. C.

If assigned to foreign duty, give such details as are permissible under censorship regulations:
Occasional

Promotions, decorations, citations, etc. (include dates)...............................

Casualties (include dates and places)...............................

Name and address of nearest friend or relative not in service:
Wife

159

Artist Elizabeth Shoumatoff was at work on this portrait of Franklin Roosevelt when the president suffered his fatal stroke.

the Harvard community filled the Memorial Church to mourn the fallen president. Willard Sperry, dean of the Divinity School, led the service. He spoke first of the tragic timing of Roosevelt's death. "He died too soon," said Dean Sperry. "He had earned the right to see victory on land and sea and in the air. He should have seen it for himself; his eyes should have beheld it, and not another. He will live in the memory of generations as one with whom his own time had dealt, if not unfairly, then austerely. He is a casualty of these costly years of war.

"He was a member of this beloved community of memory and hope," Sperry continued. "We have lost one of our own members. It would be presumptuous of us to say that elsewhere there is no sorrow like unto our sorrow. But our sorrow is touched with a humble and proper pride that this society was one of the shaping forces which fitted him for his duty and his destiny."

"Mr. Roosevelt, as he grew older, grew into younger hearts," wrote *Bulletin* editor David McCord in an editorial tribute. "He was a symbol, a cause, a reason, and an anvil of strength to youth. He was the only President this fighting generation had ever consciously known. It knew him well. He foresaw; and he acted as none but the prescient can act. That is something which youth is supremely fitted to understand. 'He belonged to this day,' as Dean Sperry so wisely said. 'He spoke the language of the hour and needed no interpreter.'

"He acted when few of us wanted to act. A master of timing—another attribute of youth—he took the steps just ahead of us, and on the schedule of divine chance. He hated war, as the generation which is fighting it hates it. And he loved and respected that generation which has made and is making the history historians now can never figure without his name."

WITHIN A FORTNIGHT, American and Russian troops made contact at the Elbe River and encircled Berlin. Italian partisans murdered the fleeing Benito Mussolini and his mistress. Hitler took his own life. On May 4, German forces began to surrender. Four days later President Harry Truman and Prime Minister Churchill announced to the world the victory of the Allies in Europe.

Harvard's noon classes were canceled and a crowd of about 12,000 gathered in the Tercentenary Theatre for a fifteen-minute service of remembrance and thanksgiving, conducted from the steps of the Memorial Church. On the flagstaffs of University Hall, the hammer and sickle of the Soviet flag stirred in the light breeze alongside the Union Jack and the Stars and Stripes. They flew at half-mast in memory of the late president of the United States.

Not since the Tercentenary of 1936 had so large an assembly gathered in the great open quadrangle. "The weather was easy and propitious," the *Alumni Bulletin* recorded, "and the audience stood bareheaded under the elms, along the walks, and across the grass . . . on seeded ground, and up the hospitable steps of Widener." Dean Sperry and Henry Bradford Washburn (A.B. 1891), vice-chairman of the University's board of preachers, conducted the service. "The Lord is great and greatly to be praised; he is to be feared above all gods," Dean Sperry began. "He cometh to judge the earth: he shall judge the world with righteousness, and the people with his truth. He maketh wars to cease unto the end of the earth."

Led by the University Choir, robed in black and red gowns, the assembly sang "Now thank we all our God, with heart and hands and voices." Dean Sperry read from the prophecy of Isaiah: "And they shall build the old wastes, they shall raise up the former desolations, and they shall repair the waste cities, the desolations of many generations." After

A naval training unit marching past University Hall on the way to a service of prayer and thanksgiving on V-E Day. The flags of three Allied powers were at half-mast in honor of the late President Roosevelt.

J. Robert Oppenheimer and General Leslie Groves, leaders of the Manhattan Project, at Ground Zero of the first atomic bomb test site, near Alamogordo, New Mexico.

prayers of remembrance and thanksgiving, all joined in singing the national anthem.

"Once again the University took up its tasks," observed the *Bulletin.* That afternoon the Russian bells in the Lowell House tower rang out in a carillon of victory. And for a few hours that evening, for the first time since the start of the war, the bell tower was bathed in light.

"Now We Are All Sons of Bitches"

IN LATE APRIL, two weeks after Roosevelt's death, President Truman received his first briefing on the Manhattan Project. The program was a year behind schedule, and was costing $1 billion a year, about thirty times more than initially projected. Physicists were still grappling with the separation of plutonium. Only a test explosion would show whether the bomb would work. Los Alamos hoped to have enough plutonium-239 for a test in July. If it succeeded, uranium and plutonium bombs could be ready for use against Japan in August.

The test, code-named "Trinity," was set for July 16, in New Mexico's desolate Jornada del Muerto Valley—an eerily apt name. Kenneth Bainbridge, who would direct the test, chose the site. George Kistiakowsky and Donald Hornig had developed the detonating device. Special seismographs designed by L. Don Leet, PH.D. '30, associate professor of geology, would gauge the test bomb's reverberations. President Conant traveled by train to witness the test.

In the tense night hours before the test, Bainbridge and Kistiakowsky stood guard at the top of the tower where the bomb was mounted. Hornig guarded and armed "the gadget." Bainbridge unlocked master switches at 0509. A twenty-minute countdown began. At base camp, twenty miles from Ground Zero, Conant waited with Vannevar Bush and General Groves. At minus two minutes he lay face down on a tarpaulin, his feet toward the shot tower. At 052945 an intense light filled the sky. Then came a thundering crash, earth tremors, and a wave of dry heat. Conant rolled over to watch the glaring light coalesce into a fireball. "Though for three years we had been told by the physicists about the ball of fire," he later wrote, "I had expected only a lightning flash on the horizon. To my stupefaction, it was more like a long-lasting white light from a giant star shell directly overhead." As a dark mushroom cloud enveloped the star shell, the men shook hands.

The euphoria faded fast. "I had gooseflesh all over me when I realized what this meant for the future of humanity," the Columbia physicist I.I. Rabi wrote later. "It's a terrible thing we made," said Robert Wilson, who had helped get the Harvard cyclotron to Los Alamos. As the mushroom cloud rose, Bainbridge turned to Oppenheimer and said, "Now we are all sons of bitches."

THE WAR'S END WAS NEAR. On July 21, a navy captain who was fluent in Japanese broadcast a message to Japan's home islands: make peace or risk total destruction. For more than six months, B-29s of the 20th Air Force had been razing Japanese cities, dropping magnesium and napalm bombs designed by Louis Fieser at Harvard's Gibbs Laboratory. In March a force of 334 B-29s had flown the most destructive bombing mission in history, scattering thousands of incendiaries over Tokyo on a windy night. The raid left some 97,000 dead, 125,000 wounded, and 1,200,000 homeless. In May, 800 B-29s burned a two-mile-wide, 21-mile-long swath from Yokohama to Tokyo. Constant air attacks were reducing Nagoya, Osaka, Kobe, and smaller cities.

Lieutenant colonel Crocker Snow '26 had been on some of those raids as a pilot and combat intelligence officer with the 21st Bomber Command, stationed on Saipan. In July he was assigned to assist General T.F. Farrell, deputy to General Groves, who had been sent to Tinian Island to direct a psychological warfare program linked to "a top secret weapon." His unit's B-29s were to help flood Japan with leaflets stressing the certainty of defeat and outlining surrender terms.

"I didn't know until after the event that two bombs had been delivered to Tinian, one by ship on July 26, the other by B-29 on August 2," Snow later recalled. "Each bomb weighed about 10,000 pounds. The first, code-named 'Little Boy,' was cylindrical, with the nuclear core at one end and a large charge of TNT at the other. The second, called 'Fat

A leaflet dropped from a B-29 near war's end is captioned "The aftermath of bombings is hell." Text on the reverse side reads in part, "Every day of added resistance will bring greater terror to you. Bombs will blast great holes in your cities." This leaflet is from the scrapbook of retired air force colonel Crocker Snow '26.

爆彈後の生地獄

Man,' was shaped like a pumpkin, with tons of TNT surrounding a small core of plutonium."

Early in August, Snow's unit began dropping leaflets with a message from President Truman. "We will not deviate from [the stated surrender terms]," it read. "There are no alternatives. We shall accept no delay." At 8:15 on the morning of August 6, a B-29 named *Enola Gay* released "Little Boy" over Hiroshima, on the main island of Honshu. The bomb burst at an altitude of 1,890 feet, obliterating almost half the city. Japanese estimates put the number of dead at 71,400, with almost as many injured. The USSR declared war on Japan the next day.

After the Hiroshima strike Snow's unit dropped more leaflets over densely populated areas of Tokyo and Nagoya. "Evacuate your cities now!" the text began, adding, "Because of your leaders' refusal to accept the surrender declaration that would honorably end this useless war, we have employed our atomic bomb."

A second atomic strike was planned for the arsenal city of Kokura on August 11. An unfavorable weather forecast necessitated an earlier date. The Manhattan Project's delivery expert, Norman Ramsey, huddled with navy captain William Parsons, an ordnance man who had headed the engineering division at Los Alamos and had armed "Little Boy" on *Enola Gay's* flight to Hiroshima. They made plans to prepare "Fat Man"—named in honor of Winston Churchill—for use on August 9. In the meantime B-29s continued their raids on Japan's home islands.

The B-29s assigned to the Kokura strike left Tinian before dawn. On the instrument plane was William L. Laurence '12, science editor of the *New York Times,* the only journalist authorized to cover the Manhattan Project from start to finish. "Does anyone feel any pity for the poor devils about to die?" Laurence would write. "Not when one thinks of Pearl Harbor and the Death March on Bataan."

Kokura, on the north coast of Kyushu, was obscured by smoke from an incendiary attack on Yawata, to the west. After three wary passes the B-29s flew on to the secondary target, Nagasaki. "Fat Man" fell at 11:01 A.M., exploding at 1,540 feet with a searing blue-white flash. Casualties were later estimated at 40,000 dead and 60,000 injured. The delivery plane, short of fuel, was routed to Okinawa, where it made an emergency landing with seven gallons of gasoline left in its tanks.

Japan sued for peace the next day, asking that Emperor Hirohito be allowed to retain his throne. Heeding the advice of Undersecretary of State Joseph Grew '02, former ambassador to Japan, and other counselors, President Truman agreed, with the understanding that Hirohito would be subject to the authority of the supreme commander of the Allied forces in the Pacific. Shortly after 7 P.M. on August 14, Truman announced to the world that the war was over. In Los Alamos, George Kistiakowsky celebrated by igniting a pile of surplus explosives.

SIX YEARS AND TWO DAYS after the German invasion of Poland, a formal ceremony aboard the battleship *Missouri* officially ended the Second World War. The date was September 2, 1945, a Sunday. Since early morning, Tokyo Bay had been churning with launches and destroyers ferrying dignitaries and journalists to the *Missouri,* flagship of

The second atomic bomb exploding over the Japanese city of Nagasaki on the morning of August 9, 1945.

Admiral William Halsey's Third Fleet. From his office above the ship's veranda deck, Lieutenant Commander John Marshall, M.B.A. '28, observed the arrivals. General Douglas MacArthur, supreme commander of Allied forces in the Pacific, was piped aboard at 0843. Japan's nine representatives came up the gangway minutes later. Proceedings started at 0908.

"We are gathered here," MacArthur began, "to conclude a solemn agreement by which peace may be restored." Straining to hear, Marshall was struck by the drama of the moment. "I could see that the general was much moved," he wrote afterward. "His hands were shaking visibly and his whole body was tense. As he read he made small but forceful gestures with his hands to emphasize his words. He spoke very briefly." Delegates from Japan and ten Allied powers signed the articles of surrender. As the formalities ended, an overflight of 400 B-29s and 1,500 carrier aircraft roared across the sky.

In the United States it was still the previous day. Harvard was not yet in session. President Conant had gone to his summer retreat in Randolph, New Hampshire, for a month of fresh air and exercise. Returning to work after Labor Day, he would find a stack of letters and telegrams. Most were expressions of approval and thanks. "Congratulations on the bomb!" began a three-page letter from Grenville Clark, a member of the Harvard Corporation. But some of the mail was sternly critical. "This bomb destroys the last shred of security in an already insecure world," wrote one correspondent. Another tasked Conant with complicity in "the greatest scientific crime in history."

B-29s and carrier aircraft overfly the U.S.S. *Missouri* in Tokyo Bay following the signing of articles of surrender on September 2, 1945.

"The Radiance of Their Deeds"

ON DECEMBER 7, 1945, Harvard commemorated its war dead at an afternoon service in the Memorial Church. Engraved in the church's memorial chamber were the names of the 373 Harvard men who had died in the first world war. The names of 697 who died in the second would later be placed on the church's south wall. Each name had its wrenching story.

The first deaths had occurred before Pearl Harbor. John Stanley Parker '13, lieutenant in the Royal Navy Volunteer Reserve, had been killed in November 1941 when H.M.S. *Broadwater* was torpedoed off Iceland. U.S. Navy captain Sherwood Picking, a former professor of naval science and tactics, had died in an R.A.F. crash in England the same month. Three members of the class of 1941 were killed in the first weeks of the war. One was Ensign Philip Gazecki, lost with the *Arizona* on December 7. Marine Corps captain and bomber pilot Willard Reed Jr. '30, a former airline pilot, had been the first Harvard aviator to die. His plane went down in the Dutch East Indies early in 1942.

The College class of 1942 lost 38 members to the war. The classes of '41 and '46 both lost 37. The Law School lost 79 alumni, the Business School 78, the schools of medicine, public health, and dentistry 25. The commander-in-chief of the armed forces was not the only Roosevelt to die in service. Brigadier General Theodore Roosevelt Jr. '09 died of a heart attack in Normandy in July 1944. He had led infantry units in

North Africa and Sicily, and was said to be the most decorated officer of the war. Major Kermit Roosevelt '12 had died in Alaska in 1943. Sons of Theodore Roosevelt, both were World War I veterans. A midair explosion killed Joseph P. Kennedy Jr. '38, older brother of the future president, in August 1944. Marine platoon sergeant Peter Saltonstall '43, one of three sons of Massachusetts governor Leverett Saltonstall, was killed in action on Guam that same month. Thomas Lamont III '46, whose father and grandfather had been Harvard Overseers, died when the submarine *Snook* was lost in Japanese waters in May 1945.

Don Richards '45, a three-letter athlete as a sophomore, had starred on the 1942 football team and had been touted as a future all-American. In August 1944 he was killed in France. In the spring of 1944 a photograph in the *Bulletin* showed Lieutenant Dana Reed '43, one of the magazine's former undergraduate columnists, with members of his flight crew. In November Reed's B-24 was lost over Italy in bad weather. Lieutenant commander Cedric Coleman, s.m. '39, and Lieutenant Robert Whitman '38, officers on the cruiser *Indianapolis*, died July 30, 1945, when their unescorted ship was torpedoed en route from Guam to the Philippines. Four days earlier the *Indianapolis* had delivered the main components of "Little Boy" to Tinian Island.

The last Harvard man to be killed while a state of war still existed was Captain James O. Clark, ll.b. '42, an air force intelligence officer. On a mission to drop supplies to prisoners of war in a Japanese camp, Clark's plane crashed on Guam on September 2, 1945.

"THEY GAVE THEIR LIVES," said President Conant at the commemorative service, "in a close and bitter struggle between two worlds: one groping towards a goal of light, the other committed to a reign of evil. The victory was decisive, but the margin was slight. . . .

"Across the street stands a reminder of the appalling slaughter of the Civil War; this church is a monument to those who died during the first World War; today we figuratively lay the cornerstone of yet another war memorial. I doubt if there will be a fourth in Harvard history. If the peace is broken once again by a major war, our cultural pattern will be warped and seared and twisted. If the wave of destruction comes and passes, it is doubtful if the continuity of our three-century-old tradition could be maintained with vigor.

"A man's life is surely measured by the quality of his spirit; not by the length in years. Many of those whose memory we salute today so lived that the impress of their integrity and courage left a lasting mark. Their surviving comrades and even their comrades' children's children will to some degree reflect the radiance of their deeds. . . . The victory they helped win has given freedom another chance. Those who must make the most of the opportunity they retrieved will find an inspiration in their example."

Opposite: Harvard's World War II roll of honor was unveiled at a service on Armistice Day, 1951. Though some had hoped that a new student center might be built as a memorial to the dead, the erection of tablets in the Memorial Church did not fan the kind of controversy that arose after World War I.

The names of the 697 alumni, students, and faculty members who gave their lives in the war were inscribed on panels of cream-colored Champville marble from France. They covered half the south wall of the church. The carving of 13,651 letters on the panels took twenty weeks; one carver spent seven weeks preparing and coloring the shields identifying the various Harvard schools. Henry Shepley '10, of the Boston architectural firm of Coolidge, Shepley, Bulfinch and Abbott, designed the tablets.

Years later, smaller tablets on the church's north wall would memorialize the seventeen Harvard men who died in the Korean War and nineteen who died in the Vietnam War.

Amazing Growth

True learning cannot go on in a vacuum; it is in constant interplay
with society . . .

—Nathan M. Pusey, *The Age of the Scholar* (1955)

AVING MASTERED THE ARTS of war, the University began relearning the ways of peace. But the temporary militarization of academic life affected Harvard in lasting ways. The wartime alliance of universities, government, and industry was perpetuated by Cold War tensions, assuring extensive funding for basic research. Continued public and private support enabled Harvard and other major universities to build new facilities, launch new programs, and attract leading scholars from around the world. It also affected the nature of scholarly inquiry—sometimes broadening the professorial role into that of consultant, entrepreneur, or even hireling, and positioning the university as a provider of experts and expertise to a post-industrial society that was increasingly complex, specialized, urban, and technological. "Conant's Arsenal" thus became an arsenal of ideas, skills, information, and advice for the nation and the Free World.

War research brought able young scholars to the fore and helped start them on productive careers. Technology developed for military uses—most conspicuously the high-speed computational machines—revolutionized fields of study. Collaborative

September 1946: A freshman class of record size–about 2,000 men–arrives to register. The presence of thousands of veterans increased total University enrollment more than threefold over the previous year. "It is the veteran's University," observed the *Alumni Bulletin*, "bulging at the doors and windows."

research, initially organized as a means to speed up wartime projects, was established as an effective way to do science. Instructional methods devised for accelerated language training, and for intensive courses in other subjects, became standard in many departments. The multidisciplinary approach and team-teaching format used to train officers at the School for Overseas Administration were widely emulated, particularly in graduate and professional education. At the College level, the war helped clear the way for a sweeping revision of educational policy based on *The Report of a Committee on the Objectives of a General Education in a Free Society*, known as "the Red Book." Published in the summer of 1945, it stimulated a national re-evaluation of educational goals and methods.

European exiles who had found places at Harvard became prominent in American education. In future years, Harvard's schools would think globally when recruiting faculty members. The number of students from abroad would grow. The 3,600 men and women who registered for College and graduate courses in September 1945 included a record 327 from other countries. Over the next half-century that number would increase ninefold. Scores of new courses, programs, and chairs would be created in international relations, comparative government and religion, area studies, economics, and languages.

In the international arena, global warfare gave way to global competition between rival political and economic systems. President Conant had viewed World War II as a death struggle between the scientific establishments of democratic and fascist nations. In the postwar paradigm, democracy and communism would contest for the "minds of men." Most American educators believed that by training a new generation for postwar responsibilities, they could help assure the triumph of democracy. American legislators shared this assumption, and over the next two decades they provided unprecedented support to the nation's educational institutions.

Cold War tensions also fostered a resurgence of the isolationism and anti-intellectualism that had gripped the nation in the interwar era. Senator Joseph McCarthy and other vigilante legislators attacked universities as breeding grounds of communist subversion. Higher education rode out the storm and soon found itself in an era of amazing growth. In the early 1960s, the administration of President John F. Kennedy '40 helped bring the postwar fortunes of American universities to a peak. But American intervention in a civil war in Vietnam brought the golden age to a jolting end.

The Veterans Encamp

NO ASPECT OF POSTWAR CHANGE seemed more radical or portentous than the opening of Harvard classrooms to thousands of returning servicemen from a wide range of backgrounds. An advance guard of five hundred veterans, their tuition fees and other expenses paid by the 1944 "G.I. Bill of Rights," were among the 3,600 registrants in September 1945. Most of the faculty members who were still in service or on loan to government agencies returned to their

OFFICIAL REGISTER
OF HARVARD UNIVERSITY
VOLUME XLII ❖ NUMBER 6
MARCH 27 1945

WHAT ABOUT HARVARD?

VE RI
TAS

"What About Harvard?"
Postwar programs for veterans were described in an 88-page booklet prepared by University officials in the spring of 1945. More than 6,000 copies were mailed to Harvard men on military leave of absence, and additional thousands to other veterans who sought information about the University. The pamphlet noted that Harvard planned to adopt a three-term calendar and "a more flexible system of admission" to accommodate men resuming their educations.

William A. Dwiggins, a celebrated typographer, designed the booklet.

classrooms that fall. As the British emigré poet W. H. Auden would saucily put it in the 1946 Harvard Phi Beta Kappa poem, "Under Which Lyre: A Reactionary Tract for the Times,"

> Encamped upon the college plain
> Raw veterans already train
>   As freshman forces;
> Instructors with sarcastic tongue
> Shepherd the battle-weary young
> Through basic courses.
>
> Among bewildering appliances
> For mastering the arts and sciences
>   They stroll or run,
> And nerves that never flinched at slaughter
> Are shot to pieces by the shorter
> Poems of Donne.
>
> Professors back from secret missions
> Resume their proper eruditions
>   Though some regret it;
> They liked their dictaphones a lot,
> They met some big wheels and do not
> Let you forget it. . . .

"Cot, chair, and ashtray": The Indoor Athletic Building's gymnasium floor became a temporary dormitory during the postwar housing crisis. To the *Alumni Bulletin*, the gym floor looked like "the hangar deck of an Essex-class carrier returning from the Pacific with military personnel due for discharge."

Inset: Freshman Paul Ode '51, of Fargo, North Dakota, bedded down on the gym's balcony.

Many of those who saw service found military organization, methods, and attitudes not only congenial but transferable to academic pursuits. As a result the customs and catchwords of American military culture were adapted to classroom discussions, exams and papers, dining hall debates, extracurricular activities, and athletics. Coaches had to deal with a new type of athlete, older and less tractable than the prewar breed. Football coach Dick Harlow, whose off-the-field interests included horticulture and collecting rare birds' eggs, was resented by veterans for his habit of addressing his charges as "dear boy."

At Harvard and every other college and university, housing was the number-one problem. The nation's student population had been less than 1.5 million before the war. Many observers had predicted that American population growth would level off and leave college enrollments on a permanent plateau. With the swift demobilization that followed the war's abrupt end in August, more than a million veterans began crowding onto the nation's three thousand campuses. The sudden influx of vets raised total enrollments to more than 2.5 million, severely taxing the capacities of American higher education.

Harvard College had granted leaves of absence to 3,500 students who had left for military service. The College had also admitted more than 1,200 applicants who had gone directly into the military from secondary school. Most of these 4,700 men would resume their studies within a single calendar year. By the fall of 1945, Harvard's counselor for veterans was also receiving more than a thousand letters a week from "new veterans," with no prior Harvard connection, exploring options for their educational futures. About 1,000 men from this group were accepted that fall. Admissions officers anticipated at least 3,000 more "good applications" from new veterans by the start of the next academic year, along with the usual submissions from secondary school candidates. The prewar size of the entire College had never exceeded 3,500. Almost 9,000 veterans enrolled in the College and the ten graduate and professional schools in the fall of 1946. The University's student population soared from 3,600 to 11,700. The size of the College rose from 1,782 to 5,400. The freshman class of 2,000 was by far the

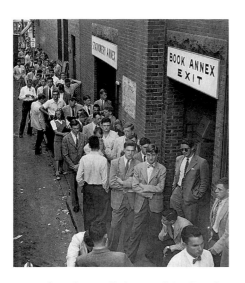

Queuing up. Below, registration day at Memorial Hall, 1946. Textbook buyers, above, waiting outside the Harvard Coop's book department.

largest ever. Enrollment in the Graduate School of Arts and Sciences rose from 400 to 1,600. The Business School's student body went from 70 to 1,400. The Law School's jumped from 162 to 1,500.

The *Alumni Bulletin* pondered the plight of the conquering hero:

> Aside from the inconvenience of living quarters which may be located at considerable commuting distance from Harvard Square, he will have to be satisfied with crowded classrooms and all the haste which goes with a University enrollment of 12,000 men [sic], a third larger than the previous peak year. His $60 or $90 a month will not go so far as a year ago in a community where sodas now cost 25 cents and suits $50; where a single furnished room is $32 a month and an apartment $75. But he has come, he is welcome, and we wish him the best of luck. We can take him if he can take us.

President Conant had written 16,000 local alumni asking for help in sheltering 3,000 married veterans and their families. His appeal elicited 99 offers of space, including a sanatorium and two country clubs. Before registration day, 1946, some 300 students living within 45 minutes of Harvard Square were told they would have to commute till the housing crisis abated. The basketball court of the Indoor Athletic Building was commandeered as a dorm for single students. Each was issued "cot, chair, and ashtray." One undergraduate anchored a small sloop in the Charles River and lived aboard. Almost 200 married veterans were housed in 33 one-story frame buildings shipped by the government from South Portland, Maine, where they had been erected for wartime shipyard workers. About 400 families bunked at Fort Devens, in the outlying town of Ayer, a three-hour round-trip train commute via Porter Square station. Their sector of the army camp was dubbed "Harvardevens Village." Another 115 families lived in apartments that Harvard leased at the Hotel Brunswick in Boston's Copley Square.

By March 1947 the crisis was subsiding, and the temporary housing office set up in Straus Hall closed its doors. The University's share of the costs of veterans' housing was estimated at more than $1 million.

THE VETERANS WERE EAGER TO LEARN. Faculty members liked their seriousness of purpose, work habits, and perspectives. Their economic and social backgrounds, war experiences, motivation, and values set the vets apart from the relatively homogeneous and more casual student body of prewar days, and made the University a much more pluralistic institution. "Harvard has never seen so able, so mature, so interesting, and so widely representative a group of students," wrote Dean Paul Buck, who had assumed the new post of University provost in the fall of 1945. "Their quality is superb." Five student veterans who spoke at a 1946 Commencement symposium personified Harvard's changing demography. Joseph Everingham '49, a 29-year-old freshman from Florida, had worked for Procter & Gamble and served in the Pacific theater as a major in the army medical corps. Jesse Dukeminier '48, a Mississippian, had spent a year at the University of Tennessee and served in Germany as an army Pfc. Charles Zettek '49, of Kansas, had seen Germany as an air force bombardier. Constantine Brelis '49,

A graduate student and his family moving into emergency public housing for married veterans. Frame buildings put up in open areas near the schools of law, divinity, and business sheltered almost 200 families.

Students housed at "Harvardevens Village" in Ayer, Massachusetts, commuted by train to the Porter Square station in Cambridge.

once a Newport restaurant worker, had been an army intelligence officer in Burma. Abe Schestopol '49, an ex-steelworker and machinist from Brooklyn, had been an air force navigator in the China theater. For most of the teachers and the taught, the years after World War II inspired new faith in the workings of democracy.

What did the returning veteran study? First and foremost, the social sciences. "He wants to discover what is happening to the world around him and discuss what he can do about it," explained the *Alumni Bulletin*. Economics A was the College's most populous course. In 1940 it had enrolled 512 students; in the fall of 1946, Professor H. H. Burbank looked across 1,092 open notebooks as he began his weekly lectures. William Yandell Elliott's Government 1 was in second place with 874 students. Mathematics A, with 778 students, ranked third; then came History 1, the most popular course of the prewar era, with 509.

Wanted: A Few Good Men, Fewer Floppy Ducklings

THE STREAM OF veterans entering postwar Harvard led Provost Paul Buck to call for changes in "the balance of the College."

"I share the often-heard view that [the] College would be improved if it had a larger share of the healthy, extrovert kind of American youth which is so much admired by the American public," Buck wrote in an *Alumni Bulletin* article in February 1946. Applications received through the Veterans Office, he maintained, "contrast favorably with the types coming through the College Examination Board."

Buck's assessments of Harvard's traditional applicant group would have shaken sensitivity-minded administrators of later eras. "I suspect 95 percent of [applicants] from the large metropolitan public high schools of New York and New Jersey are of one category—bright, precocious, intellectually overstimulated boys," he wrote.

"For another example, I suspect a large proportion of the Harvard applicants from the larger private schools of these same states are not at all representative of these schools but are weighted with the delicate, literary types of boys who don't make the grade socially with their better balanced classmates who, in turn, head for Yale or Princeton."

Harvard "has done much to supply skillful, sympathetic advice and medical treatment to the

Provost Paul Buck sought "the healthy, extrovert kind of American youth" for the College.

sensitive, neurotic boy who has some talent," wrote Buck. "The result is that solicitous parents connive with harassed schoolmasters to send their floppy ducklings our way. And the pressure to deposit them in our small pond increases in proportion as we improve their survival rate." Buck suggested "an extended organization for making contact with the 500 to 1,000 schools which now send us students, often only occasionally.... There are many boys of the kind we want in the second quarter of classes that now send us only top men.

"I do not propose that we should take any action to stop the flow to Harvard of the studious or sensitive type of boys," Buck added. "We must not lose the advantage we now have from the appeal of Harvard to the exceptional boy, even if he is a bit 'queer' from the standpoint of his fellows. When we say we believe in a vigorous and successful program of intercollegiate athletics as a healthy core of undergraduate life, we must make it clear we are neither bidding for the athletic tramp nor discouraging the boy who likes sport and can take it in stride."

Responding to Buck's initiative, the admissions office and the alumni association developed an extensive recruiting network, with some 6,000 active alumni by 1998, and the demography of the College became ever more diverse.

Enrollment in History 5 ("America from 1760 to the Present," taught by Professors Buck, Frederick Merk, and Arthur Schlesinger), rose from 219 students in 1940 to 509 in 1946.

Freshmen who were part of the Great Enrollment of '46 would be the first undergraduates to experience the new program of General Education. Not far behind Gen Ed on the University's drafting board were plans for the fields of botany, biochemistry, social relations, and engineering. The last three were new departments created early in 1946. Biochemistry was designed to integrate the fields of biological chemistry, physical chemistry, and biology. Social relations subsumed the department of sociology as well as instruction and research that had been the province of the departments of anthropology and psychology. "War experience," the *Bulletin* noted, "has shown that the study of human relations cannot be entirely segregated into separate fields without often raising undesirable barriers." A new department of engineering and applied sciences was intended to meet the postwar world's need for "research engineers well grounded in first principles." Its first chairman was associate professor Frederick Hunt, who had headed the Underwater Sound Laboratory during the war. Among its research devices were Howard Aiken's automatic sequence controlled calculator, the Electro-Acoustic Laboratory's anechoic chamber, and the physics department's supersonic wind tunnel.

The Red Book

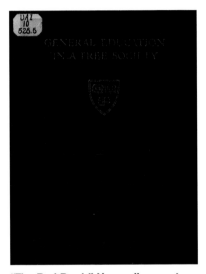

"The Red Book," Harvard's report on American general education, was published by Harvard University Press in the summer of 1945. To the dismay of Roger Scaife, the Press's director, President Conant and the Corporation decided to distribute 3,500 complimentary paperback copies to educators and government officials. Rather than killing the sale of the $2 hardcover version, as Scaife feared, the advance copies spurred demand: the Press sold almost 60,000 copies.

For faculty members who remained in Cambridge, the war years had provided both motive and opportunity to ponder the educational needs of the postwar world. At the instance of President Conant and with a grant of $60,000 from the Corporation, Dean Buck had initiated a study of "the objectives of a general education in a free society" in 1943.[1] The upshot was an extensive report issued two years later. Its recommendations reset the direction of undergraduate education at Harvard, and had far-reaching effects on postwar discourse in American higher education.

Harvard had not had a curricular overhaul since the Lowell administration. Concerns about the strategies and purposes of liberal arts colleges had become an issue in the 1930s. The shrinking job market had made college students more inclined to take courses oriented to future careers or postgraduate study. There was a growing consensus that concentration and examination requirements overemphasized specialization, and that distribution requirements allowed a haphazard approach to general studies. In the academic year 1938-39, two studies—one by a committee of the Faculty of Arts and Sciences, the other by the Student Council—had addressed the problem.

The faculty group, led by Professor Charles H. Taylor, recommended that concentrations be grouped within three broad areas: natural sciences, the humanities, and the social sciences. Suggested topics of concentration included "Ethical Values and Western Culture," "Expression and the Arts," "Human Problems of Industry." The student committee pursued the more basic question of defining the aims of a lib-

Initial Offerings

Under the chairmanship of Benjamin H. Wright, professor of government, the Committee on General Education offered the equivalent of eight full courses to freshmen and sophomores in the "Gen Ed" program's first year.

Humanities courses included three first-and-second-term pairings: "Homer, the Old Testament, and Plato" (I.A. Richards), with "Dante, Montaigne, and Shakespeare" (Theodore Spencer); "The Epic" (J.H. Finley) with "The Novel" (Harry Levin); and "Individual and Social Values in Literature": history and drama, first term; fiction and philosophy, second term (Andrews Wanning).

Natural Science courses included "Principles of Physical Sciences" (Edwin Kemble); "Understanding the Physical World" (Philippe Le Corbeiller and I. Bernard Cohen); and "Principles of Biological Science" (Edward Castle, Walles Edmondson).

Offerings in Social Sciences were "Introduction to the Social Inheritance of Western Civilization" (Crane Brinton) and "Western Thought and Institutions" (Samuel Beer).

eral education. Liberal education, the committee held, is designed to free human beings from ignorance and prejudice, and accordingly "should give the student some idea of our common tradition of human experience and also the intellectual tools with which he can confront new problems successfully." The Council suggested five required introductory courses: two in humanities, two in natural sciences, one in social sciences. Its report recommended bolstering and enlarging the tutorial system, and reiterated the longstanding undergraduate demand that teaching and tutoring ability be counted more heavily in selecting and promoting faculty.

More committee reports followed. But not until after America's entry into the war did the faculty's committee on educational policy take the bit in its teeth and introduce a proposal that "a course in American Civilization or American History, and a course in the Great Authors" be required of all undergraduates. "The idea of 'compulsion' broke like a bombshell in the Faculty," wrote Dean Buck. The plan was rejected, but as Buck noted, "all who followed the debate realized that this was not the ending but the beginning of an effort to invigorate the liberal arts curriculum by defining in clearer terms its basic objectives."

A University-wide committee on the Objectives of General Education in a Free Society was convened in the spring of 1943. Composed of twelve senior professors, it was chaired by Buck.[2] John H. Finley Jr., Eliot professor of Greek and master of Eliot House, was vice chairman. He drafted the bulk of the committee's report.

Released in the spring of 1945, the report had a powerful impact. University presidents hailed it as a pivotal document in American educational history. President Conant called it a masterpiece. "I doubt if any single volume published under Harvard auspices or written by any member of the faculty has left an impress on American education comparable to the eventual effect of this careful study," he declared.

MORE THAN HALF THE REPORT traced the history of education, and the aims of general education, in the United States. The final chapter dealt with general education in the community. Discussion of general education at the college level, and its implications for Harvard College, was limited to a single chapter.

The committee held that general education had been neglected at Harvard and other institutions. It cited the importance and value of a student's being "allowed to acquire something approximating a mastery of a particular segment of learning." The principal weakness was with introductory courses taken to meet distribution requirements. Such courses were primarily designed for those who wanted to take further courses or specialize in a given field. Any contribution they made to a student's general education was usually incidental.

The report proposed "a scheme of direct distribution" that would create a new set of courses designed "to fulfill the aims of general education exclusively and not incidentally." All students would be required to take six such courses outside their major field. At least one would be in the humanities, one in social sciences, and one in natural sciences. "The prescribed courses in the humanities and the social sciences," the report stated, "would be expected to furnish the common core, the body of learning and of ideas which would be a common experience to all Harvard students, as well as introductions to the study of the traditions of Western culture and to the consideration of general relationships." The report proposed alternative science offerings to allow for differences in preparation and ability.

Having considered the report in a series of seven meetings, the Faculty approved it by a vote of 135-10, authorizing the introduction of new courses "on an experimental basis" in the fall of 1946. President Conant himself joined the "Gen Ed" teaching staff a year later, when he gave a half-course on "The Growth of the Experimental Sciences" (Natural Sciences 11a) to a class of 169 students and many auditors. Conant was eager to test in the classroom his theory that laymen could learn to understand the scientific method if science were taught by the case history method. He had made that argument in his 1945 Terry Lectures at Yale, published in 1947 under the title *On Understanding Science*. He taught the course for two more years as Natural Sciences 4, given with such young luminaries as Leonard Nash, a resourceful chemistry teacher, and Thomas Kuhn, then a physicist, later a philosopher who advanced the influential idea of "paradigm shifts" as part of his work on scientific revolutions.

After five years of testing, Gen Ed became a required part of the curriculum in the fall of 1951. Though amended in minor ways—and restudied in detail, with lengthy debate, in 1962—it remained in its essential form until the adoption of the Core Curriculum 25 years later.

Professor John H. Finley, classicist and master of Eliot House, drafted much of the report on general education.

The Marshall Plan

HARVARD'S "VICTORY COMMENCEMENT" of 1946 had been a salute to the American military. Honorary doctorates were voted to six military and naval leaders, including Generals Dwight Eisenhower, Douglas MacArthur, and George Marshall. MacArthur and Marshall were unable to come to Cambridge to claim their degrees. But as President Truman's newly appointed secretary of state, Marshall was one of twelve honorands at the next year's Commencement. On the morning of June 5, 1947, President Conant cited him as "An American to whom Freedom owes an enduring debt

O Pioneers

The Medical School's class of 1949 was the first to include women. These twelve enrolled in the fall of 1945. In front: Ladislas Wojcik, Doris Rubin, Edith Schwartz, Martha Caires, Marjorie Kirk. In back: Jo Ann Tanner, Shirley Gallup, Edith Stone, Marcia Gordon, Dora Benedict, Raquel Eidelman, Idolene Hegemann.

The Business School accepted its first women M.B.A. candidates in 1949; the first women students at the Law School were admitted in 1950.

Wearing a plain gray suit, white shirt, and blue tie, Secretary of State Marshall was escorted in the 1947 Commencement procession by Edmund Morgan, Royall professor of law. Preceding Marshall and Morgan is Clarence Haring, professor of Latin American history and economics, and master of Dunster House.

of gratitude, a soldier and statesman whose ability and character brook only one comparison in the history of this nation."

The former General of the Army spoke at the annual meeting of the Harvard Alumni Association that afternoon. He used the occasion to propose a program of massive economic aid to war-ravaged European nations. His 1,200-word speech took less than twelve minutes. Though almost no one sensed it at the time, it would later be seen as the most important Commencement address ever given at Harvard.

From a literary standpoint the speech was unexceptional, and Marshall's oratorical style was uninspired. First-hand accounts portrayed a self-effacing orator who toyed with his glasses, kept his eyes on his text, and was sometimes inaudible. But part of the greatness of Marshall's address lay in its absence of rhetoric and its modesty of expression. It was a straightforward argument for giving generous assistance to America's global neighbors in Europe, conditional only on their willingness to join in charting their own economic recovery.

That the speech was given at Harvard was almost a matter of

chance. Marshall was also invited to speak at the University of Wisconsin and at Amherst that spring. When President Conant renewed the offer of a degree, in January 1947, Marshall was hesitant. He had just been named secretary of state and was about to attend a foreign ministers' conference in Moscow, where the reconstitution of Germany would be the main topic. During the month-long conference Marshall met privately with Joseph Stalin. The Soviet premier's intransigence heightened Marshall's anxiety about the future of Western Europe. "The patient is sinking while the doctors deliberate," he declared on returning from the failed conference. In the weeks that followed, Marshall oversaw the development of a proposal for unilateral aid to Europe, informally known at the State Department and White House as the Marshall Plan.

In early May, Under Secretary of State Dean Acheson, LL.B. '18, floated the idea of large-scale assistance to Europe in a speech to an association of businessmen, farmers, and civic leaders in Mississippi. When Acheson suggested that the time might be ripe for the secretary himself to broach the plan, Marshall asked if Harvard's Commencement would be an appropriate forum. Acheson advised against it "on the ground that commencement speeches were a ritual to be endured without hearing," but Marshall did not drop the idea. He asked his special adviser, Charles Bohlen '27, to work up a draft based on memoranda from Under Secretary Will Clayton and George Kennan, chief of policy planning. Acheson read the draft, added comments, then "heard no more."

Laird Bell '04, a Chicago lawyer, was president of the Harvard Alumni Association. Selecting Commencement speakers was one of his duties. Bell had assigned one of the two main speeches to his friend Ernest Colwell, president of the University of Chicago. At the urging of President Conant, who wanted a military figure, he had also engaged General Omar Bradley, administrator of veterans' affairs. With Commencement a week away, the State Department advised Bell that Secretary Marshall would be glad to speak briefly at Harvard. "Thus I wound up with two generals instead of none," Bell wrote later. "I did not realize how historic the occasion would be."

IT WOULD HAVE BEEN MEMORABLE in any event. An audience of about 7,000 joined the degree candidates and faculty members in the Tercentenary Theatre. President Conant awarded 2,185 degrees in course, a dramatic increase over the 583 awarded at the 1946 exercises. (One of the degrees was the hundred-thousandth conferred by Harvard since 1642). Among Marshall's fellow honorands were J. Robert Oppenheimer '26; T. S. Eliot '10; University Professor I.A. Richards, exponent of Basic English; William A. Dwiggins, typographic designer; William F. Gibbs '10, a naval architect largely responsible for the wartime mass production of ships; and Marshall's old friend James Wadsworth, former U.S. senator from New York. Marshall's LL.D. was the last one conferred.

"I will not be able to make a formal address," Marshall had written Conant, "but would be pleased to make a few remarks in appreciation

Regional Studies:
A War-Born Idea

The University's first "area studies" program began in the fall of 1947, when the Carnegie Corporation made a $100,000 grant to fund interdisciplinary research on the language, history, economics, and culture of the Soviet Union. The Russian Research Center was modeled on the research and analysis branch of the Office of Strategic Services, which brought together historians, economists, anthropologists, writers, politicians, and scientists. Its wartime chief had been Coolidge professor of history William L. Langer '15, PH.D. '22.

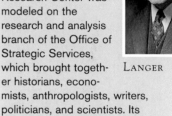

LANGER

Clyde Kluckhohn, PH.D. '36, a professor of anthropology whose field was Navajo culture, was the new center's first director.

In 1954, when a group of international oil companies agreed to fund a Center for Middle Eastern Studies, Professor Langer was assigned to plan it. After Kluckhohn resigned a year later, Langer succeeded him as head of the Russian Research Center.

As general director of regional studies, Langer also helped found a Center for East Asian Studies. These centers set the pattern for independent research institutes devoted to cognitive studies, computation, Hellenic and Renaissance studies, world religions, Latin America, urban policy, and population studies.

of the honor and perhaps a little more." At the afternoon exercises Marshall followed Laird Bell, Governor Robert Bradford '23, ll.b. '26, Bradley, Colwell, and Richards. His first words struck a note of humility that informed his entire speech: "I am profoundly grateful—touched by the great distinction and honor and great compliment accorded me by the authorities of Harvard this morning. I am overwhelmed, as a matter of fact. And I am rather fearful of my inability to maintain such a high rating as you've been generous enough to accord to me. These historic and lovely surroundings, this perfect day, and this very wonderful assembly—it is a tremendously impressive thing to an individual in my position."

Marshall then began his prepared speech: "I need not tell you that the situation in Europe is very serious." The damage to Europe's economy was far worse than anyone had expected. "It is logical," said Marshall, "that the United States should do whatever it is able to do to assist in the return of normal economic health in the world, without which there can be no political stability and no assured peace."

The speech was short on specifics. The proclamation of the Truman Doctrine in March had taken Congress by surprise, and powerful senators had resented it. Marshall must have thought that presenting a detailed plan would be counterproductive. He said nothing about the amount or duration of U.S. aid, referring only to "substantial additional help." He spoke of "our policy," but didn't give it a name. (The *Alumni Bulletin* headed the text of the untitled speech "The Marshall Doctrine.") Though the speech was clearly an initiative, its language suggested otherwise: "It would be neither fitting nor efficacious for our Government to draw up unilaterally a program designed to place Europe on its feet economically. . . . The initiative, I think, must come from Europe." And though the plan seemed likely to help block the extension of Soviet influence, the threat of communism was never cited. Marshall spoke only of "disturbances arising as a result of the desperation of the people concerned."

Marshall added two handwritten paragraphs at the end, reiterating concerns he had voiced at the start. "It is virtually impossible at this distance merely by reading or listening, or seeing photographs and motion pictures, to grasp at all the real significance of the situation," he declared. "And yet the whole world of the future hangs on a proper judgment."

Physical devastation in Münster, Germany, 1945.

General Marshall (center, hat in hand) reviewed the alumni procession before the afternoon exercises on Commencement day, 1947. In the first row, from left, are Laird Bell, president of the Harvard Alumni Association; Governor Robert Bradford; R. Keith Kane '22, Fellow of the Harvard Corporation and that year's Commencement marshal; President Conant; General Omar Bradley; former U.S. senator James Wadsworth; physicist J. Robert Oppenheimer; University Professor I.A. Richards; poet T.S. Eliot. Two rows behind Governor Bradford is Boston mayor James M. Curley.

When Marshall finished, as Laird Bell wrote later, "the applause was tremendous."

FEW HAD GRASPED THE HISTORIC DIMENSIONS of Marshall's words. Press-relations officers at Harvard and the State Department advised reporters that the address was "a routine commencement speech." A headline in the next day's *New York Times* read, "Marshall Pleads for European Unity." Conant would admit in his memoirs that he had not understood the import of the speech.

But its point was not lost in Europe. British Foreign Secretary Ernest Bevin heard portions of Marshall's speech on that night's BBC news. "When the Marshall proposals were announced," he later wrote, "I grabbed them with both hands." Over the next fortnight he and French foreign minister Georges Bidault organized a unified European response. "I can only say to other nations," said Bevin, "that when the United States throws a bridge to link the East and the West it is disastrous for ideological or other reasons to frustrate the United States in that great endeavor." Officials from sixteen European nations met in Paris to outline a joint recovery plan. Despite Bevin's injunction, Soviet Russia and nations under Communist control declined to participate.

On April 3, 1948, a year after the failed Moscow conference, President Truman signed the Foreign Assistance Act, authorizing $17 billion in grants and loans over four years. During that time the participating nations restored industrial and agricultural production, stabilized their currencies, and increased gross national product by 15 to 25 percent.

But the benefits of the Marshall Plan transcended economics. "All free peoples are at last discovering a firm, sound basis for united action," said Paul Hoffman, the plan's chief administrator, at the Commencement of 1948. Speaking at Harvard twenty years later, Prince Bernhard of the Netherlands described the plan as "an act without peer." Never before, he said, "has a strong power made it a central objective of foreign policy to create another strong power. Never in history has there been such a striking contrast with the foreign policy . . . contained in the classical maxim of *divide et impera*." In later years Marshall's address would seem all the more remarkable. The policy it bespoke was a superior example of enlightened self-interest. Both speech and policy presented the United States and its citizens in the best possible light—in a phrase that the poet Auden had applied in another context, "a friend to the future."

The Cold War

To SOVIET PREMIER STALIN, the Marshall Plan posed a challenge that demanded a response. In the spring of 1948 his troops invaded Czechoslovakia and blockaded West Berlin. The United States could do little to help the Czechs, but it did mount a tenmonth airlift to relieve Berlin. The blockade was lifted in May, and the West had an early victory in the Cold War.

That fall the USSR exploded its first nuclear device—far sooner than the West had expected—and Mao Tse-tung's Communist govern-

Peacemaker

As secretary of a United Nations commission seeking to end Arab-Israeli warfare in Palestine, Ralph J. Bunche, PH.D. '34, was thrust into the role of chief mediator when Count Folke Bernadotte was assassinated. His resolution of the conflict earned him the Nobel Peace Prize in 1950. Awarding him an LL.D. in 1949, Harvard had hailed him as "a professor of political science who has shown a practical mastery of his subject."

BUNCHE

Bunche became the UN's ablest troubleshooter, directing peacekeeping missions in the Suez in 1956, the Congo in 1960, and Cyprus in 1964. As a civil rights activist, he joined protest marches in Washington and Alabama. Resigning from the UN because of ill health in 1970, he was the organization's highest-ranking American official.

A Phi Beta Kappa graduate of UCLA, Bunche was the first African American to earn a Ph.D. in government and international relations at Harvard. (He was also the first black to win the Nobel Peace Prize.) As a professor at Howard University, he contributed to the Swedish sociologist Gunnar Myrdal's landmark study of U.S. race relations, *An American Dilemma* (1944). Bunche accepted a Harvard professorship in that year, but relinquished it in order to continue work for the State Department on colonial and trusteeship issues, and to assist in organizing the future United Nations.

ment took power in China. Exposure of a Soviet spy ring in Canada fed suspicions that the Soviets' engineering triumph was the result of espionage. The case led to the conviction of Klaus Fuchs, a physicist who had worked on the Manhattan Project. Millions of Americans were convinced that Communist agents were breaching national security and penetrating high levels of government. A rising spirit of vigilantism was reinforced by Attorney General Tom Clark's lists of organizations classed as "Communist front groups." Membership in the CP wasn't a crime, but the Truman administration adopted loyalty regulations calling for the dismissal of anyone who had been "a member, close affiliate, or sympathetic associate" of the party.

Even so, Republican politicians charged that Democrats were "soft on communism." Congressional investigators subpoenaed ex-Communists and pressured them to identify party members. The most persistent investigating bodies were the House Un-American Activities Committee (HUAC), formed in 1938 as part of a conservative backlash against the New Deal; the Senate Internal Security Subcommittee; and a subcommittee of the Senate Permanent Investigating Committee chaired by Joseph McCarthy, Republican junior senator from Wisconsin. The investigations damaged hundreds of men and women who had supported seemingly noble causes in the 1930s and 1940s. Liberal-minded academics like the astronomer Harlow Shapley and the geologist Kirtley Mather were maligned as "reds" or "pinkos." Lee Pressman, LL.B. '29, and Nathan Witt, LL.B. '32, who had held posts in the agriculture department in the New Deal days, were among Harvard alumni who gave forthright accounts of past associations. Those of other former officials, like Lawrence Duggan '27, Alger Hiss, LL.B. '29, Harry Dexter White, PH.D. '30, and Lauchlin Currie, PH.D. '31, were less clear, but the implications were assumed to be damning. Red-baiting congressmen and members of the press were quick to point out institutional ties to the "Kremlin-on-the-Charles." Hiss, who had left the State Department to head the Carnegie Endowment for International Peace, became the particular target of Richard M. Nixon, a freshman congressman from California, in much-publicized HUAC hearings that began in 1948. Many Harvard alumni gave testimonials to his character and contributed to the cost of his defense. When Hiss was convicted of perjury in 1950, Secretary of State Acheson declared that "whatever the outcome of any appeal . . . I do not intend to turn my back on Alger Hiss."[3]

THE FIRST ARMED COMBAT of the Cold War era broke out in June 1950. Almost 100,000 North Korean troops stormed into South Korea, where a small U.S. garrison had been stationed after World War II. President Truman sent warships, aircraft, and ground troops to halt the invasion, and the United Nations Security Council marshaled troops from member nations. For the first time in history, a multinational organization was using force to stop international aggression.

Equipped with Soviet-made tanks, weapons, and aircraft, the North Korean army almost dislodged the UN forces. A bold counterstrike devised by General Douglas MacArthur, supreme U.S. commander in the Far East, pushed the invading army back to the border, but brought

Alger Hiss, formerly of the State Department, was found guilty of perjury and sentenced to five years in jail after hearings held by the House Un-American Activities Committee in 1948. Journalist Whittaker Chambers, a former Communist, had testified that Hiss had been part of a spy ring. William L. Marbury, LL.B. '24 (below), a member of the Harvard Corporation, was Hiss's attorney.

The election of Marbury, a Baltimore lawyer, to the Harvard Corporation in January 1948 marked that board's first change in membership in a decade. The new Fellow was also the first to reside in a city more distant from Cambridge than New York, and the first since the seventeenth century to be elected without having attended Harvard College.

Harvard Architecture Takes a Contemporary Turn

PLANNED IN 1946 and opened in 1949, Lamont Library was the first large Harvard building designed in the contemporary idiom.

Donated by Thomas W. Lamont (A.B. 1892), who died only months before its completion, the building was not only Harvard's first modern structure but also the world's first undergraduate library. Designed by the Boston firm of Coolidge, Shepley, Bulfinch and Abbott, it cost $2.5 million to construct. A $1.5 million endowment fund was raised by subscription. The architects made extensive use of blond wood and natural light in the interior, but retained traditional red brick and white trim for the exterior.

Lamont was connected by tunnels to Widener and Houghton Libraries. Initially it housed 80,000 volumes in five levels of stacks, but its shelves eventually held more than 200,000. The Farnsworth Reading Room and the Woodberry Poetry Room were transferred from Widener Library to Lamont; the Poetry Room was designed in contemporary Scandinavian style by the Finnish architect Alvar Aalto.

---

large detachments of Chinese troops into the war. McCarthy and other Republicans made political capital out of the "police action" in Korea. "The Korean death trap," said McCarthy, "we can lay at the doors of the Kremlin and those who sabotaged re-arming, including Acheson and the President, if you please."

When Puerto Rican nationalists tried to kill Truman in November 1950, the nation's anxiety level rose again. The assassination attempt, which cost the life of a presidential guard, was timed to coincide with an uprising in San Juan. Readers of the *Alumni Bulletin* were duly informed that the president of Puerto Rico's revolutionary Nationalist Party was a Harvard graduate, Pedro Albizu y Campos '16, LL.B. '21.

BLAMED FOR "LOSING CHINA" and for failing to win in Korea, dogged by the Hiss case and by charges of influence-peddling within his administration, Truman declined to run for another term in 1952. The Democratic nominee was Illinois governor Adlai Stevenson, a Princetonian whose way with words called to mind Franklin Roosevelt's. But Stevenson's eloquence and astringent wit could not dispel the aura of anti-intellectualism surrounding the campaign. The Republican candidate was former general Dwight Eisenhower, then president of Columbia University. His running mate was Richard Nixon, by then a senator. In G.O.P. campaign parlance, Stevenson and his supporters were "eggheads." "We are tired of aristocratic explanations in Harvard words," said Eisenhower, who had smilingly accepted a Harvard LL.D. at the 1946 Commencement. In the biggest landslide since 1936, Ike

After 312 years, the all-male ranks of the Faculty of Arts and Sciences were broken in December 1948, when Helen Maud Cam was formally installed as professor of history. Professor Cam, who had previously been a lecturer at Cambridge University, gave a trenchant address on the function of her specialty, medieval history. More fully than anything else, she said, it embodies "the slow advance of erring and straying humanity."

and Nixon won by a margin of 6.5 million votes.

Eisenhower had clinched the election by vowing to go to Korea and end the war. The final accords were signed in July 1953. Some 34,000 Americans had been killed in action; almost 21,000 had died of other causes. Seventeen Harvard men were among the dead. It was not a war that many Harvard students and alumni had hurried to join.

THE G.O.P. VICTORY MEANT THAT Republican Communist-hunters could no longer concentrate their fire on the federal government. Congressional investigators had already probed the film industry. They now turned to higher education. Resistance was weak. One authority estimates that close to a hundred academics lost their jobs for refusing to cooperate with investigating committees, while hundreds more may have been eased out under other pretexts.[4]

President Conant devoted part of his annual report in 1953 to the "malicious misrepresentation" of colleges and universities. "If there are members of the staff of any university who are in fact engaged in subversive activities," he wrote, "I hope the government will ferret them out and prosecute them." He added,

> I would not be party to the appointment of a Communist to any position in a school, college, or university. There are no known adherents to the Party on our staff, and I do not believe there are any disguised Communists either. But even if there were, the damage that would be done to the spirit of this academic community by an investigation by the University aimed at finding a crypto-Communist would be far greater than any conceivable harm such a person could do.
>
> As to the charges that some professors hold unpopular political opinions, the answer is, of course, they do. It would be a sad day for the United States if the spirit of dissent were driven out of universities. For it is the freedom to disagree, to quarrel with authority on intellectual matters, to think otherwise, that has made this nation what it is today.

This was Conant's parting shot. Eisenhower had offered him the post of U.S. high commissioner to Germany, and Conant announced his acceptance in January 1953. His decision caused mild shock within the Harvard community. The anti-Communist crusade was only one of many unresolved problems confronting Harvard. New science buildings, graduate housing, and an undergraduate library had been added in the postwar years, but the institution still had many unmet needs.

For Conant the move made sense. He had led Harvard through two stressful decades. His work had been complicated by the Depression, the war years, the postwar population pressures, and Cold War tensions. Yet Conant had returned Harvard to intellectual leadership in science, reorganized procedures for faculty advancement, revised the College curriculum and the admissions system. Though fund-raising was not his strong suit, he had projected the institution's postwar financial needs and set up a development office to deal with them.[5] In his forthright way, he had also met the responsibilities of a national educational leader, speaking out unequivocally on controversial issues. In

Called a "world-tree" by its maker, sculptor Richard Lippold, a stainless steel pylon rose in the quadrangle of a new Graduate Center, adjacent to the Law School and completed in 1950. Planned by Walter Gropius, of the School of Design, the center's buildings exemplified the International Style. Within were murals by Josef Albers and Joan Miró.

The world-tree, according to Lippold, embodied a "transparent" sphere symbolizing the inner tensions of its time. It was viewed with predictable irreverence by many Harvardians, including graduate student Thomas A. Lehrer '47, whose paean appeared in the *Crimson*:

I think that I shall never see
A poem weird as a world-tree
A tree to brighten every meal
With fragrant boughs of stainless steel
A tree that may in winter grace
A skating rink around its base
A tree whose stark and spiked busem
Will scare the birdies (and confusem),
That needs not rain, or sun to rise,
That needs but love, and Simoniz.
Of all the thoughts of Mr. Gropius
This cosmic hat rack is the dopius.

recent years he had been a strong advocate of universal military training and military preparedness. His interest in educational matters had not abated, but America's role in achieving international stability had become his overriding concern.

The Corporation now faced the double-edged problem of providing interim leadership while seeking his successor. Conant was voted a leave of absence until September 1, 1953, when he would become president emeritus, and his duties were assigned to an administrative committee chaired by Provost Buck. Charles A. Coolidge '17, LL.B. '22, a Boston lawyer who had been a Corporation member since 1935, ran the presidential search. The Fellows agreed not to consider any of their own number. Within the University, possible candidates included John Fin-

In Search of a Sane Athletics Policy

A NOTABLE ASPECT of undergraduate extracurricular life in the Conant era was a change in the role of intercollegiate football and the growth of a large and healthy program of intramural athletics.

In the Lowell administration, big-time football had dominated athletics, as it did at other colleges. But ticket demand declined during the Depression, and suspension of regular competition during the war years provided an opportunity to review athletic policies. In 1945 Harvard, Yale, and Princeton joined in broadening a twenty-year-old "Big Three" agreement to include five other "Ivy Group" universities (Brown, Columbia, Cornell, Dartmouth, Pennsylvania). They agreed to avoid "the well-recognized excesses" of intercollegiate football and adopt standards governing eligibility, recruiting, and financial aid.

A string of subpar football seasons in postwar years— particularly that of 1949, when Harvard won only one game and was badly beaten by Stanford and Virginia—led to a searching look at the future of Harvard football and the cost of the athletic program. Rumors that Harvard might drop football were put to rest

"So you see, Paul, according to this theory, we're not de-emphasizing sports; they're just emphasizing them."

Cartoon by David Braaten '46 from *Inside Harvard* (1950), by Braaten and W. S. Fairfield '50.

in March 1950, when Provost Buck announced, "We are not going to go the way of Chicago.... We shall continue to seek our fair share of victories.... We want athletes in the College because we believe in a balanced student body.... We shall seek them by legitimate means."

The Athletic Committee, composed equally of graduate, faculty, and student members, was reorganized as an all-faculty group, and the gentle and well-liked Thomas D. Bolles, coach of rowing, replaced the outspoken and rigidly moralistic William J. Bingham '16 as director of athletics. The intramural program was enlarged and strengthened.

In 1951 the Ivy presidents adopted a joint policy statement affirming that "athletes shall have the same opportunities of admission and financial assistance as other students whose interests and abilities have been shown in other areas." The next year they agreed to meet on a regular basis and amended the 1945 compact to ban spring football practice and postseason games. In 1954 the presidents' group generalized football policies to cover all sports, and adopted round-robin scheduling for football and "as many sports as practicable."

ley, master of Eliot House, and Donald K. David, Erwin Griswold, Francis Keppel, and Edward Mason, deans, respectively, of the schools of business, law, education, and public administration. Buck would have been a logical candidate, but he wanted to give up administrative work. Outsiders whose names were widely mentioned included Dr. W. Barry Wood '32, of Johns Hopkins, and New York financier David Rockefeller '36. Walter Lippmann recommended McGeorge Bundy, a 33-year-old associate professor of history, former Junior Fellow, and Yale alumnus. Brown University president Henry M. Wriston suggested Nathan Pusey '28, PH.D. '37, president of Lawrence College in Appleton, Wisconsin.[6]

Wriston, a former president of Lawrence, had hired Pusey to teach there in the 1930s. After stints at Scripps College and Wesleyan University, Pusey had succeeded Wriston at Lawrence in 1944. His administration had seen a 50 percent increase in endowment and a 40 percent increase in enrollment. Pusey had installed a freshman studies program based on great books, launched an ambitious building campaign, recruited able teachers, and raised faculty salaries.

Pusey was 45. He had published little and was not a New Englander. But Corporation members warmed to him because of his strong interest in undergraduate education, his belief in the liberal arts, and his record as an administrator and fund-raiser. They also sensed a remarkable firmness of character beneath his quiet manner and youthful appearance. As a *Milwaukee Journal* reporter wrote at the time, "He is fond of people and it is hard for him to reprove them, but when he thinks he is right, he is immovable. A certain strength of mind is evident; he never loses his temper, yet few persons cross him. He is painfully honest, and scrupulous to avoid compromising himself or the school. He carries his principles with him everywhere."

Four Corporation members met Pusey for lunch at the Harvard Club of New York City. Pusey thought he was being consulted about academic issues. The real situation was made clear at a second lunch in Boston in May. Won over, the Corporation formally elected Pusey as Harvard's 24th president on the morning of June 1. At 12:30 the choice was announced to the largest gathering of newspeople that Harvard had seen since the Tercentenary.

President Conant leaving Harvard to become U.S. high commissioner to Germany in the winter of 1953. The understanding was that he would become ambassador when peace treaties were ratified.

Tilting with McCarthy

NATHAN MARSH PUSEY was the first Harvard president born west of the state of New York. From Council Bluffs, Iowa, he had attended high school there and had gone to Harvard on a scholarship for Iowa students. Pusey earned his numerals in freshman basketball, had as his tutor the poet Conrad Aiken '11, and won straight As in English and comparative literature, graduating *magna cum laude*. In his senior year he was the highest scorer in the "Harvard-Yale Brain Test," a three-hour written examination that pitted ten Harvard undergraduates against ten from Yale. (Judges from Brown, Cornell, and Princeton declared Harvard the winner.) After three years of traveling and secondary school teaching, Pusey returned to Harvard as a doctoral

Auguste Renoir, *Seated Bather* (1885)

Claude Monet, *The Gare Saint-Lazare: Arrival of a Train* (1877)

Paul Cézanne, *Still Life with Commode* (c. 1885)

A Collector's Bounty

MAURICE WERTHEIM '06 was a successful banker whose personal interests included theater (he founded the New York Theater Guild in 1919), liberal journalism (he resuscitated the *Nation*), and sport (especially fly-fishing). In 1936 he set out to assemble a small, representative collection of great French modernist works. In his quest he often relied on advice from expert friends like Paul Sachs '00, director of the Fogg Art Museum.

At his death in 1950 Wertheim left the Fogg one of America's most remarkable collections of late nineteenth- and early twentieth-century art. It included 43 paintings, drawings, and sculptures by such masters as Degas, Cézanne, Manet, Monet, Picasso, Renoir, and Van Gogh. These works formed the heart of the Fogg's holdings of Impressionist and Post-Impressionist art, and were later installed in a permanent gallery.7

student in ancient history, writing his dissertation on fourth-century Athenian law. In 1936 he married Anne Woodward, who had just graduated from Bryn Mawr. They had met when she was thirteen and Pusey, then a College student, tutored her for a summer in mathematics.

Pusey had not been a prominent member of the class of 1928. But classmates were pleased to greet him when the Puseys and their three children arrived in Cambridge a week after his election to participate in '28's twenty-fifth reunion festivities. Then the new first family retreated to Iowa for a month of relaxation at Lake Okiboji. Pusey made two major decisions that summer. In July Paul Buck arrived with a list of five

Above: Changing planes en route to Boston a week after his election as Harvard's president, Nathan Pusey had an airport encounter with his predecessor, James Conant.

Below: At his twenty-fifth reunion in June 1953, Pusey borrowed a top hat from Overseer Charles Cabot '22 (left) and displayed his class waistcoat.

candidates for the deanship of the Faculty of Arts and Sciences. The last name was McGeorge Bundy's. Pusey had admired an *Atlantic* article that Bundy had written in riposte to William F. Buckley's best-selling *God and Man at Yale*. He told Buck, "That's the guy I want to see." Slipping quietly into Cambridge in mid-August, Pusey met with Bundy, who accepted the deanship.

The president also met with John Lord O'Brian (A.B. 1896), a Buffalo lawyer active in alumni affairs. O'Brian was trying to sustain a $6 million campaign to strengthen the almost moribund Divinity School. Pusey, Harvard's first Episcopalian president, had a strong interest in religion. "I liked [O'Brian] enormously," he recalled, "and we got started." He made his first major address as president at a Divinity School convocation in September 1953.

On October 13, in the Faculty Room of University Hall, Pusey was vested with the powers and privileges of the presidency. Some two hundred guests filled the room to witness an inaugural much like Conant's. Bowls of red roses brightened the room; sunlight slanted through its large windows. Judge Charles Wyzanski Jr. '27, president of the Board of Overseers, gave the charge. "This year, in retrospect, may seem the halfway mark at which the twentieth century turned from the age of anxiety to the beginning of a justified belief in a better world," said Wyzanski. "By your courage you can give men renewed confidence that they are more nearly masters of their destiny.

"As the head of nine faculties," he concluded, "may your presence, and your and their high mission, give substance to Matthew Arnold's poetic vision: *'Tis Apollo comes leading / His choir, the Nine. / The leader is fairest, / But all are divine.*" In response, Pusey pledged

> . . . to try to keep assembled here the very best scholars and teachers that can be found, to work to ensure conditions conducive to their best efforts, and constantly to strive for more effective ways to make their activity touch, quicken, and strengthen the intellectual aspirations of succeeding generations of young people. . . . Harvard is a great intellectual enterprise founded and nourished in a great faith. It shall be my purpose, continuing in that faith, to guide it as best I can, so help me God.

THE SPIRITUAL TONE of those words contrasted with the spirit of the times. The McCarthyist furor was reaching a peak. Pusey had known McCarthy since 1945; the two men had met in the smoking car of the Appleton-Madison train when Pusey was president of Lawrence. "He was an amiable, gregarious, hail fellow who could tell stories and be awfully funny," Pusey recalled. But McCarthy had not forgiven Pusey for joining a citizens' group that opposed his re-election in 1952. When Pusey became Harvard's president, McCarthy called him "a rabid anti-anti-Communist," adding, "Harvard's loss is Wisconsin's gain." In November 1953 the senator cited Harvard as "a smelly mess" where students were "open to indoctrination by Communist professors." He had in mind Wendell Furry, a soft-spoken physicist who had declined to answer an investigating committee's questions about his membership in a Communist group from 1938 to 1947. Furry had said

that he was no longer a party member, and that he knew of no current Communist activity at Harvard. In a statement on his case, the Corporation had said it would regard "present membership in the Communist Party by a member of our faculty as grave misconduct, justifying removal." Party membership went "beyond the scope of academic freedom" because it would restrict a teacher's "ability . . . to perform duties with independence of thought and judgment." For furnishing "incomplete or false information" to investigating agencies, Furry had been given three years' probation.[8]

McCarthy sent Pusey a long telegram questioning Furry's continuing presence at Harvard. Pusey responded by calling the first large-scale press conference ever held in Massachusetts Hall. "Harvard is interested in teaching respect for freedom of inquiry, respect for the free mind, and in trying to get people to practice this kind of thing, Harvard is one of the major leaders in the war against communism," he told the press. In a reply to McCarthy he affirmed Harvard's "absolute and unalterable" opposition to communism. "I am in full agreement with the opinion publicly stated by my predecessor and the Harvard Corporation that a member of the Communist Party is not fit to be on the faculty because he has not the necessary independence of thought and judgment," wrote Pusey. "I am not aware that there is any person among the 3,000 members of the Harvard faculty who is a member of the Communist Party."

McCarthy continued to snipe at Harvard, and Pusey issued statements rebuffing him.[10] The senator's domination of the American

Joseph Welch, counsel to the army, was the modest hero of the Army-McCarthy hearings in 1954. The hearings proved to be the undoing of the unscrupulous Senator Joseph McCarthy (right).

On the television program *Omnibus* in 1956, President Pusey explained to 20 million Americans that Harvard had been founded "to advance learning and perpetuate it to posterity."

political scene came to an end in the spring of 1954, when McCarthy tried to investigate the U.S. Army. In a theatrical series of televised hearings, watched by some 20 million viewers, McCarthy and his chief counsel, Roy Cohn, were found to have intervened repeatedly and improperly to seek a commission and special favors for G. David Schine '49, a former protégé who had been drafted into the army. Schine, whose family owned a large hotel chain, had been on McCarthy's payroll as an expert on Communist subversion. The revelation that Cohn and Schine had enjoyed a whirlwind junket to Europe helped bring on McCarthy's downfall.

The strongest presence in the Army-McCarthy hearings was army counsel Joseph N. Welch, LL.B. '17, a genteel Boston lawyer and master of courtroom repartee. Welch's exchanges with McCarthy clearly revealed the senator's unprincipled nature. In a desperate last-ditch attack, McCarthy charged that a young member of Welch's firm, Fred Fisher, LL.B. '48, had belonged to a left-wing lawyers' group while at Harvard Law School. Welch's pained reply brought the hearings to a dramatic climax. "Until this moment, Senator, I think I never really gauged your cruelty or your recklessness," he began. "Have you no sense of decency, sir, at long last? Have you left no sense of decency?"

The Senate censured McCarthy; within three years heavy drinking would end his life. But the accusatory tactics that had helped him to power would resonate in the nation's political discourse, and the political power of the TV camera was now firmly established.[9]

PRESIDENT PUSEY'S STAND against McCarthy, his candor and quiet confidence, captured and held the interest of the press. Edward R. Murrow's nationally televised *Person to Person* featured a visit with the Pusey family. The president talked briefly about academic freedom; his younger son, Jamie, played "the first bagpipe solo ever to be heard on television from the President's House at Harvard." It was also the first extended appearance of a Harvard president on TV.

To the community life of the University, the Puseys gave an infusion of Midwestern friendliness. Cheerful and outgoing, Anne Pusey joined in the work of the Harvard Dames, the College Teas, and the Newcomers, groups intended to increase the involvement of faculty and student wives and family members with other members of the community. The Puseys made regular visits to regional Harvard clubs and meetings of educational leaders. The president was not a spellbinding speaker, but his earnestness and clarity of expression appealed to audiences. In his quiet way, Pusey also kept in touch with a wide range of student activities—the Glee Club, Phillips Brooks House, professional school clubs, athletics. He would greet the football team in the locker room after games, and sometimes flew with the squad on road trips.

Pusey's administrative style reflected his small-college background. He meant to run Harvard as Lowell had, without a large staff or a provost. Leaving day-to-day business operations to vice president Edward Reynolds '15, he oversaw the full spectrum of academic affairs. After six months he invited William Bentinck-Smith '37, the editor of the *Alumni Bulletin*, to become his assistant. For the next seventeen years Bentinck-Smith was virtually a one-man presidential staff. He dealt with deans and other administrators, handled correspondence and special projects, and often acted as the University's spokesman.

Most administrators and faculty members found Pusey accessible, consistent in his decisions, and a perceptive listener. Charles Coolidge, the Corporation's Senior Fellow for the first dozen years of the Pusey era, admired the president's "gift for putting round pegs in round holes, of selecting just the right person to do a job. He worked at it like a dog." Associates also discovered the Pusey firmness. It could take the form of a quick, flat turndown, or a blunt refusal to reopen a question that the president regarded as closed—both causes of a syndrome known to deans in University Hall as PPD (post-Pusey depression). But there was also a sense of humor, dry, understated, and prized by close associates. When Yale honored him with an LL.D., he acknowledged solemnly that never in his fondest dreams had he aspired to be an alumnus of Yale. And there was his famous riposte when a tipsy graduate, rising during the question period at a Harvard Club dinner meeting, referred to his son, "whose ancestors came over on the *Mayflower*, and whose father went to Harvard, and *his* father went to Harvard, and HIS father went to Harvard, and now *he…can't…get in!*"

"Well," mused Pusey, "we can't send him back—the *Mayflower* doesn't run any more."

PUSEY WAS OPTIMISTIC by nature, but the state of the nation in the early 1950s was far from encouraging. In his first Baccalaureate sermon, the new president told the class of 1954 that

> Our national life has been suffering from a peculiarly violent, festering mental ill-health, a noxious growth of irrationality, which—nourished and exploited by irrational, scheming minds—presents a spectacle radically at odds with patriotic, democratic pretensions. This illness has fostered uncertainty, accentuated division, magnified hate. . . . Little public conduct has deserved either admiration or respect. As a consequence I cannot even guess what you men think of the adult world you are moving into. . . .

Pusey was not just dubious about standards of public morality. He was apprehensive that higher education was facing a serious erosion of

Not until the mid-'50s did a woman appear on Harvard's Commencement platform. Helen Adams Keller '04 (below, with her companion, Polly Thomson), awarded an LL.D. in 1955, was the first of her sex to receive a Harvard honorary degree.

Left: Barbara Ward, Lady Jackson, assistant editor of the *Economist,* was the first woman to address a Commencement audience. Awarded a Litt.D. in 1957, she presented a ten-year retrospective on the Marshall Plan.

public support and demoralization within the teaching profession. It was not yet clear that Senator McCarthy was finished, and that for higher education, unexampled prosperity was around the corner.

The Rising Tide

NO ONE IN HIGHER EDUCATION had foreseen the dynamic growth that began in the mid-1950s. Everything fell into place. The population curve soared. Gross national product leapt upward. The orbiting of *Sputnik I* shocked America into new concern about its capability in science, technology, and general knowledge, ushering in an era in which the resources of government and citizenry were committed to higher education as never before. Public and private sources pumped billions into university-based research, enabling Harvard and other institutions to expand on a scale that would have been unimaginable in the bad old McCarthy years.

Almost every institution prospered, but Harvard did especially well. "'A rising tide lifts all the boats,'" McGeorge Bundy later wrote in an incisive review of the period.[10] "The struggle for new resources was unending, but once again Harvard was particularly lucky. Her traditional ties to the rich gave her access to private money, and at the same time her advantages of established strength made it easier for her to do well in the new competition for federal and foundation funds. The rising tide of the fifties lifted the better boats most."

The Conant administration had begun to fill gaps in the University's physical plant, and some of the graduate schools had begun their own campaigns. With endowment income of less than $150,000 a year and only four chaired professorships, the Business School had raised a near-record $14 million for endowment and two buildings. The Law School had raised $1.5 million for construction and restoration. Before Pusey took office the Corporation had authorized fund-raising programs for the schools of divinity and education. In each case the goal was $6 million. But the most pressing concerns were the long-term needs of the College and the Faculty of Arts and Sciences.

During his first months in Cambridge Pusey had toured laboratories and libraries, administrative and departmental offices, and athletic facilities. "I was distressed by the condition of the old dormitories and the number of dilapidated buildings, and appalled by the backlog of need for new space," he said later. "Everyone I talked to seemed apprehensive about Harvard's future growth and its ability to meet the demands it faced. I concluded that Harvard was in danger of dragging its feet in a period of great growth and vitality.

"Harvard had taken pride in not raising tuition," recalled Pusey, "while professors' salaries lagged in a rising market, in effect subsidizing tuition." From 1929 to 1949, when per-capita disposable income was doubling, tuition had remained frozen at $400 a year, and the real pay of a full professor declined by 20 percent. Faculty members got three across-the-board increases in the Pusey administration's first four years, bringing the average professorial salary to almost $15,000. Tuition rose to $1,000 and continued to increase more steeply than annual gains in

Learning Channel

With transmitting facilities at Harvard's Blue Hill Meteorological Observatory in Milton, station WGBH-TV brought educational television to Boston in the spring of 1955. It was an offshoot of radio station WGBH-FM, which had been on the air ("with 20,000 watts effective radiated power") since 1951.

The stations were operated by the Lowell Institute Cooperative Broadcasting Council, a consortium of ten Greater Boston educational and cultural institutions, including Harvard. The council was organized in 1946 to provide educational programs to local commercial stations.

The 630-foot height of Great Blue Hill—which gave the stations their call letters—made it possible to transmit high-quality signals over a 65-mile radius, covering a listening area with a population of almost 5 million.

Breaking ground for the School of Public Health's Nutrition Laboratory, one of thirty major buildings constructed at Harvard during the 1950s and 1960s. At left, helping President Pusey with the jackhammer, is General Foods board chairman Charles G. Mortimer. The company had pledged more than $1 million toward the cost of the new lab.

disposable income. The needs of the College were a principal topic at almost every Corporation meeting. James R. Reynolds '23, presidential assistant for development, made studies of potential financial support, sources of gifts for capital and current use, and government and foundation grants. The Overseers' committee to visit Harvard College, chaired by David Rockefeller, made two influential reports. One suggested that the College should respond to the nation's population growth, then going up at a rate of almost 3 million a year, by accepting as many as 100 more applicants per year over fifteen years. Enrollment was then about 4,450. The second report recommended the construction of three new Houses and a center for nonresident students. Other committee reports—on astronomy, athletics, chemistry, and drama—all converged on the need for new funding.

IN APRIL 1956, AS A TRIAL BALLOON, Pusey sketched out a $40 million construction program at a meeting of the Associated Harvard Clubs in Miami. The *Alumni Bulletin* described the "background of gently waving palm trees and a star-studded sky—a setting about as unlike Harvard Square as anything that could be imagined." No institution of higher education had ever sought more than $15 million, and Pusey's projection did not include funds for teaching, research, library resources, or student aid. But the club officers responded positively.

At a two-day meeting in Pulpit Harbor, Maine, that summer, the president sold Corporation members on a massive program. When specific needs were added up, the total came to $125 million. Against the advice of fund-raising professionals, who drew the line at $45 million, the goal was set at $82.5 million. A two-year Program for Harvard

In Europe, meanwhile...

President emeritus Conant, now U.S. high commissioner to Germany, accepted an honorary doctorate in natural science from the University of Hamburg in 1956.

Two years later, at 65, the tireless Conant returned to America and cast himself as the "volunteer inspector general of United States public schools."

College was announced in February 1957. Francis H. Burr '35, the Corporation's newest member, saw the goal as "utterly unobtainable." Treasurer Paul Cabot '21 was just as dubious. Only Pusey was sanguine. "I was young, or naive, or something," he said later, "but I just felt we've got to do it, so let's do it."

An appeal to past and present members of the governing boards yielded $13 million and served as a catalyst for the campaign. The drive was to end in June 1959, but by then only $67.2 million had been raised. Fund-raising was extended for six months. The end of December brought a flurry of gifts, including $5 million from fifty donors who had already made large contributions. The drive passed the $80 million mark on December 31, and in early January a pledge of $2.5 million from Harold Vanderbilt '07 put it over the top. Vanderbilt had previously pledged $1.4 million to help build a new Medical School library. Counting later gifts, appreciation, and interest, the Program for Harvard College raised about $100 million from 28,000 donors. For all of private education, it redefined the art of the possible.

The campaign produced fresh funds for faculty salaries and professorships, two new University professorships, and financial aid, as well as underwriting the cost of a half-dozen major buildings: Quincy House, Leverett Towers, and Mather House, which provided living space for 950 more undergraduates; a new health center; the Loeb Drama Center; and the Carpenter Center for the Visual Arts. The success of the Program for Harvard College paved the way for a $58 million Program for Harvard Medicine, completed in 1965, and a $49 million Program for Science, completed in 1971. These campaigns and others added more than thirty buildings to Harvard's plant.[11]

RISING GOVERNMENT FUNDING was a major development of the postwar decades. During World War II all federally funded research and training had been arranged through the University treasurer's office. When the war ended, treasurer William Claflin was ready to wind up outstanding contracts and let government-backed research fall back to its minimal prewar level. So was President Conant. "As late as 1953, when I left Cambridge, I could not have imagined asking for taxpayers' money to support any Harvard activity," he wrote in his memoirs. But Harvard's financial ties with government agencies grew tremendously in the 1950s. Federal funding became a vexed question. By the mid-1960s it was a loaded one.

In 1946 Claflin and the Corporation reconsidered their stance. An Office for Government Contracts, with a staff of three, was set up in two rooms at the Semitic Museum. This was the clearing-house for government-funded projects, identifying potential researchers and negotiating contracts. Harvard's first postwar project was a study of microwave circuits and electromagnetic radiation, an area in which physicist Edward Purcell, a 1952 Nobel Prize-winner, and others did advanced research. Other projects involved atmospheric analysis, weather forecasting, burn treatments, the homing sense in birds, beasts, and fishes, and isotope research at the Harvard cyclotron. By 1953 Harvard had more than a hundred contracts, worth $8 million, with twenty government

The clock tower of Memorial Hall went up in flames at 4:29 P.M. on September 6, 1956. The Cambridge Fire Department, just across the street, hoisted a 100-foot extension ladder and trained hoses on the blaze, but it took twelve hours to extinguish. All that was left in the morning were the tower base, smoldering timbers, and the great bell, cracked and ruined by the flames.

The spire had been undergoing restoration, and the fire was attributed to an unattended blowtorch. As its own insurer, the University set aside a repair fund of $313,000, representing the estimated damage. By the time of Memorial Hall's centennial in 1972, the principal had more than doubled. But the fund was not restricted to repair of the tower and it was eventually spent on renovations to other parts of the building. A series of gifts and pledges from alumni and friends kept alive the possibility that the tower would rise again.

The New Harvard

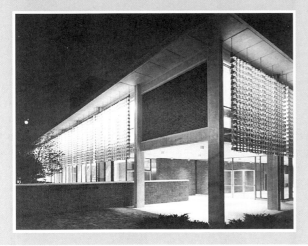

ABOUT HALF the funds raised by the $82.5 million Program for Harvard College went for new construction. In contrast to the unified Georgian Revival styling of most of the structures built in the Lowell era, Harvard now sought contemporary designs by an assortment of famous architects. Below: the courtyard entrance of Quincy House (Shepley, Bulfinch, Richardson, & Abbott, 1958). Below, left: the Loeb Drama Center (Hugh Stubbins, 1960). At left: the Carpenter Center for the Visual Arts, Le Corbusier's only building in the United States (1961).

agencies. A decade later the value of government contracts exceeded the wartime level of $30 million. Federal funds were concentrated in three faculties: medicine (almost 60 percent of budget), public health (more than 55 percent), and arts and sciences (about 30 percent). Within arts and sciences, almost 95 percent of research in the division of engineering and 90 percent of research in the physics department was government-sponsored.

No secret research was permitted. In 1949 the Corporation had approved a faculty resolution ruling out classified research except in times of "grave national emergency." In this respect Harvard was almost unique among American research universities. The University's position was that classified work should be done in government laboratories. Freedom to publish research results had to be guaranteed. Harvard faculty members could not accept government projects that detracted from regular research activities, and permanent faculty were not to be paid out of short-term research funds.

The creation of the National Science Foundation in 1951 reflected the government's increased reliance on nonprofit institutions as sources of basic research.[12] Cold War imperatives had extended the

Government-sponsored work at Harvard's synchro-cyclotron: Karl Strauch, professor of physics, oversaw a project on proton scattering.

The 150-million-electron-volt atom-smasher, completed in 1949, replaced Harvard's first cyclotron, shipped to Los Alamos during the war. Supporting funds came from the Office of Naval Research, though none of the work had military significance. In 1967 Professor Strauch succeeded Stanley Livingston, an MIT physicist, as director of the Cambridge Electron Accelerator (opposite page).

partnership that had worked so well in wartime, and educational leaders welcomed the arrangement. As Dean Bundy told a Senate subcommittee in 1955, "We believe that a steadily growing national program of basic research, through contracts unhampered by security requirements, is not only a great reinforcement to the understanding of nature and to material well-being, but also a sheer necessity in the struggle for national survival in freedom."

When Soviet Russia launched *Sputnik I*, the first orbiting satellite, in October 1957, more federal funds were committed to higher education. Training rocket scientists was not the object. America's population growth presaged an acute need for teachers and specialists in fields like health care, social services, communications, and public administration. National Defense Education Act grants encouraged graduate education to respond with new programs and facilities. By the end of the 1950s about 80 percent of American institutions of higher education were receiving some form of federal funding, and 20 percent of all financial support for higher education was from federal sources.[13]

Excessive reliance on federal funds became an increasing source of concern to Pusey and the Corporation. The government's share of the University's $58 million budget had been reckoned at 10.5 percent in 1958, but a revised accounting format showed that the actual proportion was almost 18 percent. In 1959 federal funding exceeded tuition revenue for the first time, and the next year the government's share of the budget reached 24 percent—about $18 million. The rising trend line prompted Pusey to call for an institutional self-study on the impact of federal funding. Daniel Cheever '39, PH.D. '48, lecturer on government and director of alumni affairs, was appointed to conduct it.

Cheever's report, submitted in 1961, took up such problems as the imbalance between the sciences, which got the lion's share of federal grants and contracts, and other fields; the tendency to support research rather than teaching; and the difficulty of obtaining adequate reimbursement for direct and indirect research costs. The report noted that "the Government needs from the universities something that industrial or Governmental laboratories cannot supply, the creative activity that takes place most naturally in an institution where the arts, sciences, and letters are joined in an atmosphere of intellectual freedom. The money that the government spends on specific projects will be wasted if it is not spent in ways that will sustain these special qualities of the university."

"The university no longer expects to avoid involvement in public affairs, for it is by now all too clear that free universities and free political institutions are interdependent and their futures intertwined," added Cheever. "But it will serve society well only as it remains true to its essential nature—a university, not an agency of government. It is entitled to demand complete intellectual freedom. To this end it must ask for a measure of detachment from current crises and routine procedures as necessary conditions of fulfilling its fundamental purpose in civilized society."

The report noted approvingly that "if Federal funds were to be cut off tomorrow, Harvard would be able to honor its commitments to all its permanent faculty members." But it suggested no boundary markers

Six-Billion-Volt Whirligig

T HE CAMBRIDGE Electron Accelerator was the most conspicuous example of government participation in university research during the expansive 1950s and '60s. Jointly operated by Harvard and MIT, it became a national center for the study of high-energy interactions of electrons and photons.

The CEA, engineered by Harvard and MIT physicists, took eight years to plan and build. It was completed in 1962. The $12 million construction cost and almost all of the operating costs were met by the Atomic Energy Commission. The annual budget ranged from a high of $6.2 million in 1965 to a low of $2 million in 1973. On the average, this accounted for almost half the federal funds received annually by the Faculty of Arts and Sciences.

The accelerator was housed in a large crescent-shaped structure, north of the University Museum, that took up as much square footage as the Divinity School's nearby buildings. The accelerator was capable of energizing particles to a peak value of 6 billion electron volts by sending a slender beam of electrons into orbit through a 20-million-electron-volt pre-accelerator and speeding them past a series of 48 big electromagnets arranged in a 236-foot-diameter ring. An electron could cover the course 10,000 times in one-hundredth of a second, almost the speed of light.

The mechanism was located below ground level and shielded by thick concrete walls. The

The Cambridge Electron Accelerator's experimental area was the size of a football field. The accelerator could direct as many as six electron or photon beams into the hall to accommodate as many experiments.

CEA's only major accident—one of the worst in Harvard annals—occurred on July 5, 1965, when 300 liters of liquid hydrogen blew up in the experimental hall. The explosion and resulting fire injured eight staff members; one later died.[15]

The CEA dominated the field of high-energy physics for a dozen years. In the accelerator's first years of operation, when it was producing the fastest, most intense, and most energetic beam of electrons in the world, it was used by more than two hundred physics professors and graduate students from many universities. By 1970 accelerators with higher energy ranges were in operation, and the Atomic Energy Commission transferred its support to costlier and more potent facilities at Stanford and elsewhere. The CEA was closed, and its staff and equipment dispersed, in 1973.

for federal funding. Over the next seven years the monetary value of Harvard's income from government sources would triple, with the federal component of the annual budget approaching 40 percent.

The Fourth Branch of Government

T HE COLD WAR HAD TIGHTENED financial ties between Harvard and government. As the 1960s began, the presidential administration of John F. Kennedy '40 tightened the intellectual relationship. As a Commencement speaker in 1956, Kennedy had referred to the "largely unfounded feelings of distrust" that estranged intellectuals and politicians. For the good of the nation, cooperation and understanding were needed. As president, Kennedy wanted an administration stocked with "the best and the brightest." Harvard's faculties were a prime recruiting ground. The University and the administration became so closely identified that Harvard was dubbed "the fourth branch of government."

John Fitzgerald Kennedy had entered Harvard in the Tercentenary autumn of 1936. One tutor remembered him as "a gangling young man with a lightly snub nose and a lot of flap in his reddish-brown hair." He had entered Princeton from Choate School the previous fall, but had dropped out after a few months. At the suggestion of his father, Joseph P. Kennedy '12, he spent the summer studying under Harold Laski at the London School of Economics.

Jack was the second of Joseph Kennedy's four sons to enter Harvard. Joe Junior, the oldest, was starting his junior year. Robert and Edward would graduate after the war. Initially Jack seemed more interested in sports than in studies. He played freshman and junior varsity football and was backstroker on the freshman swimming squad's medley relay team. He joined the sailing team and skippered his boat to an intercollegiate championship. As a member of Winthrop House he went in for intramural swimming, hockey, and softball. He was also a *Crimson* editor. Concentrating in history and government, he got C's in his freshman and sophomore years. In his junior year, courses taught by Professors Arthur Holcombe, Bruce Hopper, and Payson Wild ignited his intellectual interests. "Kennedy is surprisingly able once he gets down to work," wrote one teacher. His senior honors thesis was titled *Appeasement at Munich*. Expanded and retitled *Why England Slept*, it became a bestseller within a few months of Kennedy's graduation.

Kennedy joined the navy before Pearl Harbor. Injured when his torpedo boat was run down by a Japanese destroyer in 1943, he was decorated for rescuing surviving crew members (see page 163). His war record, a brief stint as an international journalist, and his father's financial backing helped get him elected to Congress. In 1952, after three terms in the House, Kennedy won the Senate seat held by Massachusetts Republican Henry Cabot Lodge Jr. '24. Three years later, recuperating from back surgery, he wrote *Profiles in Courage*, a study in political leadership that won a Pulitzer Prize in 1957.

Kennedy was now a national figure. He had narrowly lost his party's vice presidential nomination in 1956, but in 1960 his strong showing in major primary elections gained him the Democratic nomination for president. Kennedy and his running mate, Senate majority leader Lyndon Johnson of Texas, waged an aggressive campaign against Vice President Nixon and Cabot Lodge. Kennedy won by fewer than 120,000 votes out of a record 68.3 million cast. At 43, he was the youngest president ever elected and the first born in the twentieth century. He was also the first Roman Catholic to win the White House.

IN HIS ACCEPTANCE SPEECH, Kennedy declared that "we stand on the edge of a New Frontier." That a large number of New Frontiersmen would have Harvard ties had been evident since the fall, when reports in the press identified Archibald Cox '34, LL.B. '37, Royall professor of law, as Kennedy's "brain trust coordinator and recruiter." Cox had taken a year's leave from Harvard to assist Kennedy, but his ap-

Man of the Hour

Surrounded by bodyguards, police, and detectives, Premier Fidel Castro of Cuba spoke at Soldiers Field in April 1959 as the guest of the Harvard Law School Forum.

The leader of the revolution that had overthrown the Batista regime only three months earlier told a sympathetic audience of about 10,000 that his government's aim was to develop Cuban resources "to get the standard of living you have here." Speaking from a wooden platform erected in front of Dillon Field House, he answered questions after his prepared address.

Castro had dined at the Faculty Club before his speech. He wore his characteristic green fatigues and was introduced by Dean McGeorge Bundy, who respectfully called him Dr. Castro.

"The Cuban revolutionist," Castro told his hearers, "has his own ideals. He believes in them strongly—ideals of freedom, human rights, and social justice. But freedom is impossible if millions of people don't know how to read and write. A man is not free if he is hungry."

Below: Jack Kennedy (right) and his brother Joe sailed for England in 1938 with Joseph P. Kennedy, their father, who had been named ambassador to Britain. Young Joe had just graduated from Harvard; Jack was a rising junior.

Hat in the ring: Kennedy, then an Overseer, at Commencement in 1959. He won the Democratic nomination for president a year later.

pointment as solicitor general would keep him in Washington until 1965.

Kennedy had kept in close touch with Harvard. After the war he had been an elected director of the Alumni Association, and he had led the field as a candidate for Overseer in 1957. At the previous year's Commencement Harvard had honored him with an LL.D. ("Brave officer, able Senator, son of Harvard; loyal to party, he remains steadfast to principle"). During his six-year term as an Overseer, Kennedy chaired committees to visit the departments of astronomy and military, naval, and air science. He was also on committees visiting the government department and the School of Public Administration.

Two months after the 1960 elections Kennedy arrived for an Overseers' meeting and was mobbed by hundreds of students who broke through police lines to see him. "I am here to discuss your grades with President Pusey," he called out from the steps of University Hall. "I shall protect your interests." Later he went to the Irving Street home of professor of government Arthur Schlesinger Jr. and spent the afternoon making telephone calls to prospective New Frontiersmen.

"I stood on the sidelines and was rather amused by some of the people here who were so eager to get aboard," Pusey would later say. "I had some fun joking with [Kennedy] when it became clear that he was planning to take people out of here in numbers. I would be asked for opinions about people, and I'd say, 'Why don't you look someplace else?'"

Schlesinger, a campaign adviser, had signed on as a presidential assistant and official historian. Another early recruit was McGeorge Bundy, Kennedy's grade-school classmate. After seven years as dean of arts and sciences, Bundy became special assistant for national security affairs. Other faculty members who joined the administration included Archibald Cox; David Bell, A.M. '41, lecturer on economics (director of the budget); Abram Chayes '43, LL.B. '49, professor of law (counselor, State Department); and Stanley Surrey, Smith professor of law (assistant secretary of the treasury). Don K. Price, professor of government and dean of the School of Public Administration, was Kennedy's consultant on governmental structure and operations; Paul Doty, professor of chemistry, was on the White House science advisory committee. John Kenneth Galbraith, Warburg professor of economics, was named ambassador to India, and Edwin O. Reischauer, PH.D. '39, became ambassador to Japan. Law School dean Erwin Griswold complained that the New Frontier had drafted more than 10 percent of his forty-man faculty; before being tapped himself, Dean Price of the School of Public Administration countered that he had lost 100 percent of his faculty (David Bell was the school's only member who did not hold a joint appointment).

Four cabinet members had Harvard ties. Ford Motor Company president Robert McNamara, M.B.A. '39, a former assistant professor at the Business School, was named secretary of defense. C. Douglas Dillon '31, LL.D. '59, a New York investment banker who had been under secretary of state under Eisenhower, was secretary of the treasury. J. Edward Day, LL.B. '38, a California insurance man, became postmaster general. More controversial was the appointment of Robert F. Kennedy '48 as attorney general. Then 35, he had been counsel to a Senate labor-management rackets committee and had managed his brother's campaign. With the waggish wit that endeared him to the press and much of the public, the president-elect answered critics by quipping, "I don't see what's wrong with giving Bobby a little experience before he goes out to practice law." As his brother's closest adviser on domestic and foreign issues, Bobby would be the second most powerful man in the country.

Others in the White House inner circle were special assistant Kenneth O'Donnell '49, a former football teammate of Robert Kennedy, and speech writer Richard Goodwin, LL.B. '58. Paul Nitze '28 was assistant secretary of defense for international security affairs; James Tobin '39, PH.D. '47, was on the Council of Economic Advisers. *Presidential Power*, a "manual of president-craft" by Richard Neustadt, PH.D.'51, became the bible of the New Frontier. Neustadt himself served as a presidential consultant. All told, more than fifty of some 85 positions classed by President Kennedy as "high-level" were filled by Harvard alumni.

"Harvard has given presidents to this nation before," acknowledged Judge Henry Friendly '23, LL.D. '27, president of the Alumni Association, "but hardly one who seems to have so much of Harvard in his blood—and surely none who has bled Harvard so much."

"Never in history has a single university so swiftly and completely overrun the federal government," wrote Will Oursler '37 in the *Ameri-*

Among the president's men (from the top): McGeorge Bundy, assistant for national security affairs; Arthur Schlesinger Jr., special assistant; David Bell, director of the budget; Richard Neustadt, consultant; John Kenneth Galbraith, ambassador to India; and Edwin Reischauer, ambassador to Japan.

Opposite: "Oh, it's a grand day for Harvard." This Stevenson cartoon appeared in the *New Yorker*.

can Weekly. James Reston, Washington bureau chief of the *New York Times*, opined that there would be "nothing left at Harvard but Radcliffe." The only Harvard department left untouched, claimed Cowles Publications' Fletcher Knebel, was the one in charge of losing to Yale. When asked how he got his post, Secretary of Agriculture Orville Freeman replied, "I'm not sure, but I think it has something to do with the fact that Harvard does not have a school of agriculture."

KENNEDY'S ADMINISTRATION gave the nation an infusion of hope and confidence. "Let's get this country moving again" had been the senator's campaign slogan. In a resonant inaugural address, he declared that "the torch has been passed to a new generation of Americans—born in this century, tempered by war, disciplined by a hard and bitter peace, proud of our ancient heritage—and unwilling to witness or permit the slow undoing of those human rights to which this nation has always been committed, and to which we are committed today at home and around the world. . . . For there is a new world to be won."

Kennedy was determined to reassert American military and economic superiority in the world arena. His concept of the nation's international role contrasted with that of Eisenhower, who had sought military disengagement in Korea and declined to rescue the French from a colonial rebellion in Indochina. Kennedy's boldness brought him early humiliation after the Bay of Pigs fiasco in Cuba, and later led to a dramatic showdown with Soviet premier Khrushchev, who defied the West by walling off East Berlin and putting Soviet missiles on Cuban bases. But Kennedy outmaneuvered Khrushchev in the missile crisis of 1962, and scored a diplomatic coup when the Soviets joined Britain and the United States in a nuclear test-ban treaty in 1963.

Resolved to pull ahead of the Soviets in the "space race," Kennedy committed the United States to putting a man on the moon by the end of the decade. The Peace Corps, proposed in a campaign speech, sent thousands of volunteers to developing countries. The creation of the Alliance for Progress was a sign that Latin America would not be neglected.

Congressional opposition frustrated the president's hopes for a sweeping civil rights bill, but the Kennedy brothers gave full support to the desegregation movements begun in the mid-1950s. When a hostile mob threatened the Reverend Martin Luther King Jr. and his supporters in Montgomery, Alabama, the attorney general sent 400 federal marshals to protect them. When a black student was barred from enrolling in the University of Mississippi and riots broke out, the president ordered troops to the scene.

The Kennedy years were fraught with international and domestic tensions, but the president's easy manner and quick wit conveyed the sense that his administration was in control. As the first chief executive to hold regular press conferences on live television, he made the medium his own, as Franklin Roosevelt had done with radio. Jacqueline Bouvier Kennedy, a glamorous and accomplished Vassar graduate, played a signal role in making the White House a cultural center. The Kennedys

President Kennedy visited Harvard in May 1963 to view possible sites for a presidential library. In the foreground, to the president's left, is Paul Buck, professor of history, director of the University Library, and a member of a three-man committee formed to advise the Corporation on locations for the library. University police chief Robert Tonis is at Kennedy's right.

revived the lapsed tradition of White House musicales and held receptions and dinners for creative artists. One dinner honored 49 Nobel laureates and other distinguished Americans, occasioning the president's remark that the guest list comprised the White House's "most extraordinary collection of talent . . . since Thomas Jefferson dined alone."

KENNEDY SAW THE UNITED STATES as a munificent provider of ideas, goods, and services to the free world. Harvard now saw itself in the same light. "For several decades—perhaps longer—there has been growing in Harvard a sense that her mission is world-wide," wrote President Pusey in 1961. "This is not to question Harvard's essential rootage in this nation, it is rather simply to recognize that the present activities, interests and responsibilities of our country, and so also of her educational institutions, reach round the world."

Individually and in teams, scholars from Harvard and other universities shared their expertise on democratization, economic development, health care, and education with national agencies and private organizations on every continent. The Center for International Affairs, founded in 1958 to provide fellowships for academic experts on leave from government service in Europe and the Near East, set up an advisory service for developing countries. Multidisciplinary research centers studied societies in the Soviet Union, the Middle East, and East Asia; a Latin American center was in the making. Every graduate school had its international programs. New offerings in international relations, comparative government, and foreign cultures, languages, and religions enlarged the curriculum of the Faculty of Arts and Sciences. More than two thousand students from abroad enrolled at Harvard each year.

In the course of his tour of the Far East in 1961, President Pusey received a doctorate in letters at the annual convocation of the University of New Delhi. At right is Indian vice president S. Radhakrishnan, chancellor of the university.

President Pusey himself was an international figure. In the fall of 1961 he traveled to Asia, visiting six Harvard clubs and fifteen universities in Korea, Japan, Taiwan, Hong Kong, Thailand, and India, and attending an assembly of the World Council of Churches in New Delhi. That summer the Glee Club made its first world tour, with an itinerary that began in Hawaii, included twenty cities in the Far East, and ended in Athens.

Harvard had a central part in the formative years of the Peace Corps. It was one of the first institutions to provide facilities, faculty, and administrative support for Peace Corps training programs. The first group of volunteers for Nigeria trained at Harvard; by the second year of the program, 55 Harvard and Radcliffe men and women—mostly alumni, but including some undergraduates on voluntary leave—were among the 4,000 volunteers on assignment overseas. Only the University of California at Berkeley could claim a larger number.

For many of those who remained at home, the administration's emphasis on civil rights was a spur to political action. Working through the national Student Nonviolent Coordinating Committee, students and faculty members joined voter registration drives in Mississippi. A Harvard-based Civil Rights Group, in affiliation with undergraduate political and religious organizations, provided counseling, tutoring, and playground supervision in black neighborhoods. A few students became linked with Students for a Democratic Society, organized in Port Huron, Michigan, in 1962. One was Todd Gitlin '63, who succeeded

Tom Hayden as president in the spring of his senior year. Though SDS was tied to the socialist-oriented League for Industrial Democracy, its initial agenda was not radical. The primary goal was to work with single-issue groups promoting peace and disarmament, urban health and welfare, and racial and economic equality.

"A Good Time to Act Greatly"

MANY WHO WERE THERE at the time would remember early-1960s Harvard as Eden—a truly collegial place where the life of the mind was valued and everything needful was at hand. The Program for Harvard College had relieved overcrowding in the Houses and provided new facilities for the creative arts. The intellectual stimulation of freshman year had been heightened by the Freshman Seminar program, in which eight or ten students could do independent research with eminent faculty members as mentors. Begun in 1959, it was proposed and funded by Edwin Land '30, S.D. '57, the Harvard dropout who invented instantaneous photography. In departmental courses, as a future dean of arts and sciences would write, "the people who wrote the books stood at the lectern."[14] Lecturing in Nat Sci 114 was the *auteur* of behavioral psychology, B.F. Skinner. Sociologist David Riesman, a coauthor of *The Lonely Crowd*, gave a popular General Education course billed as "an attempt . . . to relate the contributions of sociology, anthropology, and psychology to those of history, economics, and political science in the study of American character and society." Hundreds competed to get into psychoanalyst Erik Erikson's large course on the human life cycle. Biology 2's resident expert on genetics was James D. Watson, who would share a Nobel Prize in 1962 for discovering the DNA molecule's structure. The physicist Edward Purcell, also a Nobel laureate, was another enthusiastic teacher. The renowned theologian Paul Tillich gave undergraduate courses on "The Interpretation of History" and "Religion and Culture."

Still active were scholars whose learning and idiosyncrasies were legendary: Arthur Darby Nock, historian of religion; linguists I.A. Richards and Joshua Whatmough; the polymath Harry Wolfson; historian

Biochemist James Watson had a key part in one of the great scientific discoveries of all time: defining the double-helical structure of the DNA molecule. With two British scientists, Watson formulated a model that showed how DNA replicated itself, leading to new revelations about the genetic basis of heredity. The three shared the Nobel Prize in medicine or physiology in 1962.

Watson (at right) joined Harvard's faculty in 1955. His *Molecular Biology of the Gene* (1965) became a widely used biology textbook. He also jolted the scientific community with a candid account of the fiercely competitive race to discover the structure of DNA. Initially titled *Honest Jim*, it was accepted for publication by Harvard University Press. But when the Press tried to obtain legal releases from Watson's British colleagues, they threatened to sue. The Press's director sought guidance from the Harvard Corporation, which advised against publication. Retitled *The Double Helix*, the book was published by Atheneum in 1968 and became a best-seller.

Samuel Eliot Morison; the English department's all-knowing Howard Mumford Jones. Visiting British savants like Isaiah Berlin, Maurice Bowra, and C.P. Snow turned up at House masters' lodgings and the Signet Society to sip sherry with tutors and undergraduates.

A postwar theatrical renaissance had diminished when the Brattle Theater Group died of financial anemia in 1952. But within a few years a second renaissance had begun, with ambitious undergraduate productions ranging from Shakespeare to Genet. The Harvard Opera Guild made its debut with productions of *The Barber of Seville* and *The Consul*. New literary magazines came and went. Café Capriccio, the ballad-singing center of Harvard Square, closed in the late 1950s but reopened as the Café Mozart, serving coffee of exotic kinds. Club 47 was the place for jazz and folk-singing. Joan Baez and Bob Dylan were among future stars of the genre who sang there. Station WHRB broadcast undergraduate picking and singing. The station's reading- and exam-period orgies diverted listeners with an eclectic mix: William Jennings Bryan's "Cross of Gold" speech, Australian aboriginal music, and a horn quartet in which all the parts were recorded by the same undergraduate musician.

BUT BEYOND THE CHARLES RIVER there was trouble. The specter of nuclear war with Russia was omnipresent. In the South, city officials were unleashing attack dogs and playing fire hoses on civil rights demonstrators. A sense of disconnection afflicted much of American society. In his 1961 Baccalaureate address President Pusey called it a "debilitating inertia . . . more a mood of dispiritedness than of despair." Though contemporary life offered "almost no hope of order, permanence, or stability in human affairs," said Pusey, "this is no time to feel sorry for ourselves. It is a worse time to blame or fear others. It is a time to act—a good time to act greatly." His hope was that some might have found at Harvard "a life-giving faith . . . to undergird and confirm the works of the mind."

The next academic year was one of increasing strain for Pusey. Early in his presidency he had temporarily added the deanship of the School of Education to his duties. When McGeorge Bundy left for Washington, Pusey decided to act as interim dean of arts and sciences. It was a tall order, especially in a year that began with a two-month trip to Asia. Flying west in October, Pusey left the oversight of his office to Senior Fellow Charles Coolidge. Lamont University Professor Edward Mason, PH.D. '25, LL.D. '56, former dean of the School of Public Administration, served as acting dean of arts and sciences. "I'll open the mail and start the machinery going on important questions," said the imperturbable Coolidge, adding that he meant to imprint most of the mail with a rubber stamp reading, "The President is expected back on December 6."

Pusey did not relish his deanship. Faculty members viewed the dean as their envoy to the central administration, and were put off by having to deal with a dean-cum-president. Pusey had seen his dual role as an opportunity to explore the faculty's inner workings, but he later admitted that he could not keep up with the administrative demands of the dean's office and had "learned a lot more about some of the depart-

Bridgman   Purcell

Nobel Laureates

J ames Watson (opposite page) was the eighth faculty member to win or share a Nobel Prize in the postwar era. The earlier laureates:

—Percy W. Bridgman (1946, physics), for studies and inventions in high-pressure physics.

—Edward M. Purcell (1952, physics), for developing the nuclear resonance method of measuring magnetic forces within the atom.

—Fritz A. Lipmann (1953, medicine or physiology), for discovering "co-enzyme A" and its role in cell metabolism.

—John F. Enders, Frederick C. Robbins, and Thomas H. Weller (1954, medicine or physiology), for growing polio virus in tissue cultures for use in vaccine.

—Georg von Békésy (1961, medicine or physiology), for research on the inner ear.

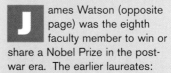

Clockwise from top: Lipmann, Enders, Robbins, Weller, von Békésy

Historian Franklin Ford, who became dean in 1962, led the Faculty of Arts and Sciences through the increasingly difficult decade of the 1960s.

To dramatize their disarmament proposal, three dozen members of a new group called Tocsin staged a daylong walk around Harvard and Radcliffe in December 1960, handing out leaflets and blue armbands. By the end of the day more than a thousand students and faculty members were wearing armbands. The style of political protest would become more frontal and strident as the 1960s went on.

ments than I wish I'd ever known." In May 1962, at the annual meeting of the Associated Harvard Clubs in Los Angeles, Pusey offered the deanship to Franklin L. Ford, PH.D. '50, a professor of history who was spending a year at Stanford's Center for Advanced Study in the Behavioral Sciences. Ford, a former senior tutor at Lowell House, began his new duties in the fall. His handling of the office reduced the pressure on Pusey and raised the morale of the faculty. Though his field was German history, Ford was attentive to the interests of the faculty's scientists. He became the principal organizer of the $49 million Program for Harvard Science, announced in 1967.

As Pusey noted in a report on his first ten years in office, issued in 1963, the University had grown impressively in a decade. Overall enrollment had risen from 11,400 to 13,700. The faculties had increased in size by 50 percent, and Harvard scholars had won five Nobel prizes. The student body had become far more diverse; the College continued to produce the largest number of Rhodes Scholars. In the first decade of round-robin play, Harvard teams had compiled the best record of any Ivy League school. Almost a hundred buildings had been constructed or renovated. The scale of the institution's financial operations had grown dramatically. The annual operating budget had gone from $39 million in 1953 to $100 million. The value of the endowment had reached $845 million. Withal, the number of personnel in the central administration had been reduced.

WERE THERE NO SIGNS that times were about to change? There were, but few knew just what to make of them.

Organized political protests had begun. In December 1960 about three dozen members of a new group called Tocsin staged an all-day demonstration in support of a U.S. moratorium on nuclear testing.

May 1961 brought the "diploma riots"—two nights of undergraduate rioting to protest the adoption by the faculty and the governing boards of a diploma written in English rather than Latin. The demonstration began lightheartedly, with a Latin oration delivered on the Widener Library steps by a toga-clad, laurel-crowned senior. A throng of about two thousand then sang "Gaudeamus Igitur," marched to President Pusey's house, and proceeded to Harvard Square chanting "Latin Si, Pusey No!" A second night of disorder ended with arrests and some restrained use of tear gas by Cambridge police. Like the spring riots of previous years, this one might have been dismissed as a compound of high spirits and a trivial cause, but many seniors felt genuinely aggrieved that the administration had ignored a series of petitions and discussions about the diploma issue. "None of the students had been consulted," noted Mark Alcott '61, the Bulletin's undergraduate correspondent, "but they hardly could have expected to be; they never have been."

In the spring of 1962 the Crimson flayed President Pusey in a series of highly critical editorials. In the Crimson's view, his leadership had been uninspired and uninspiring, and the president had alienated himself from faculty members and undergraduates. The editorials marked the first serious rift between student editors and the president.

When Radcliffe students descended on John Winthrop House in

May 1963 to stage their own version of a panty raid, another riot broke out. To *Bulletin* correspondent Edward Grossman '64, the "Great BVD Raid . . . focused a cold, hard, light on the most compelling problem in this community: the integration of Radcliffe into the academic and social company of Harvard, on equal terms and no eyebrows raised."

A week later Harvard announced the dismissals of Timothy F. Leary, lecturer on clinical psychology, and Richard Alpert, assistant professor of clinical psychology and education. Leary and Alpert had been experimenting with such hallucinatory drugs as psilocybin, mescaline, and LSD, with undergraduates (and themselves) as subjects. In the spring of 1962 the University had forbidden undergraduates to participate. Alpert was fired for continuing to administer drugs to students, Leary for failing "to keep his classroom appointments."

The fall of 1963 was spiced by a controversy over the enforcement of College parietal rules, which limited the hours when students could entertain women in their rooms. Citing a "general laxness in the observance of parietal procedures," dean of students Robert B. Watson '37 touched off the debate by describing recent infractions as potentially "scandalous" had they been made public. The dean added that "there are public laws in this state, [and] it's our positive duty to deal with fornication just as we do with thievery, lying, and cheating—by taking severe disciplinary measures against the offenders." John U. Monro '34, dean of Harvard College, echoed Watson's anxiety. To flout "decent standards of behavior," he said, was to betray Harvard's historical commitment to conservative morality. Such statements provoked astonishment, mirth, and contempt among undergraduates. "The revolution in moral premises and sexual behavior," wrote the *Bulletin's* Edward Grossman, "is not incipient or tentative, but an observed phenomenon, and so profound that it has effectively blocked communication on the subject between this generation of Harvard and all the generations which reached adulthood before World War II."[15]

Such episodes were a foretaste of things to come. By the end of the decade, political demonstrations would be a regular part of the life of American universities. Students would have at least a nominal role in institutional decision-making. Adversarial journalism would be standard procedure for the *Crimson*. Alpert would be teaching elsewhere; Leary, urging all the world to "turn on, tune in, drop out," would be the nation's most famous explorer of "inner space." Drug use in college and university settings would be ubiquitous.

And parietal rules would be on the way out. Predictably, the whiff of "sex scandals" at Harvard proved irresistible to newspapers in Boston and beyond—but not after November 22, 1963, when the world was stunned by the news of President Kennedy's assassination.

A magisterial presence: Professor John H. Finley Jr., master of Eliot House, as the judge in a Christmas production of *Toad of Toad Hall*. House drama was a flourishing art form in the early 1960s.

The University on Trial

An academic analogue to the crash of 1929.
—*David Riesman, Henry Ford II professor of social sciences, on the tribulations of American universities in the late 1960s.*

T HE BRAVURA SPIRIT of the Kennedy Administration bred a rising optimism in much of the nation. The euphoria ended when the president was assassinated in Dallas on November 22, 1963. Vice President Lyndon Johnson, who had coveted the presidency, succeeded Kennedy and advanced the civil rights initiatives that the latter had begun. But the life of the nation was increasingly troubled by deepening involvement in a counterinsurgency war in Vietnam.

The Vietnam War diverted resources from Johnson's ambitious domestic program, the Great Society, and drained governmental support from colleges and universities. Spending for higher education peaked in 1967, and declined 2 percent per year thereafter. Increased military spending brought galloping inflation; costs rose faster than incomes, and the stock market faltered. Institutional endowments declined in real value. "The boom is over," wrote sociologist David Riesman in 1968. Marginal col-

A flag of rebellion flies from University Hall, forcibly occupied by members of Students for a Democratic Society and their followers at noon on April 9, 1969.

leges were already failing. Though the college-age population was soaring, almost sixty institutions would close their doors in the next two years.

Military engagement in Vietnam coincided with the appearance on American campuses of the baby boom generation. This record cohort of students, born at a rate of almost 4 million a year, was the first to grow up watching television; many of its members were keenly attuned to political and social issues. Faculty members and administrators were unprepared for their discontent with "the system"—and for their ways of expressing it.

Increasing draft calls and a widening perception of the Vietnam War as illegal and immoral led to campus protests. Universities themselves became targets. To many students, they represented the system and were complicit in prosecuting the war.

The conduct of the war raised hard questions about the uses of technology, learning, and power. Students condemned what they perceived as the divorce of learning from morality. Some of the best and brightest assembled by the Kennedy administration now appeared to be unprincipled—or at best self-deceived—and intransigent. At Harvard and almost every other major university, the protesters went beyond the war to embrace other issues: racism, the university's impact on the community, "student power."

Universities had helped the country out of previous crises, but were now in a crisis of their own. Their students were assailing them as seats of elitism, avenues to unjustifiable wealth and power, purveyors of weapons technology to the military-industrial complex. To the public, administrators and faculty members seemed unable to keep their houses in order. Opinion polls showed a precipitous drop in confidence in American institutions, including institutions of higher education. In an era of shrinking resources, uncertainty about educational goals, and reformist pressure from students, the university was on trial.

Harvard was better off than most. Academically it was strong. Applications remained at record levels. It had an endowment of almost a billion dollars. But like other institutions, it was now confronted by students whose values, expectations, and behavioral patterns were distinctively different from their forerunners'.

The Baby Boomers

ALL TOLD, THE BABY BOOM generation comprised some 75 million young people born between 1946 and 1964. By the mid-1960s this vast group made up almost 40 percent of the American population. The boomers were not only the first generation to grow up with television and rock music. They were also the first largely raised in the new suburban sprawl of postwar America, and the first to attend (and overload) the new postwar high schools.

"They were twice as likely as their parents to go to college," wrote journalist Landon Jones in a broad generational study, *Great Expectations*, "and three times as likely as their grandparents. They forced our economy to regear itself to feed, clothe, educate, and house them. Their collec-

November 22, 1963

IT WAS A BALMY Indian summer day in Cambridge. Most students were in class or at lunch when the news broke that President Kennedy had been shot during a Dallas motorcade. At 2 P.M. word came that he had been pronounced dead. The Memorial Church bell tolled; an incredulous hush enveloped the Yard. People walked through it slowly and soundlessly, as in a dream. Traffic noises from Harvard Square seemed muted. As the afternoon passed, offices and libraries darkened and closed. Students crowded into the *Crimson* newsroom to hear news bulletins and watch the teletype machines. The varsity football squad, in New Haven for the next day's Harvard-Yale game, returned to Cambridge. For the first time, The Game was postponed.

A memorial ceremony was held the next day. Every pew of the Memorial Church was filled half an hour before the service. Latecomers crowded the vestibule and the World War I memorial chamber. The Glee Club sang the *Adoramus Te* of Clemens; then came readings from the 130th and 46th Psalms, and the University Choir singing Purcell's *Thou Knowest, Lord, the Secrets of Our Hearts.*

The Reverend Charles Price '41, preacher to the University, spoke briefly. "The President is dead, and each of us is stricken in a mortal place," he began. "We took courage from his courage, and were lifted up by the grandeur of his vision. His whole life was lived in the public service. Now he has died for his country and we died a little when he died. Words are too feeble to praise him. Only devotion to things he cared about can do

A month before the assassination, President Kennedy had watched the Harvard-Columbia football game and chatted at halftime with President Pusey.

that." Samuel Miller, dean of the Divinity School, read a final prayer: "Fix thou our steps, O Lord, that we stagger not at the uneven motions of the world, but go steadily on our way, neither censuring our journey by the weather we meet, nor turning aside at anything that may befall us." The service ended with the singing of *Our God, Our Help in Ages Past*, and a Bach organ prelude.

For two days, Harvard and the rest of the world remained transfixed as a stark sequence of events unfolded before the television cameras— the murder of suspect Lee Harvey Oswald while in custody of the Dallas police, the cortege to and from the Capitol rotunda, the funeral mass, the burial in Arlington National Cemetery, the lighting of the eternal flame. The 46-year-old president's death seemed not only a national tragedy but a personal one; the British commentator Alistair Cooke spoke of "this sudden discovery that he was more familiar than we knew."

tive purchasing power made fads overnight and built entire industries."[1]

The baby boom took America by surprise. Birth rates had declined throughout the 1920s and 1930s, hitting a modern low of 2.3 million in 1933. In the early years of World War II, births started to climb: a record 3.1 million "furlough babies" were born in 1943. ("The U.S. baby boom is bad news for Hitler," proclaimed *Life* magazine.) With the end of the war, births rose to 3.4 million in 1946 and 3.8 million in 1947. Demographers and Census Bureau statisticians claimed that these were transitional fluctuations. But births went on rising, reaching an all-time peak of 4.3 million in 1957 and exceeding 4 million a year through 1964, the last year of the boom. The maturation of the boomers had a transforming effect on the size of the applicant pool available to colleges and universities. From 1963 to 1973, total enrollments more than doubled, rising from 4.7 million to 9.6 million. Harvard College kept enrollment increases to about 2 percent per year, but the applicant pool rose from 5,100 to more than 10,000. A harbinger of change had been noted in 1960, when expanded recruiting efforts, combined with the World War II birth boomlet, produced a 56 percent jump in applications—from 3,200 to almost 5,000. Throughout the 1960s, competition for admission to Harvard, Radcliffe, and other high-prestige colleges was increasingly intense. "It is not surprising," wrote Landon Jones, "that, after surviving this Darwinian ordeal, the baby boomers later became the most fiercely anticompetitive generation in our history."

FOR ANYONE AVERSE TO COMPETITION, the Harvard of the mid-1960s was not an ideal setting. As McGeorge Bundy would write in *Daedalus*, the 1960s saw "an intensification of competitive pressures and external constraint (even without the draft)." As a result, wrote Bundy, students developed a "sense of involuntary servitude to a required framework of learning."[2] Exposure to the draft made matters worse.

The protests that began in mid-decade were primarily aimed at the nation's military involvement in Vietnam, but bundled with them were protests against educational regimentation and the canons of liberal education as defined (or left undefined) by elite institutions. Designing one's own education, through student power, was seen as the ultimate educational reform.

The baby boomers' arrival on American campuses had gone almost unnoticed at first, but cultural changes that would be identified with the boomers were already in process. Tocsin's protest marches had signaled the renewal of political activism at Harvard. The 1962 flare-up over parietal rules prefigured later demands for a fully coeducational College. A "drug culture" had appeared, as press coverage of the dismissals of Timothy Leary and Richard Alpert made clear.

But Tocsin's members had marched in coats and ties. By 1965, when U.S. forces assumed an expanded role in Vietnam, many baby boomers were bent on distancing themselves from the adult generation. Long hair, and wearing army-surplus fatigues with beads and bells, were expressions of disdain for the military. Challenging the House dining halls' coat-and-tie rules was a way to say no to educational regimentation. Leather jackets, T-shirts, and blue jeans showed their wearers' solidarity with working people. Playing rock music at high decibel levels, smoking marijuana and exhibiting sexual freedom in public places, embracing eastern religions and radical politics—all were gestures of resistance to an adult generation that was seen as conformist and hypocritical. Within two years, the easy optimism and idealism of the Kennedy era had given way to contrarianism and generational warfare.

All authority figures were suspect. Jacob Brackman '65, who wrote for the *Alumni Bulletin* as an undergraduate, described in a 1968 *Esquire* article a generation "that doesn't take the news straight, doesn't take the utterances of public figures straight, doesn't take social games straight. It suspects not only art but the whole range of modern experience." Skepticism was not novel at Harvard, nor were the Harvard-

Antiwar demonstrators staged a march when Arthur Goldberg, ambassador to the United Nations, spoke at Harvard early in 1967.

ians of the 1960s the first "to raise insubordination into a culture," in the cultural historian Paul Berman's phrase.[3] On a nocturnal bender in 1789, Harvard students had threatened to burn down the president's house; in 1834, as Samuel Eliot Morison records, "the black flag of rebellion was hung from Holworthy Hall" and a bomb was ignited in chapel.[4] But in those days rebellious students were rarely allowed to remain on the premises if they were found out. The Harvard of the 1960s would be far more tolerant of what William James had memorably called the "undisciplinables."

Only gradually did college administrators and teachers face up to the baby boomers' refusal to abide by norms of expected behavior that had governed earlier generations. Speaking to entering freshmen in the fall of 1965, dean of the College John Monro praised "the surging effort of young men and women of your age...to tackle through direct action some of the grave social ills of our time." But he also warned that anyone breaking Harvard's parietal rules or the state's drug laws would be asked to leave. "Our expectation is that you will behave like gentlemen," said Monro. The class of 1969 listened respectfully. But relatively few of its members were interested in emulating the look and behavior of "the establishment." The code of gentlemanly conduct, a borrowing from the English public school system, was on its way out. A year later Monro would tell incoming freshmen that "no two genera-

High-rise buildings, sheathed in light-colored concrete, altered the Harvard skyline in the early 1960s. Structures like these represented an effort to maximize available building space, while responding to prevailing currents in contemporary architecture. At left: William James Hall (Minoru Yamasaki, 1963), for departments in the social sciences. Top right: Holyoke Center (Sert, Jackson & Gourley, 1962), for administrative offices and a new health center. Below: Peabody Terrace (Sert, Jackson, 1964), for married graduate students.

To many students of the mid-'60s, the scale and styling of buildings like these reinforced the sense that Harvard was a technocratic and impersonal place.

tions have ever wanted or needed to talk together more than yours and mine, and no two generations have had a harder time doing it."

Under Siege

IN THE KENNEDY YEARS the United States had provided billions in aid to help South Vietnam resist the army and guerrilla forces of North Vietnamese leader Ho Chi Minh. More than 16,000 troops had been sent as "military advisers." In August 1964 an encounter between U.S. ships and North Vietnamese patrol boats led Congress to pass the Gulf of Tonkin Resolution, giving President Johnson extraordinary powers to "prevent any further aggression." In a bid to force an end to the war, Johnson ordered limited bombing of North Vietnam and authorized the use of ground troops in combat.

Draft calls soared from 100,000 in 1964 to 400,000 in 1966; troop levels in Vietnam reached 300,000, and continued to climb. A solid majority of the American public supported military intervention, but rising draft calls and lengthening casualty lists fostered an increasingly vigorous antiwar movement. On college and university campuses, groups that had organized around civil rights issues shifted their focus to draft resistance and antiwar protests. Students for a Democratic Society, formed by University of Michigan students in 1960, emerged as a new campus force. A Harvard-Radcliffe chapter was organized in 1964 by Carl Offner '64 and Michael Ansara '67. The group held its first antiwar march that year. In April 1965 the national SDS held a mass demonstration in Washington that drew some 20,000 protesters. The event brought SDS into a loose antiwar coalition of civil rights and pacifist groups, clergy, feminist organizations, and students.

In his Baccalaureate address to the class of 1965, President Pusey observed that "a new and rather disturbing seriousness of tone" had been evident in that spring's antiwar demonstrations. "It may very well be," said Pusey, "that the end of these disturbances is not yet."

In October 1965, protest marches in ninety cities brought increased attention to the student movement that journalists now called the "New Left." Coordinated by SDS, the marches brought out an estimated 100,000 protesters. En route to Boston Common, Harvard students were joined by others from nearby schools. Along the three-mile route they were taunted by spectators with shouts of "Bomb Hanoi," "We want victory," and "Why aren't you millionaires' kids in Vietnam?" On the Common, police broke up a threatening crowd of hecklers.

SDS strategists saw that radical activists could make more headway on college and university campuses than in the working-class communities they had planned to organize. In the fall of 1965 the national office formulated an antidraft program encouraging conscientious objection, an end to the submission of rank-in-class information to local draft boards, and opposition to Reserve Officers Training Corps units on college campuses. Spokesmen emphasized that SDS did not advocate illegal methods of avoiding the draft.

Denunciations of SDS by government officials, including President Johnson and Attorney General Nicholas Katzenbach, incited more stu-

Escorted by W. Averell Harriman, LL.D. '66, Jacqueline Kennedy arrived at Holyoke Center for a dinner celebrating the creation of the Institute of Politics in October 1967.

Conceived by its director, Professor Richard Neustadt, as "a meeting place for the worlds of politics and scholarship," the Institute was part of Harvard's School of Government, renamed in 1966 in memory of John F. Kennedy. Ambassador Harriman, who had been under secretary of state for political affairs in the Kennedy administration, chaired the Institute's advisory committee.

dents to join. National membership rose to about 4,000. But SDS was at a crossroads. The national group's relationship with its parent organization, the League for Industrial Democracy, had broken down. Always wary of Communist efforts to infiltrate socialist groups, the old-line socialists running the LID disliked the presence in SDS ranks of "red diaper babies" with family ties to the Communist Party. Choosing solidarity over ideological purity, SDS defied the LID by striking a Communist-exclusion clause from its constitution. In October 1965 SDS broke with the LID.

At about the same time, a three-year-old Communist youth group called Progressive Labor began to infiltrate Midwest and East Coast SDS chapters. SDS rhetoric became much more radical. Nonviolence was less often invoked. Terms like "militant action" and "physical confrontation," imported from European student movements, were increasingly heard. Harvard's first physical confrontation occurred in the fall of 1966.

SECRETARY OF DEFENSE Robert McNamara was the target. He came to Quincy House in November to participate in an off-the-record seminar sponsored by the new Institute of Politics, part of the recently renamed John F. Kennedy School of Government. Before his arrival, Harvard-Radcliffe SDS demanded that McNamara engage in a debate on the Vietnam War. When he declined, SDS members said they would stage a "disruptive" demonstration to protest the Johnson administration's Vietnam policy and McNamara's refusal to debate.

Some 300 demonstrators were there to confront McNamara as he left Quincy House. Discovering that he was being shown out the back way, some of the demonstrators lay down in front of a waiting police car. Others started to rock it. By then a crowd of almost a thousand had assembled. McNamara climbed onto the roof of a parked car and tried to take questions, but he was drowned out by shouting. "I spent four of the happiest years of my life on the Berkeley campus doing some of the things you're doing here," McNamara shouted back. "I was tougher then, and I'm tougher now!" Jumping down, he was escorted by Harvard police into nearby Leverett House, and then through the University steam tunnels to the safe haven of Harvard Law School.

Hemmed in by demonstrators in November 1966, Defense Secretary Robert McNamara climbed onto the roof of a car and tried to answer questions. The crowd outshouted him.

Harvard was taken aback by the confrontation. A resolution apologizing to McNamara "for the unruly behavior of a small group" was signed by about 2,700 students. "Mob rule is what the incident sounds like to me, and there's no place for it at Harvard College," said Dean Monro. "I'm amazed that students at Harvard could use tactics like this." But Monro was uneasy about making "any kind of political activity or demonstration a matter of disciplinary action." Reviewing the incident, the College's administrative board resumed the practice of bringing major disciplinary cases before the full Faculty of Arts and

Sciences. The faculty exacted no punishments, but warned that "obstruction of free movement" would not be tolerated if it recurred.

It recurred in the fall, when two hundred demonstrators blockaded a Dow Chemical Company recruiter in Mallinckrodt Hall. In the past eighteen months more than fifty protests had been directed against Dow, the primary supplier of napalm to the U.S. military. The blockade lasted seven hours, despite the efforts of deans, House masters, and faculty members to talk the protesters out of the building.[5]

This time the administrative board recommended that 74 students be put on probation and that 171 be admonished. At the largest meeting in its history, the faculty approved the board's rulings. Fred L. Glimp '50, PH.D. '64, who had left the admissions office to succeed Monro as dean of the College, joined President Pusey and Franklin Ford, dean of arts and sciences, at a press conference after the meeting. Glimp called the punishments "serious but not harsh." Pusey read a statement explaining that Harvard was not punishing students for their dissent, but for their way of expressing it. "This kind of conduct is simply unacceptable," said Pusey, "not only in a community devoted to intellectual endeavor, but I would assume, in any decent democratic society."

Pusey had never taken a public stand on the Vietnam War. Antiwar students supposed he was for it. In an annual report issued in January 1968, he cited "a small group of over-eager young in evidence on many campuses who feel they have a special calling to redeem society."

Safe within the sanctuary of an ordered society, dreaming of glory—Walter Mittys of the left (or are they left?)—they play at being revolutionaries and fancy themselves rising to positions of command atop the debris as the structures of society come crashing down. Bringing students of this persuasion back to reality presents a new kind of challenge to college education.

Pusey said he was not criticizing "students who are sincerely concerned about the war or who choose to participate in orderly protests for whatever reason." In the past year, he wrote, "The vast majority of Harvard undergraduates went about their essential business seriously and gaily, as students have from the beginning." In the strained atmosphere of the times, many students felt that Pusey was trivializing their feelings of political commitment. His contention that for most it was business as usual suggested to them that the president was out of touch with his College constituency.

FOR UNIVERSITIES AND THE NATION, 1968 was a tumultuous year. The Tet Offensive, launched by Communist forces at the start of the Vietnamese New Year, showed that a quick end to the war was unlikely. With the energetic support of thousands of student volunteers, Minnesota senator Eugene McCarthy ran as a peace candidate in the New Hampshire primary. He got a startling 42 percent of the vote, holding Lyndon Johnson to 48 percent. Robert Kennedy, now the junior senator from New York, jumped into the presidential race. In late March, President Johnson announced that he would devote the rest of

Fred Leavitt, recruiting for Dow Chemical, was held hostage for seven hours by antiwar demonstrators in October 1967. Below: Dean of the College Fred Glimp asks the demonstrators to leave. Leaning against the wall is SDS co-chair Michael Ansara '68.

his term to settling the war. He would not run again because the nation was not united behind him. No president since Franklin Roosevelt had advanced so much liberal legislation, in civil rights, health and welfare, and education. But because of Vietnam the Johnson administration would end on a note of failure.

Four days later the Reverend Martin Luther King Jr., who had led the nonviolent civil rights movement since the mid-1950s, was killed by a sniper in Memphis. "Let us dedicate ourselves to what the Greeks wrote so many years ago," declared Robert Kennedy in a tribute to King: "to tame the savageness of man and make gentle the life of this world." In June Kennedy was assassinated. He had just finished first in the California primary elections.

University campuses had boiled over. At Columbia 800 demonstrators had taken a dean hostage and occupied five buildings. Student uprisings occurred almost simultaneously in Europe; in parts of North and West Africa; in Central and South America, the Philippines, and Japan. Yet Harvard had a relatively calm spring. Hundreds of students who might otherwise have been drawn to radical action had decided instead to stay within the system and work to elect McCarthy or Kennedy.

Hopes of a McCarthy candidacy came to a jolting end at the Democratic convention in Chicago that August. Party regulars made Vice President Hubert Humphrey the nominee. To head off threatened disruption by radical groups, Mayor Richard Daley called out city and military police and National Guardsmen. Millions of television viewers watched Daley's forces run riot in the convention hall and the streets outside, clubbing and tear-gassing protesters, reporters, and bystanders. In November Humphrey was narrowly defeated by Richard Nixon, who promised law and order and pledged in his victory speech that he would "bring America together."

As his assistant for national security affairs, Nixon chose Henry Kissinger '50, PH.D. '54, professor of government and director of the De-

Left: Coretta Scott King leaves Sanders Theatre after making a Class Day address in June 1968. She had taken the place of her husband, the Reverend Martin Luther King Jr., assassinated two months earlier. "In a power-drunk world, where means become ends and violence becomes a favorite pastime, we are swiftly moving toward self-annihilation," King's widow told the class of 1968. "Your generation must speak out with righteous indignation against the forces which are seeking to destroy us."

Heavy rain forced that year's Commencement exercises indoors for the first time since 1904. At the afternoon meeting of the alumni, held outside, the principal speaker was Shah Mohammed Reza Pahlevi of Iran, one of eleven honorary degree recipients. Below, Commencement aides intercept a group of seniors carrying sheets reading "No degree for a dictator."

fense Studies Program at the Center for International Affairs. Daniel Patrick Moynihan, professor of education and urban politics, was appointed to the new post of presidential assistant for urban affairs.

BEFORE THE ELECTION someone had spray-painted on a wall of Harvard's Weeks footbridge, "Vote No on November 5." Facetious undergraduates announced the formation of an anarchist group called "X," "but one gets the feeling," wrote *Alumni Bulletin* undergraduate correspondent Joel Kramer '69, "there isn't even enough political feeling at Harvard this fall to support anarchy." Yet there were almost 300 enrollees in Social Relations 148, "Social Change in America," one of four avowedly radical courses introduced in the fall of 1968. More than half the section leaders were undergraduate members of SDS.

There was a sense that something was going to happen. In October, a five-man commission issued a 222-page report on the Columbia uprising. Law professor Archibald Cox, a commission member, thought Harvard had a chance of averting a similar crisis because its residential and teaching arrangements were unlike Columbia's. But Harvard would soon be treated to what Columbia faculty members took wry pleasure in calling "the off-Broadway production of the Varsity Show."

SDS was waging a national campaign to drive ROTC units off university campuses. Harvard-Radcliffe SDS members circulated petitions and held meetings to highlight the issue. Three student-government groups and the Faculty of Arts and Sciences reviewed the status of ROTC units at Harvard. In December some 200 SDS members and sympathizers tried to sit in on a faculty meeting devoted to ROTC, forcing a postponement. Dean Ford called the sit-in "the most serious offense of its kind at Harvard."

Five of those involved had been on probation since the Dow demonstration. The administrative board voted 8-7 to require them to withdraw for two terms. The faculty hesitated. Once the protesters left, they might be drafted, compounding the punishment. Samuel Beer, Eaton professor of government, argued that "we do the militant students no

The strife-torn 1960s also saw some notable moments in Harvard athletics. The 1968 heavyweight crew, above, gave coach Harry Parker his fifth straight undefeated season and was the first Harvard boat to represent the United States in the Olympic Games. The crew placed sixth when the finals were rowed in Mexico City in October.

Game of the Century

ECLIPSING THE HEROICS of Brian Dowling, Yale's great quarterback, Harvard scored sixteen points in the final 42 seconds to achieve a miraculous tie in the climactic game of the 1968 football season.

A *Crimson* headline the next day proclaimed, "Harvard Beats Yale, 29-29."

Both teams came into the game with records of 8-0. The Ivy League title was at stake. A crowd of 40,000 filled the Stadium for the epic event.

At right, end Pete Varney scores the tying points on a last-second conversion pass from reserve quarterback Frank Champi.

favor, either in their present rebellion or in their later maturity, by . . .
giving them no sense of acceptable limits." But the faculty overturned
the board's vote, approving an amendment that put two-time offenders
on continued probation. The reversal effectively finished the administrative board as a disciplinary body, but put nothing in its place.

In February the faculty voted to end academic credit for military,
naval, and air science courses, and to halt the practice of granting faculty appointments to ROTC instructors. It also voted to end ROTC's
rent-free use of Harvard buildings, and to replace scholarships that
would be lost if ROTC decamped. The Corporation refused to accept
the last two provisions, pointing out that 40 percent of the 345 members
of Harvard's army, navy, and air force ROTC units were Law School or
Business School students who were not under the jurisdiction of the
Faculty of Arts and Sciences.

"In the Corporation's view," wrote President Pusey in an open letter
to Dean Ford, "it would be shortsighted in the extreme if academic institutions were now to withdraw their cooperation from the ROTC program because of repugnance to an unpopular war." University officials,
he said, would negotiate to maintain ROTC on a noncredit basis.

THE MONTH OF MARCH 1969 was eventful. The Corporation
and Radcliffe's board of trustees agreed to begin negotiations aimed at
achieving full merger of the two institutions by fall 1970. The Faculty of
Arts and Sciences approved the proposals of a committee chaired by
Henry Rosovsky, PH.D. '59, professor of economics, for a degree program in Afro-American studies. The committee's report also called for
fellowships for black graduate students and stepped-up recruitment of
black faculty members and administrators. The Harvard Association
of African and Afro-American Students, joined by SDS, demanded
cancellation of a course called "An End to Urban Violence," taught by
a visiting professor at the School of Design. The protesters charged that
the course reflected racist assumptions. A faculty petition and a statement from President Pusey reaffirmed "the inviolability of instruction
and examination in all duly approved University courses," but the professor withdrew the offering. Nine hundred students were taking Soc
Rel 149, "Radical Perspectives on Social Change."

For two weeks an anarchist group led by King Collins, a Columbia
graduate-school dropout, kept Harvard hopping. Collins twice broke
up classes given by Alex Inkeles, professor of social relations, shouting
obscenities and trying to force a banana into Inkeles's mouth. When
Collins and his friends disrobed in the Eliot House laundry room,
House master Alan Heimert threw them out, and Collins was arrested
for trespassing when he made his next visit to Inkeles's classroom.

In late March President Pusey met with the Student-Faculty Council,
organized after the Dow episode as a forum for discussion of University
issues, to talk about ROTC. "We don't think ROTC is wicked or anything else," he told the council. "We want it here because as far as I can
see, students will want to satisfy their military obligations this way." To a
questioner, Pusey insisted that "the current notion that the military-
industrial complex is an evil thing does not correspond to reality." The

At Harvard and other Ivy League
universities, military education
would be terminated by 1971.

Crimson followed up with a long editorial-page analysis of the president's stance on ROTC. It concluded, "President Pusey's testimony . . . before SFAC represents the type of rigidity which breeds confrontation."

"On Strike! Shut It Down!"

O N THE NIGHT OF APRIL 8, 200 demonstrators left a four-hour SDS meeting at Lowell Lecture Hall, marched to the president's house, and forced their way past a police guard at the gate. Michael Kazin '70, co-chairman of SDS, borrowed a pocket knife and pinned a list of six demands to the door.

The list had been formulated that night. As usual, Harvard-Radcliffe SDS was divided. The Worker-Student Alliance (Progressive Labor) faction was for seizing a building immediately. The New Left group wanted more time to build student support. WSA leaders held out for demands opposing Harvard expansion in Cambridge and the Boston Medical Area. The New Left saw ROTC as the chief issue. Motions for a building seizure were voted down three times. Both sides finally agreed on a set of demands that combined the expansion and ROTC issues. When the meeting broke up it was almost midnight.

The next day was springlike. At noon about seventy WSA members assembled outside University Hall, the administrative headquarters of the Faculty of Arts and Sciences. Norman Daniels, a graduate student in philosophy and SDS co-chairman, mounted the northeast steps of the building and read the list of demands through a bullhorn. Passersby shouted, "No, no!" and "Go home, go home!"

"There is only one enemy here, the Harvard Corporation," Daniels went on. "It's time for us to tell the Corporation by action what we've been telling them all fall by words." Shouting "Fight, fight, fight!" about three dozen demonstrators entered the building. Fred Glimp, who was meeting with three other deans, was confronted by John Berg, a tall, bespectacled graduate student in government. "We're going to have to throw some people out," said Berg. A few administrators left voluntarily. Others, including dean of freshmen F. Skiddy von Stade '38, dean of students Robert Watson '37, and assistant dean Archie C. Epps III, B.D. '61, were forcibly evicted. Pushed out one door, Epps re-entered through another. "What in hell are you doing back here?" said one demonstrator. "We're taking over this building," said another. "You're responsible for killing people in Vietnam."

"I am not responsible for killing people in Vietnam," said Epps hotly. "You are using methods here that I thought you objected to, violence and force." Again Epps was pushed out.

Franklin Ford was the last of nine deans evicted. Warning that the occupiers would face disciplinary action, he added, "I am prepared to remain in the building, for as long as you like, to discuss things."

"There's nothing to discuss," someone shouted. "When the Corporation gives in to our demands they can issue a statement."

An SDS flag was flown from a third-floor window, and a sign reading *Che Guevara Hall* was hung outside the Faculty Room. Two or three hundred people, including a few reporters, were now in the building. A

Refusing to leave voluntarily, assistant dean Archie C. Epps III was among nine administrators hustled out of University Hall as the SDS occupation of April 9, 1969, began.

crowd of about two thousand had collected outside. Months earlier, President Pusey and the council of deans had decided that if a "sensitive" building were taken, police would be called in promptly. Within University Hall were confidential personnel files. Pusey also feared that an occupied building would become a magnet for radicals among the 90,000 Greater Boston college students housed within two or three miles of Harvard Square. At 4:15 Dean Ford appeared on the Widener Library steps to give the demonstrators a fifteen-minute ultimatum and ask everyone else to clear the Yard. Almost all the occupiers remained in University Hall, and the crowd of onlookers grew. From a high-wattage sound system in Weld Hall came the Beatles' *Revolution*.

Harvard officers met with Cambridge police and city officials to discuss plans to clear University Hall at dawn the next day. After conferring with Ford, Glimp, and other deans, Pusey telephoned Harvard police chief Robert Tonis and said, "Tell the police we want them."

At 8 P.M. the University News Office issued a statement from the president. It began, "Can anyone believe that the Harvard SDS demands are made seriously?" and ended, "How can one respond to allegations which have no basis in fact?"

A FEW MINUTES BEFORE 5 A.M. a caravan of cars and buses brought police officials and 200 state troopers into the Yard. Municipal police had begun clearing the entrances to University Hall. Demonstrators had set off fire alarms in Yard dormitories, and a crowd of almost a thousand had formed. Dean Glimp issued a last-minute warning that could not be heard inside the building. The state troopers, in baby-

Almost 300 occupiers filled University Hall's Faculty Room. Among them were outsiders who had participated in uprisings at Columbia and the Sorbonne.

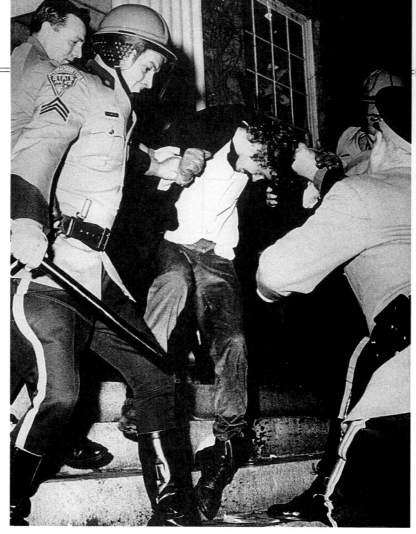

At dawn on April 10, a force of about 200 state policemen entered University Hall and began clearing the building. On the first floor, demonstrators passed out wet cloths for use against tear gas and linked arms to resist the first wave of police. Using riot gear, the state troopers broke the demonstrators into smaller groups, pushed them out of the building one by one, and took them off in buses for arraignment in Cambridge district court on charges of criminal trespass.

Nearly fifty people, including five policemen, were treated for injuries after the "bust."

blue helmets and coats, black boots, and jodhpurs, used a battering ram and chain cutters to gain entrance. Glimp and other Harvard officers followed them into the building. Holding their sticks high, cracking them against other sticks, the troopers broke the occupiers into groups, and pushed, shoved, and clubbed them out the doors and into waiting buses. The last bus left for the Cambridge courthouse at 5:25.

The court arraigned 184 persons on charges of criminal trespassing; 145 were Harvard or Radcliffe students. Almost fifty people, including five policemen, needed medical treatment. The injuries included two concussions, a minor skull fracture, and broken legs, wrists, and noses.

In the Yard people wept, cursed, and taunted the police. As the Boston police marched out they were pelted with small rocks and spittle. Students followed them to the gates shouting "Pusey's pigs!" and "Get out, get out!" College officers entered University Hall to assess its condition. Halls and offices were littered with paper. Files had been ransacked, records and correspondence photocopied, personal property taken. A hinge pin of a safe in Glimp's office had been pried out.

Outside, students began shouting, "On strike! Shut it down!"

Shocked and angered by the violence of the "bust," moderate students who had opposed the occupation did what Columbia students had done. They formed a coalition and went on strike. More than 2,000 jammed the Memorial Church at ten o'clock for an emotional four-

Dazed by the speed and violence of the building clearance, angry students shouted "Sieg heil!" and "Fascist pig!" at police officers waiting to leave the Yard. Clearing University Hall took less than a half-hour; the last contingent of police left just after 6 A.M.

hour meeting that ended in an agreement to boycott classes for three days. Classes continued to meet, though attendance was often sparse. Harvard was not shut down. Hundreds flocked to impromptu classes organized to discuss issues of the moment.

The Faculty of Arts and Sciences held an emergency meeting at the Loeb Drama Center on the second day of the strike. Dean Ford began by summarizing the circumstances surrounding "a physically repugnant and intellectually indefensible seizure," adding, "we are now faced with the predictable next chapters of what has become the stale script for the 'radicalization' of a university. . . . Some now insist that 'storm troopers entered University Hall.' This is true, but they entered it at noon on Wednesday, not at dawn on Thursday."

The administration hoped for a firm expression of support from the faculty. But many members were resentful that the faculty had not been consulted before the police action. Lengthy debate produced a resolution deploring both the occupation and the use of police to end it. The resolution asked that criminal charges against the occupiers be dropped, and established a "Committee of Fifteen" to investigate the causes of the demonstration and handle disciplinary action. The faculty met almost weekly for the rest of the spring. At variance on almost everything else, its members sought to avoid the factionalism that had wracked other universities. That they succeeded in doing so was largely

Opposite: Hours after the police action, 2,000 people jammed the Memorial Church for a mass meeting of a newly organized coalition group. After four hours of sometimes chaotic debate, they agreed to hold a three-day strike.

attributable to the organization of conservative and liberal caucuses, which negotiated agenda items before they came to the floor. Each side recognized the importance of compromise.

The Board of Overseers, at its regular meeting on April 14, "unequivocally" supported the decision to call in police. That afternoon almost 10,000 people trooped to a mass meeting at Harvard Stadium. Ably chaired by Lance Buhl, a 29-year-old history instructor, the meeting followed strict rules of order. SDS stayed away, but by a three-to-one vote those attending endorsed a set of demands that paralleled the original six. Two others were added. One called for amnesty for the University Hall occupiers, the other for student participation in administering the planned Afro-American studies program. After two and a half hours, those still on hand rejected an indefinite extension of the strike by a vote of 2,860 to 2,848. A recount showed the same slim margin: 2,971 to 2,955. "Typical Harvard," remarked an observer.

WITH THE STRIKE IN ITS SECOND WEEK, the faculty voted to reduce ROTC to extracurricular status, without rent-free housing. It was clear that these restrictions would end the presence of ROTC at Harvard. Thousands returned to the Stadium that afternoon and voted 2,411 to 1,129 to suspend the strike. Black student leaders said they would go on striking until the African-American studies demand was accepted.

Black students were invited to state their case to the faculty at two mid-April meetings. Their words implied that they might take disruptive action if their proposal went down. On April 22 the faculty broke with tradition and voted to give them a role in creating and running an academic department, including hiring and tenure decisions. That overrode the vote taken eight weeks earlier, when the faculty approved the proposals of the Rosovsky committee. To the relief of most faculty members, the vote brought the strike to an end. Rosovsky angrily quit the standing committee on Afro-American studies. "An academic Munich," he wrote later.[5] The remaining weeks of the spring term saw a series of minor disruptions. In May a Cambridge judge assessed $20 fines for criminal trespass on 170 people arrested for occupying University Hall. Most succeeded in appealing the fines. At the start of

As President Pusey left an emergency faculty meeting held to discuss the University Hall crisis, a student offered him a striker's armband. The faculty had condemned both the occupation of the building and the administration's resort to police to end it.

Thousands trooped to two mass meetings at Harvard Stadium to address issues raised by the strike. Following strict rules of order, participants in the first meeting worked out a set of eight demands and voted against an indefinite extension of the strike. The tally was recorded as 2,860 to 2,848.

Below: Two weeks after the strike's end SDS members halted a truck delivering linen at Dunster House. The student driver was roughed up and his load strewn about. The Teamsters' Union had called a strike against the linen supplier.

Commencement week, the Committee of Fifteen required sixteen students to leave Harvard for varying lengths of time. Twenty others received suspended requirements to withdraw; 102 were given warnings. When the committee held an open meeting to discuss the disciplinary rulings, angry radicals turned it into a shouting match. "If the University is to make any contribution toward reducing or overcoming the violence that prevails in the world, it must itself remain an oasis of non-violence," the committee wrote to the students it disciplined. But it also issued an interim report on the causes of the crisis that criticized the decision to summon police without delay. It called for "a sweeping reexamination and restructuring of the institutions, procedures, habits, and policies that are being challenged by many more than the disrupters."

SDS members hatched plans to invade the platform during the Commencement exercises, but the interruption was averted when senior class officers persuaded Pusey to allow a five-minute statement by an SDS member. The speaker—one of six seniors who had been required to withdraw—denounced the exercises as "an atrocity" and led a walk-out of about thirty seniors and other SDSers, who held a "counter-Commencement" in front of Memorial Hall.

Pusey would describe 1968-69 as "a dismal year" in his next annual report. His previous report, he conceded, had "failed to do justice to the widespread and varied malaise in both student and faculty populations. . . . In my view, this malaise in academic communities is not something peculiar to them, but in large measure reflects a deep and wide disquietude—born of legitimate concern, disappointment, uncertainty, frustration, anxiety, and to a degree also fear—at present characteristic of society as a whole."

Aftershocks

THE DEMONSTRATIONS OF 1969 set the pattern for protests that continued into the 1970s. The next academic year brought three building occupations by African-American students protesting "blatantly racist" hiring practices affecting painters and construction workers, and raids on the Center for International Affairs by a new faction of SDS. The spring disruptions had centered attention on

Harvard's administrative structures, and on the University's role in the community. Recommendations from various study committees were swiftly considered and acted on. A twenty-man Faculty Council was formed to help manage the business of the Faculty of Arts and Sciences. The next slate of candidates for the Board of Overseers included younger-than-average nominees—and for the first time a woman, Radcliffe trustee Helen Homans Gilbert '36. The administrations of Harvard and Radcliffe agreed on a trial of co-residence in three Harvard Houses. Plans were announced for 1,100 units of low- and moderate-income housing to be built in the Medical Area.

Fred Glimp resigned as dean of the College to direct Boston's Permanent Charity Fund, a post he had accepted a few hours before the occupation of University Hall. Ernest R. May, a professor of history, succeeded him. Professor Ford, who had suffered a mild stroke during the first week of the student strike, resigned as dean of the Faculty of Arts and Sciences to resume his teaching and research. His successor was John T. Dunlop, professor of political economy, who had chaired the Committee of Fifteen. Robert Watson, dean of students, was named director of athletics and was succeeded by assistant dean Epps.

President Pusey announced in February 1970 that he would take early retirement the following year. Appearing on *Meet the Press* after the strike, he had been asked by NBC's Lawrence Spivak '21, "Dr. Pusey, your supporters worry that these events may force you to resign. Your critics, of course, are worried that you won't resign. What are your intentions?" "I have no intention of resigning," Pusey had answered. "Anyone who has one of these jobs today must recognize that it's not just an activity that's filled with pleasure and happiness. But there are still things that are worthwhile to do."

Pusey later revealed that he had hoped for two years to yield his office to "a person who could stay with it throughout the 1970s." But four of the Corporation's five Fellows were to retire by 1970. Replacing them, Pusey felt, was a precondition. The spiraling progression of disturbances left little time to plan an orderly transfer of the presidency.

Two academics—John M. Blum '43, PH.D. '50, professor of history at Yale, and Charles P. Slichter '46, PH.D. '49, professor of physics at the University of Illinois—were elected to the Corporation in January 1970, replacing R. Keith Kane '22 and William Marbury. Boston lawyer Francis H. Burr '35 succeeded Marbury as Senior Fellow.

ESCALATION OF THE VIETNAM WAR brought a nationwide wave of protest that spring. At Harvard an era of peaceful peace marches ended on the night of April 15, when a group of 1,500 demonstrators, mobilized by an SDS splinter group called the November Action Coalition, clashed with police in Harvard Square. A four-hour riot erupted. Scores of store windows were smashed; fires were set. Police shot tear gas at the rioters, and into the Yard and House entryways. Forty policemen and 35 students were treated for injuries. The damage to some forty places of business was estimated at $100,000 or more.

In May came the U.S. invasion of Cambodia, and the killings of students at Kent State and Jackson State Universities by National Guards-

Leading 85 black students out of University Hall after a half-day occupation in December 1969, spokesmen for the Organization for Black Unity, a new University-wide coalition, read a statement. OBU occupied the building twice to press demands for changes in Harvard hiring policies.

men. After a mass meeting at Sanders Theatre, SDS members marched off to torch Shannon Hall, the ROTC building. Freshmen from the Yard linked arms to stop them. Two days later an early-morning fire destroyed 122-year-old Lawrence Hall. The abandoned building, scheduled for demolition to make way for a new science complex, had been taken over by radical students and street people as a "Free University." After a massive peace rally at Soldiers Field, SDS members marched on Shannon Hall once more; again they were headed off. Such incidents meant sleepless nights for Archibald Cox, who had agreed to act as the administration's troubleshooter during student disruptions. For months Cox had been tested by building occupations and bomb threats.

The Faculty of Arts and Sciences passed antiwar resolutions. Hundreds of students and faculty members joined demonstrations in Washington. A dozen senior faculty members called on presidential adviser Kissinger to protest the course of American foreign policy. Nathan Pusey was among eight university presidents who met for ninety minutes with President Nixon and warned him of "deep and widening apprehensions on campuses everywhere."

Pusey issued a statement sympathizing with "those who honestly find it difficult if not impossible to proceed with their regular responsibilities because of the recent dismaying turn of events in Southeast Asia." He urged University officers "to accommodate interruptions in our normal procedures [occasioned by] acts of conscience." The faculty voted to give politically active students wide latitude in completing spring-term work. Final exams were made optional in many courses.

Again SDS members planned to stop the show at Commencement. Fifteen minutes into the morning exercises—as William F. Weld '66, a candidate for the J.D. degree, gave an oration on "Political Disagreement"[6]—about thirty demonstrators mounted the dais with picket signs and a few small children. Residents of the nearby Riverside area, they had camped in the Yard the previous night. "We are the oppressed people," announced Saundra Graham, a short, peppery mother of five who spoke for the group. She used a bullhorn because the public address system had been hastily shut off. "Give us land and we will build housing on it," said Graham. "We are going to get some kind of commitment today or we are not leaving." After a ten-minute parley with other officials, President Pusey announced that two Corporation members would meet with the protesters. The exercises resumed. Never before had a Harvard Commencement been stopped in its tracks.

THE PRESIDENTIAL SEARCH that began in the spring of 1970 was the longest and most elaborate in Harvard's history. "Hooks" Burr, now the Corporation's Senior Fellow, was in charge. Some 203,000 letters soliciting nominations were mailed to alumni, faculty members, and students. "We earnestly hope that our choice, in the end, will send no shock waves through the community," Burr told reporters. "The new president has got to be received enthusiastically."

The Corporation received guidance from a recently formed Committee on Governance, chaired by Dean Dunlop. Dunlop himself was seen as a presidential contender. But the early favorite was Derek Cur-

Harvard Square was rocked by a four-hour riot in April 1970. Hundreds of rioters, including many "street people" who increasingly populated the Cambridge area, battled police, smashed windows, and looted storefronts. The first floor of a bank was burned out and a fire was set in the subway kiosk (above).

State officials described the "trashing" as one of the worst civil disturbances in Massachusetts history. Property damage was estimated at more than $100,000.

The Commencement of 1970 was halted for twenty minutes when Cambridge neighborhood residents and student demonstrators took over the platform. The protest ended when Corporation members Albert Nickerson and George Bennett agreed to meet afterward with representatives of the group.

tis Bok, dean of the Law School since 1968. Then 40, Bok had been a Law School faculty member since 1958. As a member of the council of deans he knew the University's workings, but he had not been caught up in the political toils of the Faculty of Arts and Sciences. He was reputed to be a good listener and tactful crisis manager. His field was labor and antitrust law; arbitration was a skill he had practiced as well as taught. Bok was a reluctant candidate. "I was absorbed with what I was doing at the Law School and had not been there very long as dean," he said later, "but I thought it would be presumptuous to take myself out of the running. Finally a national story came out that had me as one of the final candidates, and I thought, the time has come." Bok was at home in Belmont. It was snowing hard. He wrote Burr to say that he wished to remain at the Law School, but as he was leaving to mail the letter the telephone rang. Burr was calling to say that he was on his way to see Bok. When he arrived, he offered him the presidency.

Bok temporized. He made up his mind after a New York dinner with Yale president Kingman Brewster, one of his old Law School teachers. Brewster talked mostly to Bok's wife, Sissela, daughter of future Nobel laureates Gunnar and Alva Reimer Myrdal. She had just completed a Harvard doctorate in philosophy. "After we left," Bok recalled, "Sissela turned to me and said, 'Derek, maybe we should do this job.'"

"No shock, it's Bok," was the *Bulletin's* headline when the choice was made public. That all presidents since Leonard Hoar, A.B. 1650, had been graduates of Harvard College did not prove an obstacle to Bok's election. Though he had taken his LL.B. at Harvard in 1954, Bok had grown up in southern California and graduated from Stanford. "The fact that the Corporation and the Overseers couldn't find one of their own to take the job," the *Boston Globe*'s Bud Collins wrote gleefully, "indicates that Harvard men are a lot smarter than it appears."[7]

"An ideal president of Harvard University," said Burr of Bok.

The installation of a new president in the fall of 1971 would round out the most turbulent epoch in Harvard history. Years of recovery lay ahead. But the institution had already begun to remake itself.

Harvard and Women

T HE NATIONAL MOVEMENT for women's rights, and the effects of the sexual revolution, made it impossible to ignore the unequal status of women at Harvard. Women undergraduates were outnumbered four to one. The limitations of Radcliffe's housing facilities and scholarship funds meant that they were the only category of students whose admission was held to a fixed number. Except in the School of Education, women were underrepresented in the graduate and professional schools. Within the nine faculties, only three women held tenured positions.

Wives of presidents had exerted a lively and gracious influence on the temper of Harvard. Masters' wives played similar roles within the House system. Women filled responsible administrative positions in most parts of the University. The President and Fellows had gladly accepted a $100,000 classroom building from Anne Sever in 1879 and a $3 million library from Eleanor Elkins Widener in 1912. Yet Harvard let Radcliffe remain an appendage, and treated scholarship as an essentially male pursuit.

President-elect Derek Bok, dean of Harvard Law School, meeting the press in January 1971. At right is C. Douglas Dillon, president of the Board of Overseers.

Until the Pusey administration few women were hired as teachers. In 1970 a task force of women faculty members in arts and sciences compiled a report revealing that most of the teaching and administrative appointments held by women were in the lower ranks, and comprised less than 11 percent of all appointees. The report led to stepped-up recruiting efforts and more flexibility in policies affecting part-time teaching and maternity leaves. Though the proportion of women faculty members rose, improvement in the upper ranks occurred slowly. Openings were not frequent, and as a direct result of past attitudes, the pool of qualified women was small.

At the undergraduate level, the controversy over parietal rules had showed that partitioning of the sexes was no longer acceptable to most students. With co-residential housing as an option, bringing the male-female ratio closer to parity began to seem both fair and feasible. Federal law now prevented sex discrimination in university policies and procedures. The pros and cons of a Harvard-Radcliffe merger came in for extensive discussion in the late 1960s.

FOR RADCLIFFE'S LEADERS this was an ironic twist. Mary I. Bunting, who had succeeded Wilbur K. Jordan as president in 1960, had brought the college closer to self-sufficiency than at any time in its nine-

Left: Nadine Strossen '72 and Helen Snively '71 moving into Winthrop House for a trial run of co-residency in the spring term of 1970.

At the 1971 Commencement, Radcliffe seniors and some of their Harvard counterparts displayed armbands or banners signifying their commitment to equal admissions. At the time the male-female ratio among undergraduates was 4:1.

ty-year history. Its nine brick dormitories had been grouped into three "House centers" that borrowed some of the features of Harvard's House system. The sparkling new Hilles Library had risen beside the Radcliffe Quadrangle in 1966. Currier House, a new residence center, was completed in 1970. But at the same time Harvard was assuming an increased share of Radcliffe's educational and administrative responsibilities. Radcliffe no longer had its own health service and security force. It had given up its graduate school and traded Longfellow Hall, its only large classroom building, to the School of Education. It had also transferred the degree-granting power it had exercised since 1894. From June 1963 onward, Radcliffe seniors and advanced-degree candidates received Harvard degrees—with diplomas signed by the presidents of Harvard and Radcliffe—and became Harvard alumnae.

Mary Bunting came to share the view that a merger made sense. There were three obstacles. One was the financial burden that Harvard would have to assume to modernize Radcliffe dorms and provide financial aid to women undergraduates. (Only 27 percent of women were receiving aid, as against 42 percent of men.) There were legal questions

Love Story, **filmed in 1969, starred Ryan O'Neal as Oliver Barrett IV, a well-bred Harvard hockey player, and Ali MacGraw as Jenny Cavilleri, a terminally ill Radcliffe student. A book drawn from the screenplay by Erich Segal '58, PH.D. '65, was the nation's best-selling work of fiction for more than a year; the paperback edition had the largest printing yet recorded in publishing history.**

"Both the film and the book achieve a level of undiluted escapism," wrote the *Harvard Bulletin's* reviewer, **"creating a world where college days are happy, women are pure and faithful and men are strong but sensitive, and America is a country untroubled by social tensions."**

Could a Tennessee senator's son and his future wife, "Tipper" Aitchison, have been models for Oliver and Jenny? In 1997, as vice president of the United States, Albert Gore Jr. '69 let slip to reporters that he thought they might have. The press and its sources found the notion improbable.

about the uses of the institutions' separate endowments. Finally there was the prospect of adverse reaction from alumni of each college, and from parents wary about closer contacts between the sexes.

To Harvard and Radcliffe students these concerns meant little. Most were unreservedly in favor of mixed residential and dining facilities. Separate quarters, it was argued, did not reflect the real world. An unstated argument was that women already resided at Harvard. Undergraduate correspondent Thomas Stewart '70 wrote in the *Bulletin* that "among the five hundred women who spend the night in a Harvard room on football weekends (the informal estimate of a Harvard dean), there are several who live in the Houses more or less regularly. I know five couples living in Adams House, the bastion of liberty; so I guess there are about fifty all told." There were stories of indulgent House masters who encountered couples descending entry stairways at early hours and said simply, "Good morning, gentlemen."

A survey in late 1968 showed that 80 percent of Radcliffe students and 66 percent of Harvard students wanted trial residential exchanges "at once." In the spring of 1970, 300 students took part in an exchange between three Harvard Houses and three Radcliffe residence centers. So began the experiment that would vastly change Harvard College and its onetime Annex. The two colleges held their first joint Commencement that June.

Changing Landscapes

A NINTH RESIDENTIAL HOUSE, 21 stories high and named for Harvard's sixth president, Increase Mather, was rising east of Dunster House. It was one of four major construction projects that would top off the building boom of the Pusey years. Gund Hall, a quasi-pyramidal structure of glass and concrete, was being built for the Graduate School of Design on the east side of Quincy Street, facing Memorial Hall. A subterranean library annex with connections to Widener, Houghton, and Lamont was in the planning stage. North of the Old Yard a landscaped pedestrian overpass, constructed in 1968 at a cost of $3 million, now linked the science buildings and Law School with the Yard and the Houses. Excavations had begun for the largest, costliest building in Harvard history, the $19 million Science Center, to be located between Littauer Center and Memorial Hall.

Disruptions notwithstanding, the 1960s had been boom times for science at Harvard. "Big science," requiring complex experimental equipment, esoteric materials, and ultrasensitive electronic instrumentation, continued to alter such fields as high-energy physics, astronomy, and biomedicine. At the Cambridge Electron Accelerator (see page 203), physicists from many institutions explored the constituents of the atomic nucleus and the forces controlling them. The interaction of light and matter was the domain of senior scientists like University Professor Edward Purcell, John H. Van Vleck, PH.D. '22, S.D. '66, Hollis professor of mathematics and natural philosophy, Nicolaas Bloembergen, McKay professor of applied physics, and Julian Schwinger, professor of physics. Their work in magnetic resonance and laser spectroscopy, rec-

At left: Construction work
for a gigantic new Science Center
began in 1971.

Below: Gund Hall, the School of
Design's $10 million headquarters.
Its glass-roofed studio section
accommodated five hundred
students on five stepped levels.

Mather House, providing space for
425 undergraduates, opened in
1971. The high-rise architecture of
Harvard's ninth residential House
contrasted with the neo-Georgian
look of the original "river Houses."
It was planned by Shepley, Bulfinch,
Richardson & Abbott, successors to
the firm that designed the Houses
in the Lowell years.

ognized by Nobel Prizes, brought physics and chemistry into closer conjunction. Applications would extend to medical diagnostics and surgery, military and industrial engineering, communications, radio-astronomy, molecular biology, even the arts.

Astrophysicists, using high-frequency radio signals, were recalculating the size and age of the universe, mapping galaxies, and probing the nature of black holes. In biology, the deciphering of the structure of DNA provided a platform for further investigations by researchers like Walter Gilbert '53, professor of biophysics, and Mark Ptashne, PH.D. '68. Working independently, Gilbert and Ptashne—then a 28-year-old Junior Fellow—demonstrated the existence of "repressor" molecules that switch genes on and off. Gilbert went on to devise a rapid and accurate method of sequencing DNA's chemical bases.

Such research could not have been done without new tools like electron microscopes, radiotelescopes, and high-speed computers. The

Double Play

C hemist Robert Burns Woodward (left) and Julian S. Schwinger (right), a physicist, both won Nobel Prizes in 1965. It was the first time that two Harvard researchers in different disciplines had won Nobels in the same year.

Woodward dominated the field of organic chemistry for almost half a century. He was recognized for his brilliant laboratory syntheses of complex molecules, including quinine, cortisone, lysergic acid, cholesterol, strychnine, lanosterol, reserpine, and chlorophyll.

One of the world's leading theoretical physicists, Schwinger restructured the equations of quantum mechanics to make them fully consistent with special relativity theory.

Biochemist Konrad Bloch won the 1964 Nobel Prize in medicine or physiology for his studies of the transformation of cholesterol and fatty acids in living systems.

swiftly changing computer technology of the 1960s made Engineering and Applied Sciences the fastest-growing division of Arts and Sciences. Professor Howard Aiken had given the first computer course, Engineering Sciences 118, in 1956. A decade later, the division had an array of courses in programming and in subfields like mathematical modeling, operations research, probability theory, and game theory. Natural Sciences 110, an introductory computer course, was added to the General Education program in 1968. An Office for Information Technology was created the next year; a Center for Research in Computing Technology opened in 1971. Applied science was now closely engaged with social and political research, and the influence of computers on future generations of students was becoming discernible. Harvey Brooks, PH.D. '40, S.D. '63, dean of engineering and applied sciences, wrote in 1969 that "the creation of a universal 'computer culture' on the campus may be one of the most powerful antidotes to the present student disaffection and unrest." And in the long run it was.

TENSIONS EASED IN THE academic year 1970-71. Internal divisions began to heal. There were fewer disruptions. The only violence came in October, when a bomb shredded the top-floor library of the Center for International Affairs at 1 A.M. No one was injured in the bombing, Harvard's first since 1834. In March an ugly breach of academic freedom occurred when a conservative group tried to hold a "counter-teach-in" on the Vietnam War at Sanders Theatre. SDS and a coalition of radical graduate students and faculty members were there to drown out the speakers with shouts and bullhorns. Archibald Cox took the stage to quiet the clamor, but the shouting and chanting went on. "If this meeting is disrupted—hateful as some of us may find it— then liberty will have died a little," Cox pleaded. His brief, eloquent speech was inaudible, but was carried live by WHRB.

In "this very building," said Cox, the University had provided a platform for speakers urging Harvard's destruction. "Freedom of speech is indivisible," he declared. "You cannot deny it to one man and save it for others. . . . The test of our dedication to liberty is our willingness to allow the expression of ideas we hate. If those ideas are lies, the remedy is more speech and more debate." The shouting went on, and the speakers finally had to be led out through the steam tunnels.

Apprehensions about Harvard's stability may have been the cause of a short-lived drop in College applications, from almost 8,000 in 1969 to 6,840 in 1971. Contributions to the Harvard College Fund dipped briefly, for the first time since the Depression years, but rose to a new high of $3.75 million in 1971. In the last four months of the Pusey administration, a special campaign called "To Finish a Job" raised $9 million to help complete the Science Center and start work on the library annex, to be named the Nathan Marsh Pusey Library.

PUSEY'S PRESIDENCY HAD SPANNED an era as expansive as Lowell's. He had arrived at a time when enrollments had leveled off and the University's physical growth had been checked by depression and war. In the eighteen years of his presidency Harvard conferred more degrees than it had from 1636 to 1910; the number of living alumni rose from 95,000 to 160,000. Thirty new buildings doubled the University's usable floor space.

The number of endowed chairs for faculty members more than doubled, from 122 to 277. Almost a third of the 155 new professorships were in medical science and public health. Six scientists won Nobel Prizes in the first decade of the Pusey years, and four more were honored in the mid-1960s: Konrad Bloch, Higgins professor of biochemistry (1964, medicine or physiology); Julian Schwinger (1965, physics); Robert Woodward, Donner professor of science (1965, chemistry); and George Wald, Higgins professor of biology (1967, medicine or physiology).

The size of the University community—students, faculty, staff— grew from about 20,000 to almost 40,000. Harvard's annual operating budget rose from $39 million to $200 million, the value of the endowment from $216 million to more than $1 billion

The University had become more pluralistic and democratic. Under Wilbur J. Bender '27, dean of admissions from 1957 to 1960, the College admissions staff enlarged the orbit of recruiting efforts. Scholarship funds of about $2 million in 1960 had more than doubled by the end of the decade, ensuring what would later be called a "need-blind" admissions policy. Increasingly the College resembled what Michael Young, writing in 1959, termed a "meritocracy." Bender's successor, Fred Glimp—an air corps veteran from Idaho who had been part of the postwar influx of nontraditional Harvard entrants—had broadened recruiting initiatives aimed at finding more prospects who were nonaffluent and nonwhite. Recruitment of minority applicants was intensified after the assassination of Martin Luther King Jr. Then came coresidence and the fuller participation of women in College life.

The faculty counterpart to nationwide recruiting for undergraduates, as David Riesman observed in a review of the period, was the ad hoc committee system devised by President Conant.[8] The system sub-

George Wald played a leading role in the transformation of biology from a cellular to a molecular science. He achieved in test tubes all the known chemical reactions involved in the action of light on the pigments of the eye. His research earned him the Nobel Prize in medicine or physiology in 1967.

Wald's Natural Sciences 5, "The Nature of Living Things," was a popular General Education course. He was also an early and unflagging opponent of the war in Vietnam.

jected candidates for promotion to exacting academic standards and militated against the ascriptions of social position and lineage that survived from the Lowell era. A substantial increase in Jewish recruitment and acceptance, noted Riesman, was a significant postwar development at both faculty and student levels. By the end of the 1960s, he estimated, Jews made up a third of the faculty and a quarter of the student body. At the start of the decade, many of the faculty's best-known figures—prominent House masters like John Finley, Mason Hammond, and Elliott Perkins, lecturers like Samuel Eliot Morison and the sociologist George Homans—had been patrician in background and manner. By 1970, when Finley left Eliot House, most were retired. Dean of freshmen F. Skiddy von Stade, who had kept polo ponies as an undergraduate, was almost the last of the breed. He stayed on until 1976.

Gone for good, after 1969, was the loose paternalism that had been part of the temper and tone of Harvard. As at universities everywhere, moral codes became less rigid. Parietal rules withered away when co-residence took effect. Instances of cohabitation were unofficially tolerated. Contraceptive counseling was provided. A new informality prevailed. Coats and ties were no longer expected in class or required in dining halls. Dropping the longstanding classroom use of "Mister" or "Miss," younger teachers addressed students by their first names.

Military science courses ended in 1970, naval and air science courses the next year. The nature of research and teaching in certain fields changed markedly. Disciplines like economics and philosophy, which had come to emphasize analytical methodology, put more stress on questions of value and social utility. In areas of the humanities like English, art history, and such new fields as Afro-American studies, social criticism assumed new importance. More contemporary materials appeared on course reading lists (required reading for a course on twentieth-century English history included the Beatles' *Sergeant Pepper's Lonely Hearts Club Band*).

The University gave increased attention to community relations, especially in such areas as land use and employment practices. The professional schools developed or enlarged community-service programs. The Medical School's Harvard Community Health Plan, initiated in 1969, was a conspicuous example.

Institutional self-study was the order of the day. Professor John Dunlop's University-wide Committee on Governance churned out a series of reports: on the organization of the president's office and the governing boards, on rights and responsibilities, on Harvard and money, on the nature and purposes of the university. More were on the way.

PRESIDENT PUSEY, WHO MIGHT HAVE FOUND so much change unsettling, made peace with it in the final speech of his presidency, delivered on the afternoon of a surprisingly tranquil Commencement day. As Alfred North Whitehead had pointed out, noted Pusey, the old world is always dying, and a new one being born.

"So it is here," said Pusey. "One Harvard is passing into history and another being born. One is dying while another, burgeoning with new life, is eagerly waiting before. We salute it and welcome it."

President Pusey, President emeritus Conant, and President-elect Bok on Commencement day, 1971. Not for a century had three presidents come together at a Commencement.

Pusey continued to have an impact on higher education as president of the Mellon Foundation. Conant, then 77, had just published *My Several Lives: Memoirs of a Social Inventor*. He died in 1978.

Opposite: Degree candidates gathered, in timeless fashion, for the morning exercises.

Harvard Restored

The Harvard family is not a shy or sedate group. . . . It is out of this life of splendid contentiousness that new realities are created, and old realities are put to the ultimate test against the changing standards of time.
— *Lindsay Conner, J.D. '80, speaking at the Commencement of 1980*

AMERICAN HIGHER EDUCATION had entered an era of anxious self-scrutiny. The student movement of the 1960s had been directed against the Vietnam War and the venality of American society, but it had also been an attack on institutional codes of conduct, residential restrictions, decision-making procedures, curricula, and admissions practices that a new generation saw as outmoded or undemocratic. At Harvard and countless other institutions, special committees weighed student grievances and concluded that many were justified.

The economic outlook seemed bleak. A Carnegie Commission report warned that a thousand colleges and universities, including Harvard, were facing financial trouble.

The upheavals of the 1960s had exhausted and unseated many senior educational leaders. Derek Bok belonged to a cohort of younger college and university presidents whose common task was to heal internal divisions and restore a shared sense of institutional purpose. They would also struggle with energy crises, double-digit inflation, and shrinking government funding. Other new realities of the 1970s and '80s would include student and

Daniel Chester French's statue of John Harvard receiving a pre-Commencement rubdown.

alumni constituencies that were critical of their institutions' performance as employers and shareholders. In a variety of forms, ethical issues assumed new importance in university life.

Harvard's institutional scale grew strikingly. Over the twenty years of Bok's presidency more than 4.5 million square feet were added to its physical plant, an increase of 30 percent. The scope of the institution's activities became more international. Annual operating expenses increased sixfold, from $200 million to $1.2 billion.[1] A new investment subsidiary and a $358 million capital campaign helped raise the value of Harvard's financial assets from $1.2 billion to almost $5 billion.

Total enrollment was held at about 16,000, but the student body changed radically. Women and members of racial and ethnic minority groups arrived in ever larger numbers. An affirmative action program began the diversification of teaching faculties and administrative staffs.

The undergraduate curriculum was reviewed and revised. Systematically assessing the graduate and professional schools, President Bok prodded them to rethink their objectives and revise their curricula. He became the prime mover in establishing ethical studies requirements throughout the University. With Bok's backing, the Kennedy School of Government grew into a full-fledged professional school with extensive involvement in national and international affairs.

Computer-based technology quickened the pace of scholarly inquiry and enlarged the University's research output. Electronic indexing and retrieval programs transformed the library system. A University-wide electronic network was designed to streamline internal communications and link users with databases throughout the world.

Administratively, Harvard became more bureaucratic and professionalized. In the Pusey years a single vice president had looked after all of the University's business affairs, from financial planning to plant management. The Bok administration would have multiple vice presidents, more middle managers, more deans and subdeans. Executive responsibility would become more specialized and diffused. Harvard would become increasingly "corporate."

"To Renew a Vision of Our Future..."

THE UNIVERSITY-WIDE COMMITTEE on governance had reported that Harvard was "under-administered." Institutional growth and increasing government regulations and guidelines imposed new bureaucratic burdens. Assisted by David Robinson '47, a Carnegie Corporation vice president on loan to Harvard, Bok planned a new administrative structure in the spring of 1971.[2]

The plan called for four vice presidents and a general counsel. The last was already in place. In 1970 President Pusey had appointed Daniel Steiner '54, LL.B. '57, as Harvard's first house counsel. Steiner had practiced law in New York City and worked for federal agencies in Washington before returning to Harvard as secretary to the governance committee. Under Bok, he would succeed Archibald Cox as the administration's crisis manager. Bok's vice president for finance was Hale Champion, who had held a similar post at the University of Minnesota

Derek Bok at work in the summer of 1971. The photograph on the wall shows five of his nineteenth-century predecessors: Josiah Quincy, Edward Everett, Jared Sparks, James Walker, and C.C. Felton. Bok's desk had belonged to President Eliot.

The massive concrete walls and steel spans of the Undergraduate Science Center (1972) symbolized Harvard's shifting institutional scale. The $19 million complex rose north of the Old Yard, where the old Lawrence Scientific School once stood. In the foreground is the Holworthy Gate (1900).

The Science Center provided four large lecture halls and laboratory space for 600 to 800 students. In the basement was a giant mechanical area, its cubic volume equal to that of Boston's Symphony Hall.

and had been director of finance for the state of California. Stephen Hall, an ITT Sheraton Corporation executive, was administrative vice president; Charles Daly, formerly a vice president at the University of Chicago and before that a congressional liaison officer in the Kennedy White House, was vice president for community and governmental relations. Chase N. Peterson '52, M.D. '56, director of admissions since 1967, was named vice president for alumni relations and development some months later.

Professional skill mattered more to Bok than Harvard background. Steiner and Peterson were the only Harvard degree-holders in the new command structure. Champion, a Stanford graduate, had been at Harvard as a Nieman Fellow and as a fellow of the Institute of Politics. Hall was a Cornellian, Daly a Yale man. All were energetic and competitive in a way that recalled the days of the Kennedy White House. When the *Crimson* challenged the president and his staff to a game of touch football, Bok and nine colleagues showed up at Soldiers Field with a tub of cold beer and battled the Crimeds to a 6-6 draw. "Bok's Jocks" later had insignia T-shirts made and took on *Crimson* and women's varsity teams in touch football, basketball, softball, and tennis.

BOK'S FORMAL INSTALLATION was the plainest and smallest in Harvard's modern history. It took place in University Hall's Faculty Room on October 11, 1971, with 110 guests attending. Business attire was the rule. C. Douglas Dillon, president of the Overseers, read the charge. "Everywhere the values of the past are being questioned by a new generation," said Dillon. "Harvard is now completing a period of physical growth unprecedented in her history. The facilities needed to meet the demands of the day are largely in place, or in sight. What is now required is not more buildings, but rather a clearer view as to where we should be going, a clarity of view that in recent years has seemed to largely elude our nation's campuses. In a community of scholars such as this, diversity of interest and opinion is both natural and necessary. But man's greatest progress has occurred in periods when there was a rea-

Bok was installed as Harvard's twenty-fifth president in a simple ceremony in University Hall's Faculty Room. The Fellows of Harvard College sat at the round table. From left: Albert Nickerson, John M. Blum, Charles P. Slichter, Hugh Calkins (partially hidden), and Francis H. Burr.

Bok family members sat beneath the Harvard portraits. At far right is the president's wife, Sissela.

After the installation the Boks were serenaded by freshmen on the fire escape of Weld Hall. In the family group, from left, were Victoria, 9; her father and mother; Mrs. William Kiskadden, Bok's mother; and Hilary, 11, autograph book in hand.

The president's residence. Seeking privacy for his family, Bok broke tradition by choosing to live outside Harvard Yard. "Elmwood," a mile and a half from Harvard Square, was once the home of poet James Russell Lowell (A.B. 1838). The house, left to Harvard in 1962, had been used by the dean of the Faculty of Arts and Sciences.

sonable consensus, freely accepted, as to overall objectives. It will be your great task, Mr. President, to promote the achievement of such a consensus, while stubbornly defending the academic freedoms that have made Harvard what she is today."

"I accept this office," Bok responded, "with the hope that I can help to renew a vision of our future that will rally faculty, students, staff, and alumni to the effort that our special resources permit, and the circumstances of our times require."

A WEEK BEFORE HIS INSTALLATION, Bok made a proposal that would profoundly affect the character of Harvard College: to increase the number of women undergraduates. Bok and the governing boards had concluded that the overall size of the College should stay at about 6,000. But by increasing the size of incoming Radcliffe classes from 300 to 450, and reducing slightly the number of men admitted, the male-female ratio could be lowered from 4:1 to 2.5:1 within four years.

The Harvard-Radcliffe relationship had not been fully resolved. Radcliffe's trustees had voted in 1969 to begin merger talks, and the Corporation had endorsed full merger within eighteen months. Both parties backed off when a faculty-alumni committee concluded that full merger would require equal admissions. That would have meant an unmanageable increase in the College's size, or a sharp cut in the number of men. Radcliffe was also having qualms about letting Harvard take over programs and facilities, like the Radcliffe Institute and Schlesinger

Library, that served women's interests. The upshot was a "nonmerger" agreement in 1971, consolidating the Colleges' House and tutorial systems. Harvard would cover Radcliffe's operating expenses in return for all of its unrestricted income; the Institute and Library remained under Radcliffe's control, as did the College's physical plant, administrative offices, and endowment.* After Mary Bunting's retirement in 1972 the agreement would have replaced Radcliffe's president with a dean, but that change was opposed by some of the College trustees. A protracted search for a new president ended in Radcliffe's back yard when Matina S. Horner, assistant professor of clinical and personal psychology at Harvard, accepted the position. Married to a physicist, and the mother of three young children, Horner was a graduate of Bryn Mawr (1961) with a doctorate from Michigan (1968). At 32, she was the youngest president in Radcliffe's history.

Her installation ceremony, held at Agassiz House, was a reaffirmation of Radcliffe's institutional identity. Most of the 275 guests were women. Derek Bok sat inconspicuously in the rear of the room. Horner expressed her hope that Radcliffe could combine "the best aspects of independent single-sex and coeducational institutions." The first marshal of Radcliffe's class of '73, calling her college "a rallying ground against the evils of Harvard," exhorted her sisters to "create a Radcliffe community here at Harvard."

Matina Horner arriving to meet the press after her election as Radcliffe's sixth president in May 1972. Thomas D. Cabot '19, a Radcliffe trustee, escorted her.

An Uneasy Spring

VIETNAM STILL DOMINATED the life of the nation. An "eerie tranquility," in Yale president Kingman Brewster's phrase, had overspread American campuses in the fall of 1971. Disruptions began again in the spring of 1972. After the resumption of heavy bombing in North Vietnam, a group calling itself the People's Coalition for Peace and Justice vandalized Harvard's Center for International Affairs. Though much of the Center's research focused on disarmament and economic development, it was the third time in three years that the building had been attacked. Damage was put at $20,000.

Bok was one of nine university presidents who signed a joint statement protesting the renewed bombings and calling for withdrawal from Vietnam. With other presidents, he met with national security advisor Henry Kissinger to urge disengagement. But Kissinger and President Nixon clung to the belief that intensive bombing would force North Vietnam to negotiate peace terms.

In April about three dozen black students forced their way into Massachusetts Hall at dawn. Police cordoned off the building. Dispossessed of their offices, President Bok and his staff regrouped on the tenth floor of Holyoke Center. The occupation was not about Vietnam. The demonstrators were demanding that Harvard sell $18.5 million worth of

---

*In 1975, when the Harvard-Radcliffe agreement was reviewed, separate admissions offices were unified and a policy of equal access was adopted for future entering classes. For women this not only meant equal consideration in the admissions process, but also equality in financial aid and more nearly equal availability of prizes and fellowships.

Demonstrators marched out of Massachusetts Hall after being served with a court order in April 1972. They had occupied the building for a week.

Trouble at the Press

Losses incurred by Harvard University Press led to the Bok administration's first public relations headache, in the spring of 1972.

Over a four-year period, expansion and expenses related to new technology had produced a cumulative deficit of $1.2 million. Concluding that Press director Mark Carroll '50 was a poor businessman, administrative vice president Stephen Hall decided he had to go. The directors of the Press eventually concurred.

A terse notice in the *University Gazette* was the only announcement. A brief statement from Carroll implied that President Bok had summarily fired him.

Newspapers played up the story. Faculty members and Press authors inferred that the new administration wanted the Press run on commercial lines, and that academic freedom was at stake.

"Far from being a technocrat who looks just at the bottom line of the Press's balance sheet," Hall insisted, "my sole objective is to make the Press great."

Press author Walter Muir Whitehill '26 protested. "The abruptness of Mark Carroll's unexplained dismissal," he wrote Bok, "seems more in the spirit of a Peruvian military dictatorship than of Harvard University."

Arthur J. Rosenthal, founder of Basic Books, was brought in to succeed Carroll. He maintained the scholarly integrity of the Press and returned it to solvency. Vice-presidential responsibility for the Press was shifted back to the president's office, where it had resided until 1971.

Gulf Oil stock to protest Gulf's operations in the Portuguese colony of Angola. After a week-long occupation the protesters marched out when Harvard lawyers secured a court order making them liable to civil contempt charges. Disciplinary boards from the faculties of arts and sciences, law, and divinity considered complaints against 35 students, reached differing verdicts, and imposed only "suspended suspensions." The mildness of the disciplinary actions elicited reproofs from the Board of Overseers and from President Bok.

Similar protests had occurred elsewhere, but the Massachusetts Hall occupation brought the issue of shareholder responsibility to the fore at Harvard. The Corporation had already assayed a range of shareholder resolutions involving Gulf and other large corporations. To enlarge the decision-making process, Bok created an Advisory Committee on

Shareholder Responsibility, made up of five alumni, five faculty members, and five students. Stock divestiture would become the longest-running and most-discussed issue of his presidency.

About thirty SDS members occupied government department offices in Littauer Center in May. The building was sealed, phone lines were shut off, and the demonstrators left after a few hours. As an effective political tactic, building occupations were becoming passé.

Since the start of the year a vestigial SDS group had attacked Richard Herrnstein, professor of psychology, for a purportedly racist magazine article suggesting that intelligence might be genetically based. The Committee on Rights and Responsibilities—composed exclusively of faculty members, since students refused to serve—declined to act when Herrnstein complained that he had been subjected to intense harassment. In the spring Bok stepped in. The case went beyond the well-being of one professor, he told the Faculty of Arts and Sciences. "Every scholar has a variety of subjects to which he can devote his efforts," said Bok. "If work on one of them threatens to subject him to unpleasant personal attack, he and many like him will inevitably be tempted . . . to turn to more placid subjects where such risks are not involved. The resulting danger to scholarship will be immense."

BEFORE TAKING OFFICE, Bok had conceded in a speech to a New York Harvard Club audience that "the times are not particularly propitious for a consensus about the shape of undergraduate education." But, he had added, "it *is* a time for innovation and testing." That Harvard provided no teacher training for the hundreds of graduate students who assisted in undergraduate courses was troubling. "I fully intend to break my lance, as many presidents have before me, against the wall of better teaching," declared Bok. "This occupies me first of all." In his first months as president he followed up by raising a fund yielding $75,000 a year to support innovative teaching initiatives.

Bok also wished to make practice and performance in the arts a more central part of the academic experience. The place of the arts at Harvard had long been anomalous. Admissions officers smiled on applications from budding musicians, actors, painters, filmmakers. The colleges' choral groups, the Harvard-Radcliffe Orchestra, and the Band were known for their high performance standards. The institution had a rich theatrical tradition. Many graduates were major figures in the arts, and Harvard gave honorary degrees to performing artists, composers, painters, sculptors. But practice had never been seen as an integral part of academic work in music, dramatic literature, or the visual arts. Within weeks of his installation, Bok named a Committee for the Practice of the Arts. Its report, issued more than a year later, called for credit-bearing courses in music, visual studies, drama, and dance, fellowships in the arts, new facilities, and a central office for the arts.

Because the faculty was grappling with chronic deficits, new facilities and fellowships were out of reach. But the report did lead to the formation of a standing committee that set guidelines for course credit in the arts, and to an Office for the Arts jointly run by Harvard and Radcliffe. Myra Mayman, a Bryn Mawr graduate, was named coordinator of the

Opposite page: Artist Constantino Nivola and his daughter Claire '70 adding highlights to Nivola's bas-relief "sandscape," mounted in a corridor of the new Science Center in the fall of 1972.

Nivola had created the mural in the 1950s for the Olivetti typewriter company's Fifth Avenue display room. Working on a Long Island beach, the artist shaped sand into abstract patterns, added seashells, pebbles, fisheyes, driftwood, and handprints, and molded his designs in poured plaster. The showroom closed in 1970, but the 70-foot mural was rescued by Josep Lluis Sert, dean of the School of Design and architect of the Science Center.

Nivola, a former faculty member, was a visiting professor at the time of the installation. He augmented the sandscape's textures with paint because the natural lighting in the Science Center appeared to flatten its three-dimensional relief.

As coordinator of arts at Harvard and Radcliffe, Myra Mayman helped promote new programs in music, drama, film, dance, and visual arts.

arts in the fall of 1973. Her office developed new extracurricular programs in dance, visual arts, film, music, drama, and musical theater. Eventually, as many as 3,000 undergraduates participated each year. Mayman also launched a series called "Learning from Performers" to bring professional artists to Harvard as teachers. About twenty took part annually, coaching students in small-group sessions. The Office for the Arts became one of the great success stories of the Bok years.

Constitutional Crisis

A CEASE-FIRE ENDED AMERICA'S ROLE in the Vietnam War in January 1973. At the Office of Graduate and Career Plans, a draft counselor hung out a sign: DRAFT IS OVER! WHOOPEE! A service of prayer, thanksgiving, and penitence was held at Appleton Chapel; twelve people attended. Nineteen Harvard men had lost their lives in the war, the first in 1962, the last in 1970.

All the American troops still in Vietnam returned that spring. By that time public attention was fixed on the Watergate inquiry.

The Pentagon Papers had set off the chain of events that eventually toppled a president. On June 13, 1971, the *New York Times* began running excerpts from secret government documents exposing official incompetence and deception in the conduct of the war. At Harvard, where Commencement week was about to start, word spread that the study had been leaked by Daniel Ellsberg '52, PH.D. '63.

"Ignorance and Decision" had been the provisional title of Ellsberg's doctoral thesis. As a Rand Corporation economist, he had worked on the secret Pentagon study for Defense Secretary McNamara, and had helped formulate Vietnam options for Henry Kissinger. Now at MIT, he had become an outspoken opponent of the war. He had given copies of the 7,000-page Pentagon study to *Times* reporter Neil Sheehan '58 and to Senator J. William Fulbright (who did not make it public). After ten days in seclusion, Ellsberg appeared on a CBS-TV news program to accept responsibility for the leak. He seemed unfazed by the prospect of imprisonment as he surrendered to federal marshals in Boston on June 28, 1971. "I wonder," said Ellsberg, "if many people here wouldn't think ten years is a cheap price to end the war?"

Daniel Ellsberg, accompanied by his wife, Patricia (Marx) '59, gave himself up to federal marshals in June 1971. He had been accused of breaching security by making the Pentagon Papers public.

Solicitor General Erwin Griswold, former dean of the Law School, had moved rapidly to obtain a district court ruling enjoining the *Times* from further publication. The case went swiftly to the Supreme Court, where a 5-4 decision upheld the *Times*'s right to print the documents. By that time other newspapers had begun running them.

President Nixon, incensed by Ellsberg's act, called for a secret squad to plug further government leaks. The group became known as the Plumbers. Its first priority was to discredit Ellsberg, and its clandestine activities began with a September break-in at the office of Ellsberg's psychiatrist in an attempt to find confidential medical files. In June 1972, with an election in the offing, the Plumbers twice raided Democratic National Committee offices in Washington's Watergate complex to pilfer files and tap phones. A watchman detected the second raid and five men were arrested. A week later, in secret hearings, a federal grand jury began taking testimony on the Watergate break-in.

"No goddam Harvard men, you understand?" the newly elected Richard Nixon was said to have told aide John Ehrlichman as they began the White House appointments process.[4] But when the Watergate inquiry closed in on Nixon, Harvard men seemed to be everywhere.

Carrying every state but Massachusetts, Nixon had won the 1972 election by a record margin. Allegations of illegal campaign activities on the part of the president's re-election committee soon led to a Senate inquiry. North Carolina senator Sam Ervin, LL.B. '22, chaired the investigative panel. Ervin liked to refer to himself as "a plain old country lawyer." But when televised hearings began in May 1973, he proved adept at extracting the truth from reluctant witnesses.

The first hint of high-level conspiracy came from James McCord Jr., an ex-CIA agent convicted in the trial of the Watergate burglars. At the urging of his lawyer, Bernard Fensterwald '42, LL.B. '49, McCord met with Samuel Dash, LL.B. '50, the Ervin committee's chief counsel, and implicated White House appointees whose names had not come out in the break-in trial. One was presidential counsel John Dean.

Negotiating for immunity, Dean disclosed to Justice Department prosecutor Earl Silbert '57, LL.B. '60, that the Plumbers had raided the office of Ellsberg's psychiatrist in 1971. This revelation tainted the government's prosecution of Ellsberg, and the case was dismissed.

Nixon sought to distance himself from the widening scandal by dismissing chief of staff H.R. Haldeman, domestic adviser John Ehrlichman, and Attorney General Richard Kleindienst '47, LL.B. '50. As Kleindienst's successor he picked Elliot Richardson '41, LL.B. '44, then secretary of defense. A Boston Republican, Richardson had been under secretary of state and secretary of health, education, and welfare in Nixon's first administration. He had a reputation for probity.

The full Senate wanted the Watergate case assigned to an independent prosecutor. Richardson agreed to appoint one. He took for granted that the appointee should be an experienced prosecutor of national standing. But when seven candidates rejected the post, Richardson turned to Archibald Cox, who had taught him labor law at Harvard.[4] Cox was not a trial lawyer, but as the Kennedy administration's solicitor general he had argued a near-record number of cases before the Supreme Court, prevailing in 80 percent of them.

Cox was reluctant to leave Harvard again. President Bok assured him that the nation needed him. Cox went to work in May. He asked for and was given a budget of $2.8 million. As staff assistants he brought in Law School professors James Vorenberg '48, LL.B. '51, and Philip Heymann, LL.B. '60, both criminal-law experts. When a White House staffer revealed to the Ervin committee that Nixon's meetings and calls had been routinely recorded, Cox went to court and successfully argued for access to the tapes. Nixon balked. Weeks of legal parrying followed. In late October Nixon ordered Richardson to fire Cox. Richardson refused and resigned in protest. So did Deputy Attorney General William Ruck-

Sam Ervin of North Carolina deftly steered his Senate committee through six months of hearings on the Watergate case.

Archibald Cox, the first special prosecutor in the case, followed a trail of evidence to the Oval Office. Though he was born in New Jersey, Cox was perceived by many as a quintessential New Englander. To one member of the Washington press corps, the *New Yorker*'s Elizabeth Drew, he came across as "a folksy, tentative, Jimmy Stewart-like character."

Streaking

The clothed runner was an enterprising reporter conducting an interview. The runner in scarf and boots identified himself as a member of FUDA (Fully Unclothed Dashing Activists), "dedicated to the instant destruction of all states except for the State of Infancy." The scene was Harvard Yard.

The nation's immersion in Watergate had created a need for comic relief by the winter of 1973-74, when the streaking fad hit college campuses. Purist streakers ran with winged-foot devices. Streakers at Yale were joined by a clothed runner bearing a torch. At Harvard Medical School, two masked streakers disrupted an anatomy exam.

At 2:30 A.M. on the night of March 11, in Harvard Square, a Cambridge patrolman carrying ten pounds of police equipment nabbed a streaking sophomore after a chase of 125 yards. The streaker turned out to be the football team's kick-return specialist. "Harvard needs faster backs," huffed Cambridge district court judge Lawrence Feloney '43, dismissing the charge of indecent exposure.

elshaus, LL.B. '60. The only Justice Department official still empowered to enforce the president's ultimatum was Robert Bork, a conservative Yale law professor who had replaced Erwin Griswold as solicitor general. Bork hesitantly complied. Cox issued a brief valedictory statement: "Whether ours shall continue to be a government of laws and not of men is now for Congress and ultimately the American people to decide."

The "Saturday Night Massacre" was the gravest mistake of Richard Nixon's political life. It created a national furor and brought on the first congressional motions for impeachment. Some 450,000 mailgrams and telegrams piled up at the White House and Capitol. At the Yale-Cornell football game, Yale's band formed an "H" to salute Cox, Richardson, and Ruckelshaus. At Harvard, Derek Bok paid tribute to Cox at a service of morning prayer: "I have never known a man who took his responsibilities more seriously," said Bok, "or struggled harder to be true to his principles."

Texas lawyer Leon Jaworski, an old ally from the Kennedy era, succeeded Cox. He kept "Cox's army" in place and pressed ahead with the prosecution. Nixon engaged Boston trial lawyer James St. Clair, LL.B. '44, to lead his legal defense,[5] but on July 24, as the House of Representatives began formal debate on impeachment, the Supreme Court handed down an 8-0 decision ordering the president to surrender the relevant tapes. Self-incriminated by recorded evidence that he had obstructed justice and abused his office, Nixon resigned ten days later.

Nothing Less than a New Profession

THE ROLES OF COX, ERVIN, and others in the Watergate saga made the nightly news the major attraction at Harvard. The revelations of misdoings in high places deepened the alienation of students and had lasting effects on academic programs. Ethics courses became a requirement, first at the Law School, then more broadly. Rising concern about standards of government conduct also helped revitalize the school of public administration.

As an adjunct of the economics and government departments, the school had existed for more than three decades without faculty or curriculum of its own. It was the smallest and poorest of the professional schools. In the 1950s President Pusey had considered shutting it down. But its fortunes had improved in 1966, when the Kennedy Library Corporation pledged $10 million to endow a research center devoted to politics, and the school was renamed for the late President Kennedy.

Conceived as a center for academics, public officials in mid-career, and undergraduates, the Institute of Politics (see page 220) became the catalyst for a grandiose "Big Plan" for a riverside complex of buildings housing the presidential archives and museum, a center for international studies, the new institute, and classrooms and offices for the school of government. I.M. Pei, who was not yet widely known, was picked to design the complex. Pei suggested that it be built on a twelve-acre site long occupied by subway car barns.

The Kennedy School was also the hub of a new interfaculty program in public policy and management, launched in 1969.[6] Citing the "dolorous record" of government, President Bok announced in 1973 that he would chair a committee to expand the program, and would seek $21.3 million to fund it. "In the wake of grave public scandals," wrote Bok, "universities have a major opportunity and responsibility to set about the task of training a corps of able people to occupy influential positions in public life. What is needed is nothing less than the education of a new profession."

But finding the wherewithal proved difficult. The school had few wealthy alumni. After three years only $1 million was in hand, and the school was running a deficit of $200,000 a year. Meanwhile, the Big Plan had fallen through. Groundbreaking for the Kennedy library had been delayed because relocating the subway yards took longer than expected. Although Harvard had committed $20 million to the proposed complex, less than $5 million had been raised. Construction costs were going up, and citizens' groups were fighting the project because of its anticipated effect on Cambridge's already congested traffic. Early in 1975 the Kennedy Library Corporation announced that it would seek an alternate site.[7]

Architect I. M. Pei made a series of designs for the Kennedy Library complex from 1965 to 1974. The one above was submitted in 1970. Construction delays and community opposition later forced the Library Corporation to abandon the idea of building the complex at Harvard.

AFTER ALMOST TWENTY YEARS as the school's dean, Don K. Price stepped down in 1977. Bok picked Graham Allison Jr. '62, PH.D. '68, professor of politics, to succeed him. At 37, Allison was Harvard's youngest dean. His passion for politics, his flair for scholarly showmanship, and his entrepreneurial zeal energized the Kennedy School.

Allison had gained tenure at 29. He had been a consultant on foreign affairs to the Department of Defense and the Rand Corporation, and had published an analysis of governmental decision-making in the 1962 Cuban missile crisis. Within eighteen months, he and his small staff erased the school's deficit and raised almost $10 million. In the fall of 1978, with Kennedy family members and almost five thousand others on hand, the school opened its new Littauer Center of Public Administration, a $12 million building on the former car-barn site.

The school's new home was designed to help shape its substance and image. At Allison's insistence, the architects returned twice to the drawing board to arrive at a red-brick, slate-roofed design that incorporated stylized counterparts of the gables and chimneys of Harvard's older buildings. Unlike so much University architecture of the 1960s, this school was intended to look like Harvard. But if the exterior expressed

Five thousand guests attended the dedication of the John F. Kennedy School of Government's new building in October 1978. Also on hand were some 400 chanting, sign-carrying students who opposed naming the school's library for the late Charles Engelhard, a donor whose wealth was derived from South African gold mining interests. School officials later agreed to restrict the perpetuation of Engelhard's name to a plaque mounted inside the library.

a modern respect for tradition, the interior broke with the past. Its central feature was a three-story atrium that declared the school's public purpose. It was to serve by day as a crossroads for students and faculty, by night as a theater-in-the-round for lectures, political debates, and public policy panels. Two additional buildings were constructed in the 1980s. Joined by a small quadrangle, they gave the Kennedy School a compact red brick campus of its own.

Allison tightened the linkage between Harvard and the public life of the nation, and his twelve-year deanship saw a controlled explosion of growth. His school's endowment soared from $20 million to $150 million. The ranks of permanent faculty grew from 20 to 75; degree candidates rose from 200 to 750 a year. Nine research centers were added.

Rosovsky and the Core

LED BY A NEW DEAN, the Faculty of Arts and Sciences had addressed the need for curricular reform in the fall of 1974. After three years as dean, John Dunlop had taken leave to head the White House cost-of-living council. Bok named Henry Rosovsky to succeed him. "CHOICE OF ROSOVSKY NO SURPRISE: HE FITS THE BILL," announced the *Crimson.* Like Dunlop, Rosovsky was an economist, and a period of scarce resources was at hand. The faculty was still divided into caucuses, but Rosovsky was not identified with either. And he was strongly interested in curricular reform.

Rosovsky was 46. Born in Danzig (later Gdansk, Poland), he grew up speaking Russian and German. In 1940 the family came to the United States as refugees. Rosovsky followed his older brother to the College of William and Mary, took his B.A. in economics in 1949, and became a naturalized citizen the same year. Before college he had served with army occupation forces in Germany; as a reserve officer he was sent to Korea and Japan in 1950. That tour of duty ignited his scholarly interest in the Far East, and he added Japanese to his stock of languages.

As a Harvard graduate student, Rosovsky taught a section of Economics 10, was elected a Junior Fellow, and took his Ph.D. in economics in 1959. He taught at the University of California at Berkeley for seven years, but after the campus upheavals of 1965 he joined the "White Berkeleyans" who went east to find a more tranquil habitat. Returning to Harvard, he put in three years as chairman of the economics department and chaired the committee that wrote the first report on Afro-American studies. Three years on the Faculty Council had confirmed his belief that the College curriculum needed attention.

THE "RED BOOK" REFORMS of the late 1940s, based on the precept that liberal education should have a "unifying purpose and idea," had made the General Education program the centerpiece of the curriculum. The program's useful life had lasted a decade or so. By the 1960s, piecemeal changes had made a shambles of Gen Ed.

New undergraduate programs introduced in the 1950s—advanced standing, independent study, freshman seminars—encouraged specialization. Reviewing Gen Ed in 1963, a faculty panel urged more "inno-

Henry Rosovsky, dean of the Faculty of Arts and Sciences from 1973 to 1984, was the prime mover in reforming the College curriculum. His close rapport with President Bok, and his own forceful character, made Rosovsky a powerful figure. When he stepped down as dean he was elected to the Corporation.

vative and interdisciplinary" courses. New offerings bloomed so abundantly that the program's unifying purpose was lost in the foliage. Samuel Beer's "Western Thought and Institutions," the model Gen Ed course, now coexisted with "Scandinavian Cinema" and "Classical Music of India, Pakistan, and Bangla Desh." Course listings swelled from 55 in 1963 to 101 in 1969. Tracing the proliferation of courses in natural sciences, Shattuck professor of government James Q. Wilson would maintain that "the 'Nat Sci' requirement can be met in any number of ways which ensure that the student will not learn, or even observe from a safe distance, science."

When students of the 1960s demanded the right to design their own education, the faculty had complied by easing requirements. Even the language requirement could now be waived with a certification from the University Health Services that a student suffered from "strephosymbolia." President Bok, devoting the first of his annual reports to the state of undergraduate education, had written that recent curricular changes "almost all took the form of relaxing old requirements rather than implementing new programs," and as such were "the product of a period that has been critical of old traditions and ancient requirements, yet largely devoid of new visions for educational reform."[8]

Rosovsky sent out a 22-page letter inviting his colleagues' views. Curricular standards had eroded so much, he claimed, that the bachelor's degree amounted to little more than a certificate of attendance. "At the moment," wrote Rosovsky, "to be an educated man or woman doesn't mean anything. It may mean that you've designed your own curriculum; it may mean that you know all about urban this or rural that. But there is no common denominator." The existing curriculum, a bulging grab bag of 2,600 courses, "no longer expresses our basic aims, and does not establish a common basis for intellectual discourse."[9]

Rosovsky's political instincts told him that a faculty-wide process was needed. At Stanford, Princeton, and Yale, curricular review had been delegated to blue-ribbon panels, and thoughtful proposals had been shot down by the full faculty. He began by appointing seven task forces to study undergraduate education and College life.

The task force on curricular design was chaired by James Q. Wilson, a specialist in organizational behavior. Concluding that General Education's trinity—natural science, social science, humanities—was too broad to be useful, Wilson's group recommended replacing Gen Ed with a "core curriculum" divided into eight areas. The emphasis was to be on "approaches to knowledge," not on bodies of knowledge per se.

When the proposal reached the Faculty Council, the number of areas was reduced to five: literature and arts; historical study; social analysis and moral reasoning; science; and foreign cultures. Candidates for the bachelor's degree would earn a quarter of their credits in these areas. They would also have to exhibit competence in expository writing, a second language, and mathematics.

The Core proposals were controversial. Many faculty scientists thought the sciences were being stinted. Some 2,400 students signed a petition asking the faculty to delay its vote and allow more undergraduate involvement. The *Crimson* denounced the entire exercise as a con-

Bridge-Builder

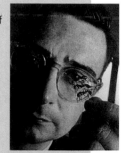

E.O. WILSON

In 1975 the evolutionary biologist Edward O. Wilson, PH.D. '55, published *Sociobiology: The New Synthesis,* a book that defined a broad new field of study and sparked heated debate about the impact of evolution on social behavior. The biological origins of animal and human behavior, wrote Wilson, made biology the logical foundational discipline of the social sciences. In later writings he continued to explore the interlocking relationships between the great branches of learning.

As a leading proponent of Harvard's Core Curriculum, Wilson argued for "some deliberate affirmation in universities of the convergence and centrality of a large part of knowledge, of methodology, and of the very techniques of reasoning." For two decades he taught the Core course on evolutionary biology.

Ants, social wasps, bees, and termites were the primary focus of Wilson's research. ("Most children have a bug period," he observed, "and I never grew out of mine.") He shared a Pulitzer Prize in 1979 for *The Ants* and won another in 1991 for *On Human Nature*. Wilson became Pellegrino University Professor in 1986.

Core Samples

Introduced in the fall term of 1979, the first Core Curriculum offerings included 55 half-courses in five broad areas. Among them:

Literature and arts
"Great Novels of the Nineteenth and Early Twentieth Centuries" (Jerome Buckley)
"The Concept of the Hero in Hellenic Civilization" (Gregory Nagy)
"Weimar Culture" (Maria Tatar)

Historical study
"The Scientific Revolution" (I. Bernard Cohen)
"Tradition and Transformation in East Asian Civilization: Japan" (Edwin Reischauer, Henry Rosovsky, Albert Craig, others)
"The Emancipation of the Jews" (Yosef Yerushalmi)

Social analysis
"Principles of Economics" (Otto Eckstein, Jeffrey Wolcowitz, others)
"Crime and Human Nature" (Richard Herrnstein, J. Q. Wilson)

Moral reasoning
"Realism and Moralism" (Harvey Mansfield)
"The Theory of the Just War" (Michael Walzer)

Foreign cultures
"Comparative Politics of South America" (Jorge Dominguez)
"Sources of Indian Civilization" (Diana Eck)

Science
"The Astronomical Perspective" (Owen Gingerich, David Lathem)
"From Alchemy to Elementary Particle Physics" (Sheldon Glashow)
"Evolutionary Biology" (E.O. Wilson)

spiracy to "clamp down on students." But when debate began in the spring of 1978, the three faculty meetings devoted to the Core were notable for thoughtful discourse and crisp repartee. Rosovsky made sure all sides had a say, insisting that the Core was "a framework, adaptable to the changing views of the faculty." His advocacy of the Core was strengthened by the fact that he had declined the presidencies of Yale and the University of Chicago some months earlier, at least partly to see the curricular review to completion. When it came to a vote, the Core proposals passed easily. The tally was 182 to 65.[10]

The new curriculum was to be phased in over a four-year period. The Core initially comprised about eighty courses, two-thirds of them new. None, perhaps, was as grandly ambitious as such first-generation Gen Ed offerings as Crane Brinton's "Introduction to the Social Inheritance of Western Civilization" or John Finley's "The Epic." But broad courses like "Comedy and the Novel," "Justice," and "Space, Time, and Motion" came close. Others were framed much more narrowly ("Chivalric Romances of the Middle Ages," "Turn-of-the-Century Austrian Culture"). Unlike early Gen Ed courses, many Core courses had a non-Western focus ("Politics, Mythology, and Art in Bronze Age China," "Sub-Saharan African Civilizations").

If the *New York Times* went too far in describing the Core as "a radical departure from established methods of undergraduate education," the new program was a distinct advance. It refreshed the existing mix of courses with dozens of new ones. It made ethical studies a required part of undergraduate education. It subsumed and extended the great reforms begun in President Lowell's era and carried forward in President Conant's. Conant, who thought knowledge had been overdepartmentalized, would have approved of the inclusion of multidisciplinary perspectives in many Core offerings. The emphasis on "broad, basic modes of understanding" was in keeping with Alfred North Whitehead's saying that "scraps of information" have nothing to do with the true meaning of culture, and with Lowell's inaugural declaration that "the essence of a liberal education consists in an attitude of mind, a familiarity with methods of thought, an ability to use information rather than in a memory stocked with facts."

Affirmative Action and Diversity

As THE FACULTY DEBATED the Core proposals, the Supreme Court was deciding *Regents of the University of California v. Bakke*, a case that tested the constitutionality of affirmative action in higher education. The University of California Medical School at Davis had reserved sixteen places per class for disadvantaged minority-group members. Allan Bakke, a 37-year-old white engineer who had twice been denied admission, sued the University of California, claiming the right to equal protection under the Fourteenth Amendment. Having lost at the state level, the university hired Archibald Cox to argue its appeal before the high court.

Cox framed his argument broadly. He wanted it to protect admissions programs at institutions like Harvard, Columbia, Stanford, and

The Blizzard of '78

O N FEBRUARY 6, a Monday, it snowed hard. Night brought winds of hurricane force, thunder, lightning, and more snow. The Blizzard of 1978 was the worst winter storm that Cambridge had seen in a century. The president and the deans of the several faculties managed to meet on Tuesday afternoon; they decided the University would be officially closed the next day. Never before had Harvard shut down because of adverse weather conditions.

All parts of the University but the Law School stayed closed on Thursday. Students indulged in

the kind of festival rites that young people on unexpected holiday tend to indulge in. Some of the frolicking took place outdoors. So many cross-country skiers took to the streets that snow-removal efforts were impaired, and the city issued a cross-country skiing ban. Snow sculptures took shape in

the Yard—a massive pyramid, a sphinx, a dragon, a Loch Ness monster, a stego- saurus, a replica of *The Thinker*.

From a ski jump on the front steps of Widener Library, free-stylers executed midair somersaults. Students in groups of twelve, hand in hand, leapt into Pusey Library's snow-filled moat. Daredevils did flips into Larsen Hall's sunken courtyard. The University Health Services treated six snow-related fractures (two ankles, two ribs, one wrist, one neck), and 27 strains and sprains.

More than a hundred students were hired to help buildings and grounds workers deal with the 27-inch blanket of snow. Cleanup crews worked round the clock for two days and nights. By Sunday paths were clear, backs were aching, and the job was done. The cost to Harvard exceeded $200,000. The city of Cambridge's cleanup bill was about $1.5 million.

"The Exhausted West"

Citing him as "a Russian writer in the tradition of Tolstoy and Pasternak . . . a courageous exponent of the unfettered human spirit," Harvard awarded an honorary doctorate in letters to Aleksandr Solzhenitsyn at the Commencement of 1978.

At the afternoon exercises, the exiled novelist spoke for almost an hour in measured Russian, simultaneously translated over a separate speaker system. The speech—Solzhenitsyn's first public statement since his arrival in the United States in 1976—was a stern critique of Western society. It was titled "The Exhausted West."

"We have placed too much hope in political and social reforms," Solzhenitsyn declared, "only to find that we were being deprived of our most precious possession: our spiritual life. In the East, it is destroyed by the dealings and machinations of the ruling party. In the West, commercial interests tend to suffocate it. This is the real crisis. The split in the world is less terrible than the similarity of the diseases plaguing its main sections."

the University of Pennsylvania—four schools that were among 120 institutions filing amicus briefs in the case. The joint brief sought to justify race as a selective factor in admissions decisions. Racial diversity, it argued, not only enriched higher education; from the standpoint of the larger society, it was needed to overcome the effects of past discrimination and ensure equality of opportunity for all races.

A statement of Harvard's policy on College admissions was part of the brief. It opposed the use of quotas and described minority status as one of many criteria used to rate qualified candidates. Race might tip the scale in an applicant's favor, "just as geographic origin or a life spent on a farm might tip the balance in other candidates' cases."

Banning all forms of reverse discrimination, Cox argued, would impede "the search for justice for all, to which this country has always been committed." By a 5-4 vote, the court ruled that a rigid quota was unconstitutional and that Bakke should be admitted—but that schools could legitimately pay "some attention" to race in admissions decisions. Justice Lewis Powell, writing for the majority, contrasted Davis's "explicit racial classification" with Harvard's more nuanced approach. Quoting extensively from the statement in the amicus brief, Powell wrote that "this kind of program treats each applicant as an individual in the admissions process, [yet] does not insulate the individual from comparison with all other candidates for the available seats."

THE DECISION MARKED a complete turnabout from the 1920s and '30s. "Race, once the undesirable factor, has become a most desirable consideration," noted Marcia Graham Synnott in *The Half-Opened Door*, published soon after the *Bakke* case. "Disadvantaged minority students may be admitted with academic records that would result in the rejection of white applicants. On the other hand, there [is] a crucial difference in purpose between discriminatory and benign quotas: the function of the former was to exclude, of the present, to include."[11]

American colleges had undertaken a massive social engineering project. Nationwide, enrollment of blacks in predominantly white institutions doubled during the 1970s. Harvard's recruiting efforts predated most private colleges'.[12] As the civil rights movement grew, the admissions office worked with the National Scholarship Service and Fund for Negro Students to double and redouble the number of black undergraduates. Admissions officers began visiting largely black urban high schools, like George Washington in New York City and DuSable and Phillips in Chicago. Undergraduates and recent graduates helped out as recruiters. The proportion of black students in the College rose from 2 percent in the early 1960s to 7 percent in 1969. Ninety blacks were admitted in the spring of 1968, when Martin Luther King Jr. was killed, compared to 51 the previous year. By the mid-1970s there were more than 500 blacks (including Radcliffe students) in a College of 6,500.

Harvard's example had helped swing the *Bakke* case, but having a model admissions policy did not ensure a fulfilling experience for all black undergraduates. Even the most academically and socially successful reported that, implicitly or explicitly, they were often made to feel that they owed their presence at Harvard to reverse discrimination and lowered academic standards.[14] For the growing number of students from segregated backgrounds, the College of the 1970s could seem an alien place. Though Harvard had an affirmative action program for faculty and staff, there were few black faculty members or administrators. College buildings bore the names of well-born white men; their portraits were plentiful. Traces of notable black graduates, like W. E. B. Du Bois (A.B. 1890, PH.D. 1895), William Monroe Trotter (A.B. 1895), Alain Locke '08, Edward Gourdin '21, Countee Cullen, A.M. '26, and Ralph Bunche, PH.D. '34, were almost nonexistent.

Like Kansas farm boys and New York furriers' sons, black students of earlier generations had often adopted the dress and manner of the New England prep-school types who were the collegiate trend-setters. But at colleges everywhere, cultural standardization was a casualty of the 1960s. Influenced by the Black Power movement, many college-age blacks now dressed and spoke in ways that emphasized their black heritage. "Black tables" were fixtures at the freshman, House, and graduate dining halls, and blacks and other minorities clustered at the Radcliffe Quadrangle in the two geographically most remote of the twelve residential Houses.

As SDS chapters lost focus and splintered, black groups came to the fore in campus protests. The 1969 report of Henry Rosovsky's faculty committee on Afro-American studies had pinpointed issues that would soon lead to militant demonstrations. In the fall of 1969, members of the Organization for Black Unity, a University-wide coalition, staged building occupations and closed off a construction site to protest hiring and contracting practices. Those demonstrations led the University to adopt an action program for minority employment, which subsequently formed the basis of its first affirmative action plan.[14] Later came the week-long occupation of Massachusetts Hall to protest Harvard investment policy (see page 251).

WITH THE INCEPTION OF Afro-American studies in 1969, that department supplanted the six-year-old Harvard-Radcliffe Association of African and Afro-American Students ("Afro") as a social and political base for black students. But the department was increasingly viewed as an academic disaster area.

More than a thousand students, including many whites, had lined up in the fall of 1969 to enroll in the new department's seven courses. Course enrollments had dropped to 314 by 1979, and there were only eight concentrators, none white. The department was notoriously contentious, and only two tenured professorships had been filled in a decade.

In a report that reaffirmed the intrinsic value of Afro-American studies, a review committee convened in 1972 had criticized the "virtual autonomy" of the chairman, Ewart Guinier '33, and the "counterproductive" presence of students on the executive committee. After hot debate, the faculty rescinded the students' voting powers.

Guinier had formerly been associate director of Columbia's Urban Center. With a background in labor and community organizing, he did not have a Ph.D. He was devoted to his department, but his assertive

Some 300 black students graduated from the College in the first five years of the Bok administration. That exceeded the number graduated from 1870 to 1970. But enlarging the ranks of black students did not guarantee a rewarding educational and social experience for all.

Insiders

We should encourage all steps that make Radcliffe undergraduates insiders," declared Dean Henry Rosovsky when a joint committee reviewed the Harvard-Radcliffe relationship in 1975. Under an agreement effected in 1975, the colleges' admissions offices were unified and a policy of "equal access" adopted. Women enrolling at Radcliffe were thereby enrolled at Harvard.

The late 1970s were a time of increasing prominence for women undergraduates. By 1979, the year of Radcliffe's centennial, the male-female ratio was 1.7:1. *Harvard Magazine*'s "Undergraduate" column noted that "the campus leaders for the coming spring are virtually all women." Writer Kerry Konrad '79 cited the presidents of the *Crimson* and the *Advocate,* the Dramatic Club, the Gilbert and Sullivan Players, the Democratic Club, the Republican Club, "and many more."

"Women at Harvard go to Harvard now, not Radcliffe, and in dramatically increasing numbers," wrote Konrad. "The point cannot be overemphasized; it is the greatest transformation of College life since the Houses were built over forty years ago."

style and thin academic credentials stymied efforts to attract the field's leading scholars to Harvard. Guinier's chairmanship ended in 1976, but the department continued to lose ground. An Overseers' visiting committee proposed in 1979 that it be replaced by a degree-granting interdisciplinary committee. Instead Dean Rosovsky renewed the quest for a ranking scholar to head the program. Columbia historian Nathan Huggins, PH.D. '62, finally accepted the assignment. Patient and soft-spoken, he held the shaky department together until his death in 1989. In the 1990s it would experience a dramatic rebirth when Henry Louis Gates Jr., the most sought-after young scholar in the field, left Duke to assume the chairmanship.

BLACK UNDERGRADUATES had led a campaign for a student-run, University-funded Third World center. Stanford, Yale, Princeton, Brown, Tufts, and other institutions had such centers. In the summer of 1980 President Bok appointed the Reverend Peter J. Gomes, B.D. '68, minister in the Memorial Church and Plummer professor of Christian morals, to head a student-faculty committee on race relations that would weigh the pros and cons of creating a multicultural center.

The committee concluded that creating a haven for minorities would not be helpful. Its report suggested instead a foundation to promote racial understanding through cultural interaction. Such an undertaking had not been tried at Harvard or elsewhere, the report noted. Proponents of a Third World center objected, but Bok approved the proposal. To direct the new venture he named S. Allen Counter Jr., a Medical School neuroscientist who had done field work in Asia, Africa, and South America. Housed in a small basement room in University Hall, the Harvard Foundation began a busy and creative existence in the fall of 1981. Counter developed a lively program of guest speakers and discussion panels, sponsored a yearly conference for women and minorities interested in science, and initiated a popular performance and food festival, held annually, called Cultural Rhythms.

Endowment-building

HARVARD AND OTHER INSTITUTIONS were hard hit by the economic upheavals of the 1970s. Steep oil-price increases in 1973 and 1978 raised the University's energy bill from $3 million to $21 million. Inflation, reaching 13 percent per year as the decade ended, eroded the real market value of the endowment by one-third. In October 1979 Harvard announced a capital campaign designed to increase its $1.4 billion endowment by at least $200 million.

With federal and foundation funding in decline, endowment income would be increasingly vital to support new areas of research, maintain buildings, meet faculty salary and financial-aid obligations, and keep tuition increases within bounds.[16] In a significant break with the University's traditionally conservative portfolio management, primary responsibility for investing the endowment had been turned over to the Harvard Management Company, an in-house subsidiary, in 1974. The new company was set up by George Putnam '49, M.B.A. '51, a Boston

The Medical Area Total Energy Plant was the costliest project ever launched by a university. Its 333-foot stack loomed over Boston's Fenway-Mission Hill district.

62-Megawatt Headache

I T B E G A N as a bold experiment in energy independence. After a decade of financial, political, and technological setbacks, it looked like the blunder of the century.

When the Medical Area Total Energy Plant was planned, in 1972, it appeared to be a visionary solution to the energy needs of the Medical School and the dozen teaching hospitals, professional schools, and research centers adjoining it. Replacing an aged power plant built in 1906, MATEP was this country's largest venture in cogeneration, engineered to produce electricity, chilled water, and steam. Saving energy by reusing exhaust emissions, the plant was expected to cut Medical Area fuel bills by almost one-third.

The cost was initially pegged at $50 million. Compared with Harvard's costliest projects of the past—the $19 million Science Center, the $15 million electron accelerator, the $12 million Holyoke Center complex—that was serious money. But multimillion-dollar construction-cost overruns, regulatory delays, community opposition, and rising interest rates inflated the final figure to $350 million. The 62-megawatt plant was largely completed in 1980, but the air-quality permit that allowed it to fire up its oil-powered generators and produce electricity wasn't granted until 1986.

Harvard had intended to transfer ownership of MATEP to a bank or lending agency, but a series of leaseback plans fell through. In 1982 a tax-exempt bond issue refinanced the plant.

A F T E R A D E C A D E of full operation, MATEP was yielding $54 million in annual revenue—enough to cover operating expenses, but not to service an outstanding debt of $330 million. Prospective deregulation promised to make the electric utility industry more competitive, enabling large users like Harvard to shop for favorable terms. But cheaper energy in the open market would also put pressure on MATEP's rates. The University's chances of recouping its investment in MATEP seemed slim. In 1998 Harvard sold the plant to a utility supplying electricity and steam to its central campus. The price was $147 million.

mutual-fund executive who had succeeded George F. Bennett '33 in the half-time position of treasurer in 1973. Putnam came from old Harvard stock—he was a great-nephew of A. Lawrence Lowell—but his ideas about money management were far from hidebound.

Since 1949 the Harvard endowment portfolio had been managed by State Street Research and Management Company, a Boston firm in which George Bennett and his predecessor, Paul Cabot, were principals. As an Overseer, Putnam had helped prepare a report on "Harvard and Money" for the committee on governance in 1970. He inclined increasingly to the view that managing the portfolio should be separated from the tasks of setting policy and reviewing performance.

To head the new Harvard Management Company, Putnam hired Walter Cabot '55, M.B.A. '59, Paul Cabot's nephew and a former member of Putnam's firm. With a staff of nine, Cabot took over $1 billion worth of endowment assets in 1974. The management of another $400 million worth of holdings was divided among five outside firms.[16]

Cabot's investment team used sophisticated techniques to play the market aggressively. Computerization was transforming the financial world, and the Management Company could turn to Harvard's Center for Research in Computing Technology for help in setting up advanced information and control systems. Putnam also brought in George Siguler, M.B.A. '74, a 26-year-old consultant versed in such technical devices as options, futures, stock lending, and bond immunization. The Management Company was the first nonprofit firm to engage in stock lending, and one of the first to get into computer-guided options trading, arbitrage, derivatives, and venture capital. Though the company was there to earn money for Harvard, donors making deferred gifts could get the benefit of its services. With a major campaign in the offing, this was a new wrinkle in fund-raising.

Treasurer George Putnam, above, and Harvard Management Company president Walter Cabot. Both were from old-line Yankee families, but were partial to new ideas in the investment field.

THE HARVARD CAMPAIGN's five-year goal was $250 million. Four universities had set higher targets, but this was the largest drive keyed primarily to undergraduate education. Half the amount sought would endow faculty salaries and student financial aid. Some $60 million would help renew physical plant: Houses, classrooms, libraries, museums, laboratories, athletic facilities, the Memorial Church. Another $20 million would fund professional-school programs in public policy.

Unlike the Program for Harvard College, which was launched in an era of dynamic growth, the Harvard Campaign began in a climate of economic adversity. But that would change.

A foreign-policy crisis in the Middle East closed out the decade of the 1970s. President Jimmy Carter had reluctantly agreed to let the deposed shah of Iran enter the United States for medical treatment. Iranian militants seized the U.S. embassy in Tehran and took 65 Americans hostage.[17] Carter had won a diplomatic triumph by mediating a peace agreement between Israel and Egypt, but his negotiators could not free the hostages. A disastrous helicopter rescue attempt doomed his chances of re-election. Ronald Reagan, ex-movie actor and former governor of California, led Republicans to a landslide victory in 1980.

The Reagan administration cut taxes and slashed spending for social and educational programs, while appropriating more than $2 trillion for an unprecedented military buildup. The United States, once the world's largest lender, became its biggest borrower. "Reaganomics" brought on a short, sharp recession, exacerbated by layoffs attributable to a new wave of technological innovation in industry. As inflation receded and Congress eased corporate tax burdens, business indices improved. By the summer of 1982 the longest period of economic expansion in American history was under way.

From Harvard's standpoint the "Reagan revolution" was a mixed blessing. Cuts in federal grants and student loans came to more than a million a year. About $20 million in new endowment would be needed to cover the shortfall. But as stock and bond markets rallied, the

Management Company posted record results: return on investment rose to 42 percent in 1983. The company's staff had grown to almost a hundred; its annual budget was more than $8 million. The endowment was now valued at $2.5 billion, a ten-year increase of 110 percent.

The Harvard Campaign surged ahead of the projected pace. Inflationary increases had undermined most of the calculations on which the campaign had been based, and the $60 million allotted to building renovations had proved to be a gross underestimate. Repairs to two of the Houses had uncovered extensive deterioration: another $40 million would be needed for the Houses and Radcliffe Quadrangle buildings alone. In the summer of 1982, the campaign's leaders agreed to raise their goal from $250 million to $350 million, a figure that had a nice resonance with Harvard's upcoming anniversary.

THE CAMPUS WAS ALREADY ASTIR with renovations and new construction. Renewal of the Houses had been planned as a seven- or eight-year undertaking, but the degree of rot and deterioration of plumbing and electrical systems was such that the pace of the project was doubled. Work on eight river Houses was telescoped into three summers, with repairs to Radcliffe Quad buildings beginning the fourth year.

Outside of the $350 million Medical Area Total Energy Plant (see page 265), the House renovations constituted the largest, most time-sensitive project that Harvard had undertaken. Electrical work—rewiring and increasing the load capacity of all the buildings—accounted for almost a third of the total cost. Electricians found pennies in fuse boxes, wires fused to conduits, and evidence of smoking wires behind fixtures. That there had been no major fires seemed miraculous.

While work on the Houses went forward, the interior of Sever Hall (1880) was refurbished. Harvard Stadium, built at a cost of $310,000 in 1903, got new steel supports and concrete seating in an $8 million overhaul. The athletics department installed a $1 million, three-layer outdoor track. The Anderson Bridge (1913) got new sidewalks. The massive Class of 1857 Gate, near Wadsworth House, was elevated by giant

Among the celebrities addressing seniors at the 1982 Commencement was Kermit the Frog, a fixture of public television's *Sesame Street*. In cap and gown, Kermit recalled his own youth, saying, "For a frog, adolescence means losing your tail. You don't know the pain of puberty until you feel your tail fall off."

The well-known Muppet's creator, Jim Henson, was in Cambridge to see his daughter Lisa '82, the first woman president in the 106-year history of the *Harvard Lampoon*.

Refurbishing the spire of fifty-year-old Memorial Church was among the home improvements made possible by the Harvard Campaign. Frank Campbell of Everett Decorators, at left, wielded his paint roller twelve stories above the Yard. Directly behind him: Canaday Hall, the Science Center, Memorial Hall.

Faces in the Yard: seniors from Cabot House–a Radcliffe Quadrangle residence previously known as South House–on the morning of Commencement day.

cranes and moved a few feet to its original position nearer Massachusetts Avenue. Allston Burr Lecture Hall (1949), its functions absorbed by the Undergraduate Science Center, was demolished to make way for a major extension of the Fogg Art Museum, designed by British architect James Stirling and later named for donor Arthur Sackler.

THE HARVARD CAMPAIGN ENDED on December 31, 1984. More than 57,000 alumni and friends had contributed a total of $358 million. Donations came in many forms. Included were a couple of yachts; land in Seattle and St. Croix; Manhattan and Los Angeles condominiums; a Copley portrait later sold to the Philadelphia Museum of Art for $790,000; and two silver dollars bought in the 1940s for $30 and sold by Harvard at auction for $14,362.50, net.

A member of the class of '21, annoyed by what he considered poor usage of the language on television, gave a scholarship for students of English. An undergraduate pledged $10,000 toward an award for excellence in teaching. Grants came in memory of former teachers and deceased friends, to support Lamont Library's Poetry Room, to help students who were single parents, to modernize the Stadium's sound system, to fund research and education on avoiding nuclear war.

The largest gift was a $7.5 million donation from John L. Loeb '24, endowing fifteen junior faculty positions. Loeb had been a mainstay of the Program for Harvard College. Donors of his generation were important to the campaign, but much of its success reflected the emergence of wealthy younger alumni who had been on the leading edge of industrial and technological change in the 1960s and '70s. Corporation member Robert G. Stone '45, a campaign co-chairman, estimated that two-thirds of the major gifts "were from self-made men. The toughest dollars to get were from inherited wealth."

As in the past, major fund-raising heightened alumni interest in University activities and quickened the institution's metabolic rate. "What a successful drive can do," observed Derek Bok in 1983, "is elicit an effort within the institution that otherwise could not occur at quite that level and pitch. The administrators work harder, the faculty do likewise. I don't think it's an accident at all that when we look back from the perspective of ten or twenty years, we will find that these few years have been one of the very few periods of maximum creativity, change, improvement, and reform within the College."[18]

THE CAMPAIGN WAS A BRIDGE that took Harvard from the uncertain 1970s into an extended period of consolidation and integration. The endowment drive and the Management Company's investment yields provided fresh capital for the 1980s. The Core Curriculum was in place. Having demonstrated formidable fund-raising strengths in the campaign, Henry Rosovsky concluded eleven years in the dean's office and returned to teaching and research as a University Professor. A. Michael Spence, PH.D. '72, professor of economics, succeeded him. The University's leaders would now turn to other issues: renewing facilities, supporting curricular change at the graduate and professional level, exploring unfolding opportunities in computer technology.

The campaign's end coincided with another generational shift in the makeup of the College. The last of the baby boomers were graduating. The fifteen years since the shake-ups of the late 1960s had been a time of sociological transformation. Women now constituted 45 percent of incoming classes. In a decade, the proportion of Asian Americans had risen from 5 percent of each class to 12 percent—and would soar to 18 percent by the end of the 1980s. Minority recruiting efforts, initially focused primarily on black students, had been extended to Hispanics, Latinos, Native Americans. "The faces in the Yard," wrote contributing editor Jim Harrison in a *Harvard Magazine* photoessay, "reveal a range of ethnicity as diverse as the first dozen names in the student telephone book—Aamoth, Aaronoff, Abati, Abbasi, Abbey, Abel, Abercrombie, Abers, Ablow, Abney, Aboodi, Abou-Zamzam."

A new wave of nontraditional students would arrive in the second half of the 1980s. These were the children of the first generation of immigrants to arrive in America after the passage of the Immigration Act of 1965, which ended the discriminatory quotas that had effectively barred Asian immigrants for four decades. Reflecting a national pattern, Harvard would see an influx of students of Chinese, Indian, Korean, Indochinese, and other Asian ancestry, and a corresponding increase in religious diversity. Islamic, Hindu, Buddhist, and other religious groups would grow in size and become more central to the life of the University. Academic rites like Class Day and the Phi Beta Kappa Literary Exercises would begin to incorporate prayers and hymns from such sacred texts as the Quran and the Rig-Veda.

High technology supplied another sort of generational marker. The baby boomers had been the first cohort to grow up watching television;

Three years in the planning stages, this Queen Anne-style guardhouse was erected in 1983 inside Johnston Gate. It was part of a plan to monitor and reduce vehicular traffic in the Yard. Architect Graham Gund, M.ARCH. '68, M.A.U. '69, did some three hundred designs before arriving at one that was equally pleasing to Harvard and the Cambridge Historical Commission. The total cost of the project came to $57,000, including landscaping. The *Boston Globe's* architectural critic, Robert Campbell '58, noted that this made it "the costliest building per square foot ever built in the Boston area."

On duty when the picture above was taken was Harvard Police officer Edward Donahue.

their successors, or at least large numbers of them, were the first to grow up using household computers.

The Computer Revolution

T
HE STRIKING STUDENTS of 1969 had demanded institutional change and called for social revolution. Fifteen years later it was the computer revolution that was changing Harvard. Derek Bok, who did not routinely use a computer, devoted his annual report for 1985 to the uses of technology in education. "In theory, at least, the new technology has the power to transform the nature of the university," he wrote. The process had already begun. Harvard's yearly expenditures for information technology were nearing $30 million, and were increasing at an annual rate of 25 percent.

"Computer" no longer meant a room-filling mainframe that cost hundreds of thousands of dollars and required a staff of experts to run. Recent years had seen an array of new hardware that ranged from the vector supercomputer to high-speed departmental computers, scientific work stations, and the "personal" computer (PC). Between 1980 and 1985 the number of computers at Harvard rose from 290 to more than 8,500; about 8,000 were PCs. Harvard's Technology Product Center, which sold computer equipment at substantial discounts, moved a record 3,900 PCs in 1985. About two-thirds were sold to students.

A vital element of PC operating systems had its genesis at Harvard's Aiken Computation Laboratory. Working night and day in the first weeks of 1975, a Currier House sophomore named William H. Gates III had used one of the lab's computers to write programming language for the limited memory space in the Altair 8800, billed as the first personal computer. With help from Paul Allen, a high-school friend from Seattle then working in Boston, and Monte Davidoff '78, a Currier House neighbor, Gates did the coding in eight weeks and sold it to the Altair's developer. Gates and Allen then formed a partnership to market programming software. They called it Microsoft. Midway through his senior year Gates left Harvard to concentrate on the venture. Based in Albuquerque, where the Altair was built, it was hugely successful. The mass-market computers that began the PC revolution—Tandy's TRS-80 (1977), the Apple II (1978), the IBM PC (1981), the Apple Macintosh (1984)—were produced with Microsoft licensing. When the company went public, Gates's holdings made him a billionaire at 31. No one in American history had become so rich at so young an age. At 42, Gates would be by far the world's wealthiest individual, worth $51 billion.

The PC was an immensely powerful tool. In addition to computational power, it offered text-generating features that made typewriters obsolete. Connected to an electronic network, it became part of a high-speed, low-cost communications medium that was worldwide in scope.

Wide-area networking had begun when the Defense Department's Advanced Research Projects Agency (ARPA) designed a research network to link local networks at universities and national laboratories. Harvard became the first node on the ARPANET when the agency delivered a Digital Equipment Corporation PDP-10 to Aiken Lab in 1969.[19]

Bill Gates '78 left Harvard to find fun and profit in software design. Below: Aiken Laboratory, where he wrote programming language for the first personal computer.

Linked to radio- and satellite-based computer communications, ARPA-NET sites became part of a global supernetwork formed in the 1980s and known as the Internet. The first practical data-sharing protocols, devised by the European Center for Nuclear Research (CERN) in Geneva to facilitate international collaboration in high-energy physics experimentation, arrived at the end of the decade, with world-shaking effect. CERN's breakthrough became known as the World Wide Web.

Computing at Harvard had evolved in typically decentralized fashion. Departments and schools developed their own technology and databases. By the late 1980s almost a dozen internal networks were in use. The Office of Information Technology (OIT) had been set up in 1971 to coordinate planning and operations, but academic computing had later decoupled from it. To provide a unified system of connectivity, OIT planned a University-wide network that would provide high-speed data and video-image exchange, while incorporating an improved telephone system. Work on the $30 million project, requiring 10,000 miles of copper and fiberoptic cable, began in 1989. Linking residential facilities, classrooms, and faculty offices, the new network supported electronic mail and bulletin boards, file transfer, interpersonal exchange, and computer-based instructional programs.

"Harvard Out of South Africa"

TRY AS HE MIGHT to promote a sense of common purpose at Harvard, President Bok could not overcome one long-lasting cause of division: the movement to end university investments in corporations operating in South Africa. No issue since Vietnam had affected American campuses so intensely. For more than a decade, student coalitions petitioned, marched, picketed, and sometimes used obstructive tactics to press their case. Divestment rallies were a sign of spring. At every Commencement, demonstrators displayed signs, balloons, and mortarboards with legends like "End Apartheid," "Harvard Out of South Africa," "Divest Now!" At the end of his twenty-year presidency, Bok would muse that "at times it seemed like one long, endless argument over divestment."

The first large-scale demonstration had come in the spring of 1978, when more than 3,000 students joined a candlelit march to protest the Corporation's acceptance of a report that opposed full divestment of University shareholdings in companies with ties to South Africa. The student-faculty-alumni advisory committee on shareholder responsibility had proposed instead that the portfolio be reviewed on a case-by-case basis to assess each corporation's capacity to improve working conditions and end South Africa's state-enforced segregation. This would provide a basis for a policy of "selective divestment." To many students, this looked like a temporizing approach.

The following spring Bok issued a series of open letters that examined the ethical responsibilities of the university in society and the possible consequences of stock divestiture. "The real power of universities stems from the force of individual ideas," he wrote in one letter, "and not from the use of their portfolios or their purchasing offices." Full

Michael Crawford's drawing of a computer-literate John Harvard illustrated President Bok's report on the educational uses of computer technology in *Harvard Magazine*'s issue of May-June 1985.

Sue Minter, Susan Karwoski, and Amy Goodman, graduating in 1984, were among those supporting divestment at their Commencement. Members of the class contributed $10,000 to a fund to be paid over to Harvard when and if it divested fully.

Below: "African shanties" put up in front of University Hall by a pro-divestment group in 1986.

divestment, Bok contended, "would almost certainly cause the University to divert millions of dollars in pursuit of a strategy that is legally questionable, widely disputed on its merits, and very likely to prove ineffective in achieving its objectives." Attempts to exert institutional pressure for political ends, argued Bok, would make the University more vulnerable to counterpressures from the outside world.

Bok endorsed other forms of institutional action. In 1979 he proposed a $6 million intercollegiate scholarship program for nonwhite South Africans, which he subsequently chaired.

Harvard eventually began to divest selectively—and quietly. In 1981 it sold $51 million in Citibank notes because the bank made direct loans to the South African government. When the sale was revealed, a spokesman explained that "it is not the primary objective of the University's investment policy to raise publicity around these issues." Harvard would later sell more than $360 million worth of holdings in companies that did not meet its standards for continued investment, but in 1985 it still held shares worth more than $500 million in about a hundred companies with South African ties. The size and fervor of protest activity increased that spring.

A crowd of 5,000 gathered in the Yard in April to hear civil rights leader Jesse Jackson denounce institutions that "preach moralism by day and get economic gratification by night." At the Quincy Street offices of the governing boards, 45 students gained entry and held a day-long sit-in. About 200 blockaded a South African diplomat attending a Harvard Conservative Club luncheon at Lowell House.

To students holding noontime vigils at the John Harvard statue, Bok suggested that lobbying in Washington would be a better means of forcing an end to apartheid. In May he made a trip to the capital himself, testifying as a private citizen in support of a bill brought by Massachusetts senator Edward Kennedy to invoke economic sanctions against South Africa. Congress enacted sanctions that summer.

Pro-divestment activists kept the pressure on. An ad hoc group called Alumni against Apartheid, based in Berkeley, California, announced that it would nominate its own slate of Overseer candidates pledged to full divestment. Gay Seidman '78, one of three candidates nominated by petition in 1986, was elected. A 29-year-old graduate student in sociology who had been the *Crimson*'s first woman president, she was the youngest Overseer in recent history. Three more petition candidates were elected over the next four years. One was South African archbishop Desmond M. Tutu, LL.D. '79, who had won the Nobel Peace Prize in 1984 for his opposition to apartheid.

"African shanties" built by a pro-divestment group rose in front of University Hall in the late spring of 1986. Adjoining them was a sixteen-foot ivory tower erected by students from the Design School. The Conservative Club countered with two nearby "gulags." As Commencement approached, both groups were asked to remove or relocate their structures. The gulags came down, but the shanties stayed up until the festivities were over.

There was more protest activity in September, when Harvard celebrated its 350th anniversary.

A Great Show

THOSE PLANNING THE 350TH CELEBRATION styled it a "family party," less ambitious in scale than the 1936 Tercentenary exercises. But the calendar of events, as announced in *Harvard Magazine*, took up thirty times the space allotted to the Tercentenary schedule in the *Alumni Bulletin* of May 29, 1936. "Still," as an editorial note observed, "the size of the family has increased since then—from some 85,000 alumni, faculty, staff, and students in 1936 to about 271,000 today—so why not the size of the party?"

"It will be a great show," wrote William Bentinck-Smith, a former *Bulletin* editor, in a retrospective account of Harvard anniversary observances. "Indeed, it will be literally a greater show than have been its predecessors." And it was. An estimated 60,000 persons attended some portion of the 350th, compared with about 15,000 in 1936. Traditional academic rites were complemented by sound and light displays, recitals by dozens of music and dance groups, drama and poetry readings, film showings, museum exhibits, a mammoth folk concert in the Yard, and a Stadium extravaganza that offered a bit of everything. Entertainment took the largest share of the 350th's $2 million-plus budget. President Bok insisted on a substantial intellectual component, and more than a hundred symposiums covered topics ranging from the structure of the

Saturday night at the Stadium. As Harvard's 350th celebration reached its eye- and ear-filling climax, the Boston Pops Esplanade Orchestra made music. "Dancing waters" played at the footlights, fireworks lit up the sky, and a fiery *Veritas* shield was hoisted a hundred feet into the air.

universe to the structure of a Beethoven quartet movement. Some 350 faculty members participated, along with scores of experts from other institutions, government, and industry.

The observance was set for early September, when rooms in the Houses would still be available for 4,000 alumni representatives and spouses. Students serving as class representatives, workers, or entertainers, about a thousand in all, were lodged in the Yard. (Dean of students Archie Epps took the lead in arranging a scaled-down 350th celebration for the undergraduate body in October.) Press credentials for the five-day festivities were issued to 1,200 reporters and photographers. Because high-ranking national and international figures were expected, security precautions were extensive. His Royal Highness the Prince of Wales was a star attraction. As a graduate of Cambridge University's Trinity College, he embodied Harvard's ancestral ties to Cambridge. Presidents of the United States had attended Harvard's last two anniversary celebrations, and the planners of the 350th had asked Ronald Reagan to speak. The invitation ignited controversy, but the president eventually decided not to attend. Secretary of State George Shultz, a Princeton and MIT graduate, agreed to stand in.

THREE FORMAL CONVOCATIONS in the Tercentenary Theatre were the central events of the 350th. The first was designated as Foundation Day. "Harvard in a Changing World" was the theme of the second day's meeting. The third was Alumni Day.

On Foundation Day, fifty flags evoking the history of the North American continent hung from poles fixed to the Yard's trees. The program included a witty reprise of eighteenth-century Harvard history by Adams University Professor Bernard Bailyn, a gracious speech by Prince Charles, and greetings from representatives of other universities. Benno Schmidt Jr., Yale's new president, spoke of Harvard's "emporium of academic freedom" as "the signal achievement we honor in your first 350 years." That dedication to academic freedom, said Schmidt,

Blocking the entrances to Memorial Hall, pro-divestment demonstrators forced the cancellation of a dinner on the second evening of the 350th celebration. Below: Claude Pepper, J.D. '24, one of 600 invited guests, reasoning with the demonstrators. The Florida congressman told them he shared their views, but that they had made their point and should now leave gracefully.

"has won the struggle of the centuries over religious orthodoxy, over political usurpation, over racial bigotry and social prejudice. And today you stand against the short-sighted zealots who would make the university the instrument of their particular political agenda, whether an anxious brand of patriotism or a fervent commitment to one or another social change."

A confrontation that evening disrupted the smooth flow of scheduled events. Arriving at Memorial Hall for a formal dinner, 600 alumni and guests were barred from entering by a hundred or so pro-divestment demonstrators. Most were students, alumni, or employees. A small contingent of Harvard police kept them from going inside, but the protesters sat down on the steps, refused to move, and began chanting, "If you want to digest, you have to divest." A few guests tried to force their way in, and scuffles broke out. After parleying with the demonstrators, Harvard police chief Paul Johnson told Bok and other officials that the blockade could not be ended without risking violence. Nearly an hour after the first course was to have been served, the dinner was canceled.

Inside Memorial Hall the refectory was festooned with balloons charged with confetti; glasses of red wine stood on the tables. The foodstuffs—cream of parsley soup, beef tenderloin with green peppercorn sauce, fresh figs and raspberries with chantilly cream—were trucked off to shelters for the homeless. The wine was poured away. Bok and his staff ordered pizza and stayed up late discussing security plans for the next day, when the presence of Secretary Shultz might provoke more protests.

President emeritus Pusey was to have presided at the dinner and to have given the main speech. He had planned to touch on the importance to Harvard of "alumni possessed of learning, motivated by deep human concern." The blockade surprised him, "but it also had a déjà vu feeling for me, because some of those characters were the same ones who were hanging around Cambridge in 1969."

For "Harvard in a Changing World," the Theatre was hung with flags of the fifty nations that sent the largest numbers of students to the University. A fanfare composed by Leonard Bernstein '39 opened the exercises. The mayor of Cambridge, Massachusetts governor Michael Dukakis, LL.B. '60, and Massachusetts congressman Thomas P. (Tip) O'Neill, Speaker of the House of Representatives, each made brief addresses. O'Neill recalled that as a lad of fourteen he had mowed lawns in the Yard. "Presently, five members of the President's cabinet, eighteen members of the Senate, fifty-one of my colleagues in the House have attended Harvard University," he continued. "And I thought when I left Cambridge that those unruly boys would never be in Washington in the droves that they're there."

While Governor Dukakis was speaking, a small airplane circled noisily overhead, towing a banner reading "U.S./HARVARD OUT OF SOUTH AFRICA—SANCTIONS/DIVEST NOW." Security agents telephoned officials at Logan Airport, and the plane was ordered away after seven passes.

Dean Michael Spence responded to the mayor, the governor, and the Speaker. The convocation next heard from a student orator, Jeffrey Rosen '86. "Harvard has always perceived itself and America to be in moral crisis," declared Rosen. If his generation had a real fault, he said, it was "a Puritanical self-righteousness and lack of charity—both for ourselves and for others." He won a standing ovation.

Poet Seamus Heaney, Boylston professor of rhetoric and oratory since 1984, read "Villanelle for an Anniversary," composed for the occasion and destined to become a Harvard classic: "A spirit moved. John Harvard walked the yard," it began. "The atom lay unsplit, the west unwon. / The books stood open and the gates unbarred."

Then came fifteen minutes of "Voices from Harvard's Recent Past," excerpted by University Marshal Richard M. Hunt from recorded speeches. The voices were those of Franklin Roosevelt, Winston Churchill, George Marshall, Robert Frost, John F. Kennedy, Martin Luther King Jr., Barbara Jordan, Mother Teresa, Art Buchwald, and Bob Hope.

The final speaker was Secretary Shultz. He denounced the "fervor for punitive sanctions against South Africa," affirming that "we are *for* a rapid end to apartheid and *for* a peaceful transition to a democratic

Speaking at the "Foundation Day" convocation, Prince Charles disarmed his audience by joking about being "an anachronism" and confessing that he had not addressed so large a group "since I spoke to forty thousand Gujarati buffalo farmers in India in 1980." The heart of his remarks concerned education–the sort that can produce "the balanced, tolerant, civilized citizens we all hope our children can become."

system." But "it is not our job," Shultz continued, "to egg on a race war or to accelerate a polarization that will lead to such a result." As he spoke, picketers chanted outside the Yard.

Shultz went on to discuss the information revolution. Leaders of the totalitarian world, he said, now faced an "agonizing choice": either "to open their societies to the freedoms necessary for the pursuit of technological advance," or to risk falling further behind the West in the post-industrial age. Neither Shultz nor the professional political scientists listening to his words would have been bold enough to predict the collapse of the Soviet Union within three years.

The banners in the image bear text: "VE RI TAS", "A-3", "A-4", "C-5"

"Alumni Day." Banners bearing the arms of Harvard, the Houses, and the graduate schools caught the sun and filled the Tercentenary Theatre with brilliant color.

THE TERCENTENARY THEATRE was thickly hung with with Harvard banners for the last convocation, designated as Alumni Day. Alice-Mary Maffry Talbot '60, the second woman to head the Alumni Association, presided. A spirit of lightheartedness prevailed. Relating the history of "a truly unique experiment in education," Radcliffe president Matina Horner concluded, "President Bok, I am here today to accept Harvard's enduring gratitude for Radcliffe's presence and her enduring contributions." Awarding a Harvard Medal to art historian Agnes Mongan, Bok inadvertently left his notes in her lap and took the medal back to the podium. Returning it, Bok quipped that "this demonstrates the historic insensitivity of Harvard to women." But in the final address of the afternoon Bok turned serious, examining "the harvest of problems our successes have brought us."

Excessive regulation, public hostility, and attempts by military and intelligence agencies, business groups, and social activists to use universities for their own purposes were among the external dangers Bok cited. Internal challenges included the difficulty of limiting growth and setting priorities, and the impact of outside demands on faculty members' academic work. In the future, said Bok, "the key ingredient on campus will not be money, important as it is. It will be time."

"All of the dangers I have described share a single characteristic," added Bok. "Each results from a failure to appreciate the proper aims of a university and the conditions essential for achieving them."

Accompanied by the University Band, the audience sang "Fair Harvard." Bok then adjourned the meeting until the year 2036.

The spirit of the 1980s. Ted Hibben, an M.B.A. candidate, took a farewell cruise in Business School waters on Commencement day, 1986.

THAT NIGHT'S STADIUM SHOW was designed to bring the 350th to a spectacular climax. It was produced and directed by Tommy Walker, a former Disneyland entertainment director who had planned extravaganzas for Superbowl games, presidential inaugurations, and world's fairs. An immense, glowing stage, incorporating two gigantic video screens, filled the open end of Harvard Stadium. About 27,000 people attended; more than 4,000 of them paid $350 a pair for "Crimson Circle" seats. Retired newscaster Walter Cronkite, the recipient of an honorary doctorate in 1980, was host and narrator. The performers included three student choral groups, the Boston Pops Esplanade Orchestra, the Harvard Band, a Hasty Pudding kickline, concert pianist Ursula Oppens '65, the Empire Brass Quintet, poet David McCord (then in his eighty-ninth year), actor John Lithgow '67, saxophonist Don Braden '85, pre-med jazz singer Fiona Anderson '88, and a dozen singing, dancing, or marching groups.

The show lasted two hours and twenty minutes, without intermission. Actors and dancers dramatized a series of historical events, a pyrotechnical moving hand signed the name of one-time Harvard treasurer John Hancock, and a torchlight procession recalled the 250th celebration of 1886. President Bok said good night and good luck. The Pops played "A Harvard Festival," arranged by the late Leroy Anderson '29. Fireworks inscribed the sky for seven ear-splitting minutes, and a blazing Veritas shield with "350" in the center was hoisted by crane a hundred feet in the air.

To those with enough stamina to get to church the next day, the Reverend Peter Gomes offered counsel. He warned against pride. He told his hearers to be guided in their pilgrimage "by the anonymous wisdom of the East wherein is given this saying: 'Seek not to follow in the footsteps of the men of old; rather, seek what they sought.'" Nathan Pusey and Derek Brewer, master of Emmanuel College, Cambridge, read the lessons. The Reverend Charles Price, former preacher to the University, ended the service with prayer: "Oh God of the unknown future, walk with us into the coming years. Bring us to trust in your unfailing providence and inspire us with hope which will not die. Put a song in our hearts that we may tell the story of these 350 years to our children and our children's children. And grant that they may in turn add to it and tell it to generations yet unborn for centuries to come."

Harvard in a Changing World

For Derek Bok, the 350th marked the completion of fifteen years in office. At 56 he maintained the athletic carriage he had as dean of the Law School, when he scrimmaged with students on the basketball court. He was now the senior Ivy League college president; surveys rated him as the most respected figure in American higher education. The University Press was about to publish *Higher Learning*, his second book on educational issues. Bok took a sabbatical leave, his first in almost thirty years at Harvard, for the first three months of 1987. Henry Rosovsky, who had been elected to the Corporation in 1985, served as acting president. Bok and his wife, Sissela, visited India, Israel, and Spain. They reached Madrid at a time when university students were holding a general strike. "It's exhilarating," Bok said later, "to sit on your hotel balcony watching thousands of students march by below, and realize it has nothing to do with you."

His travels, Bok said, had made him "more acutely aware of the opportunities that Harvard has abroad." That spring he appointed a special assistant to improve links with alumni in a dozen nations. In that year's Commencement address he floated an avowedly fanciful vision of a globalized Harvard with branch campuses in twenty countries, admitting one foreign student for every two Americans, and requiring overseas work-study experience for the bachelor's degree.

Bok had returned to find Harvard in its usual springtime ferment. Divestment was still a vexed issue. Tenure disputes at the Law School dramatized the rift between older faculty members and adherents of Critical Legal Studies, an ideology that portrayed existing legal institutions and much legal scholarship as tools of social control. Leaders of a newly formed Harvard Union of Clerical and Technical Workers were planning a grass-roots drive to organize Harvard's 3,500 clerical and technical workers, more than a third of the University's total work force. Organizing efforts were to start in the fall of 1987.

On October 19, 1987, the New York Stock Exchange crashed. Panic selling wiped out $500 billion in stock values, and the Dow Jones Average dropped 508 points. The 23 percent decline almost doubled that of October 1929. The economy held up and Wall Street recovered, but "Black Monday" marked the end of the Reagan bull market.

Harvard's endowment had increased from $2.2 billion to more than $4 billion in five years. Only 40 percent of the portfolio was invested in securities when the crash occurred, and the short-term drop in the endowment's market value was less than $300 million. When the fiscal year ended, Harvard Management Company reported a 6 percent increase in the endowment's value.[20] But Black Monday was a reminder of the stock market's influence on the financial status of a large educational institution. Professional and volunteer fund-raisers had campaigned for five years to add almost $300 million to Harvard's en-

A National Labor Relations Board ruling cleared the way for a vote on union representation of Harvard's 3,500 support staff members in the spring of 1988. The Harvard administration opposed unionization, but the employees approved it by a narrow margin. Contract talks began early in 1989, with former dean John Dunlop as the University's chief negotiator.

The union-management contract affirmed that support staff members were entitled to participate in what had become a cooperative process of University governance.

Bionic Mice

Reversing an earlier policy, the U.S. Patents and Trademark Office ruled in 1987 that genetically engineered multicellular organisms, including animals, were eligible for patenting. A year later Harvard received the world's first patent for a mammal: a genetically altered mouse developed by Philip Leder '56, M.D. '60, Andrus professor of genetics, and Timothy Stewart, senior scientist at Genentech Inc., and former Harvard researcher.

PHILIP LEDER   Engineered to develop breast cancer, the transgenic mouse served as a biological "research model" for scientists testing methods of treating the disease.

Another strain of mouse, in which males developed enlarged prostate glands, was engineered by Leder and former postdoctoral fellow William Muller, of Canada's McMaster University, and patented in 1993.

Exclusive licenses to produce the bionic mice were assigned to E.I. du Pont de Nemours and Co.

Licensing arrangements represented a potentially limitless revenue source for research institutions. By the mid-1990s, universities in the United States and Canada were receiving an estimated total of almost $600 million a year from royalties and licensing. Harvard's share came to $7.6 million in 1996.

---

dowment. On a very bad day in the market a paper loss of that magnitude could occur within hours.

Three weeks before the crash, financial vice president Thomas O'Brien had left Harvard to become dean of the business school at the University of Massachusetts. Administrative vice president Robert Scott, an MIT graduate who had previously directed the Office for Information Technology, succeeded O'Brien. Harvard gained its first woman vice president when Sally H. Zeckhauser assumed Scott's duties. For nine years she had been president of Harvard Real Estate Inc., formed in 1979 to manage more than $100 million worth of residential and commercial real estate in Cambridge and Boston.

The Bok administration's highest-ranking women had been Patricia Albjerg Graham, dean of the Graduate School of Education since 1982, and Sally Falk Moore, appointed dean of the Graduate School of Arts and Sciences in 1985. Now more women were reaching the top rungs of administration and scholarship. Judith Richards Hope, J.D. '64, a Washington lawyer, became the Harvard Corporation's first woman member in 1989. A year later Helen Vendler, PH.D. '60, a scholar of English and American poetry, became the first woman to hold a University Professorship. She had also been the first woman Senior Fellow of the Society of Fellows.

Matina Horner, Radcliffe's president since 1972, stepped down in 1989. The Harvard-Radcliffe agreement of 1977 was now subject to termination at any time, but the Radcliffe relationship remained a sensitive issue and there was no attempt, as there had been in 1971, to revise the existing administrative structure. After a sixteen-month search the Radcliffe trustees elected Linda S. Wilson, vice president for research at the University of Michigan, as Horner's successor. A graduate of Sophie Newcomb College, Wilson had a doctorate in inorganic chemistry from the University of Wisconsin. She made it clear that Radcliffe would not be allowed to wither away while she was in charge.

THE PRESIDENTIAL ELECTION of 1988 had pitted George H. W. Bush, Ronald Reagan's vice president, against Massachusetts governor Michael Dukakis, LL.B. '60. Dukakis, who had taught at the Kennedy School, had drawn heavily on Harvard in forming his election team. Susan Estrich, J.D. '77, a Law School professor, was his campaign manager; former financial vice president Hale Champion, now the Kennedy School's executive dean, was his State House chief of staff. A half-dozen faculty members were key economic and foreign policy advisers.

Bush, who had graduated from Yale in 1948, tried to make political capital out of his opponent's Harvard ties. Dukakis's ideas, said Bush, came from "Harvard Yard's boutique." Harvard itself was "a philosophical cult normally identified with extremely liberal causes." Sidestepping the fact that he had been elected to the elite Skull and Bones society and that his father, uncle, brothers, and sons were all Elis, Bush said of Yale that "You don't inherit your way into it or get into it because of birth."

None of this could have made much sense to the electorate. Dukakis proved an ineffective campaigner, and Bush won a landslide victory.

Nobel Laureates

FROM 1971 TO 1990, Harvard faculty members averaged almost one Nobel Prize per year. Eighteen won Nobels, bringing the total since 1914 to 33. The laureates:

Economics

1971 SIMON KUZNETS. For developing the concept of using gross national product as a measure of change in the nation's economic growth.

1972 KENNETH ARROW. For contributions to general economic equilibrium theory and welfare theory.

1973 WASSILY LEONTIEF. For input-output analysis, used in economic forecasting and planning.

Chemistry

1976 WILLIAM LIPSCOMB. For research on boranes, advancing the understanding of chemical bonding.

1980 WALTER GILBERT. For a method of rapidly decoding base sequences in DNA.

1986 DUDLEY R. HERSCHBACH. For developing techniques of observing collisions between pairs of molecules and tracing the results.

Herschbach

1990 ELIAS J. COREY. For devising precepts for making complex new molecules from ordinary chemicals.

Physics

1977 JOHN H. VAN VLECK. For applying quantum mechanics to the study of magnetism.

Bloembergen

1979 SHELDON GLASHOW and STEVEN WEINBERG. For mathematical hypotheses explaining electromagnetic and "weak" interactions.

1981 NICOLAAS BLOEMBERGEN. For work in laser spectroscopy allowing atoms to be studied with greater precision.

1984 CARLO RUBBIA. For research on previously undiscovered subatomic particles and their properties.

1989 NORMAN RAMSEY. For work enabling precise measurements of molecular and atomic interactions.

Medicine

1980 BARUJ BENACERRAF. For research on the genetic basis of the immune system.

1981 DAVID HUBEL and TORSTEN WIESEL. For research on information processing in the visual cortex.

Hubel and Wiesel

1990 JOSEPH MURRAY. For developing new procedures for organ transplants.

Peace

1985 DR. BERNARD LOWN. Co-founder, in collaboration with DR. EVGUENI CHAZOV of the Soviet Union, of International Physicians for the Prevention of Nuclear War.

Once in office he named more than a dozen Harvardians to high-ranking posts in his administration. They included Nicholas Brady, M.B.A. '54, secretary of the treasury; Elizabeth Dole, M.A.T. '60, J.D. '65, secretary of labor; and Richard Darman '64, M.B.A. '67, director of the Office of Management and Budget.

Bush had a flair for international diplomacy, but his administration was hobbled by the enormous debt load incurred during the Reagan years. It had reached $4 trillion, and by 1990 the nation was in a deep recession. Corporate layoffs raised white-collar unemployment to new highs, and "downsizing" became a byword of the 1990s.

Harvard felt the pinch. As its annual operating expenses reached $1 billion, the stalled economy slowed endowment growth. Information technology had pushed the annual cost of equipment and supplies to $130 million, triple the level of a decade earlier. The cost of benefit programs tripled over the same period. By a margin of 44 votes, support staff members had voted to unionize in the spring of 1988; the University agreed to grant across-the-board raises of 16 percent, spread over three years. The contract also required increased health plan and pension fund contributions. Wage increases alone added $2 million to the $6 million-a-year deficit of the Faculty of Arts and Sciences. Dean Spence wrote faculty members in the spring of 1989 that "it is necessary to begin now the process of raising additional funds, probably within the framework of a capital campaign of substantial magnitude." Such a suggestion would once have seemed outlandish: only five years had passed since the last campaign. But times were changing.

THE OLD ORDER BROKE UP in 1989. In April China's leaders sent soldiers in tanks to suppress a mass protest by 100,000 students and workers camped in Beijing's Tiananmen Square to demand reforms. Mikhail Gorbachev's policies of glasnost and perestroika set the stage for the emancipation of the Soviet Union's Eastern European satellite nations and the fifteen republics that made up the USSR. Poland became the first Iron Curtain country to form a non-Communist parliament. Czechoslovakia's "Velvet Revolution" toppled a hard-line government and replaced it with one headed by the dissident playwright Václav Havel. In South Africa, President P. W. Botha gave up his office to F. W. deKlerk, who pledged to negotiate political change with the country's black leaders. In November Berliners tore down the wall that had partitioned their city since 1948.

Suddenly, unexpectedly, the Cold War was over.

NO ONE KNEW WHAT would happen next. But it was clear that the reconfiguration of Eastern Europe, the rise of the Pacific Rim nations as a world economic force, and freer global interchange would add impetus to Harvard's continuing efforts to enlarge and extend its programs in international studies. In the fall of 1989 Michael Spence named Joseph Nye Jr., PH.D. '64, professor of government and a former State Department official, as associate dean for international affairs. "President Bok sees the University in a world setting," said Nye, "and the Faculty of Arts and Sciences is responding."

But neither Spence nor Bok would guide Harvard into a more international future. In March 1990 Spence announced that he would leave in June to become dean of the school of business at Stanford. Though he had been expected to play a major role in the coming campaign, Spence wrote in a letter to faculty members that the drive's duration "will be such that I could not remain as dean for the entire period." "With Mike's departure," stated Bok, "I will lose a close advisor and good friend. He will be very difficult to replace."

Two months later Bok announced that his presidency would end in June 1991. His decision surprised even close associates. "As Harvard plans for the challenges of the 1990s and prepares to launch a major capital campaign," said Bok's statement, "it is time for me to step down and allow a new president to provide fresh energy and continuity of leadership throughout the next decade."

Opposite: Charles River ice thawed, adventurous kayakers took to the water, and other citizens emerged to enjoy the sun on the first warm day of the first post-Cold War spring. The buildings in the background are Eliot House (left) and Weld Boat House.

Millennial Harvard

The University must accommodate itself promptly to significant changes in the character of the people for whom it exists.
—*Inaugural address of Charles William Eliot (1869)*

I N T H E F I N A L Y E A R S of the nineteenth century a quick victory over Spain had made the United States a world power. It had emerged from World War II as a superpower; as the century neared its end the demise of the Soviet Union made it the only superpower. What that meant was unclear. "The world that went to pieces at the end of the 1980s was the world shaped by the Russian Revolution of 1917," wrote the British historian Eric Hobsbawm.[1] "The end of the Cold War suddenly removed the props which had held up the international structure and, to an extent not yet appreciated, the structures of the world's domestic political systems. And what was left was a world in disarray and partial collapse, because there was nothing to replace them."

The United States was soon showing its strength, with President George Bush enlisting 27 nations in an alliance to roll back Iraq's conquest of Kuwait. Space-age technology enabled American air and ground forces, in combat in the Mideast for the first time, to win the Persian Gulf War in six weeks. Fewer than 200 American lives were lost, against an estimated 100,000 Iraqi deaths; but the Iraqi dictator Saddam Hussein remained in power.

A timely reminder: Branden Cunningham Miller, millenarian master of divinity, at the Commencement of 1998.

Ethnic and religious warfare in the former Yugoslavia and the African nations of Somalia and Rwanda resisted quick resolution, and exposed the limitations of external intervention in settling such conflicts. "The Cold War had filled the world with arms to a degree that beggars belief," wrote Hobsbawm; when the U.S. and UN tried to bring food and peace to the Balkans and Africa, "it proved harder than flooding the country with guns."

After World War II, Marshall Plan aid had rebuilt Europe's battered economies on terms that stressed partnership. The Cold War's end called forth no similar program, though it did create a demand for Western specialists who could rewrite the constitutions of former socialist countries and aid their transition to market-oriented capitalism.* Largely unprepared for the suddenness of the Soviet collapse, political scientists and economists temporized. One of the first to suggest a schematic for the future was Samuel Huntington, PH.D. '51, Weatherhead University Professor. In "The Clash of Civilizations," an essay published in *Foreign Affairs* in 1993, Huntington foresaw a tense, often hostile face-off between the West and the "challenger civilizations," Islam and China, with Russia, Japan, and India counterposed as "swing" civilizations.[2] This triadic configuration recalled the three irreconcilable superstates of Oceania, Eastasia, and Eurasia that George Orwell, writing in 1948, had envisioned in *1984.*

In the final year of his presidency, Derek Bok called for programs to make Harvard more international in composition and scope. Members of the Faculty of Arts and Sciences balked at some of his proposals, and the faculty's rising deficit made it an inopportune time for new ventures. Moreover, a presidential search was in progress. Exploring further international initiatives would be left to Bok's successor.

Integrating Harvard's component parts more closely, negotiating the maze of information technology, and leading the biggest capital campaign any university had yet attempted would also be left to the next president. These responsibilities would devolve on Neil Leon Rudenstine, PH.D. '64, who had taught English at Harvard before becoming an administrator at Princeton, his alma mater, and then, for three years, executive vice president of the Andrew Mellon Foundation.

Rudenstine Redux

AGAIN THE CORPORATION sought to democratize the presidential selection process, adding three Overseers to the search committee. Every president since 1654 had been picked by the Corporation alone. The committee's staff mailed 258,000 letters inviting recommendations from members of the Harvard and educational communities. They elicited 1,536 replies and 763 nominations.

Early speculation favored Corporation member Henry Rosovsky, then acting as interim dean of arts and sciences. Rosovsky, then 63, removed himself from consideration. In late November he went to New

---

*One of the busiest was Jeffrey Sachs '76, PH.D. '80, Stone professor of international trade, an adviser to the governments of Poland, Russia, Mongolia, and other former socialist countries.

York to sound out Neil Rudenstine. Startled by what seemed "an impossible idea," Rudenstine responded tentatively.

Rudenstine was 56, older than any prospective president since 1869. He had left Harvard to become dean of students at Princeton in 1968, had gone on to be dean of the college, and had then served ten years as provost. His administrative experience commended him to the search committee. He had overseen Princeton's planning and budgeting process, had been centrally involved in the college's transition to coeducation, and had helped run a $400 million fund-raising drive. His scholarly field was Renaissance literature. His wife, Angelica Zander Rudenstine, was an accomplished art historian.

Rudenstine's family background was unlike any earlier Harvard president's. His grandparents had been immigrants, Russian Jewish on his father's side, Italian Catholic on his mother's. His father, a federal prison guard in Danbury, Connecticut, had worked part-time jobs nights and weekends. His mother worked in a restaurant. Rudenstine was a scholarship student at the nearby Wooster School, graduated *summa cum laude* from Princeton, and won a Rhodes scholarship. At Oxford he met his wife-to-be.

Members of the search committee met twice with Rudenstine after Rosovsky's call. In February the committee shrank its candidate list to three: Rudenstine, Baker professor of economics Martin Feldstein '61, and Gerhard Casper, provost of the University of Chicago. Long meetings were held with each. In March the committee had a final meeting in New York. Rudenstine was everyone's choice. After a week of "thinking, self-learning, and excitement," he agreed to serve if elected. The Corporation and Overseers convened in New York to formalize his selection.

Winding up his work at the Mellon Foundation, the president-elect shuttled between New York and Cambridge during the spring. A prodigious note-writer, he used his flight time to answer letters from thousands of well-wishers. In June he made his first long-term appointment, naming Jeremy R. Knowles, Houghton professor of chemistry, as dean of the Faculty of Arts and Sciences. A former fellow of Wadham College, Oxford, Knowles had joined the faculty in 1974. Known for his research on enzymes, he was the first natural scientist to hold the deanship. He would inherit from Henry Rosovsky the task of paring the faculty's spiraling deficit, which had reached $12 million.

Commencement 1991: President-elect Neil Rudenstine and retiring president Derek Bok, as the latter concluded his valedictory address.

THE COMMENCEMENT OF 1991 rounded out the twenty-year presidency of Derek Bok. The principal speaker of the day was former Soviet foreign minister Eduard Shevardnadze, who called for the speedy completion of arms control measures and for a global ban on nuclear-weapons testing. In his valedictory speech, Bok addressed the social responsibilities of American universities. The last of his annual reports, issued that spring, had warned of hazards that threatened the basic values of Harvard and other universities: politicization, overextension, commercialization. His Commencement talk concerned the institution's social mission. "If any single thread connects many of the initiatives I have tried to take at Harvard," said Bok, "it is the effort to strengthen our work along these lines. It is our social mission that animates much of the Core Curriculum and the emphasis placed on moral reasoning, ethics, and community service in the College and professional schools. It was this mission that inspired the building of a Kennedy School that could attract able people to public service and train them to govern wisely. It was this mission that spurred our efforts to strengthen the schools of Education, of Public Health, of Divinity—each of them faculties weak in material resources but strong in their orientation toward serving human needs. And it was this mission, finally, that led to the creation of active centers of research to work on poverty, arms control, Third World development, AIDS, housing, public education, delivery of health care, and soon, I hope, the environment as well."

Bok had been treated to a round of farewell receptions and dinners. At his last faculty meeting, acting dean Rosovsky read, in Latin, a proclamation that Harvard's Danforth Center for Teaching and Learning would be renamed for Bok. More than $5 million had been contributed in Bok's honor to augment the work of the center.

The Overseers presented Bok and his wife, Sissela, with antique vases. The Council of Deans gave them a silver tray. Bok's freshman advisees gave him a beach ball and fluorescent swimming trunks.

THE BOKS LEFT CAMBRIDGE in the fall to begin a year of research and writing as fellows at Stanford's Center for Advanced Study in the Behavioral Sciences. They returned in October for Rudenstine's installation. More elaborate than the installations of Bok, Pusey, and Conant, it climaxed a two-day program that featured literary readings and music, special museum and library exhibits, and eleven faculty symposiums on subjects that ranged from the nature of revolutions to the dynamics of educational reform, from the miracles of molecular medicine to threats to the planet's ecosystem. For the finale, Rudenstine gambled on the weather and opted for an outdoor ceremony, open to all. It would be Harvard's first alfresco installation since 1909. A downpour dumped an inch of rain on Cambridge the previous night, but the skies cleared and the folding seats in the Tercentenary Theatre had been wiped dry when the afternoon proceedings began.

About 15,000 attended. In the academic procession, clad in many-splendored gowns, were delegates from approximately a hundred colleges and universities, including Emmanuel College, Cambridge, and Oxford, the new president's second alma mater. Rudenstine wore the simple black gown traditionally favored by Harvard presidents. Members of the Corporation and Board of Overseers wore business attire. The president of the Overseers, Franklin D. Raines '71, J.D. '76, delivered the charge of office.

As an undergraduate Raines had been a spokesman for moderate students during the 1969 strike. A White House staff member in the Carter administration, he was now associated with Lazard Frères, the New York financial house. "Every generation or so," Raines began, "the president of the Board of Overseers has the honor of presenting the insignia of office to a new president of Harvard College. My most recent predecessors, two and four decades ago, remarked on the sweep-

Presidential insignia: keys (1846), charter (1650), seals (1843, 1885).

ing changes facing both the world and Harvard at the beginning of those presidential terms. In 1953 the Cold War with communism was fully joined, and in 1971 the collision with a new, large, and different generation of students reverberated throughout this Yard. Now in 1991 wondrous transformations have become commonplace. The motherland of communism has embraced democracy, and one who called for a student strike from the steps of Widener Library now inaugurates the University president on the steps of Memorial Church."

The presidency, declared Raines, "requires that its occupant not only preserve Harvard but also renew her. I charge you to be unafraid to think unorthodox thoughts or to explore alternative visions of Harvard's future." He then handed the new president two ancient, foot-long silver keys, two seals, and the earliest College record book.

The Corporation's Senior Fellow, Charles Slichter, came forward to hand Rudenstine a facsimile of the Harvard charter of 1650 and escort him to the hitherto vacant president's chair, an odd triangular affair used at Harvard ceremonials since the eighteenth century.

In his inaugural address, Rudenstine noted that the broad national consensus about the value and quality of American universities had weakened. Criticisms had intensified. Universities needed to strength-

Above: Derek Bok, left, and Nathan Pusey, right, presidents emeriti, waited with Neil Rudenstine for the start of the installation ceremony.

Below: Franklin Raines, president of the Overseers, handed over the College's first record book, a symbol of authority.

en relations with their communities, the private sector, and governmental institutions. They needed to be more self-critical, to control expenses, to moderate tuition increases. Undergraduate education at Harvard deserved high priority; improving it would mean enlarging the faculty. The natural sciences, applied sciences, and technology required special attention. The times called for a University-wide agenda and "a stronger University-wide consciousness."

At a brief press conference after the ceremony the questioning was gentle, the new president's answers self-effacing. "You've received glowing report cards from everybody so far," said one reporter. "How would you describe yourself?" "I guess I see myself at the bottom of a pretty big hill, a pretty awesome hill," replied Rudenstine. "I have no idea how it will go, quite honestly."

The Business School's Class of 1959 Chapel. It was the last of three projects–including a gymnasium, Shad Hall, and the renovation of faculty offices in Morgan Hall– begun in the early 1990s to fulfill the original campus plan.

Architect Moshe Safdie designed the cylindrical chapel. The sanctuary (above) had Shaker chairs; prisms by artist Charles Ross created patterns of colored light on the walls.

THE NEW PRESIDENT'S WARMTH, accessibility, enthusiasm, and long hours became familiar topics of conversation within the University community. Seemingly tireless, Rudenstine spoke at countless student, staff, and faculty gatherings, visited Harvard clubs, sat in on classes, danced with delighted freshmen during orientation week. He held monthly office hours for students. He answered some 5,000 congratulatory letters and kept up a barrage of formal and informal correspondence. Appointing administrators took up much of his time. Four deanships and two vice presidencies were open, or about to become open, when he took office.

In the spring of 1992 he named Jerry Green, Wells professor of political economy, as University provost. Harvard's only previous provost had been historian Paul Buck, who had held the post from 1945 to 1953. Green, 46, had joined the economics department in 1970. As principal University-wide planning officer he would be the "key steerer," in Rudenstine's words, of a collaborative process designed to involve all ten faculties in setting Harvard's future course and erecting the intellectual platform for a fund-raising effort of historic proportions.

Harvard's long-standing policy, expressed in the old Yankee maxim "Every tub on its own bottom," had been to let each faculty set its own agenda and provide for its own needs.[3] Some schools had prospered; others struggled. Interchange between schools was limited. Bok's administration had encouraged new joint degree programs and interdisciplinary research centers, but decentralization remained one of Harvard's defining attributes. Under Rudenstine's academic planning procedure, deans of the faculties met with other deans, officers of the central administration, and faculty members in a series of collegial sessions. The entire process required forty meetings, and four retreats for the full planning group.

The planning process promoted a closer and more productive relationship among Harvard's faculties. Rudenstine sought to reduce decentralization not by curbing the autonomy of his deans, but by giving them more prominent parts in central decision-making. Helping to chart the future of other schools increased their influence at the center, while requiring them to coordinate their schools' needs and initiatives with those of other schools and the institution itself.

"EVENTS WILL NOT ALWAYS flow smoothly," Rudenstine had stated at his installation. "There will inevitably be some breakage, some tensions and problems." When a series of race-related incidents produced tense exchanges in the letters columns of the *Crimson*, Rudenstine held a "summit meeting" with black and Jewish students. "We have to think of this as a jointly managed human process that will continue," he told *Crimson* reporters.

Three weeks after the new president's installation, the conservative student publication *Peninsula* put out an issue condemning homosexuality. The Bisexual, Gay, and Lesbian Students Association answered with a rally on the steps of the Memorial Church. Among the speakers was the church's minister, the Reverend Peter J. Gomes, who was strongly applauded when he came out publicly as "a Christian who happens as well to be gay."

A Harvard Gay and Lesbian Caucus had been formed in 1983. Some of its members' concerns were now on the institutional agenda. The Faculty of Arts and Sciences was severing its last ties with ROTC programs because of the Pentagon's ban on homosexuals in the military; in May 1993 Rudenstine endorsed a proposal to grant health coverage to same-sex partners of Harvard employees. The Pentagon ban became a heated issue that spring, when General Colin Powell, former chairman of the Joint Chiefs of Staff, was announced as the principal Commencement speaker.

Because Powell had defended the Pentagon policy, his selection—predating Rudenstine's presidency—was seen by some as a slight to gay members of the Harvard family. Meeting with representatives of protesting groups, Rudenstine and Margaret Marshall, his recently appointed general counsel, worked out ground rules to permit nondisruptive expressions of protest. The general got a standing ovation from the Commencement crowd of 30,000 when he received an honorary degree at the morning exercises. When he delivered his speech, some audience members and a few of those onstage stood in silent protest. Rudenstine

Before the 1993 Commencement, scores of people stayed up late inflating 7,000 helium balloons with the legend "Lift the ban." General Colin Powell, former chairman of the Joint Chiefs of Staff (right), was to be the main speaker; a group called "Commencement Pride" had mobilized to protest the Pentagon's ban on homosexuals in the military.

spoke that night at the Gay and Lesbian Caucus's annual dinner, attended by 300 alumni, faculty, and staff members.

Reaching Higher, Thinking in Billions

PLANNING FOR A CAPITAL CAMPAIGN of epic size had been under way since 1988. Initially set for 1993, its start had been delayed to allow time for the academic planning process. In the meantime an enlarged Development Office concentrated on building up a pre-campaign "nucleus fund" that would almost double the $358 million raised during the Harvard Campaign of 1979-84.

The academic planning group had sorted out campaign priorities at a retreat in the fall of 1992. The Faculty of Arts and Sciences planned to realign its physical facilities to improve exchanges between scholars with complementary interests, while adding new professorships, enlarging science facilities, modernizing the library system, expanding financial aid, and completing a networked computing environment for faculty, students, and staff. Most of the professional schools planned major changes in teaching methods and curricular design. All were interested in extending their international scope. The planning group also agreed on five topical areas for interfaculty or "cross-school" collaboration: ethics and the professions; environmental studies; health policy; schooling and children; and "mind, brain, and behavior." University provost Green described the first four topics as "crisis" issues.

The planning documents filled more than 2,000 pages. Rudenstine assigned himself the task of preparing a summary report; he began drafting it on a thirty-hour return flight after an Asian trip in the spring of 1993. The 24,000-word document went to the Board of Overseers in the fall. In May 1994 some 750 alumni volunteers, prospects, and institutional leaders assembled for the official start of the five-year, $2.1 billion University Campaign, Harvard's first university-wide appeal.

No educational institution had sought as much. Almost half the target amount would go to the Faculty of Arts and Sciences. Some $860 million would be allotted to the professional schools. A $285 million "University Fund" would provide unrestricted capital for new academic initiatives, and for "underendowed or hard-pressed schools that may have

A two-day conclave in May 1994 marked the start of the $2.1 billion University Campaign. It included a candlelit dinner for 750 guests at the Gordon Track and Tennis Center.

At the opening session of the conference, Deans Albert Carnesale (government), Daniel Tosteson (medicine), and Jeremy Knowles (arts and sciences) addressed campaign volunteers and prospective donors on behalf of their faculties.

difficulty securing external support." At the opening session of the two-day conference commencing the drive, Corporation member and campaign co-chair Robert G. Stone Jr. announced that $652 million in gifts and pledges was already in hand.

Speaking at the closing session, President Rudenstine drew on Harvard history to describe "the dynamic between the University and its many supporters." The institutional record attested, said Rudenstine, that Harvard had "not only challenged itself—and its graduates and friends—to reach higher. It soon found that those very graduates and friends were in turn challenging the University to become even better than it was, to scale heights that went beyond its own ambition, and at a pace that was often faster than seemed possible to absorb."

THAT THE PRESIDENT would be the University's most effective campaigner was clear, but associates worried about his self-denying work habits. He put in 120-hour weeks, booked his calendar densely, wrote a staggering number of personal messages, and spent untold hours composing and fine-tuning speech drafts.

At the topmost level, there had been attrition within his administrative staff. John Shattuck, vice president for governmental and community relations since 1984, had resigned early in 1993 to become under secretary of state for human rights in the newly elected Clinton administration. After seventeen years in key positions at Harvard, financial vice president Robert Scott submitted his resignation the following fall. Just a month before the kickoff of the University Campaign, a statement from the president's office announced that University Provost Jerry Green would step down at the end of the term.

Green had been a principal architect of the campaign, and had led committees reviewing information technology, fringe benefits, faculty retirement policy, and administrative and financial computing. The statement said Green would resume his research and teaching as the first holder of a new professorship, but neither Green nor Rudenstine would speak publicly about what appeared to have been a falling-out.[4] Three days before the campaign conference, the president named Albert Carnesale, 57, dean of the Kennedy School of Government and Price professor of public policy, to succeed Green.

When economist Jerry Green (right) resigned as provost in the spring of 1994, he was succeeded by Albert Carnesale (below), dean of the Kennedy School of Government since 1991. Carnesale had a Ph.D. in

nuclear engineering and had worked for the U.S. arms control and disarmament agency before joining the school of government's faculty in 1974.

While preparing for the campaign, Rudenstine had been centrally involved in a review of benefits policies. The cost of benefits, amounting to more than one-fifth of the University's $612 million payroll, had tripled in a decade. Revisions in the existing program, approved by the Corporation in June 1994, were aimed at eliminating a $10 million annual shortfall. At a tense faculty meeting in October, senior professors charged that contributions to the faculty's pension plan had been cut back without adequate consultation or notification. Rudenstine, presiding at the meeting, bore the brunt of the criticism.

On the Monday after Thanksgiving, reporters called to a press conference at the Faculty Club were told that the president had begun a medical leave of absence. "He is suffering from fatigue and exhaustion," said a statement from the Corporation. "In his absence, the Provost of the University, Albert Carnesale, will serve as acting president." Accounts in the press interpreted the news as dramatic evidence that university presidents of the 1990s were dangerously overworked. Rudenstine's medical leave lasted thirteen weeks. He rested at home, conferring regularly with Carnesale, for most of that time.

It was a hard spring. Harvard made headlines again in April, when the admissions office rescinded its acceptance of a Cambridge high school senior whose application had not disclosed the fact that she had killed her mother. There were three student suicides, followed by a shocking murder-suicide that occurred just as the term ended. On a Sunday morning in late May, Sinedu Tadesse, a junior from Ethiopia, fatally stabbed her sleeping roommate, Trang Phuong Ho, a refugee from Vietnam. She then hanged herself. "We mourn the loss, we weep with the bereaved," said the Reverend Peter Gomes at a memorial service five days later, "and we will always wonder what forces beyond all reason or pity brought down this terrible conclusion upon young lives filled with promise."

Commencement week, 1995, evoked other difficult times: World War II, in which many members of the fiftieth reunion class fought, and the Vietnam War, which churned the lives of a later generation. Speaking on Commencement day, Czech president Václav Havel touched on war and the need for a "spiritual dimension" in the post-Cold War world. President Rudenstine contrasted the mood of hope and confidence that had followed World War II with the uncertainty of the present—"the most hazardous moment with respect to federal support for higher education in this country during the postwar period."

On a lighter note, Rudenstine apologized to the class of 1995 at its Baccalaureate service: he and they had entered Harvard together, said the president, but "I will not be graduating on Thursday. Evidently my attendance this year has been appalling."

RETURNING FROM HIS LEAVE, Rudenstine had announced the largest donation ever made to Harvard by living benefactors: a deferred gift of $70.5 million from John L. Loeb '24, LL.D. '71, and his wife, Fran-

Charles P. Slichter '45, PH.D. '49, retired as the Corporation's Senior Fellow in June 1995. A physicist at the University of Illinois, he had been a Fellow of the Corporation for 25 years, serving with three Harvard presidents.

Václav Havel, president of the Czech Republic since 1993, advocated spiritual politics, personal responsibility, and American engagement with the world in a Commencement address in 1995. The Alumni Association's outgoing president, Barry Williams '66, J.D./M.B.A. '71, led a standing ovation at the end of Havel's address.

ces Lehman Loeb. John Loeb, then 92, was one of New York's most prominent financiers. He had helped lead five Harvard capital campaigns and had made more major gifts to schools and departments than any donor in Harvard history. His $7.5 million gift to fund junior faculty positions had been the largest donation to the Harvard Campaign. The magnitude of the Loebs' new gift showed how greatly the scale of institutional fund-raising had changed.[5]

Stanford had launched the first ten-figure drive in 1986, exceeding its $1.1 billion goal by almost $600 million. Columbia, Cornell, Pennsylvania, and Yale had since mounted billion-plus campaigns. Harvard was the first to seek as much as $2 billion. The University's annual budget had reached $1 billion in 1990, but thinking in billions was still new to most people at Harvard. When the campaign goal was set, Rudenstine noted that it worked out to more than a million dollars a day.

The $2.1 billion goal was almost six times that of the Harvard Campaign, completed a decade earlier. Total annual giving now exceeded $200 million, so the challenge to Harvard's fundraisers was to find a billion in new money during the campaign's five-year run. That meant redefining the term "major gift."

Boston venture capitalist William F. Thompson '50, M.B.A. '54, one of the campaign's co-chairmen, had given the nucleus fund $15 million "to break through the $10 million gift ceiling." From the Countess Albina du Boisrouvray, granddaughter of a Bolivian tin tycoon, the School of Public Health got a record gift of $20 million to create a center for health and human rights in memory of her son. The Medical School got a gift of similar size from New York businessman Warren Alpert, M.B.A. '47. Retired publisher Walter Annenberg, giving $120 million apiece to the University of Pennsylvania and two other schools, found another $25 million for Harvard's Faculty of Arts and Sciences.

Soon after the campaign announcement, broadcasting executive Leonard Goldenson '27, LL.B. '30, and his wife, Isabelle, assigned 90 percent of their estates, valued at more than $60 million, to the Medical School for cerebral palsy research. The Center for International Affairs received a $21 million gift from Albert Weatherhead III '50 and his wife, Celia. The forty-year-old center was renamed for the Weatherheads. The Divinity School received $10 million, the largest benefaction in its history, from Nevada entrepreneur Robert Jones. From Gustave Hauser, LL.B. '53, and Rita Hauser, L'58, the Law School received $13 million, the largest cash gift to any law school. Rita Hauser later created a $15 million matching fund to encourage giving by women donors.

On the afternoon of the 1998 Commencement, co-chair Robert Stone announced that the campaign had raised $1.84 billion, or almost 88 percent of the $2.1 billion goal. With a year and a half to run, the campaign was nine months ahead of schedule and seemed certain to exceed its target. More than 165,000 donors—44,000 of them women—had contributed.

Sustained growth in the economy and financial markets had helped Harvard fund-raisers rally campaign support from alumni and friends. The bull market had also enabled Harvard Management Company's

Financier and philanthropist John Loeb '24 and his wife, Frances, capped a long list of major donations to Harvard with a deferred gift valued at $70.5 million in 1995.

SEAMUS HEANEY

Prize Poet

Irish poet and essayist Seamus Heaney, Boylston professor of rhetoric and oratory since 1984, won the Nobel Prize in literature in 1995. The Swedish Academy of Letters conferred the $1 million prize "for [poetic] works of lyrical beauty and ethical depth, which exalt everyday miracles and the living past."

Raised on a farm in County Derry, Ireland, Heaney began writing poetry as a scholarship student at Queen's University, Belfast. While teaching at Harvard he continued to live for part of each year in Ireland.

T.S. Eliot '10 had been the only writer with Harvard ties to receive the Nobel Prize in literature. He won it in 1948.

Opposite: A $12 million restoration, completed in 1995, returned the great hall of Memorial Hall to its original use as a refectory.

investment specialists to add successive billions to the endowment. President Walter Cabot, sidelined by a heart attack in 1989, was succeeded in June 1990 by Jack R. Meyer, M.B.A. '69, treasurer and chief investment officer of the Rockefeller Foundation. Meyer reorganized the staff, instituted new investment benchmarks,[6] and rewarded asset managers with seven-figure performance bonuses. The endowment's value was $4.7 billion when Meyer arrived. When the University Campaign was announced in May 1994, it stood at more than $6 billion. Four years later, as the campaign neared the $2 billion mark, the endowment had grown to a formidable $13 billion.

The University's annual financial reports typically included caveats that future rates of return were unlikely to match those of recent years. Yet the size of the endowment had changed dramatically in a short time. Five-year total return had reached an annualized rate of 19 percent, putting Harvard at the forefront of peer institutions. Over the same period, expenses had risen less than 5 percent per year, and the portion of expenses met by endowment income grew from 18 to 22 percent. Harvard now had an enviably large cushion against constrained research funding, moderated tuition growth, and other fiscal realities of higher education at the end of the century.

Transformations

THE UNIVERSITY CAMPAIGN's immediate impact could be seen in alterations to Harvard's physical plant, in the extension of advanced information technology to libraries and classrooms, and in periodic announcements of new professorships.

Large-scale donations supported the renovation of two landmark buildings, Memorial Hall and the Harvard Union. These ambitious and costly projects, designed to increase the utility of both buildings, brought to a final stage the extensive renewal program that had started with work on the Houses in 1982 (see page 267). That was followed in the '90s by a five-year, $65 million overhaul of the sixteen freshman residence halls and other Yard buildings. More recent structures, among them Holyoke Center and William James Hall, were reconditioned as well. New construction went forward at the Business School (see page 290), the Law School, and the Medical Area. Student-faculty housing for the College went up near Quincy and Leverett Houses, and Harvard's real estate arm built the Inn at Harvard on a triangular site east of the Square that had been occupied since 1940 by a pseudo-Colonial Gulf gasoline station.

As part of a $50 million restoration and reconstruction of Memorial Hall, the 122-year-old building's imposing Alumni Hall resumed its original role as a refectory, replacing the Union as the central dining facility for first-year students.[7] Restoration of the great hall was funded by $12 million of Walter Annenberg's $25 million gift; the hall was renamed in memory of Annenberg's son Roger '62. On the building's lower level, a $10 million gift from Katherine Bogdanovich Loker, the widow of Donald Loker '25, created Loker Commons, a student center with fast-food service and nooks for eating or studying. Under a plan to

Above: The Lowell House bell tower. Paint came off and rot came out in a project completed in the summer of 1996. The cost: $750,000.

Right: The new central stairwell of the Harvard Union, reopened in the fall of 1997. In the background is a seminar room, with fireplace, in what had been the eastern end of the building's great hall.

promote transdisciplinary exchanges, a $23 million makeover turned the Harvard Union into the core of a new humanities complex. The Barker Center for the Humanities, funded in part by a $13 million gift from Robert R. Barker '36, sheltered a dozen formerly far-flung departments in the Union, Burr Hall (originally the Varsity Club), and Warren House.

The Union renovation, stoutly opposed by an ad hoc group of tradition-minded alumni who sought to halt it by legal action, greatly altered the 96-year-old building's interior, but preserved some original architectural elements attributed to the great Charles McKim. Dividing the palatial dining hall into two large seminar rooms and a skylit central stair hall, the remodeling created classroom space and offices for almost a hundred faculty members, about one-sixth of the full Faculty of Arts and Sciences. The new center opened in 1997. After renovations to 140-year-old Boylston Hall, west of Widener Library, five other humanities

Left: Paintings and sculpture were displayed in the elegant special collections reading room and other parts of the Law School Library in Langdell Hall, renovated in a $36 million project that took fifteen months to complete.

Below: At Soldiers Field, the century-old Carey Cage was razed to make room for a $15 million racquets facility providing sixteen squash courts, six tennis courts, a weight room, and offices for the department of athletics. The donor was New York State investment banker Michael Murr '73, a former varsity football player.

departments took up residence there a year later. Within Widener, the first major renovations in the huge building's 83-year history were underwritten by an additional gift of $17 million from the generous Katherine Loker. The building would be equipped with climate controls, extending the lives of the books on its shelves, and with new wiring, lighting, and fire-detection and -suppression systems.

New construction projects were planned. An international studies center, described by President Rudenstine as "the first significant visible presence . . . of our commitment to international studies," was projected on a site east of the School of Design's Gund Hall. It would be named for Sidney Knafel '52, M.B.A. '54, a New York venture capitalist who pledged $15 million to help fund it. The center was to be part of an uneven row of social sciences buildings running from the Littauer building to William James Hall, adding a semblance of order to the jumble of buildings north of the Yard.[8] At the northeast corner of the Law

Aiken Computation Laboratory, where information technology was nurtured at Harvard, was reduced to rubble in the summer of 1997.

Planned by Coolidge, Shepley, Bulfinch & Abbott and built on a wartime budget in 1946, the lab had been expanded in 1964 by adding a superstructure on concrete piers.

Above: Replacing the Aiken Lab, Maxwell Dworkin Laboratories was scheduled to open in 1999.

School's Holmes Field quadrangle, wreckers demolished the fifty-year-old Aiken Computation Laboratory to make way for a new computer sciences and electrical engineering building. Funded by a $25 million gift from Microsoft Corporation chairman William H. Gates III '77 and executive vice president Steven Ballmer '77, it would stand on the site where Gates, as a sophomore, wrote the coding that helped launch Microsoft. The $20 million structure bore the maiden names of the donors' mothers: Maxwell Dworkin. The balance of the Gates-Ballmer gift endowed a professorship in computer science. Each seat in the new lab's three classrooms would have its own data jacks and power outlets.

Such wiring systems would be a routine part of future classroom and library design. When the Law School Library reopened in 1997 after a fifteen-month, $36 million renovation of Langdell Hall, its elegantly refurbished interior had 854 places for users to plug in their laptops. A

$21 million overhaul of the Medical School's 35-year-old Countway Library transformed one floor into an electronic "knowledge laboratory" networked to multimedia classrooms, remote bench sites throughout the school, and affiliated hospitals and other institutions. As part of a $185 million construction and redesign program that would remake its entire campus over a six- to eight-year period, the Business School planned to renovate Baker Library at a cost of $35 million to $50 million, making full use of electronic media.

AS SENIOR SENATOR from Tennessee, Albert Gore '69 had been the prime mover in securing congressional passage of the High Performance Computing Act of 1991. That legislation marked the start of an era in which information technology developed by and for the worldwide research community was extended to commercial and individual Internet users, revolutionizing existing patterns of communication and information-gathering.

As a fast, cheap medium of local or long-distance communication, electronic mail caught on quickly. In 1993, when Harvard Yard was tied into the 2.7 million feet of fiberoptic cabling that formed the University's high-speed data network, members of the class of 1997 became the first in Harvard history to be bonded electronically. By plugging her computer into a wall jack, a freshman could send e-mail to other students, faculty members, and any of the 15 million computer users then linked globally by the Internet. Over the next five years, e-mail traffic within the Faculty of Arts and Sciences grew from a few thousand messages a day to more than 325,000 daily in 1998. "When I was an Oxford undergraduate, there were four mail deliveries a day," mused Dean Jeremy Knowles. "You could write little notes that could be answered in hours. The Internet has made this possible once again. The Harvard community is being drawn back together."

The Internet's global reach and information-gathering power had a catalytic effect on scholarly inquiry in every field, condensing the time required to produce and assimilate new findings. Electronic networks also reshaped the instructional process. The traditional lecture system survived, but students now used the Internet to upload papers and problem sets to their teachers and to download comments and corrections. Faculty members held electronic office hours; study groups worked together on-line. Science courses put simulation programs on the World Wide Web for students to use in working problem sets.

Because the Web supported the transfer of text, images, sound, and video via the Internet, it made possible the transmission of complex multimedia "courseware" for interactive learning programs. By 1998 about 300 courses in arts and sciences had sites on the Web; the number was expected to reach 1,000 within two years. Students created their own home pages and searched in cyberspace for course-related materials. In 1995 the Web surpassed e-mail as Harvard's most-used electronic service. Over the next three years the number of "hits" recorded by the arts and sciences website alone rose from 150,000 to 3.2 million a month. "Harvard Gateways," the Alumni Association's website, opened the University to alumni (and others) around the

The Joys of Economics

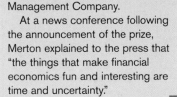

MERTON

Business School theory and Harvard Management Company practice intersected in the work of Robert C. Merton, Baker professor of business administration, who won the 1997 Nobel Prize in economic sciences with Stanford professor Myron Scholes.

With the late Fischer Black '59, PH.D. '64, Scholes created a formula for valuing stock options. Merton, who came to the Business School from MIT in 1988, applied the theory to a wide range of financial derivatives—options and futures traded in volume by institutional investors like the Management Company.

At a news conference following the announcement of the prize, Merton explained to the press that "the things that make financial economics fun and interesting are time and uncertainty."

world. *Harvard Magazine*'s home page had visitors from more than a hundred countries in its first year. With computing speeds still doubling every eighteen months at least through the early years of the twenty-first century, electronic technology would be an ever more powerful engine of change in research and teaching. But planning for the changes ahead remained a notoriously dicey proposition. The short history of information technology had not been characterized by accurate forecasts of its future. This was a field in which "anything older than three months is pre-history, anything further ahead than three years is science fiction."[9]

Millennial Harvards

AT THE TURN OF THE LAST CENTURY, as the final decade of Charles William Eliot's presidency began, the University was already a fast-growing institution. Eliot claimed to be "unable to keep up in mind or memory" with its expansion. Its principal parts were Harvard College, five graduate and professional schools, four museums, and Radcliffe College. Harvard owned almost sixty buildings and had an endowment of $10 million. Its library held 543,000 books. The University had an enrollment of 4,300 students, 230 faculty members, and about 25,000 living alumni. Even then, some feared that Harvard was getting too big.

Eliot, in the words of Professor John Finley, "had made the epochal American invention of superimposing on the Anglo-Saxon college the European structures of graduate learning. The result had been nearly a second founding of Harvard." Lawrence Lowell had renewed the College by reforming the curriculum and creating the House system. He had put up many of the structures that gave physical form to the modern University. The presidency of James Conant had, as Professor Finley put it, "more and more united Mr. Eliot's with Mr. Lowell's changes." Conant's national scholarships brought fresh talent to Harvard; the House system bulwarked the increasingly national College.

By the 1936 Tercentenary, the University of Eliot's time had more than doubled in size. The Houses filled much of the area between Yard and river, the Yard was enclosed, satellite campuses flourished in Boston and Allston. There were now nine faculties. Enrollment exceeded 6,500; permanent faculty members numbered 515. The library system had added a million books. The endowment stood at $120 million. The Tercentenary planners emphasized Harvard's international stature.

The mobilization required by World War II led to new techniques of research and teaching. After the war the G.I. Bill changed the composition and nature of the College's student body. Despite Cold War tensions and McCarthyist vendettas, the presidency of Nathan Pusey spanned a postwar epoch of prosperity and good feeling. That epoch was explosively shattered by the upheavals of the Vietnam era.

The early 1970s were a perilous time for free speech and common concern for the University's welfare. The restoration of civility and institutional morale was in part a product of broad-based deliberations

Harvey V. Fineberg '67, M.D. '71, M.P.P. '72, PH.D. '80, became the Rudenstine administration's third provost in the spring of 1997, when Albert Carnesale was appointed chancellor of the University of California at Los Angeles. Fineberg, 51, had been dean of the School of Public Health since 1984.

Fineberg was an authority on the application of decision sciences to health care. The School of Public Health had grown rapidly during his deanship; he had launched centers and institutes devoted to AIDS, cancer, cardiovascular disease, children's health, health and human rights, and risk analysis.

involving all branches of the Harvard family. The steady leadership of Derek Bok quickened the healing process. No president had been called on to balance so many competing interests. It helped that Bok quickly formed an effective partnership with the tough-minded but conciliatory Henry Rosovsky, his dean of the Faculty of Arts and Sciences, as Conant had with Paul Buck and as Pusey had with Deans Bundy and Ford. Harvard enlarged its commitment to institutional pluralism, and its constituent parts became more genuinely democratic as the representation of women and minority members rose.

Integrating the scholarly work of those constituent parts was a prime goal of the Rudenstine years, as evidenced by the collaborative academic planning program, the cross-cutting themes of information technology and internationalization, and the five interfaculty research initiatives. Gifts to the University Campaign raised the number of University Professorships, invented by President Conant for scholars "'without portfolio,' free from departmental restrictions," from twelve to nineteen during the first four years of the campaign.

The process of democratization continued. More women advanced to high-ranking administrative positions: by 1997 three of the University's five vice presidents were women, as were two of the Corporation's five Fellows.[10] Of the thirty Overseers, eleven were women. Change within academic ranks was more gradual. In the academic year 1997-98, the deans of Harvard's ten faculties were all white males. But the University's most recent affirmative action report revealed that in the past five years the number of women in senior faculty positions had risen from 90 to 147, a gain of 63 percent, while the number of minority members in senior ranks increased from 73 to 98. When affirmative action came under attack from the right in various regions of the country, President Rudenstine prepared a systematic defense, titled "Diversity and Learning," as a report to the Board of Overseers.

The institutional role of Radcliffe College became a vexed question. Radcliffe had ceded responsibility for the instruction and housing of women undergraduates to Harvard in 1971; though most saw themselves as Harvard students, women were still formally enrolled in both colleges. Ending Radcliffe's existence as an undergraduate college, while advancing its work as a research institute focusing on women's interests, was seen by many on the Harvard side as a way to affirm the equal standing of women undergraduates and reduce bureaucratic overlap. With a $100 million fund-raising campaign under way, Radcliffe administrators defended the status quo. President Linda Wilson, addressing an Alumnae Association audience in June 1998, described as "inconceivable" a future that "would eclipse our commitment to . . . undergraduates."

International studies gained renewed attention as the $2.1 billion University Campaign rolled on. In his 1997 Commencement address, Rudenstine called for expanded programs in international studies. Later that month he spoke at alumni meetings in London, Paris, Berlin, and Düsseldorf, as Harvard officialdom made its first formal visit to Western Europe in fifteen years. The European alumni community numbered more than 15,000. New Harvard clubs had sprung up in Croatia, the

Cynthia Friend, below, became the chemistry department's first tenured woman in 1989. In 1998 she was still the only woman member of the department's faculty. Increasing the proportion of women in fields like chemistry and physics remained a slow process.

Friend did award-winning research on the application of surface chemistry techniques to the investigation of catalysis: observing how solids interact with individual molecules to accelerate chemical reactions.

Czech Republic, Hungary, and Russia; Europe now had more than two dozen.

The Pacific Rim and its almost 8,000 alumni claimed an increasing share of the president's time. In 1993 he had visited Japan and Hong Kong. Early in 1998 he went to Hong Kong, Beijing, and Taipei; in June he visited Tokyo, Seoul, and Shanghai. His visits to China, the first by a sitting Harvard president, included meetings with Chinese university presidents and with President Jiang Zemin. Jiang, visiting the United States in 1997, had spoken at Harvard in November. A new Asia Center, designed to foster research and international exchanges on a University-wide basis, opened in 1998. The Business School announced that spring that it would soon open a research office in Hong Kong, with similar offices to be established in Europe and Latin America.

THOUGH THE UNIVERSITY WAS EXPANDING in all directions, the College remained at its center. Since the addition of the Memorial Church in 1932, the look of the Yard had remained much the same. But the look, style, and expectations of College students had changed.

"For the C man owns the college and sets the college tone," Judge Robert Grant (A.B. 1873, LL.B. 1879) had written in a whimsical poem composed for a Boston Harvard Club smoker in 1909. "The height of his ambition is respectably to pass, / And to hold a firm position in the middle of his class." In a day when barely 20 percent of graduating seniors took honors, the C man might have been archetypal. But by the end of the century a representative student at Harvard College could as easily be a female. She might be Asian American, and her grades would be A's and B's. In the modern era, fewer than 20 percent of candidates for the baccalaureate did not take honors.

Women made up a record 48.5 percent of the millennial class of 2001. Since the merger of the Harvard and Radcliffe admissions offices in 1975, applications had risen from 12,700 to a high of 18,180 in 1996; women applicants accounted for almost all the growth. Nearly 35 percent of the 2,040 men and women in the class of 2001 were from ethnic minorities. By far the largest subgroup (almost 18 percent) were those broadly classified as Asian American. About 8.6 percent of the class were Hispanic, 8 percent black, and 0.7 percent Native American. Seven percent came from other countries.

With the achievement of greater ethnic, religious, and social diversity had come even higher academic achievement. In the annual competition for Rhodes and Marshall scholarships, one index of academic strength, Harvard continued to outdistance other colleges.[11] In 1996 the number of summa cum laude graduates reached 116, or 6.8 percent of the class, breaking the record of 4.8 percent set in 1992—and prompting the faculty to stiffen departmental summa requirements. Grade inflation could be blamed, but it was also true that undergraduates of the '90s took on research projects and thesis topics that would have been the preserve of graduate students a decade earlier.

The admissions office announced in the spring of 1998 that the "yield" for the class of 2002—i.e., the proportion of admitted applicants choosing to enroll—had been 80 percent, the highest figure in 25 years

The new model Harvard graduate: Brindisi Chan '97, of San Francisco and Quincy House, captain of women's fencing, honors graduate in East Asian studies.

Demonstrating that there was no cutoff date for formal education, Mary Fasano began high school at 71. Taking one course per semester for seventeen years, she earned a Harvard degree in extension studies in 1997, when she was 89.

An earlier record for seniority was set by Thomas Small, who received a master's degree from the Extension School in 1983. He too was 89.

and far higher than other colleges'.* What made Harvard so alluring to so many accomplished students? To thousands of aspirants and their parents, Harvard was a symbol of talismanic strength, promising entrée to prestigious graduate schools and access to "a global network of alumni in business, government, and academia who might open the door to a better job and a higher salary," as a 1998 *Boston Globe* series put it. But the College also offered an exceptionally rich landscape for individual exploration and growth. Undergraduates could pick from 42 fields of concentration and a catalog listing 3,000 courses. Extracurricular organizations—about 250, all told—included more than thirty "ethnic, cultural, or international" groups; a wide variety of religious, preprofessional, political, and media organizations; and a lengthy roster of performing troupes and ensembles. Almost seventy arts groups joined in the 1998 version of "Arts First," a weekend-long spring gala introduced by the Office for the Arts in 1993. The office's records indicated that 3,000 students, or almost 45 percent of the College, participated in some form of arts activity every year.

A similar number took part in intramural sports. "Athletics for all" had been a Harvard watchword since the 1920s. The department of athletics oversaw 29 club sports, from aikido to ultimate frisbee; at the varsity level, Harvard had the nation's most extensive intercollegiate program, with 21 men's and 20 women's teams. Though Harvard had never awarded athletic scholarships, nearly a dozen teams competed at national levels. Capacity crowds at the Stadium were ancient history,

*This despite an increase in tuition and fees to $31,132—an amount that would have staggered students and parents of the 1900s, when a year at the College cost well under $1,000. With an annual financial-aid budget of $40 million, Harvard was one of a handful of colleges maintaining a policy of need-blind admissions. More than 70 percent of undergraduates received some form of financial aid, with 46 percent qualifying for scholarships.

A toe-tap for luck. Alden Strock '96, of New York City and Lowell House, passing the John Harvard statue on the way to graduation exercises.

but the 1997 football team made up for a long stretch of so-so seasons by defeating all of its Ivy League foes. No Crimson squad had done that since the league was formed in 1956, and the team's 9-1 record was the best since the fabled Rose Bowl season of 1919.

Community service remained an important focus of extracurricular energy. Seven out of ten College students performed some social service work, usually channeled through Phillips Brooks House, in their undergraduate years. President Eliot, who conceived the true American university as "a school of public spirit," would have been gratified.

THE CONGESTION OF HARVARD SQUARE, the pace of late-twentieth-century life, the size and complexity of the University, might startle even the imperturbable Mr. Eliot. Though many lived beyond Cambridge's borders, the immediate Harvard community now had more than 40,000 members, as against 5,000 or so in his time. There were 18,700 full-time students from 130 countries, enrolled in almost forty degree programs. Tenured and untenured faculty numbered more than 2,200. The roll of staff members and other employees had gone up from 300 or so in Eliot's day to 9,500; Harvard was now the state's fifth-largest employer. The alumni body had grown to 280,000.

The University owned more than 500 buildings, a third of them residential. Within Harvard's original bailiwick there was no more room to expand. Allston, south of Soldiers Field and the Business School, was a probable setting for further growth: since the late 1980s, the University had quietly spent $88 million to purchase property there.

The library system held 13.5 million volumes and documents. Within the nine faculties were more than fifty research or academic centers; "allied or affiliated" institutions included seven museums of art or natural history, an arboretum, a forest, the American Repertory Theatre, and the Harvard Institute for International Development, whose $44 million budget was bigger than those of four of the professional schools. The Division of Continuing Education now had 13,000 extension students; in 1998, some 16,440 professionals were enrolled in forty executive education programs at half a dozen of the University's schools.

WRITING IN 1901, MR. ELIOT HAD REMARKED on Harvard's "want of unity." Almost a century later, Harvard was still far from unitary: it was more properly seen as an extended family of complex organizations, diversely constituted and competing for resources, whose boundaries increasingly overlapped. Electronic networking, uniform data-management methods, collaborative planning, and the creation of spaces for interdisciplinary exchange were new departures that promised to improve efficiency, foster a sense of cohesiveness, and advance the scholarly enterprise. But the fullness of time might also confirm that decentralization had worked in its own ungovernable way to ensure institutional vitality. As a new century unfolded, the challenge confronting Harvard—and the global family of nations and cultures—would be to reconcile competition and cooperation in ways imaginative enough to achieve and maintain a world worth living in.

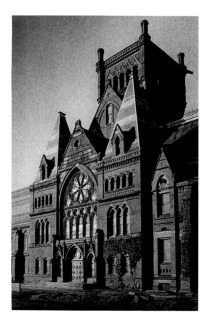

More than forty years after the fiery loss of Memorial Hall's tower (page 200), admirers of the great building could take heart: to mark the completion of the University Campaign, the tower was expected to be restored. The cost, estimated at more than $3 million, would be met with the help of a $2 million grant from Katherine Bogdanovich Loker, a campaign co-chair. She had made earlier gifts, aggregating $28 million, to create a student center beneath Memorial Hall and to underwrite renovations to Widener Library.

Opposite: From the age that is past to the age that is waiting before, the College clock on the western side of Massachusetts Hall, in place since 1725, has put a dignified face on unfolding history. In 1997, the College officially changed the words of its anthem from "Fair Harvard! thy sons to thy jubilee throng," to "Fair Harvard! we join in thy jubilee throng"--just the latest example of calm rising through change and through storm.

Notes

CHAPTER 1: THE REFORMERS (pages 13-58)

1. The elective principle was first introduced at Brown by President Francis Wayland in 1850, but was abandoned when Wayland resigned five years later.

2. Eliot and five fellow oarsmen rowed in the first racing shell built in America. Eliot, who stood six feet and weighed 138 pounds, was the lightest man in the boat. For the 1858 Boston City Regatta he and Benjamin Crowninshield (A.B. 1858) purchased crimson silk bandannas for Harvard's crew. "A color for each college had not then been thought of," Eliot wrote later. In 1910 the Corporation designated the crimson hue of the bandannas as Harvard's official color.

3. Eliot never gave up on the three-year A.B. "It stirs me up very much to hear college students say that two hours of work a day is all they have time for," he wrote Dean Briggs. A three-year residency requirement, he argued, would put pressure on the slackers. In the last of his annual reports, issued in 1908, Eliot wrote that "the present standard of labor for many lazy and unambitious young men who spend four years in Harvard College is deplorably low, or, in other words, the standard which the College itself sets for mere pass-work is so low that it can hardly be said to call for labor in any proper sense."

4. The 1904 deficit of $43,000 would be equivalent to at least $2 million in today's terms.

5. Eliot did not believe Harvard presidents should beg for funds. Following his lead, Presidents Lowell and Conant did not involve themselves directly in fundraising, though Lowell himself contributed more than $2 million to Harvard. Eliot did bend his own rule on occasion. He once wrote Edward Austin, a Boston merchant, to seek a gift for the Divinity School. Austin responded, "I do not give a damn for the Divinity School but the President of Harvard College ought not to write a letter for less than one hundred dollars and I enclose my check for that amount."

6. Annual rentals at the private residence halls ranged from $300, about twice the going rate in the College dormitories, to $700 or more.

7. Supporters of the League included Thomas Nixon Carver, professor of economics; William Z. Ripley, professor of economics and author of an influential book, *The Races of Europe* (1901); Nathaniel Southgate Shaler, professor of geology and dean of the Lawrence Scientific School; Henry Lee Higginson, a member of the Corporation; Henry Cabot Lodge (A.B. 1871), who served three terms as an Overseer; and author Owen Wister (A.B. 1882), twice an Overseer. Three years after becoming president of Harvard, A. Lawrence Lowell accepted the vice presidency of the League.

8. President Eliot had not wished to divert "a single penny" of University funds for a stadium. The class of '79's gift began a tradition of twenty-fifth reunion giving that started at the $100,000 level, reached $1 million in 1973, and broke $16 million in 1998.

9. Quill was one of three law school students on Yale's team. He claimed that Harvard's K. F. Brill, a 25-year-old sophomore, had incited his anger by biting him.

10. Eliot devoted substantial parts of his last seven annual reports to critiques of football, and never ran out of arguments. Football was excessively brutal. It exhausted participants. It distracted players and student spectators from their studies. It fostered commercialism and gambling. It was a waste of money (athletic expenses would have paid the salaries of twelve full professors in 1904-05). It taught the wrong values. It did not protect players against "immorality and vice," or equip them for careers. Ever the optimist, Eliot predicted that "the barbarous stage of public opinion and college opinion concerning athletics, which in this country has been partly the result of inexperience in competitive sports, and partly of the general predisposition to exaggeration in pleasures which characterize Americans, will pass away before many years."

11. Laurence R. Veysey, *The Emergence of the American University* (Chicago: University of Chicago Press, 1965), pp.350-351.

12. The Medical School's dean recorded in 1877 that "two valuable donations have been received,—one of a microscope, from Arthur Chadwick Howard; the other of a skull, from Dr. G. S. Jones."

13. In both cases the architect was the industrious Charles Allerton Coolidge (A.B. 1881), whose Boston firm took over H. H. Richardson's practice after his death in 1886. Coolidge worked in a variety of styles. He was principal architect of the Romanesque campus of Stanford University, completed in the first decade of the century; twenty years later he planned the neo-Georgian buildings of Harvard's residential House system.

14. The critics included the irrepressible gadfly John Jay Chapman (A.B. 1884), who saw the Harvard Classics as evidence of the increasing commercialization of the University. "The spreading of the influence of Harvard," he wrote in *Science*, "is what the trustees had in mind—the making of a little money and the doing of a great deal of good is what Dr. Eliot had in mind: the making of a great deal of money and the doing of a little good is what *Collier's* had in mind. But here is the point: Once launched, *Collier's* is in control."

15. Wilson's dour assessment of the state of American higher education contrasted with Eliot's. "I give myself no anxiety whatever about the shortcomings of the American college," the retiring president had told officers of the Associated Harvard Clubs in May. "If ever an institution justified itself to any nation in the whole history of the world, the American college has justified itself to American society."

16. Veysey, *op. cit.*, p.252. "Those who replaced [the great figures] seemed, to many contemporary eyes, a lesser breed of men," Veysey added. "When Eliot had spoken, all had at least listened; now no one who could command such a universal audience seemed to hold power. As a result, issues themselves, though discussed with mounting urgency, seemed to lose their focus. The academic twentieth century, with its anxious,

hazy talk about crisis, its less clearly visible counter-parts of opinion, and its often unspoken assumption that institutional rather than intellectual factors determine the central course of educational development, had now arrived."

17. Various plans for improving the Riverside area had been broached since the 1890s. Most had a boulevard linking the riverfront with the Yard. The plans are described in Bainbridge Bunting and Margaret Henderson Floyd's invaluable *Harvard: An Architectural History* (Cambridge: Harvard University Press, 1985), pp.180-183.

18. The committee also suggested that unlike Gore Hall, whose main entrance faced Massachusetts Avenue, a new library building should face the Yard. Without this reorientation, as Bunting and Floyd pointed out, "the Tercentenary Quadrangle could never have emerged as the heart of the University."

19. In 1915 the Nobel Prize stipend was $40,000. In addition to his work on atomic weights, Richards also explored atomic compressibility, chemical equilibrium, electrochemistry, and thermochemistry.

20. Lowell's classmate Edward S. Martin (A.B. 1877), a founding editor of the *Harvard Lampoon*, ran this summation on his editorial page in the old *Life*:

> The lion with the lamb lies there,
>   And neither one inside;
> The Harvards skip a lot of care,
>   The Techs conserve their pride.
> Instead of spending heaps of dough
>   Each other's weal to check,
> The Techs at Tech to Harvard go,
>   The Harvards tech at Tech.

21. Hecker cited a litany of pranks (omitting to mention that vandals had blown up the College pump in the spring of 1901):

> In 1898 the John Harvard statue was daubed with paint for the second time; in February, 1904, the College Library was broken into and badly damaged; in May of the same year there was a serious depredation in Sever; on May 20, 1905, the bronze memorial tablet to Phillips Brooks was carried away, and a skeleton, taken from Dr. Darling's laboratory, was suspended over Massachusetts Avenue....Signs and souvenirs of all sorts were stolen to adorn undergraduate rooms. Class dinners, held at Boston hotels, left a trail of broken crockery, noisy demonstrations, and street cars with trolley poles off their wires and sometimes shattered windows. Freshmen were bullied by upper classmen on "Bloody Monday." Some of the roughhouses at Memorial and Randall [dining halls] beggared description. Not infrequently a professor would sound the call for bluebooks and an examination on the spot to quell the riot which interrupted his lecture. Blasé young gentlemen now and then varied the monotony of reading newspapers in certain "cinch" courses by throwing pennies at the assistant.

22. From "Almost Thirty," written by Reed in 1917 and

published by the *New Republic* in 1936. Reed's positive view of the College's intellectual climate was not universally shared. "The 'average undergraduate' is undoubtedly a barbarian, and so are most of the exceptional ones," wrote Philip J. Roosevelt '13 in a 1912 issue of the *Harvard Advocate*.

CHAPTER 2: THE GREAT WAR (pages 61-87)

1. The late Arlen J. Hansen's *Gentlemen Volunteers* (New York: Arcade Publishing, 1996) recounts the wartime activities of American ambulance services. The majority of the 3,500 volunteer drivers came from Ivy League universities and Eastern boarding schools; a tabulation in late 1917 showed that Harvard had the most representatives (348) among American Field Service drivers. Next came Yale (202), Princeton (187), Cornell (122), California (70), and Stanford (58).

2. The American Fund for French Wounded, the largest emergency relief organization formed specifically for the European war, "had its own corps of drivers, all women," writes Hansen, and the American Women's Hospital, "formed by female doctors who had been turned down by the all-male U.S. Army Medical Corps, had its own section of women ambulance drivers." By the war's end, some 90,000 women had served in more than fifty relief organizations.

3. The accounts of Cunningham and other participants in the war appear in the five-volume *Memoirs of the Harvard Dead in the War against Germany* (Harvard University Press, 1920-1924), compiled by M.A. deWolfe Howe, editor of the *Alumni Bulletin* from 1913 to 1919.

4. Münsterberg's adversary was Clarence Wiener, a would-be soldier of fortune and entrepreneur who did not have the wherewithal to make a $10 million bequest. He committed suicide in 1930.

5. The other 400 volumes were lost when Old Harvard Hall was destroyed by fire in 1764. *Christian Warfare* was out on loan (and overdue) at the time.

6. The club's censored message to coach Haughton, as recorded in the diary of member Tracy Putnam '15, was, "A la veille de vôtre combat, salut! Serrez vos ceintures, fixez vos baionettes, chargez vos fusils grenades à main, et en avant les gars! On vous regarde même des sommets des Vosges." Two days later Putnam recorded, "The Harvard-Yale score was announced, 41-0. The Harvard Club of Alsace Reconquise celebrated mildly, for Doyle (our only Yale man) was away."

7. Roosevelt began by telling Wilson that "what I have said and thought and what others have said and thought is all dust in a windy street." Wilson's noncommittal response to his plan for a volunteer regiment discouraged TR. "I don't believe he will let me go to France," he told Colonel E. M. House, Wilson's adviser. "I don't understand. After all, I'm only asking to be allowed to die." House was said to have replied, "Oh? Did you make that point quite clear to the President?"

8. The French contingent's junior officers included Lieutenants André Morize, who remained at Harvard as a professor of French literature, and Jean Giraudoux,

who became a distinguished playwright, novelist, and essayist. Giraudoux had been enrolled in the Graduate School of Arts and Sciences in 1906-07.

9. Dr. Richard P. Strong, professor of tropical medicine, was detached from duty in Paris to serve as chief of a Red Cross commission fighting a typhus epidemic in Serbia. On his staff were George C. Shattuck '01, M.D. '05, assistant professor of tropical medicine; Dr. Andrew Sellards, associate in tropical medicine; and Francis Grinnell '09, M.D. '13, instructor in preventive medicine and hygiene.

10. The SATC did give "thousands of young men their first contact with college life, and many finished college even when they were discharged from the SATC," as Calvin B. T. Lee pointed out in *The Campus Scene: 1900-1970* (New York: David McKay, 1970).

"The Khaki College" (pp.84-86) is largely based on "The Ivory Boot Camp," by Jonathan Frankel '91, *Harvard Magazine*, September-October 1991, page 71.

CHAPTER 3: BETWEEN THE WARS (pages 89-134)

1. Under the salary schedule of 1905, full professors earned $4,000 to $5,500 a year; assistant professors $2,500 to $3,000; and instructors $1,200 to $1,500.

2. Between 1918 and 1925, John Price Jones Inc., managed fourteen fund-raising campaigns for institutions of higher education. Merle Curti and Roderick Nash state in *Philanthropy in the Shaping of American Higher Education* (New Brunswick, N.J.: Rutgers, 1965) that "at a cost of $1,576,731 (2.34 percent) these raised nearly $68 million for endowments and plant."

3. Former Corporation member Robert Bacon, who had died of blood poisoning after a mastoid operation in May, was awarded a posthumous LL.D. Having driven an ambulance in 1914 and helped set up a British typhoid hospital, Bacon resigned from the Corporation in 1917 to serve as aide-de-camp to General John J. Pershing. He later became British Field Marshal Haig's liaison officer with American troop units.

4. "If they had censured you," Lowell wrote Chafee long afterward, "I suspect the whole, or a large part, of the Faculty of the Law School, including the Chair [Lowell himself] might have gone overboard." To another correspondent he wrote that "if one wants to maintain free speech, and open-minded justice, one will find one's self first and last at odds with every element in the community."

5. Lowell conceded privately that his reply to Bruce was "unfortunate," but he was obdurate. "I am having a hideous time here now," he wrote to the British historian James Ford Rhodes, "and I feel like Saint Sebastian, stuck full of arrows which people are firing at me. I believe that to compel white men and negroes to live in the same building and eat at the same table… would not only hurt Harvard as a national institution, but so far as it had an influence upon the treatment of negroes elsewhere, it would cause reprisals."

6. The Jewish presence had been enlarged by the "New Plan" of admissions and by wartime draft laws. The New Plan, adopted in 1911, made admission almost automatic for applicants with high scores on entrance exams. When the draft age was lowered to eighteen in 1918, many of those still in College were academically advanced underclassmen who had matriculated at sixteen or seventeen. In these overlapping groups were substantial numbers of Jews.

7. Henry James, New York lawyer, biographer of President Eliot, and son of the philosopher William James, was one of the few Overseers critical of Lowell's attempts to reduce the proportion of Jews in the College, but ultimately he supported the president's proposal to limit the size of incoming classes.

8. Participating in the Olympics kept Gourdin from attending the 1924 Commencement, when his LL.B. was conferred; he thus missed seeing 145 of his 1921 classmates, in white robes and pointed hoods, burlesquing the Ku Klux Klan on Class Day. "The hit of the afternoon," reported the *Boston Herald*.

9. Marcia Graham Synnott's *The Half-Opened Door* (Riverside, Ct.: Greenwood Press, 1979), a meticulously researched study of discrimination in the admissions processes of Harvard, Yale, and Princeton from 1900 to 1970, provides a clear and thorough narrative of the complex quota debate in 1922-23.

10. Based on research by film archivist Paul Killiam '37, whose pastiche of Harvard films, *John Harvard: Movie Star*, was a feature of the 350th celebration in 1986. Later films in which Harvard settings or characters were prominent included Bob Hope's *Son of Paleface* (1952), *Love Story* (1970), and a sequel, *Oliver's Story* (1971), *The Paper Chase* (1973), *A Small Circle of Friends* (1980), *Soul Man* (1986), *Run* (1991), *With Honors* (1994), and *Good Will Hunting* (1997).

11. Eliot died in August 1926, aged 92.

12. The older Baker donated securities worth about $4 million; his son gave another $1 million. The name of the school was later formally changed to "Graduate School of Business Administration, George F. Baker Foundation."

13. Lowell insisted on the term "house" rather than "college" because he did not want alumni to suppose that his plan would diminish the importance of Harvard College. His correspondence shows that he had been angling for a Harkness gift at least since June 1928, when the Yale faculty was still deliberating Harkness's offer to provide a residential college system.

Four years earlier Harkness had funded a drama department at Yale, and the stellar Professor George Pierce Baker and his "47 Workshop" had been lured away from Harvard to New Haven.

14. The first House masters were Julian Lowell Coolidge (A.B. 1895), a mathematician and relative of the president, at Lowell House, and Chester Greenough (A.B. 1898, PH.D. '04), who taught English, at Dunster. Historian Roger Merriman (A.B. 1896), a former Oxford don, was master of Eliot House. Other original masters were Kenneth Murdock '16, PH.D. '23 (Leverett, English); Edward Whitney '17, A.M. '22 (Kirkland, history and literature); James Phinney Baxter, PH.D. '26 (Adams, history); and Ronald Ferry '12 (Winthrop, biochemistry).

15. "Consequently," wrote Marcia Graham Synnott (*op. cit.*), "admission to the Houses became secondary in importance only to admission to the College itself." Though students were initially given free choice in applying, apportionment based on cross-sectioning principles was adopted within a few years. Synnott's research showed that each House kept records of Jewish students admitted; a 1930s memorandum on "Suggested Procedures for Assignment to Houses" advised masters to take care that "the total of Jews accepted does not exceed what 'the traffic will bear.'"

16. The Fund's success was largely due to executive secretary David T. W. McCord '21, A.M. '22, whose urbane and literate solicitation letters helped redefine that form of educational fund-raising.

17. University groundskeepers and other employees did take pay cuts, and Harvard took a beating in the press when a group of Widener Library scrubwomen were laid off in the fall of 1930. The University had refused a state minimum wage commission order to increase their pay from 35 cents to 37½ cents an hour. At Christmas a group of alumni organized by Thomas Lamont's son Corliss '23 presented the women with a purse of $3,000.

18. Because the Depression reduced the cost of food, the dining services showed an unexpected profit of $40,000 in 1932. Lowell used the funds to start Harvard's first student employment program, providing about 270 part-time clerical jobs in administrative and library offices in 1932-33.

19. The names of Fritz Daur, Konrad Delbruck, Kurt Peters, and Max Schneider, alumni who died serving the Central Powers, were later memorialized by a tablet in the church itself. A Latin inscription by Arthur Darby Nock, then a lecturer at the Divinity School, read: *Academia Harvardiana non oblita est filiorum suorum qui diversis sub signis pro patria spiritum rediderunt:* "Harvard has not forgotten its sons who under other flags gave life for country."

20. Quoted by Ronald Steel, A.M. '55, in *Walter Lippmann and the American Century* (Boston: Atlantic-Little, Brown, 1980), p.300.

21. See Bessie Zaban Jones, "To the Rescue of the Learned: The Asylum Fellowship Plan at Harvard, 1938-1940," *Harvard Library Bulletin*, Summer 1984.

22. Others receiving permanent appointments were Willi Appel and Hugo Leichtentritt, musicologists; Otto Benesch (art history); Herbert Bloch (classics); applied mathematician and communications scientist Philippe le Corbeiller; Karl Deutsch and Carl Friedrich (government); Ernst Kitzinger (art history); Gottfried Haberler (economics); Richard von Mises (mathematics); Robert Ulich (education); Karl Viëtor (Germanic art and culture); and archaeologist George M. A. Hanfmann and mathematician Stanislaw Ulam, who came as Junior Fellows. At least three dozen other exiles also taught, lectured, or visited at Harvard.

23. Even with present funds, Conant thought the College could manage a small-scale trial of scholarships geared to intellectual merit rather than pecuniary need. Ten grants of $1,000 were offered in 1935 to students in midwestern states; the program was soon extended to southern and southwestern regions.

24. Morison's prodigious output of Harvardiana included *The Founding of Harvard College* (1930), *Harvard College in the Seventeenth Century* (1935), *The Development of Harvard University 1869-1929* (1930), and *Three Centuries of Harvard* (1936), all published by Harvard University Press.

25. Also unsealed was a packet of letters collected at the time of the 1836 Bicentennial. Most were predictably kind, but one from a Philadelphia alumnus read, "Excuse me for this frank expression of my feelings. I owe nothing to the President, professors and tutors of Harvard College in office from A D 1810 to A D 1814."

26. This was less than half the amount sought. Of the $2.8 million raised, more than $1 million was earmarked for national scholarships and $524,000 for University professorships. The first professorships went to Roscoe Pound, who had retired as dean of the Law School in 1936, and classical philologist Werner Jaeger, late of the University of Berlin.

27. Laurence McKinney '12, a master of light verse and noted wit, was the originator of the jest (see *Harvard Alumni Bulletin*, July 1, 1968, p.64).

28. Other members of the panel were Professors Harlow Shapley, Arthur Schlesinger, Felix Frankfurter, and Kenneth Murdock, who served as secretary.

29. Littauer had been one of Theodore Roosevelt's closest advisers. He had served for one season as Harvard's first volunteer football coach, and in 1925 had established a chair in Jewish literature and philosophy in honor of his father, who had come to America from Poland as a glove peddler.

30. The hold of the Communist Party on Harvard was slight. Out of some 2,000 teaching appointments, no more than twelve to fifteen men, "all in the lower grades," were enrolled in the faculty unit of the party when the radical historian Granville Hicks was hired as counselor in American civilization in 1938. Most members dropped their affiliations in disgust over the Nazi-Soviet pact of 1939. Students in the Harvard branch of the Young Communist League deplored the conservatism of their elders.

31. Again FDR failed to carry his alma mater. Republican Wendell Willkie received a comfortable majority in all but one of the Houses. Socialist Norman Thomas, making the final speech of his campaign, drew a large throng to New Lecture Hall.

CHAPTER 4: CONANT'S ARSENAL (pages 137-172)

1. The Communications School trained an elite class in coding for the top-secret navy cryptographic section in Washington. Oswald Jacoby, later a famous bridge master, was enrolled in 1942. With Donald Menzel, professor of astronomy and amateur cryptographer, he decided to test the security of the vaunted ECM (electrical coding machine) in Littauer Center. Persuading the officer in charge to look the other way for two hours, Jacoby and Menzel cracked the ECM's en-

coding method in an hour and fifty minutes.

2. With conscientious objectors volunteering as subjects, depressurization chambers were used to test the effects of rarefied atmosphere on the human voice.

3. Dean Buck had promised the President and Fellows "to prevent co-education from spreading to the lower classes. I think myself that no Radcliffe freshmen and sophomores should ever be admitted to Harvard classes and that upperclass students should be admitted only to advanced courses with small enrollments." To help make the arrangement palatable to his faculty, Buck proposed a salary increase of 20 percent for all teaching ranks, with the exception of professors receiving the maximum of $12,000.

4. One of President Conant's favorite postwar quips described the new relationship as "not coeducation in theory, only in practice"; another humorous saying was that "Harvard is not coeducational, but Radcliffe is."

5. Faculty members and graduate students were well represented in the Office of Strategic Services and its Board of Analysts. Headed by James Phinney Baxter, PH.D. '26, LL.D. '38, president of Williams College, the board included economist Edward S. Mason, PH.D. '25, LL.D. '56, and historians William Langer, PH.D. '23, LL.D. '45, Donald McKay, PH.D. '32, and Crane Brinton '19. Another member was Franklin L. Ford, PH.D. '50, who would later join the Harvard faculty, serve as dean of Arts and Sciences from 1962 to 1970, and hold the McLean chair of ancient and modern history.

6. As Churchill described the honorary-degree ceremony at Bristol University, many of the university authorities had been up all night fighting fires that German bombs had ignited in adjacent buildings. In the morning they had pulled their academic gowns over their "begrimed and drenched" fire-fighting outfits and gone on with the academic ritual "with faultless…decorum."

7. As rhetoric, "The empires of the future are the empires of the mind" was an inspired Churchillian line. But the utopian idea of shared "estates" was predicated on the unlikely notion that America might take joint proprietorship of Britannia's expiring empire.

8. Because German scientists had led in theoretical nuclear physics, it was supposed that the Nazis would capitalize by mounting an all-out effort to develop atomic weapons. "German science is at its peak in this matter," propaganda minister Goebbels wrote in his diary in March 1942. "It is essential that we be ahead of everybody, for whoever introduces a revolutionary novelty into this war has the greater chance of winning it." In actuality, German nuclear research went nowhere because Hitler did not give it high priority. Albert Speer, minister of armaments and war production, would write that the concept of an atomic bomb "quite obviously strained [Hitler's] intellectual capacity," adding that the Führer sometimes spoke of nuclear science as "Jewish physics" (Speer, *Inside the Third Reich*, New York: Macmillan, 1970, pp.227-229). The Germans also lacked a cyclotron—though Harvard physicists had previously shared with some of their German counterparts the plans for their 85-ton atom-smasher, completed in 1939 (see page 159). Europe's only cyclotron was in Paris.

Leading German physicists, including Nobel laureate Werner Heisenberg, advised Speer that the Reich could not produce an atomic bomb in time to affect the war's outcome. Though plans to construct a cyclotron went forward, Speer wrote that "on the suggestion of the nuclear physicists, we scuttled the project to develop an atom bomb by the autumn of 1942."

9. Harvard announced the impending return of the cyclotron when the war ended, but by then it was no longer state-of-the-art, and it remained at Los Alamos. It was rebuilt and used until the late 1970s; its main magnet was then stored at the laboratory's medium-energy Meson Physics Facility. Harvard was without equipment for high-energy nuclear research until 1949, when a 700-ton, million-dollar "synchro-cyclotron" was built north of the University museums.

10. Frank would be the organizer, in 1944, of an "Inter-Scientific Discussion Group" that sought to unify the perspectives of scientific disciplines. It included mathematicians George Birkhoff and Philippe le Corbeiller, physicist Percy Bridgman, economist Wassily Leontief, and astronomer Harlow Shapley. (See Peter Galison '77, PH.D. '83, "The Americanization of Unity," *Daedalus*, Winter 1998, p.45.)

CHAPTER 5: AMAZING GROWTH (pages 175-213)

1. The $60,000 funding for the study of general education was given by Mrs. Bonwit Teller.

2. The other members were Raphael Demos, professor of philosophy; Leigh Hoadley, professor of zoology and master of Leverett House; Byron S. Hollinshead, research fellow in education; Wilbur K. Jordan, professor of history and president of Radcliffe; University Professor I. A. Richards; Philip J. Rulon, professor of education and acting dean of the Graduate School of Education; Arthur M. Schlesinger, professor of history; Robert Ulich, professor of education; George Wald, associate professor of biology; and Benjamin Wright, professor of government.

3. Hiss served 44 months in prison and was released in 1954. When the files of the Soviet secret police (KGB) were opened in 1992, the Russian chairman of an archival commission reported that he had found no evidence that Hiss had been a Soviet agent.

4. Ellen Schrecker '60, PH.D. '74, *The Age of McCarthyism* (New York: St. Martin's Press, 1994), p.84.

5. At the 1947 Commencement, Conant had declared that Harvard would need $90 million "to realize its potentialities" in the decade ahead.

6. Lawrence, which had pioneered in American coeducation, was named for Amos Lawrence (A.B. 1835), Harvard treasurer, Overseer, and Lawrence Lowell's great-uncle. He had given $10,000 to help start the college.

7. Harvard initially declined the bequest: "Too good for a teaching museum" was the Corporation's reported objection. The indignant protests of Provost Paul

Buck eventually brought about a grudging reversal.

8. Three other cases involving allegations of Communist activity made headlines in 1953. Leon Kamin '49, teaching fellow in social relations, took the Fifth Amendment when questioned by a Senate committee in March. He had been a party member from 1947 to 1950 and a writer for the *Daily Worker*. Helen Deane Markham, assistant professor of anatomy at the Medical School, declined to answer the questions of House investigators. The Corporation took no action against Kamin and agreed to retain Markham for the remaining ten months of her appointment.

Law School students Jonathan and David Lubell were subpoenaed by the committee that investigated Kamin. Both had been radical organizers as Cornell undergraduates, but not at Harvard. The Lubells refused to testify fully, setting off a heated conflict within the Law School faculty. A motion to expel them was tabled after intense debate, but both were forced to resign from the *Law Record*. David had to withdraw from the Legal Aid Bureau, and Jonathan was denied election to the *Law Review*, though his grades would have qualified him.

9. The Army-McCarthy hearings were the subject of a powerful documentary, *Point of Order!*, produced by Emile de Antonio '40 and Daniel Talbot.

10. McGeorge Bundy, "Were Those the Days?", *Daedalus*, Summer 1970, p.539.

11. Not a campaign contribution, but accepted by the Corporation in December 1959, was Harvard's most romantic possession: the sixteenth-century Florentine Villa I Tatti. Bernard Berenson (A.B. 1887), connoisseur of Italian Renaissance art, had lived there for sixty years and had long dreamed of conveying it to Harvard as a center for Renaissance studies—a "lay monastery for leisurely culture." Berenson died in 1959 and left his $1.5 million estate to endow I Tatti, its collection of a hundred early Italian paintings, and its library of 50,000 books and thousands of photographs. Justifiably worried that the endowment income would prove insufficient, the Corporation accepted the bequest reluctantly. In 1993 I Tatti's endowment was supplemented by a $17 million fund established by Lila Wallace, co-founder of *Reader's Digest*.

12. As the National Science Board's first chairman, President Conant had a leading role in establishing the National Science Foundation.

13. About three-quarters of all federal funding for higher education in the 1950s came from the multi-billion-dollar budget of the Department of Defense.

14. Henry Rosovsky, *The University: An Owner's Manual* (New York: W. W. Norton, 1990), p.21.

15. The seminal event of the sexual revolution, the introduction of a birth-control pill in 1960, occurred as the vanguard of the baby boom generation (see p. 216) reached maturity. The Pill owed its existence to the finding of John Rock '15, M.D. '18, in collaboration with Celso-Ramon Garcia and Gregory Pincus, SC.D. '27, that synthetic hormones could induce a physiological state resembling pregnancy, making conception impossible. Rock was a Boston surgeon and founder of a Brookline reproductive clinic. A Roman Catholic, he saw the Pill as "a truly natural method of birth control" and became a leader in the campaign to halt population growth.

CHAPTER 6: THE UNIVERSITY ON TRIAL (pages 215-242)

1. Landon Y. Jones, *Great Expectations: America and the Baby Boom Generation* (New York: Coward, McCann & Geoghegan, 1980), p.1.

2. Bundy, *op. cit.*, p.556.

3. Paul Berman, *A Tale of Two Utopias* (New York: W. W. Norton, 1996), p.8.

4. Morison, *Three Centuries of Harvard*, p.252.

5. Unrecognized by those sitting-in was Louis Fieser, the inventor of napalm, looking on from his nearby office.

6. Having given the Latin Oration, "De Puellis Radcliffiensibus," as a senior, the future governor of the Commonwealth was the only graduand in recent memory to orate at two Commencements. He gave a Class Day speech at the Commencement of 1998.

7. At the 1971 Commencement, President Pusey legitimized his successor by conferring on Bok an honorary A.B., "so he can set it beside his degree from Stanford, and treasure it the way the rest of us do."

8. Seymour Martin Lipset and David Riesman, *Education and Politics at Harvard* (New York: McGraw-Hill, 1975), pp.307-308.

CHAPTER 7: HARVARD RESTORED (pages 245-282)

1. The budget had also grown sixfold in the previous twenty-year period, from $30 million to $200 million.

2. This in itself was a break with the past. Bok's predecessors had run Harvard without the assistance of administrative consultants.

3. Several high-level appointees in Nixon's first administration did have Harvard affiliations. Among them were Henry Kissinger '50, PH.D. '54, professor of government, national security adviser; Daniel Patrick Moynihan, director of the Harvard-MIT Joint Center for Urban Studies, chairman of the White House Council on Urban Affairs; Elliot Richardson '41, LL.B. '44, former attorney general of Massachusetts, under secretary of state; Robert Seamans '40, an MIT professor, secretary of the air force; and John Chafee, LL.B. '50, secretary of the navy. Henry Cabot Lodge '24, LL.D. '54, Nixon's running mate in 1960, headed the U. S. negotiating team at the Paris peace talks of 1969.

Nixon himself had won the Harvard Book Prize as a student at Whittier (California) High School.

4. "If Richardson had searched specifically for the man whom I would have least trusted, he could hardly have done better," Nixon wrote in *RN: The Memoirs of Richard Nixon* (New York: Grosset & Dunlap, 1975).

5. Twenty years earlier, St. Clair had gone to Washington as a young member of Joseph Welch's staff during the Army-McCarthy hearings.

6. The Kennedy School's Public Policy Program was planned in the late 1960s by John D. Montgomery,

PH.D. '51, the University's first professor of public administration; Richard Neustadt, PH.D. '52, director of the Institute of Politics; and Don K. Price, the school's dean since 1957. As dean of the Law School, Derek Bok was an early supporter. He had supplemented his own legal training with postgraduate work at the Ecole des Sciences Politiques in Paris and believed in the value of interdisciplinary studies.

7. The Kennedy library and museum had been expected to attract 600,000 visitors a year. They were eventually located at the new campus of the University of Massachusetts-Boston at Columbia Point, Dorchester.

8. Unlike his predecessors, whose annual reports to the Board of Overseers summarized major developments of the past academic year, Bok issued reports that examined the quality and direction of undergraduate and graduate education and took up such broad issues as financial aid, university ties to business and industry, and the state of American higher education. Bok's 1979 report questioned the Business School's appointments process, doctoral training, and reliance on the case method of teaching. In 1983 he called on law schools to address "the failings of a costly and almost inaccessible legal system." Turning to medicine the next year, he evaluated plans for an experimental curriculum at the Medical School. Not since Eliot's time had a Harvard president addressed the state of the graduate and professional schools so systematically.

9. Rosovsky also maintained that undergraduates were not getting a fair share of faculty time. While the size of the faculty had doubled since 1952, he noted, the student population had grown only 14 percent—and the proportion of courses with undergraduate enrollment had declined. More faculty time was going into specialized small-group instruction at advanced levels; tutorials and introductory courses were increasingly taught by graduate students. Could that be squared, Rosovsky asked, with the cost of four years at Harvard (then approaching $20,000)?

10. Phyllis Keller, an associate dean at the time, gave a detailed account of the Core Curriculum's evolution in *Getting at the Core* (Harvard University Press, 1982).

11. Synnott, *op. cit*, p.200.

12. In 1949, when the College had fewer than twenty black students, veterans' counselor (later dean of the College) John Monro had urged that recruiting "really excellent Negro students" would help "materially on one of the country's sorest social problems."

13. Many black students enjoyed highly successful undergraduate careers. Among those enrolled in early 1970s classes were Harvard and Radcliffe class marshals, two presidents of Phillips Brooks House, a member of Phi Beta Kappa's Junior Twelve, a Glee Club manager, a president of WHRB, a D.U. Club president, winners of Fulbright, Shaw, and Rockefeller Fellowships, a Crimson Key president, and captains of football, men's and women's basketball, fencing, and lacrosse.

14. President Bok asked Clifford Alexander '55, who had just been elected an Overseer, to devise an action program for minority employment. A partner in the Washington law firm of Arnold & Porter, and black himself, Alexander was former chairman of the federal Equal Employment Opportunities Commission. His guidelines formed the basis of Harvard's first affirmative action plan.

15. Tuition increases had been an annual event since 1970. The rate of increase tended to outstrip the inflation rate and reached 15 percent in 1982, when tuition, room, board, and fees rose to $12,100.

16. The company's overall goal was to achieve a long-term total return, including income and capital gains, of at least 8 percent. Half would be distributed to units of the University to help meet operating expenses; the other half would be added back to capital to maintain the value of the endowment in the face of inflation.

17. Among the hostages were John Limbert '64, PH.D. '74, a State Department political-affairs officer, and Elizabeth Swift '62, a senior Foreign Service officer.

18. The campaign had a galvanizing effect on other fund-raising programs. The Harvard College Fund, suspended during the campaign, had raised $7 million in 1979; when it resumed in 1985, the bar was reset at $17 million. Annual giving by Harvard parents rose from a level of $70,000 at the start of the campaign to $400,000 in 1984.

19. Bill Gates later used the same PDP-10, funded by the Defense Department, to write code for the Altair. His use of the computer for unauthorized ends reportedly led to a reprimand from the College administration.

20. The crash notwithstanding, the University enjoyed the second best fund-raising year it had ever had. The Harvard College Fund reported total contributions of $24 million, with ten out of twelve reunion classes setting giving records.

CHAPTER 8: MILLENNIAL HARVARD (pages 285-307)

1. Eric Hobsbawm, *The Age of Extremes* (New York: Pantheon Books, 1995), pp.4, 255.

2. Huntington developed his thesis at book length in *The Clash of Civilizations and the Remaking of World Order* (New York: Simon & Schuster, 1996).

3. The "tub system" took its name from a statement attributed to President John Thornton Kirkland (1810-1828). "It is our rule here for every tub to stand on its own bottom," he is supposed to have said of the new and struggling Divinity School. Because of the tendency of financially powerful individual and corporate donors to support the institutions most closely connected to their interests, the tub system historically favored the larger and stronger schools.

4. Green was said to have felt that he was not receiving the consultation and backing he needed to bring major projects to fruition.

5. Stock bequeathed to Harvard by Edward Mallinckrodt '00 of St. Louis was valued at $75.5 million in 1982. At the time it was announced, the Loebs' benefaction was the twelfth largest private gift ever made to an institution of higher education.

6. Since 1983 the Management Company had measured the performance of its investment portfolio against a

composite index split 65-35 between domestic equity and domestic bonds. In 1991 HMC analysts set up a more diversified "policy portfolio" comprising domestic equities (40 percent), foreign equities (18 percent), domestic bonds (15 percent), venture capital (12 percent), real estate (7 percent), commodity-based assets (6 percent), foreign bonds (5 percent), and high-yield securities (2 percent).

7. Memorial Hall's Alumni Hall functioned as a dining commons from 1874 to 1925, when it closed because of declining patronage. The hall continued to be used for examinations in large courses, banquets, smokers, dances, and (later) blood drives.

8. A science cluster already existed north of the Yard, and Quincy Street formed the north-south axis of a fine-arts row made up of the Carpenter Center for the Visual Arts, the Fogg, Werner Otto Hall, and Sackler art museums, and the School of Design's Gund Hall. Lowell Lecture Hall, renovated as a performance center in 1994, faced Sanders Theatre, Harvard's main concert hall, and stood half a block from the Paine Hall music building.

9. Martin Trow, "The Development of Information Technology," *Daedalus*, Fall 1997, p.293.

10. Elizabeth Huidekoper became financial vice president in 1996; Anne Taylor became vice president and general counsel in 1997. Sally Zeckhauser had been administrative vice president since 1986. Women members of the Corporation were Judith Hope, J.D. '64, elected in 1989, and Hanna Holborn Gray, PH.D. '57, former president of the University of Chicago, who succeeded Henry Rosovsky in 1997.

11. The high-water mark for Rhodes Scholars was set in 1987, when Harvard had ten. From the extension of the program to American students in 1904 through 1997, Harvard has produced by far the most U.S. Rhodes Scholars (290), ahead of Yale (192), Princeton (181), West Point (69), and Stanford (67).

Acknowledgments

ANYONE WRITING ABOUT Harvard's past is deeply in debt to Samuel Eliot Morison for his magisterial histories. I am also beholden to a dear friend and editorial predecessor, William Bentinck-Smith, who devoted many years to revising and updating Morison's *Three Centuries of Harvard*. That ambitious task remained unfinished when Bill died in 1993. Access to his drafts and notes, which include his own indexing of the *Harvard Alumni Bulletin* and *Harvard Magazine*, helped guide the planning and research for *Harvard Observed*. Immediate evidence of Bill's determined efforts to subdue so much institutional history was a continuing source of inspiration.

Laura Freid, *Harvard Magazine*'s publisher from 1989 to 1996, was *Harvard Observed*'s original sponsor. Agreeing that a book would be an appropriate adjunct to the magazine's centennial observance, she worked out a plan that let me tackle it as a special project. Catherine Chute, her successor, gave the undertaking her full support and handled the final publishing arrangements. John S. Rosenberg, my successor as editor, gave textual help and unstinting encouragement. Managing editor Christopher Reed and associate managing editor Jean Martin, my longtime colleagues and close friends, assisted in many ways; my particular thanks to the latter for her thoughtful and meticulous copy-editing and proofreading.

Daniel Aaron, exemplary scholar, critic, and friend, took a solicitous interest in the book from its inception and was an unfailingly generous source of advice and moral support. For helpful comments and cheering words at various stages of the writing I also thank Christoph Irmscher, Richard Marius, and Daniel Steiner.

For factual data and illustrations I leaned heavily on the Harvard University Archives, curated by Harley Holden. Staff members Patrice Donoghue, Talar Kizirian, Robin McElheny, Brian Sullivan, David Ware, Edward Haynes, and Jeff Bull gave ever-gracious aid. The Archives' recently unsealed files of Harvard's World War II archivist, the late Sterling Dow, were an important source for segments of chapter four, "Conant's Arsenal."

Support from John de Cuevas and Sarah and Daniel Hrdy helped meet part of the cost of illustration-gathering. My warmest appreciation to them.

For caffè latte in the morning, copyreading and editorial advice at all hours, and empathy in the evening, I am abidingly grateful to the incomparable Helen Bethell; for pep talks I thank Sara Bethell, Hugh Bethell, Sarah Gannett, and Thomas Bethell; for various forms of help and/or moral support, my gratitude to Wallace Dailey, Franklin Ford, Elizabeth Gombosi, Danielle Green, Sandra Grindlay, Elizabeth Hansen, Jim Harrison, Marvin Hightower, Suzanne Holland, Christopher Johnson, Paul Killiam, Craig Lambert, Donald Lamm, John Mich Jr., Madeleine Mullin, Marianne Perlak, Jane Reed, Elizabeth Repenning, Nish Saran, Mark Silber, William Sisler, Deborah Smullyan, Genny Smyers, Jennifer Snodgrass, Crocker Snow, Sandra Spanier, Rick Stafford, Sara Stillman, John Tobin, Marc van Baalen, John Veneziano, Catherine Verdi, John Walsh, Joe Wrinn, Sally Zeckhauser, and Hiller Zobel.

PRODUCING THIS BOOK was a stiffer task than one might think. Much of the mechanical preparation was done in-house at *Harvard Magazine*, by colleagues who were always subject to competing deadlines. Art director Elaine Bradley planned the typography, improved the author's rough layouts, and built electronic files. Susan Doheny, a professional researcher, was brought in to provide illustration-gathering help at a point that seemed perilously late; with uncommon composure, she rounded up more than four hundred images. Associate editor Jonathan Shaw came in early to digitize them and urge the rest of us on. When Elaine Bradley left to take a new position, Jennifer Carling and Bob Bethune completed what she'd begun. Without these hard-working collaborators there would be no book.
—J.T.B.

Illustration Credits

The prefixes HU and UA identify illustrations from the Harvard University Archives. The abbreviations HAB and HM identify images reproduced from the picture files or back issues of the *Harvard Alumni Bulletin* and *Harvard Magazine*.

THE REFORMERS: 12 A.W. Elson, HUV 240 PF. 14 HUP Lowell (5b). 15 Theodore Roosevelt Collection, Harvard College Library. 16 Brown Brothers. 17 *left* HUP Eliot (2); *right* HUK 610A. 18 *left, from top* HUP Wendell; HUP Kittredge; HUP Copeland; *bottom* HUP Lanman (3). 19 HUP Harvard Portrait Collection (H246); *top right* HUP Santayana (2); *lower right* HUP Briggs (8b). 20 *top left* Fogg Art Museum/Harvard Portrait Collection (H111); *top center* HUV 15(3-2); *top right* HM; *bottom* Detroit Publishing Co./Cambridge Historical Commission. 21 *top left* HUV 166 (6-4); *top center* Brown Brothers; *top right* UAV 170,270,2p/f Athletic Association Baseball, box 1; *center, left* Radcliffe College Archives; *center* Franklin D. Roosevelt Library, Hyde Park, N.Y.; *right* HUV 172 (2-1); *inset* HUP Sargent (6). 22 *top* HUP Adams (3a); *below* HUP Lawrence (4). 23 Detroit Publishing Co./Cambridge Historical Commission. 24 HUP Nolen (1). 25 *top* Harvard Portrait Collection (H189); *bottom* HUV 144(1-5). 26 *top* HUP-SF Hasty Pudding (54); *below* HUP-SF (N) Psychological Labs, Hugo Münsterberg; *bottom* HUP-SF Student rooms. 27 *top* HUK 363p fig. 8; *below* HAB. 28 HUA. 29 *top* HUP-SF Football (135); *below* HUK (Harvard Engineering Journal). 30 *top* HUV 1331 (4-1); *below*, HUP Reid. 31 HUP Shaler (9n). 32 *top* HUP McKay (2); *below*, HUV 15(4-2). 33, 34 Brown Brothers. 35 Harvard Medical Library, F.A. Countway Library of Medicine. 36 *top left* HUV 179 (1-6); *below left* HUV 325 (1-2); *bottom* Radcliffe College Archives; *inset* Brown Brothers. 37 Arnold Arboretum. 38 *top* HUP Taussig (3); *below* HUP Gay (1) *bottom* HUK 305. 39 Harvard Portrait Collection (H192). 40 HUV. 41 *below* HUP Lowell (1a). 42 *top* HUV 169 (1-5); *below* Seeley G. Mudd Manuscript Library, Princeton University. 43 *top* HUP-SF. *below* HUA. 44 *top* HUP Greene (1b); *bottom* HUA. 45 HUV 1940 (2-1). 46 University Archives. 47 Boston Elevated Railway Collection, Cambridge Historical Commission. 48 HUP Forbes. 49 HUP Sidis. 50 *top left* HUV 48 (23-6n); *lower left* HUV 48 (23-4); *top right* HUV 49 (27-6); *lower right* HUV 49 (27-1B). 51 *top* HUV 49a (26-5a); *right* HUV 49 (25-2); *below* HUV 49 (25-5); HUP Widener. 52 *top* UAV 297 (10-6); *below*, HUP Francke (3). 53 *top* HUP Richards (20); *bottom* HUV 723 (1-1). 54 *top* HUK 410.66; *below* HUA. 55 *top* From *Brahmins and Bullyboys: G. Frank Radway*, copyright © 1973 by Stephen Halpert and Brenda Halpert, reprinted by permission of Houghton Mifflin Co.; all rights reserved. *Bottom* HUD 200 PF. 56 *top* HUA; *bottom* Harvard Theatre Collection, Houghton Library. 57 HUP Eliot (46). 58 AP/Wide World. 59 HUA.

THE GREAT WAR: 60 Courtesy of the President and Fellows of Harvard College. 62 Culver Pictures Inc. 63 *top* The William L. Foley Collection. 64 Houghton Library, Harvard University H795.148.25F, box 29. 65 *right, below* HUA ACC 13628; *bottom* HAB. 66 *below* HUA ACC 13628. 67 HUP Seeger. 68 HUA ACC 13628. 69 *top* HUP 48 (23-4); *inset* HAB; *below* HUA. 70 *top* HUP Münsterberg; *below* Brown Brothers. 71 *top* private collection; *below* HUP Cushing (1). 72 *left* HUV240 PF; *top* Boston Globe. 73 HAB. 74 Theodore Roosevelt Collection, Harvard College Library. 75 HAB. 76 *top* HUA; *below* HAB. 77 From *Brahmins and Bullyboys: G. Frank Radway*, copyright © 1973 by Stephen Halpert and Brenda Halpert, reprinted by permission of Houghton Mifflin Co. 78 HUE 60.600 PF. 79 National Archives. 80-81 *top left* HUP Morgan (1); 81 *top right* HUP Whittlesey PF; all others HUA ACC 13628. 82 *top* Howard Chandler Christy/Museum of the City of New York; *below* Laura Brey/Harry Ransom Research Center Art Collection, University of Texas at Austin. 83 *bottom* F.H. Davis Co. Collection, Cambridge Historical Commission; *right*, HUP Jones (1). 84-85 HUP-SF ROTC (6). 86 University Archives. 87 Courtesy of the President and Fellows of Harvard College.

BETWEEN THE WARS: 88 HUV 297 (10-6). 90 AP/Wide World. 92 HUD 3167.219. 93 *top* Underwood & Underwood/Corbis-Bettmann; *right, top* HUP Laski; *below* Christopher S. Johnson. 94 *top* HUP Hinton; *below* Radcliffe College Archive, MC278.786-10. 95 *top* Old Oregon Magazine, University of Oregon; *right, top*, painting by Boardman Robinson (detail)/Special Collections Department, Harvard Law School Library; *below* HUP Byrne (1). 96 *top* Society for the Preservation of New England Antiquities; *left* HAB. 97 Boston University Library Special Collections. 98 *right* Museum of Modern Art/Film Stills Archive. 99 *top* HUP Eliot (72); *right* HUA. 100 *top,bottom* Baker Library, Harvard Business School; *center* AP/Wide World. 101 Fogg Art Museum. 102 *left* HUP Harkness (1); *right* HUP Drinker (1). 103 *top* HUV 662; *right* Christopher S. Johnson. 104 HUP Amberson; *below* HUV 604 (1-3a). 105 HUA. 106 *Owen, Dixon, Devens*, Harvard Sports Information Department; *Jones*, Wide World. 107 Brown Brothers. 108 *top* Sports Information Department; *below* HAB. 109 HUV 316 (4-8). 110 *left* HUV 53 (3-9a); *top* HUV 2332 PF(HAR5N); *bottom* HUV 53A (1-3). 111 HUB 1555.2, box 22. 112 *left* HUP Lowell (43); *bottom* Society of Fellows. 113 HUV 15 (13-3). 114 HUP Conant (33b). 116 *left* HUP Minot (1); *right* HUP Murphy (1b). 117 *right* HAB; *bottom* HUP-SF Commencement 1934 (8). 118 HUP-SF China

(14b). 119 *top* Franklin D. Roosevelt Library; *right* AP/Wide World. 120 UPI/Corbis-Bettmann. 122 Harvard Theatre Collection. 123 *top* Harvard Portrait Collection. 123 *right* HUV 55 (1-9b). 124-125 HUP-SF Tercentenary (133). 126 *top* HUP-SF Tercentenary (19); *inset* Franklin D. Roosevelt Library. 127 Harvard Theatre Collection. 128 HUP-SF Tercentenary (38). 129,130 HUA. 131 *top* Houghton Library, pf MS AM 1964 (41); *right* HAB. 132 UAI 15.898.80p. 133 *right* Otto Hagel/Life Magazine © Time Inc.; *bottom* HUP-SF WWII 1941 (1). 134 *top* UPI/Bettmann; 135 HAB.

CONANT'S ARSENAL: 136 UAV 605.442p 1943-45 (2-N90). 138 UAV 605.442p 1943-45 (2-106). 139 HAB. 140 HUP-SF WWII 96-104. 141 HAB. 142 HUP-SF WWII 58-66. 143 U.S. Army Signal Corps. 144 *top* UAV 605.270 (774-776); *bottom* HUP Stevens (2). 145 *top* HUP Bridgman (27); *right* HUP Fieser. 146 *top left* HUV 193; *bottom left* HUP Beranek (1a) *top right* HAB. 147 HUP Aiken (66); *bottom* HUP-SF Computers (4) 605.442p. 148 *top* HAB; *bottom* 605.270.5p, box 2, Cohn (JF 369-73). 149 *left* HUP Buck (7b); *top right* HUP Smith (1a); *bottom right*, HUP Claflin (1-2); *outside right*, HUP Perry (33). 150 HAB. 151 HUP Lowell (39a). 152 *top* HUA; *bottom* HM. 153 UAV 605.270.5 PF 186-188. 155 *top* Harvard News Office; *right* UAI 5.168, box 246. 156 HUA, 158 HUP Oppenheimer (1a). 159 Harvard Cyclotron Laboratory. 160 Los Alamos National Laboratory. 161 HUA. 162 HUP-SF Commencement 1944 (1b). 163 HAB. 164 AP/Wide World Photo. 165 HUP Sachs (4). 166 *left* Elizabeth Shoumatoff, courtesy of the Franklin D. Roosevelt Library. *top* UAV 874.126p. 167 UAV 605.270.1.3p. 168 UPI/Corbis-Bettmann. 169 Courtesy of Crocker Snow. 171 FPG International. 173 HUA.

AMAZING GROWTH: 174 HUP-SF Student life (38). 176 HUA 945-93. 177 *top* HUA; *inset* HUP-SF Student life (46). 178 *top* HUD 3137.3000.6p, Harvard Coop; *bottom* HUP-SF WWII (248). 179 HAB. 180 HUP Buck (7b). 181 HUA UAI 10-528.5. 183 *right* HAB; *bottom* Countway Library. 184 Harvard University News Office. 185 HUP Langer (15). 186 *left* © Archive Photos; *bottom* HUA. 187 HUP Langer (15). 188 *top* AP/Wide World; *below* HUP Marbury (2). 189 HUV 49C (19-2); *right* HUA. 190 HAB. 191 HUD 2950.26. 192 HAB. 193 Courtesy of the Harvard Art Museums, Bequest of Collection of Maurice Wertheim, Class of 1906. 194 *top* HAB/Fay Photo Service Inc.; *below* International News Photos. 195 *top* John Loengard, Harvard Crimson. 196 *above* AP/Wide World; *below* HAB. 197 *right* HUP Keller (1); *bottom* HUP-SF Commencement (14a). 198 HUP-305. 199 Countway Library; *right* HAB. 200 Byron Blanchard. 201 *top left* Harvard News Office; *lower left* Joseph W. Molitar; *lower right* Shepley Bulfinch Richardson & Abbott, photo by Gottscho-Schleisner Inc. 202 HAB. 203 HUA. 204 HUP Castro (1). 205 *left* HAB; *top right* John F. Kennedy Library; *below right* HUP-SF Commencement (61). 206 *Bundy*, HUA; *Schlesinger*, HUP Schlesinger (8b); *Bell, Neustadt*, Jane Reed/Harvard News Office; *Galbraith, Reischauer*, HM. 207 James Stevenson © 1961 from The New Yorker Collection. All rights reserved. 208 HUP Kennedy (27b). 209 HAB. 210 HUP Watson. 211 *top left* Paul H. Donaldson/Cruft Laboratory, Harvard University; *top right* HUP Purcell (3); Lipmann, HUA; Enders, Harvard News Office; Robbins, UAV 605.295.10p; *Weller*, HUP Weller; *Von Békésy*, HUP Von Békésy (3b); 212 *top* HM; *below* HAB/Beardsley Ruml III. 213 HUD 3137.3000.6p, Christmas 1962.

THE UNIVERSITY ON TRIAL: 214 Mark Silber. 217 HAB/David Duhme. 218 David H. Hunsberger. 219 *left* Christopher S. Johnson; *upper right* HUV 95 (5-11); *lower right* HM. 220 David H. Hunsberger. 221 Julien Levy. 222 Chuck Hagen. 223 HAB. 224 Harvard Sports Information Department. 225 Mark Silber. 226 UAV 605.408 3p. 227 Mark Silber. 228 *left* Michael Nagy. *right* Ted Dully/Boston Globe. 229 Tom Ittelson. 230 *left* Mark Silber; *bottom* HM; UPI/Corbis-Bettmann. 231 Mark Silber. 232 *top* Ted Polumbaum, Life Magazine © Time Inc.; *below*, HAB. 233, 234 Rick Stafford. 235 Gwendolyn Stewart Brooks. 236, 237 *left* Christopher S. Johnson; 237 *right* Judith Parker. 238 *top* Photofest; *below* HUA. 239 *top* Harvard News Office; *right* Steve Rosenthal/Harvard Development Office; *below* Shepley Bulfinch Richardson & Abbott/photo by Phokion Karas. 240 *left* HUP Bloch (3c); *top* HUP Woodward (8); *top right* HUP Schwinger (3a);. 241 HUP Wald (11); 242 W.H. Tobey. 243 Timothy Carlson.

HARVARD RESTORED: 244,246 W.H. Tobey/Harvard News Office. 247,248 Christopher S. Johnson. 249 HUP Bok (3a); *right* Judith Parker. 250,251 Rick Stafford. 252 Lilian Kemp. 253 Alex Rhinelander. 254 Rick Stafford. 255 *top* UPI/Corbis-Bettmann; *below* HM. 256 Rick Stafford. 257 *right* Photo by Thorney Lieberman for Pei, Cobb and Free/John F. Kennedy Library; *bottom* Jim Harrison. 258,259 Rick Stafford. 261 *top, below left* Rick Stafford; *below right*, 262 Martha Stewart. 263 Jim Harrison. 264 Judith Parker 265 Christopher S. Johnson. 266 *top* HM; *below* Jim Harrison. 267 Joe Wrinn/Harvard News Office. 268 Jim Harrison. 269 *top* Jane Reed/Harvard News Office; *below* HM. 271 Michael Crawford. 272 *top* John Nordell; *below* Jim Harrison. 273 Jim Harrison; *below* Mike Quan/Harvard News Office. 274 Joe Wrinn/Harvard News Office. 275 Jim Harrison. 276-277 Cynthia Tollen. 278 Boston Globe. 279 Rick Stafford. 280,281 Harvard News Office. 283 Gene Peach.

MILLENNIAL HARVARD: 284 Jim Harrison. 290 Steve Rosenthal. 291 *top* Stu Rosner; *below* Jim Harrison. 292,293 *top* Jim Harrison; *below* Flint Born. 294 Jim Harrison. 295 Dorothy Alexander. 296 Joe Wrinn/Harvard News Office. 297 Steve Rosenthal. 298 *left* Flint Born; *right* Donald Farrell. 299 *top* Anton Grassl; *below* Jim Harrison. 300 *inset* Dongik Lee; *right* Flint Born. 301 Harvard News Office. 302 Jane Reed/Harvard News Office. 303 Marc Halevi/Harvard News Office. 304,305 Jim Harrison. 306 Christopher S. Johnson. 307 Jon Chase.

Muck, Karl, 82
Muenter, Erich, 74
Münsterberg, Hugo, 70,81
Murdock, Kenneth, 112,114,128, 129
Murphy, Dr. William, 116
Murray, Dr. Joseph, 281

Napalm, 144,169,222
National Defense Research Committee, 133,142,157,160
National scholarships, 116
Neilson, William Allen, 41
Networking, 246,271,301
Neustadt, Richard, 206,220
Nieman Fellowships, 131
Nitze, Paul, 160,206
Nivola, Claire, 252,253
—Constantino, 252,253
Nixon, Richard, 188,189,204,223, 234,245,254-256
Nobel Prize, 53,116,145,158,209, 210,211,239-241,281
Nolen, W.W., 24
Norton
—Charles Eliot, 18
—Richard, 64
Noyes, Alfred, 71
Nye, Joseph, 282

O'Brien, Thomas, 280
O'Neill, Thomas P., 275
Oppenheimer, J.R., 158,161,168, 169,185,186
Overpass (1968), 238
Overseers, 8,95,97,251,286-288, 292,303
Owen, George, 106
Oxford, 45,49,103,287

Paine, John Knowles, 18
Palmer, G.H., 18,19
"Palmer Raids," 94
Pankhurst, Emmeline, 58
Parietal rules, 213,218,219,236,242
Peabody Museum, 52
—Terrace,219
Peace Corps, 208,209
Pearl Harbor, attack on, 134,157
Pei, I.M., 256,257
Peirce, Waldo, 64,73
Pellissier, Robert, 68,79
Peninsula, 291
Pennypacker, Henry, 97
Perkins, Elliott, 46,153,242
Perry, R. B., 16,129,133,149
Pershing, J.J., 83
Peterson, Dr. Chase N., 248
Petrow, Chris, 164
Pierce, John, 146
Pierian Sodality of 1808, 56
Plattsburg camps, 72
Plaut, James, 165
Powell, Gen. Colin, 291,292
President's house, 52,226
Price, Charles P., 217,278
Don K., 206,257
Prince Charles, 274,275
Prince, Norman, 65,79
Pritchett, Henry, 31
Program for H. College, 199,200, 210,266
Psycho-Acoustic Lab., 144,146
Ptashne, Mark, 239

Public Administration, School of, 205,256
Public Health, School of, 54,113, 142,148,199,201,295
Purcell, Edward, 145,210,211,238
Pusey, Anne, 193,196
—Library, 238,241
—Nathan, 192-200,202,205,209, 211,212,220,222,225,227,230, 234,235,242,256,275,278,289, 302
Putnam, George, 264-266

Quincy House, 200,201
Quine, W.V., 112,146

Radar, 145,158,
Radcliffe College, 13,36,52,151, 152,213,225,233,236,237,238, 249,250,264,302-304
Radio Operators' School, 78
—Research Lab., 142,144
Raines, Franklin D., 288,289
Ramsey, Norman, 160,170,281
Reagan, Ronald, 266,274
"Red Book," 154,176,181
Reed, Dana, 172
—John, 55,56
Refugee scholars, 116,176
Reid, W.T. Jr., 29-31
Reischauer, E.O., 206,260
Religious diversity, 269
Residence halls, 23-26
Rice, Dr. A.H., 72,109
Richards, I.A., 182,185,186,210
—Theodore, 18,52,53,114,116
Richardson, Elliot, 255,256
Riesman, David, 210,215,241,242
Rinehart, J.B.G., 20
Riots, 92,108,212,233
Riverside, 49,234
Rockefeller, David, 192,199
—family, 33
Rogers, Thomas, 45
Roosevelt, Eleanor, 28
—F. D., 19,21,28,72,90,112,114, 115,118-122,127,128,133,151, 275,157,163-168
—Quentin, 81,89
—Theodore, 14-16,29,33,54,71, 72,74-76,89,90
—Theodore Jr., 121,171
Rose Bowl, 95
Rosenthal, Arthur, 251
Rosovsky, Henry, 112,225,230,258- 260,263,264,269,279,286-288,303
ROTC, 76,138,141,142,220,224- 226,234,242,291
Royce, Josiah, 18,19
Rubbia, Carlo, 281
Rudenstine, Angelica, 287
—Neil L., 286-295,299,303,304
Rutherford, Ernest, 52

Sabine, Wallace, 32,40,
Sacco-Vanzetti case, 101
Sachs, Paul, 116,128,165,193
Sackler Museum, 268
Sage, Mrs. Russell, 49
Saltonstall, Leverett, 93,150,154, 172
Santayana, George, 18,19,55
Sargent, Dudley, M.D. 21
—John Singer, 61,87

SATC, 84-86
Schiff, Jacob, 33
Schlesinger, Arthur Jr., 112,205
Schmidt, Benno Jr., 274
Schwinger, Julian, 145,238,240,241
Science Center, 238,239,247
Scott, Robert, 279,293
SDS, 209,215,220,221,224,227,230, 232,234,240,253,263
Sears family, 35
Seeger, Alan, 56,66-68,79
Seidman, Gay, 272
Sert, Josep Lluis, 253
Sessions, Roger, 49
Shah of Iran, 223,266
Shaler, N.S., 31,32
Shapley, Harlow, 116,117,147
Shepley, Henry, 172
Shareholder issues, 251,253,271, 272
Shattuck, H.L., 107
Shaw, G.B., 127
Shultz, George, 274-276
Sidis, W.J., 49,92
Sigourney, David, 132,163
Skinner, B.F., 112,210
Slichter, C.P., 233,248,289,294
Smith, A. Calvert, 149
—George, 24
Snow, Crocker, 169,170
Society of Fellows, 111-113
Soldiers Field, 25,47
Solzhenitsyn, Aleksandr, 262
Spanish-American War, 10,37
Spence, A. Michael, 269,275,282
Sperry, Willard, 166,167
Stadium, H., 28,29,44,267
Stanton, Herbert, 164
Stein, Gertrude, 54
Steiner, Daniel, 246
Stevens, S.S., 144
Stillman, James, 33
Stock market, 90,106,107,279,280
Stone, Edward, 68
—Robert G., 268,293,296
Story, Moorfield, 95
Strauch, Karl, 202
Straus family, 51,101
Street, J.C., 145,159
Strock, Alden, 305
Student Council, 103,150,181
Sturgis, Alanson, 56
Sturtevant, Albert, 80
Sullivan, Mark, 99
Summer School, 36,37
Swain, G.F., 47
Sweezy-Walsh controversy, 129

Talbot, Alice-Mary M., 277
Taussig, Frank, 18,37,38,40
Taft, W.H., 14,39,55,91,99
Telephones, 21
Thayer, W.R., 24
Three Hundredth Fund, 117,127
Three-year A.B., 19
Titanic, 51
Tosteson, Daniel, 292
Tozzer, Alfred, 37
Trumbauer, Horace, 51,109
Tuition, College, 20-22,99,198,305
Tutu, Archbishop Desmond, 272
Tweed, C.H. 35

Underwater Sound Lab., 142,146

University Campaign, 292,293,295, 296
"Up or Out" policy, 128-130

Valentino, Rudolph, 98
Vanderbilt, Harold, 101,200
Vanserg Building, 144
Van Vleck, J.H., 238,281
Varsity Club, 52,298
Vaughan, Norman, 104
Veblen, Thorstein, 37
Vendler, Helen, 280
Veterans at H., 176-181
Veysey, Laurence, 34
Vietnam War, 176,215,216,220,240 245,250,254
Von Stade, F.S., 226,242

Wald, George, 147,241
Ward, Barbara (Jackson), 197
Warren, Dr. J.C., 35
Watergate, 254
Watson, James D., 210
—Robert B., 213,226,233
Weems, Katharine Lane, 109
Weinberg, Steven, 281
Welch, Joseph, 196
Weld, W.F., 234
Wendell, Barrett, 18,42
Wertheim, Maurice, 193
West End Railway, 20,47,49
WGBH, 198
Wheelwright, Edmund, 23
Whipple, Fred, 145,146
White, William Allen, 133
Whitehead, A.N., 111,112,242,260
Whitney, Richard, 107
Whittlesey, Charles, 81
WHRB, 211,240
Widener, Eleanor E., 51,71,72,109, 236
—Harry, 51,72
—Library, 51,261
Wiener, Leo, 49
—Norbert, 49
Wiesel, Torsten, 281
Wigglesworth Hall, 104
Wild, Payson, 153
Wilhelm II (Kaiser), 52,62,86
William James Hall, 219,299
Williamson, George, 67,68
Wilson, E.Bright, 144,158
—E.H. ("Chinese"), 37
—E.O., 112,259,260
—James Q., 259,260
—Linda S., 280,303
—Robert, 158,159,169
—Woodrow, 40,49,62,69,71,75, 76,89,91
Winthrop House, 69
Wood, Leonard, 72-74,90
—W. Barry, 108,192
Woodward, Robert, 148,240,241
World War I, 61-87,89,90
World War II, 137-172
World Wide Web, 271,301
Wyzanski, Charles, 194

Yard residences, 24,49
Yeomans, Henry, 94

Zeckhauser, Sally H., 280